D1760377

University of Edinburgh

FIN DE MILLÉNAIRE
FRENCH
FICTION

The Aesthetics of Crisis

RUTH CRUICKSHANK

OXFORD
UNIVERSITY PRESS

OXFORD
UNIVERSITY PRESS

Great Clarendon Street, Oxford OX2 6DP

Oxford University Press is a department of the University of Oxford.
It furthers the University's objective of excellence in research, scholarship,
and education by publishing worldwide in

Oxford New York

Auckland Cape Town Dar es Salaam Hong Kong Karachi
Kuala Lumpur Madrid Melbourne Mexico City Nairobi
New Delhi Shanghai Taipei Toronto

With offices in

Argentina Austria Brazil Chile Czech Republic France Greece
Guatemala Hungary Italy Japan Poland Portugal Singapore
South Korea Switzerland Thailand Turkey Ukraine Vietnam

Oxford is a registered trade mark of Oxford University Press
in the UK and in certain other countries

Published in the United States
by Oxford University Press Inc., New York

© Ruth Cruickshank 2009

The moral rights of the author have been asserted
Database right Oxford University Press (maker)

First published 2009

British Library Cataloguing in Publication Data

Data available

Library of Congress Cataloging in Publication Data

Data available

Typeset by SPI Publisher Services, Pondicherry, India
Printed in Great Britain
on acid-free paper by
the MPG Books Group, Bodmin and King's Lynn

ISBN 978-0-19-957175-8

1 3 5 7 9 10 8 6 4 2

For my family

Contents

List of abbreviations

VC   Christine Angot, *Vu du ciel* (Paris: L'Arpenteur, 1990)
NTB   Christine Angot, *Not to be* (Paris: L'Arpenteur, 1991)
LT   Christine Angot, *Léonore, toujours* (Paris: L'Arpenteur, 1994)
INT   Christine Angot, *Interview* (Paris: Fayard, 1995)
LA   Christine Angot, *Les Autres* (Paris: Fayard, 1997)
SA   Christine Angot, *Sujet Angot* (Paris: Fayard, 1998)
I   Christine Angot, *L'Inceste* (Paris: Fayard, 1999)
QV   Christine Angot, *Quitter la ville* (Paris: Fayard, 2000)

NT   Jean Echenoz, *Nous trois* (Paris: Minuit, 1992)
LGB   Jean Echenoz, *Les Grandes Blondes* (Paris: Minuit, 1995)
UA   Jean Echenoz, *Un An* (Paris: Minuit, 1997)
JMV   Jean Echenoz, *Je m'en vais* (Paris: Minuit, 1999)

EDL   Michel Houellebecq, *Extension du domaine de la lutte* (Paris: Maurice Nadeau, 1994; Paris: J'ai lu, 1997). All quotations are from the 1997 *poche* edition.
PE   Michel Houellebecq, *Les Particules élémentaires* (Paris: Flammarion, 1998)
INV   Michel Houellebecq, *Interventions* (Paris: Flammarion, 1998)

S   Marie Redonnet, *Silsie* (Paris: Gallimard, 1990)
CS   Marie Redonnet, *Candy Story* (Paris: P.O.L, 1992)
N   Marie Redonnet, *Nevermore* (Paris: P.O.L, 1994)
VR   Marie Redonnet, *Villa Rosa* (Charenton: Flohic, 1996)
AP   Marie Redonnet, *L'Accord de paix* (Paris: Grasset, 2000)
JG   Marie Redonnet, *Jean Genet, le poète travesti: Portrait d'une œuvre* (Paris: Grasset, 2000)

Acknowledgements

It is a great pleasure to be able to thank my family, friends, and colleagues for their help in bringing this project to fruition. I am indebted to Colin Davis, who from the outset has given me invaluable inspiration, support, and guidance. Margaret Atack, Martin Crowley, Elizabeth Fallaize, Alison Fell, Toby Garfitt, Ann Jefferson, Shirley Jordan, Roger Pearson, Keith Reader, Gill Rye, and Emma Wilson have also been extremely generous in offering insight, time, and encouragement during the writing of my thesis and this book. I have also been blessed with the support, kindness, and wisdom of so many friends, and in particular, Sarah Cant, Jill Capstick, Clare Connors, Olivier and Nathalie Deparis, John Corrigan, Mina Gorji, Emma Herdman, Katherine Lunn-Rockliffe, Celia Mills, Jan Moyses, Nathalie Price, and Katherine Wyatt.

In addition to thanking colleagues for their support, I would like to express my gratitude for the research funding I have received from Royal Holloway, University of London, The Queen's and St Anne's Colleges, Oxford, and the Faculty of Modern and Medieval Languages and Literatures at the University of Oxford. I am also grateful for the expertise of the staff of the Bibliothèque Nationale de France, the Bibliothèque Marguerite Durand, the Bodleian Library, and the Taylor Institution.

Some material in Chapter 3 and Chapter 5 has been published in a different form in the following, and I am grateful for permission to reproduce intersecting material: 'Sex, Shopping and Psychoanalysis: Houellebecq and Therapy', in *Le Monde de Houellebecq*, edited by Gavin Bowd (Glasgow: University of Glasgow French and German Publications, 2006), pp. 199–212; 'Marie Redonnet, the Question of Resistance, and the Turn-of-the-Millennium Novel', *Modern & Contemporary France*, 12:4 (2004), 497–511; and '*L'Affaire Houellebecq*: Ideological Crime and *Fin de millénaire* Literary Scandal', *French*

Cultural Studies, 40 (2003), 101–16, published in definitive version by
SAGE Publications Ltd. All rights reserved. [The Owner]; see <http://
frc.sagepub.com/cgi/reprint/14/1/101>.

I also am grateful to Les Éditions de Minuit and Jean Echenoz; and to
Flammarion and Michel Houellebecq for permission to reproduce
quotations from *Les Grandes Blondes* and *Les Particules élémentaires*.

Unless indicated otherwise, all translations are my own.

Introduction

THE FRENCH EXCEPTION AND THE
FIN DE MILLÉNAIRE

When in 1987 a digital clock was erected outside the Pompidou Centre
to begin a symbolic countdown to the third millennium, the gesture
appeared to be one of French cultural confidence and faith in technological progress. On 14 July 1988 President François Mitterrand an-
nounced a further *Grand Projet* to join the Arche de la Défense, the
Opéra Bastille, and the Grand Louvre. Underpinning the interconnec-
tedness of literary production and French identity, Mitterrand unveiled
plans for the world's biggest library, the Bibliothèque National de
France which would 'couvrir tous les champs de la connaissance, être
à la disposition de tous, utiliser les technologies les plus modernes de
transmission de données, pouvoir être consultée à distance et entrer en
relation avec d'autres bibliothèques européennes'.[1] The re-election of
Mitterrand and the subsequent victory of the Socialist Rocard government in 1988 ended four years of *cohabitation* with a right-wing
Chamber of Deputies led by Jacques Chirac. With the Communist
Party effectively sidelined, Mitterrand appeared to be engineering a form
of centrist politics that might reconcile Republican values and French
exceptionalism with the neoliberal ideology of an increasingly globalized
market economy. Celebrations of the bicentenary of the 1789 Revolution
sent out a bullish message: France was preparing to enter the third
millennium as a beacon of modern culture. As the Berlin Wall came
down and the Cold War ended, it seemed that France was not only
turning its back on historical divisions, but was also preparing to play a
key economic and political role at the centre of Europe at the turn of the
millennium, and a prominent cultural role on the global stage.

---

[1] 'Naissance de la BnF', <http://www.bnf.fr/PAGES/connaitr/naissanc.htm> (accessed
22 May 2009): 'cover all fields of knowledge, be open to all, use cutting edge information
technology, provide remote access, and link up with other European libraries'.

The year 2000 is but a contingent marker on the Western calendar, yet as the Beaubourg countdown clock and the illuminated day-by-day countdown on the Eiffel Tower which replaced it suggest, it retains a symbolic power. Moreover, as millennial celebrations drew nearer, their symbolism intensified the sense that France was experiencing an intersection of social, political, and economic crises. In 1993 unemployment reached 12 per cent. *Cohabitation* returned for the last two years of Mitterrand's presidency before Chirac was elected President in 1995, and ostensible political consensus was increasingly criticized as a homogenizing *pensée unique*. Successive scandals discredited high-ranking officials—past, present, and indeed presidential—with a notable convergence of *affaires* revealing involvement in atrocities of the Occupation and the Algerian War. If the appointment of France's first female Prime Minister, Édith Cresson, in 1991 suggests a positive turn in gender politics, Pierre Bérégovoy replaced her a year later, and 95 per cent of political offices in 1995 were held by men. A postcolonial crisis was evidenced by the rise of the Front National, growing unrest in the *banlieues*, the anti-racism petitions and rallies of 1997, and a series of highly mediatized legal battles over the right to wear the Muslim headscarf in Republican schools.

This convergence of tangible crises in 1990s France intersected with a resurgence of crisis discourses, suggesting that France was experiencing more than a periodic moment of self-questioning. Crisis tropes recurred in rhetoric, images, and conversations, spanning institutional organs and the field of cultural production. This return to crisis is particularly marked in perceptions of *l'exception française*, a nexus of identity narratives—economic, political, diplomatic, cultural, and indeed, literary—felt to be under increasingly severe threat from global market economics. In particular, the fear was of the impact of neoliberalism, which David Harvey links to crisis production, identifying 'an inner connection [. . .] between technological dynamism, instability, dissolution of social solidarities, environmental degradation, deindustrialization, rapid shifts in time-space relations, speculative bubbles and the general tendency towards crisis formation within capitalism'.[2] French responses to neoliberalism and its perceived role in the ongoing set of processes of

[2] David Harvey, *A Brief History of Neoliberalism* (Oxford: Oxford University Press, 2005), p. 69.

globalization (the parallel enlargement of a world marketplace and of worldwide communications systems dominated by audiovisual and digital mass media and information technology) are epitomized by increasingly urgent, sometimes contradictory, and typically anti-American discourses. These argue that multiculturalism counters the notion of 'la République une et indivisible'[3] and that the entrepreneurialism and privatization inherent in the neoliberal goal of economic accumulation go against the ethos of *liberté, egalité, fraternité*. In the 1990s enduring economic exceptionalism (exemplified by the 1992 referendum that saw France join the European Union by the tiniest of margins and the 1998 introduction of the thirty-five-hour working week) was increasingly underpinned by discourses more clearly expressing a fear of being subsumed into the global market (epitomized by José Bové's stand against McDonald's in 1999).

French cultural exceptionalism (often accompanied by a sense of cultural superiority) has long played a key constitutive role alongside economic, political, and diplomatic protectionism in the construction of the *exception française*. If the 1994 *Loi Toubon* protecting the French language follows a long exceptionalist tradition, its quest to resist the market- and media-driven invasion of Anglicisms exemplifies a dominant strand of French crisis discourses surrounding globalization: the sense of a tangible threat of cultural neo-imperialism and its perceived vehicles: neoliberalism, the mass media, and multinational corporations. Whilst throughout the 1990s critiques of the French field of cultural production continued to follow the convention of the apocalyptic declaration of a waste ground brought about by now established avant-gardes, a new set of crisis discourses became increasingly urgent. These variously described French culture as having become the victim of global market forces, homogenized into a mass media product, and succumbed to the putative dominant aesthetic of postmodernism (a nebulous perceived condition linked to the development of late capitalism, the mass media, the questioning of totalizing discourses, and the relativist celebration of the impossibility of the turning point).

---

[3] 'the one and indivisible Republic'.

Certainly the removal of the countdown clock outside the Pompidou Centre in 1997 and its replacement by a less outmoded display on the Eiffel Tower underpinned how the exponential development of new technologies had rendered the mechanism—and arguably French cultural confidence—an anachronism. Indeed if there was revolution in France in the decade after the celebration of the *bicentenaire* of 1789, it was that brought about by the combined impact of the global market economy, the mass audiovisual and digital media, and information technology. These unprecedented changes met with a concert of contradictory crisis discourses, from declarations of the end of history to terminal prognoses for French literature, hitherto an important constituent narrative of the French exception. The delayed opening of the research section of Mitterrand's *Très Grande Bibliothèque* in 1998 resonated with this questioning of the state of the French intellectual nation and its perceived threats from within and without.

This study investigates this culturally and temporally specific return to the trope of the turning point. It examines the relationship of literary returns to crisis with the inherent aesthetics of crisis of language and the self; the tangible crises of 1990s France; and the production and manipulation of crises and crisis discourses by the global market and the mass media. The book analyses the currency of the model of crisis as a turning point in both theoretical and fictional approaches at a time when the cultural dominant is perceived to be a putative postmodern aesthetics of crisis without end, and when French identity discourses are perceived to be threatened by global market economics and the mass media. Challenging such perceptions, it examines contrasting prose fictions within their conditions of production, assessing how crisis is reflected, responded to, perpetuated, and, at times, challenged. So this book seeks to tease out how prose fictions intervene in debates about the mass media, neoliberalism, global market economics, and sexual and postcolonial identities, while also gauging the enduring agency—critical and creative—of literature itself.

THE *FIN DE MILLÉNAIRE* AESTHETICS OF CRISIS

A 'long twentieth century' of crisis thinking can be traced spanning Freud, Marx, Nietzsche, and Saussure, the Frankfurt School, materialist feminism, structuralism, poststructuralism, difference feminism, discourses labelled as postmodern, and those which seek to counter them. As the millennium drew to a close, French thinkers and writers responded at once to the crises of language, representation, and legitimation, and to the new conditions produced by the mass media and the global market. These attempts are mediated by the understanding of language as an arbitrary medium which can but articulate its own crisis. And if language is understood to constitute the subject and to be the flawed tool that mediates all human representations of the world, then human experience—the crisis of the self—must equally be understood as aesthetic. The aesthetics of crisis are therefore inscribed in all human experience, linguistic practices, and cultural production. Nonetheless, aesthetics cannot be separated from questions of ethics and ideology— not in the mid-twentieth-century sense of political commitment—but rather in the sense that language (and therefore literature) is always already inscribed in the system it may seek to transcend or criticize.

The trope of the turning point should not be considered as unproblematic. Instead its contradictory manifestations and the different, often hidden ways in which crisis is produced and manipulated are brought to the fore in the following analyses. In this book, the concept of the aesthetics of crisis provides a loose critical framework which offers a new way of considering the late twentieth-century French field of cultural production, and raises questions of the enduring potential of the trope of crisis both in terms of aesthetics and of political intervention in literary and other forms. The analyses challenge the notion that the dominant discourse in turn-of-the-millennium France is that of a perceived postmodern perpetual crisis variously described in terms of the suspicion of totalizing narratives, relativism, the demise of the ethical, and the subsuming of the cultural into the conditions of production. Nonetheless, the intention here is not to attempt a stable definition of an intrinsically slippery term. Nor is it to construct binary oppositions of postmodernism and the *fin de millénaire* aesthetics of crisis, or of postmodernism and modernism. Rather, this book aims to show how the understanding of the postmodern condition as one where the trope of the turning point no longer has any sense-making or ethical potential corresponds neither to the particular convergence of crises and crisis discourses in turn-of-the-millennium France, nor to those represented and used by the thinkers and writers discussed in this study; nor, indeed, to discourses commonly described as postmodern.

6   *Fin de millénaire* French Fiction

The term *fin de millénaire* is not simply intended to denote the date of the turn of the third millennium. It refers to a culturally specific phenomenon that coincides with that symbolic turning point, but has its roots in France's intellectual tradition and the country's particular experience of modernity, of the development of the mass media, and of global market economics. As used here *fin de millénaire* resonates with the notion of the *fin de siècle* but also intersects with descriptors such as *la société du spectacle* (after Guy Debord);[4] *la société de consommation* and *l'hyperréel* (after Jean Baudrillard);[5] post-industrial society (after Daniel Bell);[6] late capitalist society (after Ernest Mandel);[7] the Third—or Fourth—Machine Age (after Fredric Jameson);[8] *la société postmoraliste* (after Gilles Lipovetsky);[9] post-traumatic culture (after Kirby Farrell);[10] *la condition postmoderne* (after Jean-François Lyotard);[11] post-Marxist, post-feminist, media, or information society. The *fin de millénaire* aesthetics of crisis, then, designates the discreet intersection in France 1990–2000 of tangible crises and apocalyptic discourses with the crisis discourses further produced and manipulated by the global market and the mass media; and also refers to the representation of those processes and the appropriation of the trope of the turning point by French writers of prose fiction.

THE *FIN DE MILLÉNAIRE* DOUBLE BIND

One of the distinguishing factors of the *fin de millénaire* aesthetics of crisis is a multifaceted double bind that is temporally and culturally specific, and faced by critical discourses, prose fictions, and the analyses

[4] Guy Debord, *La Société du spectacle* (Paris: Buchet-Chastel, 1967).
[5] Jean Baudrillard, *La Société de consommation: Ses Mythes, ses structures* (Paris: Gallimard, 1970); *Simulacres et simulation* (Paris: Galilée, 1985).
[6] Daniel Bell, *The Coming of Post-industrial Society: A Venture in Social Forecasting* (London: Heinemann, 1974).
[7] Ernest Mandel, *Late Capitalism*, trans. Joris de Bres (London: Verso, 1978).
[8] Fredric Jameson, *Postmodernism, or The Cultural Logic of Capitalism* (London: Verso, 1991).
[9] Gilles Lipovetsky, *Le Crépuscule du devoir: L'Éthique indolore des nouveaux temps démocratiques* (Paris: Gallimard, 1992).
[10] Kirby Farrell, *Post-traumatic Culture: Injury and Interpretation in the Nineties* (Baltimore: Johns Hopkins University Press, 1998).
[11] Jean-François Lyotard, *La Condition Postmoderne: Rapport sur le savoir* (Paris: Minuit, 1979).

in this book alike. Of course, the following discussions confront the double bind faced by every critical analysis: the risk of becoming totalizing in its own right and of being recuperated by the system from which it cannot maintain a critical distance. Indeed, crisis discourses all risk becoming clichés (as is arguably the case with the notions of the spectacular, simulacra, and the hyperreal). Both critical and normative discourses are inextricable from their conditions of production. However, turn-of-the-millennium contestatory narratives also run the risk of being commodified and appropriated by the mass media and the global market, yet are dependent on them in order to have a voice. Thus they risk perpetrating what Bourdieu calls symbolic violence: the imposition of categories of thought and perception upon dominated social subjects who then internalize them and so are co-implicated in underpinning and perpetuating the dominant order.[12]

A further distinguishing factor of the *fin de millénaire* aesthetics of crisis is that the trope of the turning point is continually generated and manipulated by the media and the market in order to perpetuate the global market economy. Marketing discourses and media images generate idealized stereotypes that are crisis producing because they are impossible to attain. Promotional techniques promise ostensible 'turning points'—*purchase-crises*—which necessarily fail to provide lasting fulfilment in order to continually produce ongoing demand. Reality television feeds on and produces crisis. Mainstream cinema, news reports, true-crime dramas, and video games commodify and stoke consumer appetite for trauma. What is more, these processes multiply the commodification of women, producing and disseminating new misogynist images: mass-mediatized, market-driven symbolic violence.

These multiple modes of crisis production and manipulation effectively redouble the double bind of the (mass-mediatized) recuperation of critical discourses. This study's exploration of the aesthetics of crisis of *fin de millénaire* French prose fiction recognizes that its own use of the trope of the turning point and that of the thinkers and writers it draws on are also subject to these processes. The extent to which any form of cultural production—and prose fiction in particular—can escape the

---

[12] Pierre Bourdieu and Jean-Claude Passeron, *La Reproduction: Éléments pour une théorie du système d'enseignement* (Paris: Minuit, 1970); Bourdieu, *La Distinction: Critique sociale du jugement* (Paris: Minuit, 1979).

double bind of recuperation and commodification is recurrently called into question. Nonetheless, the book aims (as, it argues, do some of the texts it analyses) to examine crisis narratives whilst also deploying them as self-reflexively as possible and as possible tools for negotiating the problematics of representation, interpretation, and contestation. Hence, by examining the relationship between tangible crises, crisis discourses, and the sense-making trope of the turning point, the following analyses offer a new way of evaluating of the potential of the literary to make interventions in debates about neoliberalism, globalization, the mass media, and postmodernism. Providing a platform for critiquing theoretical and literary approaches that challenge—or fail to challenge—the problematic of the production and manipulation of crisis by the global market and the mass media, this book renews the question of the politics of literature.

FIN DE MILLÉNAIRE PROSE FICTION: RETURNS TO CRISIS

Prose fiction today is a highly self-aware form of linguistic practice, which seeks to represent and make sense of human experience; develops in response to changes in human experience; and, arguably, changes that experience. It therefore provides a particularly pertinent way of considering the *fin de millénaire* aesthetics of crisis. Although the novel is the genre most frequently pronounced to be in crisis in late twentieth-century France, a time when the qualification 'roman' is used less frequently as generic boundaries become increasingly blurred, prose fiction remains the dominant French literary form. It therefore offers a vantage point from which to gauge the impact of global market economics and the mass media, from television and film to advertising, video games, and the Internet.

France's pride in its *grands écrivains* as agents of revolution (both in terms of historical events and cultural avant gardes) is a tenet of French exceptionalism. What is more, from the inception of the genre, the sense that French literature is in crisis has been both a symptom of and motor for literary innovation, with predictions of the imminent death of the novel countered by writers rejecting the aesthetics of their predecessors. And whilst the ascribing of a perceived literary waste ground to fallout from previous literary and intellectual avant-gardes is a key part of French literary regeneration, a questioning of the evolving ideology and institutions of capitalism has also provided an impetus for the exploration of the relationship between the aesthetic and the political in prose fiction, as evidenced by Balzac, Flaubert, Zola, Gide, Céline, and Sartre for example. During the *Trente Glorieuses* a convergence of prose fictions represented burgeoning consumer culture from critical perspectives.[13] These include Christiane Rochefort's *Les Petits Enfants du siècle* (1961), Georges Perec's *Les Choses* (1965), Simone de Beauvoir's *Les Belles Images* (1966), Annie Ernaux's *Les Armoires vides* (1974), and René-Victor Pilhes's *L'Imprécateur* (1974) amongst others.[14] However, as this study demonstrates, a different and diverse set of modes of representing, manipulating, challenging, and perpetuating the discourses of the media and the market is a particular feature of the *fin de millénaire* literary field. Here Christine Angot, Jean Echenoz, Michel Houellebecq, and Marie Redonnet provide the contrasting focuses of individual chapters, but other examples include Frédéric Beigbeder, François Bon, Catherine Cusset, Didier Daeninckx, Marie Darrieussecq, Annie Ernaux, François Maspero, Marie Nimier, Daniel Pennac, Vincent Ravalec, and Jean-Philippe Toussaint.

Whilst in the 1990s some literary critics follow in the decrying of erstwhile avant-gardes (most often the legacy of the *nouveau roman*, structuralism, and poststructuralism) there is a striking focus on the impact on literary production of neoliberal ideology and of the audiovisual and digital media. A preoccupation with the recuperation of prose fiction as a homogenized commodity is clear in questions asked in the 1997 *Quinzaine Littéraire* dossier 'Où va la littérature française?':

---

[13] 'the Thirty Glorious (Years)'.
[14] Christiane Rochefort, *Les Petits Enfants du siècle* (Paris: Grasset, 1961); Georges Perec, *Les Choses* (Paris: Julliard, 1965); Simone de Beauvoir, *Les Belles Images* (Paris: Gallimard, 1966); Annie Ernaux, *Les Armoires vides* (Paris: Gallimard, 1974); René-Victor Pilhes's *L'Imprécateur* (Paris: Seuil, 1974).

on accuse souvent les médias (et tout particulièrement la télévision) d'entretenir une grande confusion des genres et des valeurs au seul bénéfice d'un marché du livre dont les préoccupations seraient de moins en moins littéraires. [. . .] La vie littéraire et la critique vous semblent-elles condamnées? La notion même d'écrivain vous semble-t-elle en train d'évoluer en France?[15]

Whilst most writers surveyed respond by asserting the enduring critical and creative capacities of literature, these questions typify how the *crise du roman* at the end of the twentieth century articulates a fear of the transformation of prose fiction into a consumer product that neutralizes critical discourses. A perceived fragmentation of the literary field also recurs in discussions. In a dossier 'Romanciers d'aujourd'hui' in literary journal *Dix-neuf/Vingt*, Bruno Blanckeman ascribes fragmentation to a late twentieth-century intellectual crisis: 'La crise de la fiction française [. . .] ne relève pas de la littérature, mais de la représentation, en panne de modèles plus que d'œuvres.'[16] Yet Marc Dambre sees heterogeneity as vitality: 'La crise, si crise il y a, est non de pauvreté mais d'abondance.'[17] Contradictory prognoses abound, from the terminally negative to Dominique Viart's assertion of literary regeneration identifiable in provisional returns to history, the subject, story telling, and the real.[18] Yet amidst these crisis discourses and the identification of potentially regenerative returns, the significance of the phenomenon of the return to the trope of the turning point in literary texts and in competing discourses has yet to be examined.

---

[15] 'Où va la littérature française?: 24 écrivains des années 90 répondent', *La Quinzaine Littéraire*, 1–15 March 1997, and *La Quinzaine Littéraire*, 16–31 March 1997: 'the media (especially television) are often accused of causing massive confusion of genres and of values, fuelling a book market where literary concerns become ever less important. [. . .] Do you think that literature and literary criticism are doomed? Do you think what it means to be a writer is changing in France?'

[16] Bruno Blanckeman, 'Aspects du récit littéraire actuel', *Dix-neuf/Vingt*, 2 (1996), 233–52, at p. 233: 'The crisis of French fiction [. . .] is not a crisis of literature itself, but of modes of representation. The problem is not that books are not being written, but that they are not being written in new ways.'

[17] Marc Dambre, 'Parier aujourd'hui', *Dix-neuf/Vingt*, 2 (1996), 149–50, at p. 149: 'The crisis, if there is a crisis at all, is not because there are not enough works being written, but because there are so many.'

[18] See Dominique Viart, ed., *Écritures contemporaines 1: Mémoires du récit* (Paris and Caen: Lettres Modernes Minard, 1998); Viart and Jan Baetans, eds, *Écritures contemporaines 2: États du roman contemporaine* (Paris and Caen: Lettres Modernes Minard, 1999); Viart, *Le Roman français au XXe siècle* (Paris: Hachette, 1999), p. 13.

It is this multivalent but culturally and temporally specific return to crisis which provides the springboard for the following analyses of contrasting *fin de millénaire* prose fictions. Situated in the context of social, economic, and political crises and competing crisis discourses, these investigate the status—and potential agency—of the turning point. Drawing on a 'long twentieth century' of crisis thinking, the study examines the problematic of the role of the notion of crisis and its importance within contemporary discourses, and identifies the processes whereby this sense of crisis is perpetuated and naturalized. The aim is not to add to surveys of late twentieth-century French writing, to identify new 'schools' of French fiction, or to falsely commodify a heterogeneous field. Rather, the discussions draw out contradictions. Such contradictions include those inherent in the blurring of generic boundaries and the market-led impulse to categorize literary production; in claims that postmodern perpetual crisis is the cultural dominant whilst the trope of the turning point is harnessed by thinkers and writers labelled postmodern; and in the way marketing and media discourses produce and disseminate unrealizable stereotypes and promise turning points but systematically fail to fulfil them.

Particular attention is paid to the representation of women and the role of cultural production in discourses of misogyny, revealing how mediatized forms of sexual commodification disseminate misogynist discourses and images and create new unrealizable stereotypes. Nonetheless, whilst foregrounding such symbolic violence, the following analyses of *fin de millénaire* prose fiction also investigate how the crisis discourses of the mass media and the global market may also be harnessed—knowingly or unwittingly—as a motor for both aesthetic development and for raising ethical (so therefore political) questions.

CRITICAL CONTRAST: ANGOT, ECHENOZ, HOUELLEBECQ, AND REDONNET

Selecting a range of contrasting texts published in 1990 to 2000, this study necessarily takes risks. In 1975 Derrida noted that identifying an avant-garde is only possible in retrospect: 'L'effet d'avant-garde est toujours déchiffrable après coup. L'avant-garde est donc, s'il y en a, l'imprésentable.'[19] In 2001 Mireille Calle-Gruber discusses how the risk of making value judgements concerning the very recent past is compounded by a perceived manipulation of critical perception by the dominant ideology and a changing relationship with time: 'risque [...] de tomber dans le piège du contemporain. Car, paradoxe suprême, bousculés dans notre prêt-à-penser et notre prêt-à-jouir, nous avons le plus grand mal à être nos propres contemporains.'[20] Moreover, beyond the risk of 'getting it wrong' that haunts certain literary critics, the categorization of an author or work as symptomatic of a 'period' of literature paradoxically reflects the mechanics of the fictional process: the imposition of a structure on time and space, and the creation of causality and linearity out of plurality and contingency.

Whilst knowingly risking falling into the double bind of drawing attention to—and therefore underpinning—the manipulation of crisis by the media and the market, the choice of texts for this study also necessarily confronts a number of structural paradoxes. To restrict analysis to texts published between 1990 and 2000 is to impose an artificial framework. Yet it is a function of the argument that a temporally and culturally specific convergence of tangible crises and crisis discourses marks the decade. To assume that heterogeneity, literary scandal, or indeed representations of the mass media, the global market, and neoliberalism are evidence of resistance per se is a simplistic oversight. Nonetheless, the diversity of the field and the multiple ways in which writers of prose fictions harness, represent, and engage with crises and crisis discourses suggest that literature continues to bring the possibility of a turning point into question. Indeed, this study investigates the problematic and problematizing status of *fin de millénaire* prose fiction. It examines the different ways in which writers counter the perception of perpetual crisis as the cultural dominant, and harness

---

[19] Jacques Derrida, 'Trente-huit réponses sur l'avant garde', *Digraphe*, 6 (1975), 151–64, at p. 152: 'The impact of the avant-garde is always felt in retrospect. So the avant-garde, if such a thing exists, is the unrepresentable.'

[20] Mireille Calle-Gruber, *Histoire de la Littérature française du XXᵉ siècle; ou, Les Repentirs de la littérature* (Paris: Honoré Champion, 2001), p. 14: 'the risk of [...] falling into the trap of the contemporary. Because the ultimate irony is that as we lurch from ready-made thought to ready-made pleasure, we find it enormously difficult to be our own contemporaries.'

the critical leverage in contemporary contradictions. Yet at the same time, it identifies how prose fictions may perpetuate the symbolic violence and misogyny of the mass media and the global market.

The choice of Christine Angot, Jean Echenoz, Michel Houellebecq, and Marie Redonnet in itself raises questions. Together, these writers do not fit any of the perceived trends identified by critics, publishers, and writers of turn-of-the-millennium prose fiction. However, their prose fictions have been selected from a particularly heterogeneous literary field not only because of their representation and manipulation of crisis and crisis discourses, but also because they afford intersecting and diverging perspectives on the discreet phenomenon of the *fin de millénaire* aesthetics of crisis. If Angot, Echenoz, Houellebecq, and Redonnet are major literary figures, they also attract often violently contradictory critical assessments. Literary critics in their own right, they develop their own contrasting stances with regard to contemporary cultural production and the agency of literature in the twenty-first century. As writers of prose fiction and as critics, and in both the form and content of their writing, Angot, Echenoz, Houellebecq, and Redonnet are concerned with the problematic of representational practice. They also offer contrasting representations and narrative strategies which may be read as implicit critiques of global market economics and the mass media. Often self-reflexively, they recuperate the discourses of the media and the market whilst also returning—strikingly and diversely—to the trope of the turning point. Indeed, in different ways their fictions are imbued with and performative of the *fin de millénaire* aesthetics of crisis. Recurrently, however, they counter the putative postmodern aesthetic of crisis without end, and pose, invite, and beg the question of the enduring agency of the notion of crisis in literary and competing discourses.

Echenoz's literary reputation was already established by 1990 as a ludic master of subversion of popular literary genres. However, critical discussions of his writing as 'minimalist' or indeed postmodern elide the ways in which 1992 marks a distinct turning point in the scope of his literary project. Whilst the pleasure of the text remains a priority, from implicitly critical perspectives (ranging from the local to the global), Echenoz's *fin de millénaire* prose fictions reveal patterns of crisis production and manipulation. Echenoz represents, and in some cases perpetuates the production of unrealizable stereotypes and other forms of market-led and often misogynist symbolic violence. However, these texts self-reflexively call into question the agency of prose fiction and that of a wide range of more or less commodified modes of cultural production, from reality television to cinema, and from modern art to ethnic artefacts. The co-implication of the cultural producer and often of the consumer in symbolic violence markedly, if not always deliberately, comes to the foreground.

Houellebecq is France's most notorious writer and is variously labelled as head of a perceived new literary school; as a *grand écrivain*, exponent of postmodern barbarism; or little more than a *succès de scandale*. At the centre of the biggest French literary *affaire* of the late twentieth century (in itself arguably an indicator that fiction may yet have some agency) Houellebecq is not only provocative in his dealings with the media, but also from within his prose fictions via the contradictory and troubling discourses (notably misogynist, racist, and homophobic) that feature in them. The trope of the turning point is harnessed to develop a totalizing theory to account for the crisis of the late twentieth-century subject: the production of desire by what are represented as the dual sexual and material economies of neoliberalism. Houellebecq also appropriates a wide range of narrative strategies from the *roman à thèse* and poetic interludes to scientific tracts, advertising slogans, self-help mantras, and mail order catalogues. From the turgid life of the middle-aged middle manager, via failed love stories, representations of intellectual failure, and the dangerous potential of science, Houellebecq uses crisis tropes to project—and perhaps to warn against—the definitive turning point: the end of the human race.

Angot's *fin de millénaire* prose fictions actively mount an attack on the media and the (literary) market, yet demonstrate a contradictory dependence on them. These texts are often described using the homogenizing term *autofiction*, but in fact destabilize such market-driven labels. Although also categorized by dint of her gender, Angot's writing can by no means be described as feminist. Instead it sometimes deliberately but often unintentionally exposes the misogyny occluded by ostensibly post-feminist discourses. The representation and sometimes unwitting performance of co-implication that recurs in Angot's figuring of incest invites urgent questions about the responsibility of the writer, cultural producer, and consumer. Transgressive juxtapositions link the manipulation of crisis by the media with incest, sexual abuse, personal relationships, and genocide, intersecting with contemporary developments in trauma theory and with the commodification of trauma by the audiovisual media. Their deeply problematic status notwithstanding, these prose fictions emphatically articulate how, despite the media generation of a voyeuristic consumption of violence, trauma is enduringly elided.

Although Redonnet's *fin de millénaire* prose fictions receive less media attention, and are sometimes considered as following in the wake of practitioners of *écriture féminine*, they diverge from that now arguably commodified notion, and foreground (whilst also sometimes perpetuating) enduring and market-driven modes of misogynist oppression. Redonnet's texts are set in increasingly recognizable contemporary contexts and, intersecting with the thought of the Frankfurt School, seek to resist not only the discourses of the global market and the mass media, but also those associated with postmodernism. So Redonnet's *fin de millénaire* texts refute those critical assessments which, from the 1980s, have classified her fiction as exemplary of postmodern aesthetics. Whilst also categorized by some critics as part of the putative minimalist school, Redonnet's *fin de millénaire* prose fictions exceed language games. They evidence a quest to warn against the recurrence of the traumas of the past in the present and the future, and attempt not only to represent but also to make a travesty of the discourses of the global market and the mass media. Indeed beyond her fiction, Redonnet discusses her work as a new form of literary commitment, inviting the question of the agency of what she describes as literary acts of resistance.

Thus whether courting or taunting the media (Houellebecq and Angot); remaining distant from it (Echenoz); or falling out of the marketing orbit and figuring literature as a means of resisting the perceived spectacularization of the *fin de millénaire* literary field (Redonnet); these writers perpetuate, appropriate, expose, and challenge the discourses of the mass media and global market economics. Whilst neither agents nor commentators of the May 1968 *événements*, they share a common heritage of social and intellectual change: a turning point in the French relationship with consumerism and the mass media converging with an intense questioning of universal values; teleology; the transparency of language; the immutability of the subject; and the narrative of history. None of these writers can be categorized as embodying a particular ideological or theoretical position, although the relative absence of feminist discourses is a key concern of this book.

Indeed, Redonnet and Angot are not discussed in terms of 'women's writing' (and the two women themselves make a point of rejecting such categorization). Instead discussions identify, amongst other features, the two female writers' concern for the critical capacity of women as (writing) subjects and the ways in which they may more or less unwittingly perpetuate misogyny, comparing this with the representations of women by Echenoz and Houellebecq.

Establishing the critical framework of the *fin de millénaire* aesthetics of crisis, the study begins with a chapter which traces a 'long twentieth century' of crisis thinking, spanning the crises of belief, history, the self, and language articulated by Nietzsche, Marx, Freud, and Saussure and developed by the Frankfurt School and late twentieth-century French thinkers associated with structuralism, poststructuralism, feminism, postmodernism, and its counter discourses. This examination of crisis thinking is paralleled by an elucidation of the manipulation of crises and crisis discourses by the mass media and the global market economy, and its impact—real and perceived—in late twentieth-century France.

The enduring role of prose fiction in the identity narratives that constitute the *exception française* is also explored, and, establishing how literature is subject to and influenced by economic, social, and political change, the structures and commercial dictates of the French literary field are analysed. An analysis of discourses labelled postmodern and those seeking to counter that perceived aesthetic gives the lie at once to artificially paradigmatic distinctions between modernism and postmodernism and to the notion that perpetual crisis is culturally dominant. Finally, countering critical impulses towards commodification, the heterogeneity of the late twentieth-century literary field is discussed. Thus readers are equipped to situate the following chapters on the work of selected writers in the context of their aesthetic and commercial conditions of production.

Individual chapters devoted to the prose fictions of Angot, Echenoz, Houellebecq, and Redonnet draw upon the discussions of the *fin de millénaire* aesthetics of crisis in the opening chapter. Each is designed at once to set up contrasts between the writer and the broader field of cultural production; to introduce readers to the writer; and to examine the extent to which—deliberately or unwittingly—their prose fictions afford critical perspectives on, challenge, resist, and perpetuate components of the *fin de millénaire* aesthetics of crisis. Identifying how they represent and manipulate tangible crises, crisis discourses, and the trope of the turning point, the chapters devoted to Angot, Echenoz, Houelle-becq, and Redonnet investigate the diverse ways in which these writers develop narrative strategies of resistance, recuperation, and counter-resistance that differ from a putative postmodern sense of perpetual crisis and from the manipulation of crisis tropes by the mass media and the global market. Harnessing contrasting modes of crisis thinking and identifying how these writers deliberately and unwittingly intersect with them, the analyses evaluate not only the aesthetic potential of the literary but also its potential to intervene in converging debates about gender, sexuality, race, and the impact of the mass media, neoliberalism, and globalization. Thus this study seeks to build a platform from which to critique ways in which, on the eve of the twenty-first century, different theoretical and fictional approaches confront the problematic of the manipulation of crisis discourses and renew the question of the politics of literature.

1

Crisis, critical perspectives, and *fin de millénaire* prose fiction

TURNING POINTS AND SENSE-MAKING FICTIONS

The notion of crisis as a turning point is central to Western thought. It structures the Judeo-Christian apocalypse; the Enlightenment narratives of progress, reason, and history; the ruptures of modernity; and the Marxist dialectic. Evolving in response to its socio-historical context, the trope functions simultaneously as a means of shaping perceptions of the past; rationalizing the difficulties of the present; and providing a perspective for the future. In Frank Kermode's interpretation of end-directed fictions the turning point is the underlying structure of all sense-making narratives: 'Such moments punctuate and measure our time and our lives; they are the ancestors or congeners of the many other fictions we use to make sense of our worlds and our lives.'[1] With its degraded present, its radical turning point, and its promise of a redemptive future, the apocalyptic narrative is the crisis trope par excellence. The Old Testament stages a succession of apocalypses, but it is the Book of Revelations (20: 4–6) and the visions of John of Patmos that provide the blueprint for the Western intellectual tradition. Here crisis—the turning point of the Apocalypse—is followed by the millennium: one thousand years of peace, prosperity, and good government when Christ returns to reign over the City of God. For the early Christians this narrative made sense of the struggle against the repression of the Roman Empire (the Antichrist), keeping faith, and encouraging patience and

[1] Frank Kermode, *The Sense of an Ending: Studies in the Theory of Fiction with a New Epilogue* (Oxford: Oxford University Press, 2000), p. 90.

courage by projecting a turning point when the City of God (the Church) would triumph over the City of the World (Rome). However, by the seventh century Christianity was no longer a beleaguered minority religion, and Saint Augustine proposed a pragmatic understanding of the Apocalypse. Augustine endowed life on earth with meaning by describing it as the eternal conflict between the City of God (the Church which had, at Pentecost, already entered into the millennium) and the City of the World (ruled by Satan). In this sense-making narrative, judgement and eternal bliss—or eternal punishment for the citizens of the World—would come at the death of the individual, rather than with the advent of the Saviour.

Such is the modern configuration of crisis, a trope that shapes both literary and temporal fictions: a shift from an understanding of crisis as imminent and collective, to that of crisis as immanent and personal. The apocalyptic narrative at once drives and makes sense of the process of socio-political change, entering into a symbiotic relationship with ideologies that depend on the trope. Indeed the notion of crisis as a turning point has great ideological potential. It provides the structure for myths of empire and of decadence, and the trope of the turning point is appropriated both by dominant ideologies to rationalize the suffering of the present and by dissenting movements as a rationale for rebellion.

By the Enlightenment, the religious connotations of the apocalyptic trope had given way to the secular. This notion now fuelled the narrative of progress, with its therapeutic crises endowing time with purpose and history with the utopian end of a better world. The 1789 French Revolution is the epitome of the secular apocalypse, complete with Judgement Day and messianic promise of regeneration in the shape of *liberté, égalité, fraternité*. Indeed, Max Silverman suggests that post-Revolutionary France led the Western world in developing this rational model of end-directed crisis thinking:

The Revolution of 1789 was the political blueprint for transforming those concepts [French Enlightenment philosophy] into 'natural' law and became the model adopted by nascent nationalisms elsewhere. The spirit of French republicanism [. . .] symbolized the persistence of that Utopian dream of a shared humanity throughout the second half of the nineteenth century and the first half of the twentieth century. This was a dream founded on a passionate belief in the power of reason and science to usher in the new dawn. And which nation state had greater faith in reason than France?[2]

Historian Daniel Milo suggests that the symbolic power of the century as a turning point came into its own in the aftermath of the French Revolution: 'En 1800, la cassure révolutionnaire a fait émerger le siècle pour dire l'opposition radicale entre présent et passé antérieur.'[3] In nineteenth-century France successive revolutions, regime changes, millenarian movements, and apocalyptic thinkers such as Charles Fourier, Pierre Leroux, and Henri de Saint-Simon, dramatized the agency of crisis as a turning point in the process of socio-political change. The *fin de siècle* rhetoric of crisis articulated a sense of spiritual dereliction that jarred with both the unprecedented material progress of the time and confidence in an ability to change the future. Yet as Eugen Weber points out in his 2000 study of millennial beliefs, the *fin de siècle* concept shaped both the events it described and the critical perspectives of the twentieth century.[4] Likewise for Kermode, *fin de siècle* operates as a sense-making fiction, which, although attached to an arbitrary temporal landmark, marks an epistemological break:

Ends and beginnings, round numbers and sacred numbers, anniversaries and jubilees entrap the mind, arouse attention, and suggest figures of speech and thought that turn metaphor into reality. The image of *fin de siècle* was a case in point, and the marriage of decadence and end followed naturally. Its offspring were all around: a flood of novels, poems, plays, articles, and sermons about twilight, endings, deterioration, degeneracy, and decay.[5]

Meanwhile, in his history of 'end of the world' narratives Jean-Paul Clébert also identifies a convergence of 'endist' discourses at the end of the second millennium: 'En cette fin du XXe siècle [. . .] [o]n nous annonce successivement la fin de l'histoire, du politique, des idéologies (et même des démocraties), des intellectuels, de la science, des valeurs

    [2] Max Silverman, *Facing Postmodernity: Contemporary French Thought on Culture and Society* (London: Routledge, 1999), p. 1.
    [3] Daniel S. Milo, *Trahir le temps: Histoire* (Paris: Les Belles Lettres, 1991), p. 10: 'In 1800, the rupture of revolution ushered in the new century with a radical opposition of the present and the past anterior.'
    [4] Eugen Weber, *Apocalypses: Prophecies, Cults and Millennial Beliefs through the Ages* (London: Pimlico, 2000), pp. 236–7.
    [5] Kermode, *The Sense of an Ending*, p. 25.

morales, de la religion catholique.'[6] Contradicting postmodern scepticism of future-oriented discourses, such 'endism' continues in the
tradition of the apocalyptic trope, described by Pascal Bruckner as 'le
mystique des points culminants'.[7] Just as the perceived degeneration at
the temporal marker of the *fin de siècle* coincided with an intellectual
turning point that generated a new aesthetics of crisis, the convergence
of crisis discourses at the turn of the third millennium invites the
question of the enduring currency and potential of the trope of the
turning point.

A 'LONG TWENTIETH CENTURY' OF
CRISIS THINKING

The turn of the twentieth century coincided with a crisis of the Western
intellectual tradition. The narratives of reason, progress, and history and
the concepts of truth and knowledge were brought into question at a
time when burgeoning industrialization and technological advance
changed ways of perceiving the world. Scientific discovery further
undermined the tenets of religious belief whilst furnishing humankind
with the tools for its own destruction. Meanwhile, the development of
mass markets and media threatened the ability of culture to maintain a
critical distance, the autonomy of art, and its potential as a vehicle for
political struggle. Both responding to and fuelling this convergence of
anxieties, the 'maîtres du soupçon',[8] as Vincent Descombes describes
Nietzsche, Freud, and Marx, critically influenced—in the sense of
bringing into crisis—Western thought. From intersecting perspectives,
they shattered confidence in universal values of the Enlightenment,
transcendental belief systems, and the understanding of the subject as
immutable. Their insights radically affected the sense-making narratives

[6] Jean-Paul Clébert, *Histoire de la fin du monde de l'an mil a l'an 2000* (Paris: Belfond,
1993), p. 262: 'At the end of this twentieth century [. . .] one after another, we are told
of the end of history, of politics, of ideology (and even of democracy), of the intellectual,
of science, of ethics, of Catholicism.'

[7] Pascal Bruckner, *L'Euphorie perpetuelle: Essai sur le devoir de bonheur* (Paris: Grasset
et Fasquelle, 2000), p. 139: 'the mystique of the turning point'.

[8] Vincent Descombes, *Le Même et l'autre: Quarante-cinq ans de philosophie française
(1933–1978)* (Paris: Minuit, 1979), p. 13: 'the masters of suspicion'.

produced by Western culture, raising questions as to its unquestioned reliance on the trope of the turning point and on language as a transparent medium.

Friedrich Nietzsche (1844–1900) claimed the absence of objective, universal, absolute values, thus identifying Christian doctrine (or any belief, text, or discourse) as interpretative. Asserting that life is determined by the individual's will to power rather than by any preordained or transcendental force, Nietzsche at once exhorted his contemporaries to break free from dogmatism, and opened up a new, plural world of textual interpretation. This challenge intersects with that of Sigmund Freud (1856–1939), who theorized the operations of the unconscious, shattering the notion of the self as a unified entity. Conceiving of the Oedipus complex, Freud argued that individuation is the result of separation from the mother, an unresolved crisis which is repressed in the unconscious, whose unruly drives disrupt the conscious through psychotic and neurotic symptoms, or through slips of the tongue. Hence self-identity is a fiction betrayed by language and Freudian psychoanalysis is akin to literary analysis, decoding stories that mask or reveal repressed crisis.

Where Freud challenged the understanding of individual selfhood, the intellectual turning point precipitated by Karl Marx (1818–83) destabilized the understanding of history, language, culture, and collective agency. Challenging the Enlightenment notion of history as a narrative of progress, Marx argued that it should not be understood as a preordained process. He described history as the product of patterns of human exploitation, patterns which precipitate crises: dialectical struggles for control of the material conditions that determine power. He also identified language as a social practice, a vehicle for ideology rather than a transparent medium, and art as a commodity subject to the conditions of material production, albeit one that could be harnessed to revolutionary ends.

The influence of Ferdinand de Saussure (1857–1913) should be considered alongside these thinkers who at once responded to and generated crisis. Saussure's *Cours de linguistique générale* was published posthumously in 1916, but did not make its intellectual impact until the 1950s. However, his crisis thinking intersected with that of the 'masters of suspicion', demonstrating how language operates as a system of differences, with no causal link between signifier and signified. Thus

Saussure's *sémiologie* exposes the contingency behind the illusory transparency of language, with radical implications for the conceptualization and articulation of crisis, and for perceptions of sense-making narratives.

Intellectual developments in the wake of Nietzsche, Freud, Marx, and Saussure may be read as a 'long twentieth century' of often mutually influencing crisis thinking. Thus distinguishing 'schools' of thought or intellectual movements is an artificial construct. It is one which this study at once challenges in its discussion of the tropes of the turning point associated with modernism and postmodernism, and utilizes pragmatically to investigate different modes of crisis thinking. For example, psychoanalytical theory and its harnessing of the insights of Saussure exemplifies the interlinking and mutually influencing impact of these crisis thinkers on the development of twentieth-century thought as it responded to and produced new crisis discourses. If Freud's Oedipus complex is a literary metaphor that seeks to describe the traumatic turning point whereby the infant renounces its sense of union and desire for the mother, Jacques Lacan recast the Oedipal crisis in linguistic terms. Building on the work of Freud and of Saussure in his seminars during the 1960s and 1970s, Lacan describes the pre-verbal phase as the realm of the imaginary and the Oedipal crisis as the 'mirror stage', which precipitates entry into the symbolic. This entails the constitution of the unconscious, the place where lack—desire for the mother—is repressed. With entry into the symbolic comes the acquisition of language, the medium through which human beings are placed within culture, ruled by the phallus: *le Nom du père* (the Law of the Father). Where Freud's linguistic focus is on the verbal evidence of desire breaking through into the conscious, in 'L'instance de la lettre dans l'inconscient, ou la raison depuis Freud' (1957) Lacan asserts that the unconscious is structured like a language, a network of fragments of memories, emotions, and experiences.[9] For Lacan as for Saussure, language is arbitrary and relative, moving from and between one signifier and another, and can never be fixed to a concept. So he argues that in the unconscious, desire moves from object to object such that there is no transcendental, final signifier: no resolution of the crisis of repressed

---

[9] Jacques Lacan, 'L'instance de la lettre dans l'inconscient ou la raison depuis Freud', in Lacan, *Ecrits I* (Paris: Seuil, 1970), pp. 249–89.

lack. Such by the end of the twentieth century is the notion of the crisis of the self.

From the 1950s, Saussure's discussion of the arbitrary nature of the link between signifier and signified and description of language as a network producing meaning through difference provided new perspectives for French structuralist thinkers who drew on these insights to identify relational signifying systems. Anthropologist Claude Lévi-Strauss compared the myths and social relations of primitive cultures with the rules of language.[10] Roland Barthes demonstrated how 1950s French cultural phenomena operated as 'mythologies', ideologically constructed sign systems underpinning the dominant bourgeois order.[11] Dismissing the notion of transcendental literary genius, Gérard Genette and Barthes identified formal structures constituting the specific 'internal language' of literature.[12] Meanwhile, A. J. Greimas, a Russian structuralist linguist living in France argued that meaning was constructed through binary oppositions.[13] Precipitating an intellectual turning point which parallels Lacan's development of Freud's thought, Jacques Derrida took such structuralist meta-languages and their basis in Saussurean linguistics still further. Moving beyond Greimas's theory that meaning is produced within dichotomies, Derrida seeks to show how language operates not by opposing terms, but through *différance*, a neologism indicating how meaning is always already different, always already deferred. This suggests that meaning is never truly present: it is only constructed through an infinite process of the presence of one signifier and the absence of others.

Thus, developing Saussurean insights, thinkers such as Derrida expose the arbitrary nature of all signifying systems, revealing the hierarchical oppositions of Western metaphysics to be ideological constructs. This late twentieth-century mode of crisis thinking has been labelled deconstruction or poststructuralism (and associated with the discourses labelled postmodern). It seeks to identify and expose risks of generalization, reification, and, ultimately, totalitarianism. In *De la grammatologie*

[10] Claude Lévi-Strauss, *Mythologiques 1–4* (Paris: Plon, 1964–71).

[11] Roland Barthes, *Mythologies* (Paris: Seuil, 1957).

[12] Barthes, *Le Degré zéro de la littérature* (Paris: Seuil, 1953); Gérard Genette, *Figures I, II and III* (Paris: Seuil, 1966–72).

[13] A. J. Greimas, *Sémantique structurale* (Paris: Larousse, 1966).

Derrida challenges the Western privileging of speech over writing and argues that literature and philosophy are not opposing terms, but necessarily co-implicated.[14] Although the notion of literature as a unified entity with transcendent agency is undermined by deconstructing these binary oppositions, writing (or textuality) encapsulates *différance*, the play of the signifier, and retains some potential agency.

Barthes's analyses evolved similarly, as articulated in his declaration of the figurative 'Death of the Author'.[15] Having previously identified literature as a system of linguistic structures, Barthes moved on to describe it as part of an infinite tissue of texts, constituted by arbitrary linguistic uses that are not the product of an individual author but are inscribed in an endless wealth of possible interpretations mediated at once by the author and by readers. Intersecting with Barthes, Julia Kristeva, founding member of the poststructuralist journal *Tel Quel* conceived of the phenomenon of 'intertextuality', the overlapping and interlinking of sign systems and meanings in an infinite weave of texts, a phenomenon she identifies as particularly evident in literature.[16] Accordingly, poststructuralist thought privileges relativism, demonstrating heterogeneity rather than falsely premised uniformity. Whilst articulating the late twentieth-century understanding of the crisis of language, deconstructive strategies have both therapeutic potential and radical implications for the understanding of the construction and potential of textual systems in general, and literary texts in particular.

Beyond France, twentieth-century turning points in the understanding of the self and of language have also prompted new ways of figuring relationships between the unconscious, crisis, and cultural production. Slavoj Žižek's reading of Lacan identifies how popular cinema and fiction may exemplify, betray, or sublimate the linguistic operations of desire and its manifestations in narratives.[17] Lacanian psychoanalytic theory has also been harnessed to raise questions about the possibility of the processing of tangible crises and trauma through language. Whilst Freudian psychoanalysis seeks to understand

[14] Jacques Derrida, *De la grammatologie* (Paris: Minuit, 1967).
[15] Barthes, 'La Mort de l'auteur' (1968), reproduced in *Le Bruissement de la langue* (Paris: Seuil, 1984).
[16] Julia Kristeva, *La Révolution du langage poétique* (Paris: Seuil, 1974).
[17] Slavoj Žižek, *Looking Awry: An Introduction to Jacques Lacan through Popular Culture* (Cambridge, MA and London: MIT Press, 1991).

the conscious by using language to capture the truth of an experience hitherto unknown in the unconscious, intersecting with Cathy Caruth, Shoshana Felman, and Dori Laub bring Lacan's insight to bear on the possibility of recounting and of working through the effects of trauma, offering new aesthetic and ethical perspectives on the potential of cultural production that seeks to confront the crises of the past: personal and collective.[18] They suggest that trauma—from individual experiences to the Holocaust—is irretrievable, and that 'acting out' through testimony cannot resolve its effects, only bear witness to its irrevocable, inexpressible impact. Yet in terms of mental health, and from an ethical imperative, witness must be borne. This ethical issue becomes all the more urgent in what Kirby Farrell calls 'post-traumatic culture'.[19] Farrell identifies this as a development from the 1990s, shaped and perpetuated by Hollywood and mass media narratives, converging on the one hand with the development of theories of Post-Traumatic Stress Disorder, and on the other, with the phenomenon of compassion fatigue. He describes how trauma is transformed into a trope, articulating the radical unease of subjects in a world in which they have no control over power relations. As the following analyses demonstrate, the manipulation of crisis and the transformation of trauma into a trope by the mass media and the global market invite urgent questions; all the more urgent given that forms of cultural production that seek to counter dominant commodifying trends are recuperated by the order they seek to destabilize.

MODERNISM, POSTMODERNISM, AND THE TROPE OF THE TURNING POINT

Albeit artificially, twentieth-century crisis thinking is often described in terms of two contrasting aesthetics. On the one hand, a late nineteenth- and early to mid-twentieth-century modernist break with the past which

---

[18] Shoshana Felman and Dori Laub, *Testimony: Crises of Witnessing in Literature, Psychoanalysis and History* (New York and London: Routledge, 1992); Cathy Caruth, *Unclaimed Experience: Trauma, Narrative, and History* (Baltimore, MA: The Johns Hopkins University Press, 1996).

[19] Kirby Farrell, *Post-traumatic Culture: Injury and Interpretation in the Nineties* (Baltimore: The Johns Hopkins University Press, 1998).

retains either a nostalgia for or a belief in finding a means of making sense of the world. On the other, a late twentieth-century postmodern scepticism of totalizing narratives linked to the development of late capitalism and paralleled by the privileging of discourses without teleological or temporal end. Certain commentators argue that in the 1970s the modernist model of the turning point evoked by Nathalie Sarraute as the *ère du soupçon*, shifts to a sense of perpetual postmodern crisis, described by Gilles Lipovetsky as the *ère du vide*.[20] This invites the questions of the particular nature of crisis discourses described as postmodern, the crisis tropes associated with modernism, and their relationship with competing crisis discourses and tangible crises.

Analysis of the work of thinkers frequently described as postmodern reveals a concern with a new, reflexive understanding of the trope of the turning point. Jean-François Lyotard's 1979 *La Condition Postmoderne* considers the status of science, technology, and the arts, and how recent developments have affected the way information and knowledge are controlled in Western capitalist society.[21] He argues that knowledge has undergone a change of status since the nineteenth century, identifying a particular acceleration in this process since the late 1950s. However Lyotard does not seek to identify a turning point in modernity that would mark the genesis of a postmodern aesthetics of crisis. Instead, he describes the postmodern as a necessary condition of modernism, of the turning points that motivate the modernist aesthetic of the sublime, the nostalgic quest to represent the unrepresentable. Hence the postmodern is that element of the modern which foregrounds the unrepresentable in its very mode of presentation, bearing witness to difference and thus countering the terror created by totalizing discourses that aim to account for the unrepresentable. Accordingly, Lyotard identifies *grands récits* (as he describes totalizing grand narratives), ideological discourses constituted by—but necessarily concealing—the inherent relativity of language. By contrast, in Lyotard's postmodern aesthetic knowledge has no external referent, or discourses any authority, so he conceptualizes postmodernity

---

[20] Nathalie Sarraute, *L'Ère du soupçon* (Paris: Minuit, 1956) 'the age of suspicion'; Gilles Lipovetsky, *L'Ère du vide: Essais sur l'individualisme contemporain* (Paris: Gallimard, 1983) 'the age of the void'.
[21] Jean-François Lyotard, *La Condition Postmoderne: Rapport sur le savoir* (Paris: Minuit, 1979).

in terms of a crisis not only of representation, but also of legitimation. Nonetheless, he does not reject the notion of the turning point. Rather, he figures the subject as free to make up new rules. Lyotard's concept of localized *événements* envisages modest, therapeutic crises. And, whilst calling for scepticism towards grand narratives, Lyotard advocates a new relationship with language to harness its ethical potential for countering totalizing discourses by developing provisional and local *petits récits.*

So in the last decades of the second millennium not only do language and representation remain preoccupations, but the ethics of the turning point is also a key concern. Similarly, Derrida's deconstructive moves at once seek to precipitate an ethical change in logocentric Western thought and are inescapably apocalyptic and *knowingly* implicated in the grand narratives they seek to challenge. Hence his *mise en scène* in *D'un ton apocalyptique adopté naguère en philosophie* of both endist and deconstructive discourses as always already inscribed in the endless play of language, unable to escape their own apocalyptic—that is in both its etymological and in Derrida's text performatively *revelatory*—dynamic.[22] In *Spectres de Marx* Derrida goes on to express a scepticism of self-justifying neo-conservative discourses which articulate the triumph of Western capitalism and thus the end of ideology. Instead, rehabilitating the potential of Marxism, he figures writing as a political act of resistance. Although (and because) it may intervene in an untimely manner, the philosophical text has a political manifestation: it may express uncertain contemporary relationships with the nature and the possibility of returns, evoking out-of-time turning points that may have potential in the present: 'Le propre d'un spectre, s'il y en a, c'est qu'on ne sait pas s'il témoigne en revenant d'un vivant passée ou d'un vivant futur, car le revenant peut marquer déjà le retour du spectre d'un vivant promis. Intempestivité encore, et désajustement du contemporain.'[23]

---

[22] Jacques Derrida, *D'un Ton apocalyptique adopté naguère en philosophie* (Paris: Galilée, 1983), pp. 59–60.

[23] Derrida, *Spectres de Marx: L'État de la dette, le travail du deuil et la nouvelle Internationale* (Paris: Galilée, 1993), p. 162: 'It is a proper characteristic of the spectre, if there is any, that no one can be sure if by returning it testifies to a living past or to a living future, for the *revenant* may already mark the promised return of the spectre of a living being. Once again, the untimeliness and the disadjustment of the contemporary', idem, *The Derrida Reader: Writing Performances*, ed. Julian Wolfreys (Lincoln: University of Nebraska Press, 1998), p. 143.

Gilles Deleuze and Félix Guattari's anti-Oedipal analysis of desire in capitalist society attempts to refigure Marx's history of production into a history of desiring production, seeing in art revolutionary, schizophrenic potential, figuring *déterritorialisation* as a means of countering the capitalist reconfiguring of empty signifiers as exchange value.[24] Seeking to valorize individual tactics for negotiating the oppressive script of capitalism, Michel de Certeau figures provisional, personal modes of poaching on the strategic capitalist infrastructures of everyday life.[25]

Michel Foucault's analysis of the texts and discourses that construct power, knowledge, madness, and sexuality also investigates the possibility of precipitating a turning point by changing perspectives on totalizing narratives. Although focusing on an earlier phase of capitalism, Foucault's thought prompts a contemporary questioning of what kind of knowledge is constitutive of power in the virtually and digitally dominated global markets. The ideological implications of the dominant audiovisual aesthetic are also brought into focus in Foucault's analogy of Bentham's Panopticon, the circular prison that Foucault presented as an architectural figure of power in modern society.[26] Identifying how order is imposed by the sense of being watched—an internalization of the mechanisms of surveillance—Foucault provides a prescient perspective for considering the omnipresence not only of the audiovisual media, but also of virtual and digital technology and CCTV, and the role of their figurative incarceration of consumers. In an intersecting development, Paul Virilio has developed critiques of the acceleration of technology identifying the risk of the loss of control over the mass media and information and digital technology.[27]

If the notion of postmodernism is considered by some critics to conflate the cultural and the socio-political and to negate attempts to bring about turning points in human understanding and history, the

---

[24] Gilles Deleuze and Félix Guattari, *Capitalisme et schizophrénie*, vol. 2, *Mille plateaux* (Paris: Minuit, 1980).
[25] Michel de Certeau, *L'Invention du quotidien*, vol. 1: *Arts de faire* (Paris: Gallimard, 1980).
[26] Michel Foucault, *Surveiller et punir: Naissance de la prison* (Paris: Gallimard, 1975).
[27] Paul Virilio, *L'Art du moteur* (Paris: Galilée, 1992); idem, *La Vitesse de la libération* (Paris: Galilée, 1995).

term may also be used to refer to a privileging of heterogeneity that challenges totalizing narratives and allows them to be exposed as potentially dangerous ideological constructs. This last description suggests a development of the modernist ethos of the struggle, suggesting that what is labelled postmodern need not be dismissed as a celebration of a radical 'free for all', a nihilistic proclamation of perpetual crisis. Rather, it offers a potential means of revealing how the narratives of reason, progress, history, and phallocracy can lead to totalitarianism. Indeed certain *fin de millénaire* critical discourses are both ethical and therapeutic in intention, raising questions of the nature and autonomy of cultural production; of the possibilities of critical distance and agency; and of the enduring potential for challenging and resisting late capitalist ideology. So a clear turning point between modernism and postmodernism cannot be established. Indeed such falsely commodifying paradigms and labels should be questioned.

The trope of the turning point is also used by a number of French thinkers who position themselves against the perceived influence of the mass media and the global market in the putative intellectual dominant of postmodernism. Régis Debray introduced the critical science of *médiologie* in 1979, plotting the transferral of symbolic power in France away from academia and publishing to the media, and then in 1991 from the *graphosphère* to the *vidéosphère*.[28] For Alain Finkielkraut the market, the media, and digital technology generate a globalized addiction to empty images, and replace human relationships with virtual reality: 'Grâce à la mise hors de jeu de la topologie par la technologie, l'expérience humaine, trop humaine, du voisinage cède la place à l'ivresse olympienne d'une universelle équidistance. L'homme n'est plus vernaculaire, il est planétaire. Son environnement n'est plus local, mais digital.'[29] Addressing such wide-ranging issues as inequalities inscribed in education, sexual politics, ethnicity, and cultural fields; symbolic violence; and access to symbolic capital, Pierre Bourdieu's

---

[28] Régis Debray, *Le Pouvoir intellectuel en France* (Paris: Ramsay, 1979); idem, *Cours de médiologie générale* (Paris: Gallimard, 1991).

[29] Alain Finkielkraut, *L'Humanité Perdue: Essai sur le XXe siècle* (Paris: Seuil, 1996), p. 152: 'Because technology has made topology obsolete, the experience of human interrelations, all too human, has been superseded by a dizzy Olympian universal equidistance. Man no longer lives in the vernacular, he lives globally. His environment is no longer local, it is digital.'

sociologie réflexive seeks to precipitate turning points in the struggle for the rights of those marginalized by neoliberal ideology. In the 1970s and 1980s Bourdieu developed the notions of economic, symbolic, and cultural capital as ways of critically interrogating late capitalist society. Here, consumerism no longer fits Marxist class distinctions, or the notion of the alienation of worker from the use value of their work, and of the bourgeois exploitation of surplus value and the worker's reproduction of needs. In an increasingly post-industrial world, Bourdieu describes interlinked modes of differentiation: not only by economic capital (command over money and goods), but also social capital (resources based on group membership and networks of influence), and cultural capital (forms of knowledge and skill). Instead of alienation, the dominant and the dominated are co-implicated in the symbolic violence inherent in these processes: the imposition of categories of thought upon dominated social subjects who then internalize these unthought structures and thus are co-implicated in perpetuating them. Symbolic violence, therefore, is pervasively insidious because it imposes the idea of the legitimacy of the dominant order, and is embedded in the modes of being and the thought processes of individuals. For Bourdieu, all forms of cultural production are potentially vehicles of symbolic violence, and, especially in the era of globalized mass communication, the audiovisual media.

In his 1998 collection of essays *Contre-feux: Propos à la résistance contre l'invasion néo-libérale* Bourdieu critiques the logic of the global market and neoliberal ideology, its levelling of cultural autonomy, its invasion of the public sphere, and its inherent symbolic violence.[30] This was anticipated in 1996 by *Sur la Télévision*, aiming to rehabilitate the ethical responsibility of the intellectual.[31] While generating precisely the kind of controversy that boosts media profile, here Bourdieu attacks media-courting *philosophes-journalistes* (notably Finkielkraut and Bernard-Henri Lévy), exhorting cultural commentators to shun or manipulate television appearances to counter the commodification of the subject by the audiovisual media. In an intellectual field dominated

---

[30] Pierre Bourdieu, *Contre-feux: Propos à la résistance contre l'invasion néo-libérale* (Paris: Odile Jacob, 1998).
[31] Bourdieu, *Sur la Télévision; suivi de L'Emprise du journalisme* (Paris: Raisons d'agir, 1996).

by clichéd visions of spectacularization, the inertia of the masses, the perceived collapse of the real, and the ubiquity of the *intellectuel médiatique*, Bourdieu's pamphlet brought the ethical responsibility for precipitating turning points back up the intellectual agenda.

Such debate is testimony to a resurgence of the investigation of possibilities for resistance and change, countering the perceived climate of relativism, and fears of the submerging of the public sphere by global market economics, whilst demonstrating the enduring potential for autonomous cultural dissent. Likewise a furore caused by a more overt attack on postmodern thought: the *affaire Sokal* surrounding the 1997 publication of Sokal and Bricmont's *Impostures intellectuelles*.[32] The spoof article and subsequent book aimed to expose French 'poststructuralist superstars' such as Deleuze, Kristeva, and Lacan as symptomatic of a nihilistic postmodern relativism and abstraction. The resulting polemic evidences an apprehension of a need for an intellectual turning point, described by John Marks as an 'urgent call for accessibility, commitment, rationality and clarity within certain sectors of the French political class'.[33]

Other voices criticizing what they perceive as the aesthetics and ethics of postmodernism include Cornelius Castoriadis, Marc Fumaroli, and Olivier Mongin. Beyond France, prominent examples include Zygmunt Bauman, Terry Eagleton, Jürgen Habermas, Christopher Norris, and Richard Rorty. Meanwhile Stephen Best and Douglas Kellner describe postmodern aesthetics as a sense-making response to the crises of modernity.[34] Hal Foster's *The Return of the Real* identifies an 'ethnographic turn', a resurgence of social and anthropological concerns in contemporary art.[35] Jameson's *A Singular Modernity* identifies a convergent set of relationships evolving out of the development of Western capitalism which produces a set of aesthetic and ideological norms and practices shared by avant-gardes labelled modernist and postmodern.[36] Jameson argues that these norms were conceived during

[32] Alan Sokal and Jean Bricmont, *Impostures intellectuelles* (Paris: Odile Jacob, 1997).
[33] John Marks, 'L'Affaire Sokal', *French Cultural Debates*, ed. John Marks and Enda McCaffrey (Melbourne: Monash Romance Studies, 2001), pp. 80–93, at p. 80.
[34] Stephen Best and Douglas Kellner, *The Postmodern Adventure: Science, Technology, and Cultural Studies at the Third Millennium* (London: Routledge, 2001).
[35] Hal Foster, *The Return of the Real* (Boston: MIT, 1996).
[36] Fredric Jameson, *A Singular Modernity* (New York: Verso, 2002).

the Cold War and retroactively projected onto 'high modernist' art, and thus the ideology of modernity (and hence postmodernity) cannot be separated from the evolution of Western late capitalism.

So, putative practitioners, critics, and commentators of postmodernism take frequent, if differently motivated recourse to the trope of crisis as a turning point. Thus the notion of postmodern crisis without end is neither ubiquitous nor without challenge. Crisis is refigured—no longer a decisive moment within a grand narrative, it is accorded a more local role, as a kind of constitutive untimeliness and rupture within the present, which has a provisional critical potential. Moreover, some of the most prominent intellectual debates of late twentieth-century France and contemporary thought which more or less overtly challenge the ideology of the mass media and the global market are predicated on the trope of the turning point. Indeed, clear distinctions cannot be made between its 'modernist' and 'postmodern' incarnations.

CRISIS DISCOURSES, MISOGYNY, AND SYMBOLIC VIOLENCE

Outstripping perceived distinctions between modernism and postmodernism and linking crisis narratives and the question of political agency, in the second half of the twentieth century women sought to precipitate turning points by developing and challenging the analyses of Nietzsche, Freud, Marx, and Saussure. In France female thinkers marked the second half of the twentieth century by their attempts to challenge the phallocentric structure of (late) capitalism and its dominant discourses: intellectual, political, and economic. In 1949 Marxist and Existentialist thought (with its Nietzschean premise of freedom) informed Simone de Beauvoir's *Le Deuxième sexe*, an analysis of femininity as socially constructed by patriarchal society (and complicit in that construction) through its myths, educational systems, and literature.[37] Beauvoir's materialist description of the ideological constitution of women as inferior provided a springboard, via Lacan and Saussure, for women who from the 1970s have been described as difference

---

[37] Simone de Beauvoir, *Le Deuxième sexe* (Paris: Gallimard, 1949).

feminists. Whilst tending to reject such homogenizing descriptors, and to elide Beauvoir's argument that women may in bad faith contribute to their own oppression, thinkers such as Hélène Cixous, Luce Irigaray, and Julia Kristeva nonetheless build on Beauvoir's insights and converge in their focus on language and writing as potential modes of resisting and moving beyond the false binary opposition of male superiority and female inferiority and the Lacanian Law of the Father. Thus, just as a discernible turning point between modern and the postmodern aesthetics cannot be identified, so difference feminism and materialist feminism are inextricably linked.

Although distancing herself from the label 'feminist', Kristeva describes poetic language as a pre-condition for a general revolution in Western patriarchal thinking, creating the concept of the Semiotic, the rhythmic, tonal language of pre-Oedipal *jouissance* that challenges Lacan's conception of the phallocentric symbolic order and the determining influence of the Law of the Father.[38] Meanwhile, adopting an overtly feminist stance, Cixous develops Beauvoir's insights, Lacanian theory, and Derridean *différance*, seeking to challenge and move beyond patriarchal ideology and oppression. Her neologism 'phallogocentric' is an amalgam of 'phallocentric', describing how patriarchal society is centred around the male, the phallus; and 'logocentric', Derrida's description of how Western culture privileges the use of the spoken word, 'logos', over writing.[39] Cixous's aim is to find a new language that she describes as writing 'said to be feminine', that has become known as *écriture féminine*. At once undermining but claiming to be untainted by the patriarchal logic of opposition, of power, and subordination this voice performs the pre-linguistic *jouissance* of fusion with the mother. Such language seeks to bring about crisis in phallogocentric linguistic and social structures and to transcend them.

Nonetheless, by the 1990s in a world often misleadingly described as post-feminist, and a country that tends to look back on the heady days of the *MLF* and *écriture féminine* as an anachronism, the notion that feminism has precipitated a definitive turning point may be disputed. This begs the question of whether the turning points sought by

---

[38] Julia Kristeva, *Semeiotike: Recherches pour une sémanalyse* (Paris: Seuil, 1969).
[39] Hélène Cixous, *La Jeune née* (Union générale d'éditions, 1975); idem, 'Le Rire de la Méduse', *L'Arc*, 61 (1975).

French women in the 1970s and 1980s have been achieved. A question also underpinned by Bourdieu's description of misogynist symbolic violence:

Since the foundations of symbolic violence reside not in a mystified consciousness that needs to be enlightened, but rather in tendencies adjusted to the structures of domination of which they are the product, the symbolic revolution that the feminist movement seeks cannot be reduced to a conversion of consciousness. We cannot simply wait for a severing of the complicitous relationship that the victim of symbolic domination allows the dominant. Only a radical transformation of social conditions can predispose the dominated to adopt a viewpoint toward the dominant and toward herself that is none other than the viewpoint of the dominant.[40]

Indeed, of all European countries apart from Greece, turn-of-the-millennium France had the fewest number of women holding political office (5 per cent in 1995), and legislation on parity of numbers of male and female parliamentary candidates was not passed until June 2000.[41] There thus remains a need, and arguably the critical potential to precipitate crises in enduringly patriarchal institutions and in the global market and the mass media. In 1998 Christine Delphy articulated a need to return to the offensive, exposing the misogynist political economy of neoliberalism; its failure to put into practice the ostensible legal gains of the women's movement; the continued exploitation of women; and women's co-implication in it at home and in the workplace. Delphy combines what might be considered a postmodern argument for the necessity for plural battles against the falsely homogenizing discourses of Republic and neoliberalism with a materialist quest to rehabilitate the women's movement. In doing so, she argues that patriarchal domination and its oppression of women is perpetuated by the media, on the one hand producing false claims of 'l'égalité déjà là', and on the other producing an anti-feminist backlash

---

[40] Bourdieu, trans. Margaret Colvin, 'Symbolic Violence', in Roger Célestin, Eliane DalMolin, and Isabelle de Courtiviron, eds, *Beyond French Feminisms: Debates on Women, Politics and Culture in France 1981 to 2001* (New York and Basingstoke: Palgrave, 2003), pp. 23–6, at p. 26.

[41] Roger Célestin, Eliane DalMolin, and Isabelle de Courtiviron, 'Introduction', in *Beyond French Feminisms*, p. 5.

via the negative stereotyping of feminist political activism.[42] Drawing on feminist thought, past and contemporary, this study pays particular attention to the representation of women and the discourses of misogyny. The aim is at once to contribute to debates on gender and sexuality and to analyse the role of different modes of cultural production in perpetuating or challenging misogynist symbolic violence.

CRITICAL PERSPECTIVES AND CONSUMER CULTURE

Mass consumerism dates back to the end of the nineteenth century, when technological advance intersected with advertising and growing distribution and communications networks to bring new consumer goods to the wealthy. After the Second World War, patterns of consumption previously enjoyed by the elite became more widely accessible (notably in France white goods promoted by the phallocentric *politique nataliste*). From the 1970s, in addition to a more or less democratized access to material goods, there was an ever-growing emphasis on the satisfaction of individual desires and the pursuit of well-being, leisure, and experience. In the wake of the 'democratization' of consumerism (from which the socio-economically marginalized in the West and most of the developing world remain excluded), from the 1960s and 1970s cultural critics followed more or less overtly in the tradition of the 'Frankfurt School', and in particular Walter Benjamin, Theodor Adorno, and Max Horkheimer who from a Marxist perspective investigated the impact of capitalism on cultural production and on the critical capacity of the consumer. Benjamin's 1935 essay 'The Work of Art in an Age of Mechanical Reproduction' argued that the instant access afforded by mechanical reproduction necessarily entails the loss of what is immanent and vital in the work of art.[43] This loss of 'aura' implies a loss of critical capacity, and a distancing from the realm of tradition. However, Benjamin also suggested that harnessed positively,

[42] Christine Delphy, *L'Ennemi principal: Économie politique du patriarcat* (Paris: Syllepse, 1998): 'already achieved equality'.

[43] Walter Benjamin, *Illuminations*, ed. Hannah Arendt, trans. Harry Zohn (New York: Harcourt, Brace & World, 1968).

mass production had the potential to democratize the image, offering an escape from the capitalist framework in which the original was conceived (Benjamin particularly identified film as offering new possibilities for human perception). Thus the role of art in precipitating crisis— or in Marxist terms, revolution—remains a possibility, and raising awareness of the potential for resisting the commodification of critical capacity, an imperative.

In their 1944 analysis 'The Culture Industry' Adorno and Horkheimer posited that the Enlightenment narrative of progress had transformed culture into an industry, so critical difference is lost because the products of the Culture Industry have become the benchmark against which autonomous art is defined, appropriating the critical potential of culture in the process.[44] In the immediate aftermath of the Second World War, Adorno considered the Holocaust in the context of the reification of cultural life in capitalist society, arguing: 'to write poetry after Auschwitz is barbaric'.[45] By these terms, language—here in the form of literature—is not barbaric per se, but rather as the mediator of ideology, it is the potential source of barbarism. Yet, at the same time, it is also the potential source of efforts to counter barbarism. Adorno therefore foregrounded the question of the capacity of language at once to recuperate and to resist the horrors of its own creation, a question which continues to have a decisive influence on French thought and literature. For Adorno resisting this reification—the commodification of cultural discourses—should become part of the Marxist dialectic. So albeit intended as an exposition of negative potential, Adorno's analysis, like that of Benjamin, retains the sense of a critical turning point. And an ever-increasing relevance, as with the development of the global market, cultural production becomes more and more sophisticated and diffuse, and so the dangers of co-implication and commodification increase.

Henri Lefebvre's analysis of the alienation borne of the capitalist colonization of everyday life and Louis Althusser's conception of the

[44] Theodor Adorno and Max Horkheimer, 'The Culture Industry: Enlightenment as Mass Deception', in *Dialectic of Enlightenment: Philosophical Fragments*, ed. Gunzelin Schmid Noerr, trans. Edmund Jephcott (Stanford, CA: Stanford University Press, 2002), pp. 94–136.
[45] Adorno, 'Cultural Criticism and Society', in *Prisms*, trans. Samuel and Shierry Weber (Cambridge, MA: MIT Press; 1967), pp. 17–34, at p. 34.

media as an 'Ideological State Apparatus' that reproduces ideology also build on Marxist analyses intersecting with the thought of the Frankfurt School.[46] So too do Guy Debord and Jean Baudrillard, arguably France's foremost post-war critics of consumer culture. Although addressing the question from different perspectives, and evolving in different directions, they converge in identifying a blurring of fiction and reality in late capitalist cultural production. Debord's *La Société du spectacle* (1967) attacks the organization of society around the spectacular: the systematic production of images, events, and institutional infrastructures as commodities that relegate the subject to passivity whilst obscuring capitalism's powers of domination.[47] For Debord when the aesthetic is consumed as spectacle, it loses its potential as critical function, or as a means of precipitating change. Yet this analysis was not intended to be nihilistic, for a year before the crises of May 1968, Debord's tract called for the orchestration of radical turning points, or *détournements*, to outwit the oppression of the spectacle. However, by 1988 he posited that as a result of the increasing power of television, in the *spectaculaire intégré* life is dominated by images, and voices of dissent are turned into products of the market. So in *Commentaire sur la société du spectacle* Debord's confidence in the possibility of engineering turning points appears to have been lost.[48]

Baudrillard's thought evolved in parallel, initially drawing on Marx, the Frankfurt School, and Saussure, then taking a turn more overtly intersecting with poststructuralism, and establishing a reputation as an exemplar of postmodernism. In *Le Système des objets* (1968), *La Société de consommation: Ses Mythes, ses structures* (1970), and *Pour une critique de l'économie politique du signe* (1977) Baudrillard proposed a political economy of the sign whereby due to the privileging of consumption, human relations were being replaced by relationships between signs.[49] However, from the 1980s, the audiovisual media (and from the mid-1990s digital technology) provided the focus for Baudrillard's concept of hyperreality. Baudril-

[46] Henri Lefebvre, *Crtique de la vie quotidienne I, II, III* (Paris: L'Arche, 1961); Louis Althusser, 'Idéologie et appareils idéologiques d'État', *La Pensée*, (1970), 3–36.

[47] Guy Debord, *La Société du spectacle* (Paris: Buchet-Castel, 1967).

[48] Debord, *Commentaire sur la société du spectacle* (Paris: Gérard Lebovici, 1988).

[49] Jean Baudrillard, *La Société de consommation: Ses Mythes, ses structures* (Paris: Gallimard, 1970; idem, *Le Système des objets* (Paris: Gallimard, 1968); idem, *Pour une critique de l'économie politique du signe* (Paris: Gallimard, 1977).

lard argues that in a culture dominated by television, films, and the news media, the idea of a true or a false copy of something is destroyed, leaving only simulations of reality, no more or less 'real' than the reality they simulate. For Baudrillard this is the realm of the hyperreal—the collapse of the real with the imaginary—whereby production is replaced by the social reproduction of simulacra with no relation to any reality whatsoever.[50]

This conception of a crisis of representation such that simulated media output constitutes the 'real' of human experience is notoriously exemplified in Baudrillard's 1991 *La Guerre du Golfe n'a pas eu lieu*. The essay argues that the first Gulf War was not so much reported by television cameras as constructed for them. Thus, despite accusations of nihilism, late twentieth-century French thinkers tackling questions of cultural production continue to investigate the potential of the turning point.[51] Nonetheless, such investigations—like those of writers of prose fiction—risk falling into the *fin de millénaire* double bind of the recuperation of critical discourses: that of becoming commodified by the market and the media, upon which they nonetheless depend to have a voice, and the power of which they underpin. They also risk perpetrating and perpetuating symbolic violence by representing tropes, discourses, stereotypes, and idealized images without overtly problematizing or maintaining a critical distance from them.

CRISIS, THE GLOBAL MARKET, AND THE MASS MEDIA

One of the defining characteristics of the *fin de millénaire* aesthetics of crisis is the simultaneous generation and manipulation of tangible crises and crisis discourses by the mass media and the global market which redoubles the double bind of the recuperation of critical discourses. Whilst in their different ways Christianity, the Enlightenment narrative of progress, Marxism, and Freudian psychoanalysis aim to control, manage, or channel desire, late capitalism at once deliberately generates and frustrates it. Debord's argument that consumer society produces

---

[50] Baudrillard, *De la Séduction* (Paris: Denoël, 1979); idem, *Les Stratégies fatales* (Paris: Grasset, 1983); idem, *Simulacres et simulation* (Paris: Galilée, 1985).
[51] Baudrillard, *La Guerre du Golfe n'a pas eu lieu* (Paris: Galilée, 1991).

spectacle, and Baudrillard's notions of simulacra and hyperreality both figure modes of suppressing the possibility of precipitating a critical turning point. However, this study demonstrates how whilst crisis endures as a sense-making trope, it is also a primary product, generating an economy of desire for novelty that can never be satisfied.

In order to produce consumption-generating, but unrealizable promises, marketing discourses position the acquisition of consumer products as therapeutic turning points: '*new!*', '*improved!*', and even '*revolutionary!*' Yet the implied regenerative future is never reached, for the turning point systematically leads back to the production of subsequent *purchase-crises*. The perpetual production of promises of turning points results in neither resolution nor catastrophe. Concomitantly, peer and promotional pressure and the constant introduction of new products render all consumer goods and services inherently obsolete. Meanwhile unrealizable stereotypes are produced to feed an increasingly globalized market economy, receiving ever greater dissemination through the mass media.

This *fin de millénaire* economy of desire is by no means egalitarian, for at the same time as it precipitates purchases (and so crises in consumers inasmuch as desire is produced until it culminates in a turning point that leads to purchase), it produces economic marginalization. These discourses also doubly commodify women. For, if as argued above the struggle for equality is erroneously presented as a crisis resolved, the generation of consumer desire promises women fulfilment that is impossible to attain, yet at the same time produces misogynist stereotypes of idealized femininity which are equally impossible to achieve. The manipulation of crisis by marketing and media discourses is therefore a form of symbolic violence. And both a patriarchal and particularly misogynist form, on the one hand generating male consumer desire for women, and on the other, imposing idealized images which encourage women to seek—necessarily unsuccessfully—to simulate. Accordingly, throughout this book, representations of such symbolic violence and the potential for perpetuating, exposing, or challenging it are brought into question.

In *Policing the Crisis* (1978) Stuart Hall and his colleagues at the Birmingham Centre for Contemporary Cultural Studies argued that the news media turn chaotic crises into ordered concepts.[52] The media

---

[52] Stuart Hall et al., *Policing the Crisis: 'Mugging' the State and Law and Order* (London: Macmillan, 1978).

appear to reflect reality but in fact are constructing it, defining events and reinforcing a consensual viewpoint whilst appearing to voice public opinion. Hall's book has clear intersections with Debord's spectacle, whilst similar ideas are developed in Baudrillard's conception of the hyperreal, and a more recent apprehension of this process in France is evidenced in a convergence of late twentieth-century analyses of May 1968. For Finkielkraut, the *événements* represented a turning point at which French culture was subsumed by the audiovisual media and the leisure and entertainment industries.[53] Meanwhile, for Pierre Nora, the failure of May 1968 to bring about significant change is symptomatic of the commodification of the crisis trope of revolution.[54] Such media crises are therefore not 'real' events but discourses structured as 'reality'. As the news media structure reality as crisis, so commodified apocalypse becomes part of daily life.[55] This constant, contradictory diet of media crises provides an impression of progress, serving not only to uphold the dominant order, but also to suppress any threat of resistance and dissimulate the fallout from *purchase-crises* without resolution.

If May 1968 marked a watershed in the media manipulation of crisis in France, mass media coverage of the 'millennium bug' perceived to threaten the global computer systems exposed the structural contradictions of the *fin de millénaire* aesthetics of crisis. News reports produced crisis by disseminating apocalyptic prophecies of doom, yet simultaneously tried to play down what threatened to be a 'real' crisis. The panic provoked by *la bogue* and the media (mis)management of it not only demonstrate the enduring power of millenarianism, but also the contradictory manipulation of crisis required to sustain consumption by simultaneously hiding the dissatisfaction that is the necessary outcome of this contradictory mode of production. From the anamorphic perspective of Žižek's reading of Lacan, this contradiction, like the detail that sticks out in the crime scene of classic detective fiction, operates as the 'place-holder of the lack', the element that reveals

[53] Alain Finkielkraut, *La Défaite de la pensée* (Paris: Gallimard, 1987), p. 135.
[54] Pierre Nora, 'L'Ère de la commémoration', in Pierre Nora et al., eds, *Les Lieux de mémoire III: Les France*, vol. 3, Édition Quarto (Paris: Gallimard, 1992), p. 980.
[55] Marc Raboy and Bernard Dagenais, 'Introduction: Media and the Politics of Crisis', in *Media, Crisis and Democracy: Mass Communication and the Disruption of Social Order*, ed. Marc Raboy and Bernard Dagenais (London: Sage, 1992), pp. 1–15.

the apparently coherent narrative to be a deceptive secondary revision.[56] What is more, in the context of this book's concern for assessing the agency of crisis discourses, such contradictions in the manipulation of the trope of the turning point stick out to offer critical opportunities, indicating the potential for leverage, contestation, and resistance.

With the impact of global market economics and the advent of the Internet and the digital media, the audiovisual image and the digital image co-exist in an increasingly virtual realm. French critical reception of this revolutionary technology has followed a similar pattern to reactions to the advent of information technology. Initially hailed as 'une agora informationnelle',[57] these new media are increasingly viewed as a threat to national identity and social structures. This intersects with an intensification of intellectual debate in France concerning the effects of reality television, popular factual programming originating in America and with roots in the development of tabloid journalism, television documentary, forensic crime fiction, and crime reporting. France's first reality show was the *Psy show* in 1983. Here subjects exposed their problems in front of a psychoanalyst and presenter. Despite vehement criticism and TF1 initially dismissing *la télé réalité* as 'la télé poubelle', *Moi, je* followed on Antenne 2 in 1986, and the popularity of such programmes swiftly spurned imitations on TF1 and France's other public and private channels, moving from late night slots to prime time. The genre took off in 1990 with *Perdu de vue* on TF1, modelled on the US hit show *Missing Person*. Shows dramatizing legal wrangles, couples in crisis, and victims of illness, prejudice, and addiction followed such as *Témoin No 1, L'Amour en danger, Mea Culpa,* and *Bas les masques.* All aired the most personal of traumas with the ostensible purpose of achieving resolution, but delivering spectacularized and (cod) psychologized exposure of the intimate crises of the 'ordinary' subject.

Dominique Mehl identifies some potentially positive outcomes of this new televisual aesthetic. At best, public space is remodelled by the developments in the mediascape, providing a new forum for public debate, the expression of social issues and the private self, foregrounding

---

[56] Žižek, *Looking Awry*, p. 49.

[57] Alain Minc and Pierre Nora, *L'Informatisation de la société* (Paris: La Documentation Française, 1978), p. 124: 'an information agora'.

the importance of family relationships, encouraging cultural liberalism, and filling the void left by the loss of inherited value systems. Yet Mehl also highlights detrimental effects including the banalization of horror; the commodification of the poor and the suffering; and the promotion of narcissism. She describes the burgeoning of reality television in France as a symptom of the breakdown of communities; of the failure of mediation between institutional and private life; of a disjunction between mental health provision and levels of psychiatric distress; and of a lack of communication in what is often called 'communications society'. It is therefore as both cause and symptom that she identifies reality television as a '[m]icro-réceptacle de crises contemporaines'.[58]

Moreover, as a reflection of and contributor to the *fin de millénaire* aesthetics of crisis, reality television challenges and changes conceptions of reality, authenticity, and communication. It also brings about linguistic change with the more-or-less accurate entry of psychoanalytical concepts into the vernacular, and disseminates the notion of a recoverable self. It creates a new form of 'star' but then debunks 'stars' by demonstrating their constructedness, so celebrity becomes unhinged from talent. Thus reality television arguably also turns individuals' crises and their bodies into products, whilst recasting viewers as *quasi*-panoptic consumers of a compelling but disturbing form of intimacy. This invites questions about exhibitionism and voyeurism, and the growing commodification and consumption of trauma.

Changes in expectations of realist representation have been brought about by the apparent unscriptedness, immediacy, truth claims, and false intimacy of reality television formats. Indeed the descriptor 'reality' is a paradox, for reality television constitutes at the very least a highly influenced narrativization of reality. Damien Leguay argues that the images produced by reality television have a far greater suggestive power than those of written news media or fiction and that although viewers know that reality television involves the manipulation of reality, they take it for real.[59] Hence television at the *fin de millénaire* brings a new crisis of reality based on a *mise en scène* that imposes formulae for experience on consumers, adding to the discourses which effectively

---

[58] Dominique Mehl, *La Télévision de l'intimité* (Paris: Seuil, 1996), p. 12.
[59] Damien Leguay, *L'Empire de la téléréalité; ou, Comment accroître le temps de cerveau humain disponible* (Paris: Presses de la Renaissance, 2005), pp. 20–1.

redouble the double bind of the (mass-mediatized) recuperation of critical discourses.

CRISIS THINKING AND *THE END OF HISTORY*

Both the recuperation of critical discourses by the media and the emphatic return to the trope of crisis in the French cultural field is demonstrated in the polemic sparked in 1992 by American academic Francis Fukuyama's pamphlet *The End of History and the Last Man*.[60] Although criticized as the epitome of postmodern nihilism, Fukuyama's thesis is an implacable grand narrative. It argues that the commitment to end-directed history has led to most of humankind's problems and conflicts, and thus the obsession with dialectical struggle and progress should be renounced. For Fukuyama, the victory of Western capitalism over communism represents the end of mankind's ideological evolution and so a world free of conflict. Intersecting with the enduring influence in France of Russian thinker Alexandre Kojève's seminars on Hegel in 1930s and crystallizing growing French anti-Americanism, Fukuyama's claims were resoundingly criticized. Indeed, accusing Fukuyama of advancing a (totalitarian) totalizing theory, in a marked suspension of incredulity towards its own xenophobic grand narratives, France defended its enshrined Republican values to assert the *exception française* by contesting this pæan of praise to liberal democracy. Thus, like the *affaire Sokal*, and the controversy over Bourdieu's *Sur la Télévision*, the French reception of *The End of History* brought into focus an intellectual field where the notion of the critical turning point was far from obsolete (as does Fukuyama's volte-face in *Our Posthuman Future* in 2002).[61]

The End of History elicited responses from Baudrillard and Derrida, bringing their reputations as symptomatic of a putative postmodern rejection of the critical turning point into question. Derrida's *Spectres de*

---

[60] Francis Fukuyama, *The End of History and the Last Man* (London: Verso, 1992); published in France as *La Fin de l'histoire et le dernier homme*, trans. Denis-Armand Canal (Paris: Flammarion, 1992).

[61] Fukuyama, *Our Posthuman Future: Consequences of the Biotechnology Revolution* (New York: Farrar, Straus, and Giroux, 2002). Here Fukuyama argues that since humans have not reached the end of science, the potential to modify human behaviour may yet affect change in liberal democracy.

Marx incorporates both a direct and a performative critique of Fukuyama's thesis.[62] Debunking Fukuyama's claims for the *End of History* as a neo-imperialist view that retrospectively justifies the putative triumph of Western capitalism in the post-Cold War era, Derrida self-reflexively returns to the Marxist dialectic in a qualified quest for a new ethics. Baudrillard's *L'Illusion de la fin; ou, La Grève des événements* (1992) and *À l'Ombre du millénaire; ou, Le Suspens de l'an 2000* (1998) also respond to Fukuyama.[63] Although these two essays feature hypotheses seeking to account for a perceived loss of bearings in a hyperreal world, a careful analysis shows how both nonetheless bring the potential of the turning point into question. Rather than figuring the end of history as the victory of liberal democracy, in *L'Illusion* Baudrillard advances three hypotheses to account for its loss, all using the trope of the turning point. Baudrillard later returns to the trope of the turning point in *À l'Ombre*, identifying the removal of the Beaubourg countdown clock and the decoding of the human genome as symbolic of an inverse millenarianism. He describes the contemporary obsession with retracing origins as a commodification of cultural memory, and the event as a turning point as an empty symbolic product. The whitewashing of events to re-align them in an expiated, politically correct narrative thus heralds a progressive exhaustion of all critical capacity and human specificity.

Moreover, if both *L'Illusion* and *À l'Ombre* consistently draw upon the symbolism of millennia and tropes of apocalypse and crisis, they also both conclude by raising the question of the enduring potential of an epistemological break. Hence, Baudrillard further belies his reputation as France's foremost postmodern prophet of doom by mooting the possibility of critical turning points in the future. At the end of *L'Illusion*, Baudrillard's hypothesis for the ramifications of the loss of history is described in terms of a unique adventure. Whilst his description of freedom from cause and effect as a privilege begs urgent ethical questions, Baudrillard nonetheless considers language—and in particular, *literary* language—in terms of its creative potential for resisting the complete loss of critical capacity: 'Contre ce mouvement d'ensemble, il reste l'hypothèse complètement improbable, et sans doute invérifiable,

---

[62] Derrida, *Spectres de Marx.*
[63] Baudrillard, *L'Illusion de la fin; ou, La Grève des événements* (Paris: Galilée, 1992); idem, *À l'Ombre du millénaire; ou, Le Suspens de l'an 2000* (Paris: Sens & Tonka, 1998).

d'une *réversibilité poétique des événements*, dont nous n'avons quasiment pour preuve que l'existence de cette même possibilité dans le langage.'[64] Drawing attention to the critical potential of language also suggests the possibility of developing new turning points. This implied linguistic exploration distances Baudrillard from the notion of postmodern perpetual crisis. Similarly *À l'Ombre* concludes with contradictory urgency, juxtaposing a negative analysis of the loss of reality with a questioning of the regenerative possibility of an inversely dialectical mode of critical thought: 'Y a-t-il place pour une autre pensée—une pensée paradoxale—[qui] ne poserait que des problèmes insolubles ...? Qui reproblématiserait au contraire toutes les solutions déjà trouvées, contribuant à maintenir le monde sous tension énigmatique?'.[65] Here the sense of critical leverage lies not in the mode of crisis resolution (of questions that invite conclusive answers), but in the problematiza-tion of that mode, the investigation of the notion of the regenerative turning point.

THE FRENCH EXCEPTION AND THE
ROMAN NATIONAL

The end of the twentieth century saw a convergence of turning points including the fall of the Iron Curtain; the decoding of the human genome; the exponential development of global market economics; the explosion of the audiovisual media; and the advent of the Internet and digital media. France's attempts to negotiate these changes were beset not only by its historical legacy and the crisis discourses of the past but also by real crises, in turn subject to manipulation by the mass media and the global market. Domestically, the sense of living through

---

[64] Baudrillard's emphasis, *L'Illusion de la fin*: p. 158: 'Against this movement in both directions at once, there is the completely improbable, and certainly unverifiable hypothesis of a *poetic reversibility of events*, and almost the only proof we have that it may exist is the possibility of this in language.'

[65] Baudrillard, *À l'Ombre*, p. 31: 'Is there room for another way of thinking—a paradoxical way of thinking—which would only pose insoluble problems [. . .]? Which instead would re-problematize all the solutions that have already been found, helping to keep the world in an enigmatic tension?'.

the worst yet of the 'décennies "piteuses"'[66] is rendered all the more keen by the stark comparison with (and the consequences of) what Jean Fourastié called the *Trente Glorieuses*: the period of exceptionally swift modernization in France spanning the 1950s, 1960s, and 1970s.[67] For Kristin Ross, the rapidity of modernization in France constitutes an event, the palpable impact of a turning point:

> The speed with which French society was transformed after the war from a rural, empire-oriented Catholic country into a fully industrialized, decolonized, and urban one meant that the things modernization needed burst onto a society that still cherished pre-war outlooks with all of the force, excitement, disruption, and horror of the genuinely new.[68]

This unprecedented period of expansion was marked by a tension between modernity and tradition, and the advent of consumerism and the *événements* of May 1968 expressed not only a frustration with intellectual and social structures, but also a contradictory avidity and anxiety regarding American-style consumerism.

The *fin de millénaire* sense of crisis is therefore rooted in economic change within and beyond France. On the one hand the perception of a threat to French national identity is articulated in anti-American critiques of the cultural relativism perceived in the discourses of the *politiquement correct* and the *tout culturel*. On the other by the mid 1990s, globalization had come to be considered in France less as a challenge than as a threat.[69] In 1996 Viviane Forrester's *L'Horreur économique*[70] sold 350,000 copies in two months, at once reflecting and spreading French fears of an economic genocide brought about by global market economics. In 1999 to 2000, *Le Monde* printed no fewer than 2,375 articles on globalization, and a 2000 Sofres opinion poll recorded that 72 per cent of French people were 'suspicious' of globalization, whilst 65 per cent believed it to be a

[66] Jean-Michel Gaillard, 'Le Dernier quart de siècle: De 1975 à nos jours', in Georges Duby, ed., *Histoire de la France en trois volumes III: Les Temps nouveaux, de 1852 à nos jours* (Paris: Larousse-Bordas/HER, 1999), pp. 444–513, at p. 446: 'the pitiful decades'.

[67] Jean Fourastié, *Les Trente Glorieuses ou la révolution invisible de 1946 à 1975* (Paris: Fayard 1979).

[68] Kristin Ross, *Fast Cars Clean Bodies: Decolonization and the Reordering of French Culture* (Cambridge, MA, and London: MIT Press, 1995), p. 4.

[69] Vivien Schmidt, *The Futures of European Capitalism* (Oxford: Oxford University Press, 2002).

[70] Viviane Forrester, *L'Horreur économique* (Paris: Fayard, 1996).

direct cause of rising social inequalities.[71] Such fears are at the core of the perception of a threat to French cultural specificity—*l'exception fran-çaise*—a nexus of identity narratives in which literary and philosophical discourses play key constitutive roles alongside economic and political policies.

Fin de millénaire exceptionalist discourses converge in expressions of the need to resist the impact of the mass media (audiovisual and digital) and neoliberalism. Gathering pace from the 1980s, neoliberalism is described by David Harvey as the defining figure of global market economics, characterized by the championing of free markets, deregu-lation, privatization, and the notion that entrepreneurialism is the route to individual fulfilment.[72] Rather than harnessing the critical leverage inherent in the contradictory neoliberal promotion of individualism and production of homogeneity, or confronting the ambivalence of late twentieth-century France's simultaneous rejection and embracing of American-style liberal democracy, French crisis discourses surrounding neoliberalism often return to the arguably obsolete ethos of the 1789 Revolution. Neoliberal individualism and deregulation is considered to counter the ethos of the one and indivisible Republic and the values of *liberté, égalité, fraternité* enduringly viewed—despite the social, eco-nomic, and political crises besetting France—to be the bedrock of French exceptionalism. Nonetheless, this resistance counters Fredric Jameson's assertion that there is no alternative to the dominance of American late capitalism.[73] Instead, exemplifying Harvey's analysis of globalization as an incomplete, uneven, and ongoing process, critical leverage can be perceived in the French crisis discourses surrounding the global market and the mass media.

Yet turn-of-the-millennium France did not witness any attempts at political revolution on the scale of those that had punctuated modern French history. Analyses on the thirtieth anniversary of May 1968 at best highlighted the stability and at worst the atrophy of French political life. In 1998 the *black, blanc, beur* multi-ethnic French national team

[71] Timothy B. Smith, *France in Crisis: Welfare, Inequality and Globalization since 1980* (Cambridge and New York: Cambridge University Press, 2004), p. 55.

[72] David Harvey, *A Brief History of Neoliberalism* (Oxford: Oxford University Press, 2005).

[73] Fredric Jameson and Masao Miyoshi, eds, *The Cultures of Globalization* (Durham, NC, and London: Duke University Press, 1998).

won the soccer World Cup, to the joy of a host nation that seemed united in patriotic fervour. Yet this belies the very real social crises at the heart of French society such as those represented in Mathieu Kassowitz's 1995 film *La Haine*, which bought a crisis of integration and marginalization to international audiences. Indeed, by the 1990s declaring crisis was, as Silverman notes, a dominant discourse of the nation-state whose identity is inextricably bound up with the *Lumières* narrative of progress:

The sense of crisis in France today therefore frequently appears sharper than in other countries because of the widely held perception in France that that model—founded on universalism, progress, the political nation, republicanism, the word, Culture—is being resolutely effaced by contemporary trends.[74]

To what extent then, is this sense of crisis and the discourses that sustain and produce it underpinned by tangible crises?

By the 1990s crisis in the French political sphere came not in the shape of attempted revolution, but in the stagnation perceived in *cohabitation* and the *pensée unique* and by successive scandals revealing institutionalized corruption. The 1992 *affaire du sang contaminé* added to the real medical crisis of caring for AIDS victims and averting the spread of HIV. Institutional manipulation of crisis was revealed in the government's failure to legislate effectively against the use of donated blood likely to be HIV positive, and in that the ministers responsible escaped trial, and three out of the four doctors who served as scapegoats were acquitted. Just as France appeared to be grappling with the implications of the Second World War—collaboration, the *Épuration*, and the French role in the Holocaust—the responsibility of the contemporary political class was recurrently brought into question. In 1991 prefect René Bousquet was charged with crimes against humanity for his role in the *Vél d'Hiv* round up of Jews in July 1942, crimes for which he had been tried and acquitted in 1949. Bousquet was assassinated before he came to trial, but in 1994, amidst questioning of Mitterrand's own activities during the Occupation, it transpired that the President had attempted to protect Bousquet. In a grisly performance of the return of

---

[74] Max Silverman, *Facing Postmodernity: Contemporary French Thought on Culture and Society* (London: Routledge, 1999), p. 6.

institutionally repressed violence, the trial in 1997 and 1998 of Maurice Papon revealed his co-implication in repeated, institutionalized crimes: the deportation of 1,700 Jews between 1942 and 1944 (an activity he doubled with playing the role of resistance sympathizer); colonial repression as Prefect of Constantine in Algeria; and as Prefect of Police in Paris, presiding over the CRS repression of a peaceful demonstration by Algerians in October 1961 which resulted in the covered up murder of upwards of two hundred Algerians.

Meanwhile, as the social, political, and ethical consequences of France's colonial and postcolonial legacy began to be publicly debated (the Algerian War was not formally recognized as a war until 1999) the crisis of assimilation of immigrants and second and third generation descendants was played out in ever more evident signs of *marginalisation* and rioting in the *banlieues*. Successive *affaires du foulard* were precipitated by the exclusion of female Muslim pupils from schools for refusing to remove the *hijab*, a sign of religious affiliation deemed incompatible with the Republican principle of *laïcité*. Islamic headscarves (and all other signs of religious affiliation) were subsequently banned in 2004, after a highly mediatized polemic that drew attention to political and social disunity rather than to the Republican cohesion and equality the measure purports to enshrine. Likewise the rise of the Front National and the terror campaign believed to have been orchestrated by Algerian extremists during the 1980s and 1990s which included a fatal bomb attack on the Paris Métro on 25 July 1995 are eloquent examples of a dangerous manipulation of crisis discourses.

However as the above analysis of *fin de millénaire* French crisis thinking demonstrates, the perceived climate of crisis without end is not borne out in the French intellectual field. Nor is it evident at a grassroots political level. The 1990s witnessed a politicized return to the crisis trope exemplified by anti-globalization demonstrations and by campaigning for writing off the debt of developing nations. French political activist muscles have been increasingly flexed in the arena of *altermondialisme*, seeking to make impact upon economic and ecological crises with very real global consequences. Although activism drawing attention to the dangers of global warming, pollution, over-population, and the depletion of natural resources may only have precipitated extremely limited policy changes, it certainly generates an increase in eschatological perceptions of the imminent threat of world-scale disaster. In France, José Bové's iconic stand against McDonald's brought the notion of the dialectic back into the political arena.[75] Aveyron farmer, spokesperson for the *Confédération paysanne*, and hero of the French anti-American campaign against *la malbouffe*, Bové attracted huge media coverage for the movement to resist the spread of multinationals in France and the effects of globalization on small national producers, and thus by association, a perceived French way of life. He was amongst five protesters campaigning against US restriction on the importation of Roquefort cheese who were incarcerated for obstructing the building of a new McDonald's in Millau on 12 August 1999.

A modest return to the political engagement of the artist was indicated in 1996 with the 'Appel des 234' calling for legal recognition of homosexual couples and signed by two hundred and thirty four prominent figures in French cultural production and criticism including Bourdieu, Cixous, Derrida, and Redonnet. This was again apparent in February 1997, when a petition was published in *Les Inrockuptibles* and *Le Monde* signed by sixty film-makers protesting against the Debré laws on immigration. Petitions by writers, musicians, and artists followed, and many attended the huge anti-racism rally of 22 February 1997. In literature, film, and the print media there is a discernible trend towards the retrospective analysis of crises of the second half of the French twentieth century: the Occupation; the Holocaust; May 1968; and latterly France's colonial and postcolonial legacy. If cultural production throws up such contrasting returns to the agency of the trope of the turning point, what, then of the *roman national*,[76] in nationalistic, protectionist, and literary terms?

Fears for the *exception française* are articulated in critiques by Lipovetsky, Philippe Muray, and Nora.[77] They intersect with Baudrillard in perceiving a neutralization of the crises of the recent past by a consum-

---

[75] José Bové and François Dufour, *Le Monde n'est pas une marchandise: Des Paysans contre la malbouffe* (Paris: La Découverte & Syros, 2000).

[76] 'the national novel'.

[77] Nora, 'L'Ère de la commémoration', in Pierre Nora et al., eds, *Les Lieux de mémoire III: Les France*, Édition Quarto (Paris: Gallimard, 1992), pp. 977–1012; Lipovetsky, *Le Crépuscule du devoir: L'Éthique indolore des nouveaux temps démocratiques* (Paris: Gallimard, 1992); and Philippe Muray, *Après l'histoire II* (Paris: Les Belles Lettres, 2000).

erist culture of remembrance, which elides rather than confronts the legacy of the crises and crisis discourses of the past. Nora's *Les Lieux de mémoire* devotes three volumes to the question of the constitution and protection of French cultural identity and memory—'le roman national'[78]—and calls for resistance against the threats perceived in the mass media; the acceleration of the pace of late twentieth-century life; and the obliteration of cultural difference by globalization. Nora bemoans a contemporary 'mémoire intensément rétinienne et puissamment télévisuelle'.[79] This he conceives as presenting a grave threat to memory as a repository of national identity, and to the crisis tropes—historical and literary—that had thus far functioned as its guarantors. Indeed Nora's analysis of the interplay of historical narratives and literary narratives in the constitution of French identity seeks to operate both as a warning and as an investigation of the potential of the co-implicated narratives of history, literature, and identity.

This *literary* metaphor for national identity in crisis clearly has a particular resonance in France at the turn of the third millennium. Paul Yonnet uses the term to situate the sense of a compromising of French identity and the concomitant rise of racism.[80] Olivier Mongin posits that the French 'roman familial' is threatened by the influence of neoliberalism.[81] Jean-Marie Domenach links the incursion of American neoliberalism in French politics to a perceived 'interruption du "roman national"'.[82] So, this belief in the *exception française*—a grand narrative the legitimacy of which continued to be vehemently defended in the 1990s—is still very much bound up with literary narratives, and for certain commentators, a sense of the crisis of French literature.

The desire to preserve the French exception through cultural protectionism is reflected by the commissioning of reports including Alain Minc's *La France face à l'an 2000* in 1994, and Patrice Bloche's *Le Désir de la France: La Présence internationale de la France et la francophonie*

[78] Nora et al., eds, *Les Lieux de mémoire*, pp. 1659–60.

[79] Ibid., p. 35: 'an intensely retinal and potently televisual memory'.

[80] Paul Yonnet, *Voyage au centre du malaise française: l'Antiracisme et le roman national* (Paris: Gallimard, 1993).

[81] Olivier Mongin, *La Peur du vide: Essai sur les passions démocratiques* (Paris: Seuil, 1991): 'the family novel'.

[82] Jean-Marie Domenach, *Le Crépuscule de la culture française?* (Paris: Plon, 1995), p. 74: 'an interruption of the "national novel"'.

dans la société de l'information in 1998 (a title tellingly translated as *A Yearning for France*), and a Ministère de la culture et de la communication commissioned report on leisure activities in France from 1989 to 1997.[83] The equivalent 1973–89 survey notes the introduction of colour television, but emphasizes what the French read and where they went in their leisure time, and reflects the concern that French television and cinema would be flooded with American imports. However, the 1997 survey acknowledges a need to account for vast changes in television programming and the advent of the home computer, and reflects a real concern for the influence of American televisual and cinematic formats on the French field of cultural production. The frequency of book reading continued to fall, with a marked feminization of reading (unfortunately not matched by a marked increase in female writers).

Successive governments have introduced protectionist legislation designed to support the French publishing market against the perceived threat of global market economics and the audiovisual media. The *Loi pour le Prix unique du livre* was passed in 1982 in response to pressure from independent publishing houses and booksellers seeking protection from competition from French chains (notably the FNAC) and multinationals. The ban on television advertisements for books was maintained throughout the 1990s to protect smaller publishing houses. The commissioning of Patrice Cahart's report, *Le Livre français a-t-il un avenir?* in 1988 and the questions Cahart sets out to answer speak volumes of fears in France for the role of literature in the construction of identity in a globalized marketplace: 'Le Livre français est-il malade? Doit-il continuer d'être vendu selon des règles particulières? La France a-t-elle encore une production digne d'elle?'.[84]

---

[83] Patrice Bloche, *Le Désir de la France: La Présence internationale de la France et la francophonie dans la société de l'information* (Paris: Textes de référence, 1998); Olivier Donnat, *Les Pratiques culturelles des Français: Enquête 1997* (Paris: La Documentation Française, 1998), pp. 169–74; Alain Minc, *La France de l'an 2000: Rapport au Premier ministre* (Paris: Odile Jacob/La Documentation Française, 1994).

[84] Patrice Cahart, *Le Livre français a-t-il un avenir: Rapport au ministre de la Culture et de la Communication* (Paris: La Documentation Française, 1988), p. 7: 'Is French literature ailing? Should book sales continue to be subject to specific regulations? Does France's literary output still befit her reputation?'.

FIN DE MILLÉNAIRE PROSE FICTION:
THE CONDITIONS OF PRODUCTION

The discourse of the *crise du roman*—a rejection of current literary practice and erstwhile avant-gardes which paradoxically motivates literary innovation—has been the counterpoint of modern French literary history. From this perspective, the ascribing of a literary waste ground to fallout from the *nouveau roman*, Oulipo, structuralist, and poststructuralist thought follows in a rich, regenerative tradition. And if no *grand écrivain* or critically acclaimed avant-garde emerged in the 1980s and 1990s, and there had been a decline in works overtly labelled *roman*, *fin de millénaire* prose fiction is remarkable in its heterogeneity in terms of both form and content. The hybridity of literary narratives spans *autofiction*, biography, minimalism, *noir*, true-crime, documentary, essay, history, and travel (and often a combination of these). This blurring of generic boundaries counters declarations of a terminal decline.

Nonetheless fears concerning the impact of the audiovisual media and global market economics on French literary production add a different emphasis and a new sense of urgency to the *fin de millénaire* discourse of the *crise du roman*. In 1995 Noguez warns of the flooding of the literary market with books by media personalities and *intellectuels médiatiques*. 'Plus d'écrivains. Plus que des livreurs.'[85] In a 2001 *NRF* dossier *Avenir de la fiction* Benjamin Berton describes the French reading public as '*lectoconsommateurs*'.[86] This invites an investigation of the impact of the conditions of production of the French literary field.

In the final decade of the twentieth century, the average print run for a novel fell from 15,000 to 8,929; as few as 2,000 copies were printed for little-known authors; 25 per cent of all books were returned unsold

---

[85] Dominique Noguez, 'Présentation: Dossier: "Écrivains, non programmables"', *L'Infini*, 42 (1995), 3–5, at p. 3: 'They are not writing books any more. They just deliver products.'

[86] Benjamin Berton, 'Des plans sur la comète: Panorama prospectif du roman français moderne', *Nouvelle Revue Française*, 561 (2002), 161–8, at p. 161: '*reader-consumers*'.

to distributors, the most part for pulping,[87] and sales of 30,000 qualified for bestseller status.[88] The literary field was increasingly monopolized by major groups (Hachette and Havas controlled 75 per cent of the French publishing market in 1998), leaving smaller publishers unable to compete. Houellebecq, for example, published *Extension du domaine de la lutte* with Maurice Nadeau, but left for Flammarion as the independent lacked the budget to publish both his poetry and *Les Particules élémentaires*. Following his 1998 and 2001 successes and the writer's dissatisfaction with the handling of film rights, Houellebecq's 2005 *La Possibilité d'une île* was published by Fayard, following a 'transfer fee' rumoured to be in excess of one million Euros. A highly mediatized—and no doubt market-led—move, since Hachette/Lagardère's portfolio includes Fayard and a film production unit, corresponding to Houellebecq's reported desire for a hands-on role in the film adaptation of his fourth novel. Flammarion nonetheless continued to benefit from Houellebecq's notoriety, in 2008 publishing *Interventions 2*, an augmented version of previously published essays, and, with Grasset, *Ennemis publics: Correspondance de Michel Houellebecq et Bernard-Henri Lévy*.[89]

Contradictions in the literary field abound. If the proliferation of prizes suggests a vibrant literary culture, the most prestigious are perceived to be dominated by the publishing market leaders Gallimard, Grasset, and Seuil—'Galligrasseuil'—and are often beset by sales-generating scandal. Bernard Pivot's groundbreaking literary programme *Apostrophes* was accused of encouraging the commodification of the literary field by inviting authors with appropriate media profiles to appear on the show (36 per cent of book sales were recorded by a 1980 IFOP poll as influenced by *Apostrophes*).[90] On the one hand, the last *Apostrophes* in 1990 has been interpreted as Pivot turning his back

[87] See Pascal Fouché, ed., 'Introduction', in *L'Édition française depuis 1945* (Tours: Electre-Éditions du Cercle de la Librairie, 1998).

[88] Marie-Gabrielle Slama, 'L'Effet Pivot', in *L'Édition française depuis 1945* (Tours: Electre-Éditions du Cercle de la Librairie, 1998), pp. 616–19.

[89] Houellebecq, *Interventions 2* (Paris: Flammarion, 2008); idem and Bernard-Henri Lévy *Ennemis publics: Correspondance de Michel Houellebecq et Bernard-Henri Lévy* (Paris: Flammarion/Grasset, 2008).

[90] Hervé Delouche, 'La Rentrée littéraire: De la Littérature selon le réel', *Regards*, 49 (1999), <http://www.regards.fr/archives/1999/199910/199910cre09.html> (accessed 19 March 2004).

on a moribund literary scene, and his subsequent show *Bouillon de culture* had a broader cultural remit (though a similar effect on sales). Yet on the other, the *effet Pivot* is testimony to the enduring importance of literature in French cultural life. The final *Apostrophes* scored impressive audience ratings of 9 per cent, and talk shows revolving around literature have become an established feature of the French televisual landscape (including Patrick Poivre d'Arvor's *Vol de nuit* and *Ex-libris* on TF1 and Guillaume Durand's *Campus*, which replaced Bernard Pivot's *Bouillon de culture* on France 2 in 2001, opening with an interview with Houellebecq).

Meanwhile, the much-feared obliteration of the book-selling market by cinema, television, the Internet, computer games, or the ephemeral threat of the 'e-book' has not transpired. Three months after it was published, sales of Houellebecq's *Les Particules élémentaires* exceeded 350,000 in France alone (the novel has also been translated into thirty-five languages, bringing French fiction back onto the international literary stage). Independent publishing houses such as Minuit and P.O.L continue to survive and to introduce innovative French fiction. The *rentrée littéraire* provides an annual testament to the nation's enduring interest in reading and writing prose fiction, and in 1999, it saw the launch of a record 334 new French novels. For all the attractions of the small screen—television, computer, or games console—the *rentrée littéraire* continues to provide readers with opportunities to attend readings and discussions with prominent writers, reflecting the enduring potential for cultural exchange.

The contradictory discourses claiming the end of French prose fiction or proclaiming its definitive regeneration and the aforementioned urge to categorize into putative trends (rarely, however, in the same combinations) also beg the question of a crisis of criticism. *Le Monde*'s Frédéric Badré counters assertions of irreparable literary decadence by describing Houellebecq as the harbinger of 'une nouvelle tendance en littérature'.[91] Whilst ostensibly positive, this and other attempts to designate Houellebecq at the vanguard of a literary movement variously described as 'en prise directe avec le réel', 'le post-naturalisme', or 'le nouveau réalisme'[92] belie at best a

---

[91] Frédéric Badré, 'Une Nouvelle tendance en littérature', *Le Monde*, 3 October 1998, p. 14: 'a new trend in literature'. Marie Darrieussecq, Houellebecq, and Vincent Ravalec are cited as examples.

[92] 'plugged into reality', 'post-naturalism' or 'neo-realism'.

commodifying trend and at worst a desperate desire to identify a new, redeeming school amidst the heterogeneity of the *fin de millénaire* literary field. Indeed, *Le Monde des livres* editor Jean-Luc Douin criticizes this critical tendency for occluding a range of aesthetic and ethical concerns:

S'il existait actuellement une tendance dans la littérature française, ce serait celui du désordre; la frénésie à mêler les genres, tâter autant du roman que de la poésie, du récit de voyage, de nouvelle; la tentation de l'introspection autant que celle de la réhabilitation des autres, oubliés de l'Histoire; le souci de refléter les effets de l'horreur économique, du sida, de la fracture sociale, du chômage.[93]

Jean-Philippe Domecq overtly diagnoses a crisis of criticism, epitomized, he argues, by the celebration of Echenoz, Michel Rio, and Philippe Sollers as *grands écrivains*. According to Philippe Muray critics are constrained by paradigmatic perspectives imposed from above (academic and poststructuralist criticism), and from below (commercially driven television and press journalism).[94]

Certainly, the turn of the millennium ushered in a flood of literary *états des lieux*. Whilst some seek to celebrate the contemporary literary field, a convergence of titles betrays anxiety, for example Jean-Marie Domenach's *Le Crépuscule de la culture française*; Domecq's *Le Pari littéraire*; Bertrand Leclair's *Théorie de la déroute*; and Alain Nadaud's *Malaise dans la littérature*.[95] In *La Confusion des lettres*, Michel Crépu presents the *fin de millénaire* field as a late twentieth-century quarrel of Ancients and Moderns, exemplified by the *affaire* surrounding Houellebecq's *Les Particules élémentaires*.[96] In *L'Industrie de la consolation: La Littérature face au 'cerveau globale'* Bertrand Leclair bemoans the influence of the digital

---

[93] Jean-Luc Douin, 'Contre la société ou tout contre?', *La Revue des deux mondes* (2001), 42–7, at p. 43: 'If there is any discernible trend in contemporary French literature it is disorder. This is evidenced by a frenzied blurring of genres, mixing the novel with poetry, travel writing, and the short story; by writers caught between the pulls of introspection and of rehabilitating the memory of those forgotten by History; by attempts to reflect the impact of economic troubles, AIDS, the breakdown of society, and unemployment.'

[94] Philippe Muray, 'Le Propre de la critique', *L'Atelier du roman*, 6 (1996), 17.

[95] Jean-Marie Domenach, *Le Crépuscule de la culture française?* (Paris: Plon, 1995); Jean-Philippe Domecq, *Le Pari littéraire* (Paris: Editions Esprit, 1994); Bertrand Leclair, *Théorie de la déroute* (Paris: Verticales/Seuil, 2001); Alain Nadaud, *Malaise dans la littérature* (Paris: Champ Vallon, 1993).

[96] Michel Crépu, *La Confusion des lettres* (Paris: Grasset, 1999).

and audiovisual media on literary production worldwide.[97] Looking back on the 1990s, Michel Waldberg's *La Parole putanisée* bemoans the state of French literature in general and Houellebecq in particular, providing an extensive list of what *not* to read.[98] Pierre Jourde's *La Littérature sans estomac* polemically lays emphasis on the influence of market-driven editorial and critical control in French literary production.[99]

The titles of dossiers in literary journals also belie an anxiety at the heart of otherwise positively framed surveys: 'Où va la littérature française?: 24 écrivains des années 90 répondent', *La Quinzaine Littéraire*, 1–15 March 1997, and *La Quinzaine Littéraire*, 16–31 March 1997; 'Que peut le roman?', *Le Débat*, 90 (1996); and 'Questions du romans, romans en question', *Europe*, 820–1 (1997). Yet all these dossiers identify vitality, heterogeneity, and a faith in the enduring potential of prose fiction. Indeed the November 2000 issue of *Magazine littéraire* 'La Relève des avant-gardes' posits a literary renaissance focusing on non-mainstream fiction with features on trends and authors including the first-person narratives of Mehdi Belhaj Kacem; 'Les Trashys' (Virginie Despentes); 'La Littérature homosexuelle' (Marie-Hélène Bourcier, Barbara Brèze, and Hervé Brizon); 'La Poulpe'; cyber-science-fiction writer Maurice G. Dantec; and new *enfant terrible*, Houellebecq. Beyond France, the Spring 2002 special issue of *Nottingham French Studies*, 'French Fiction in the 1990s', features articles on contemporary *noir* fiction, Jean-Marie Le Clézio, Paule Constant, Annie Ernaux, Houellebecq, Michel Rio, Jean Rouaud, and 'Lesbo-Erotic' fiction. *Contemporary French and Francophone Studies/Sites* devotes three issues to 'Writing in French in the 90s' featuring Angot, Echenoz, and Houellebecq along with Pierre Bergounioux, François Bon, Renaud Camus, Eric Chevillard, Jean-Marie Le Clézio, Catherine Cusset, Régine Detambel, Sylvie Germain, Pierre Michon, Marie Ndiaye, Jacques Roubaud, Lydie Salvayre, Leïla Sebbar, and Philippe Sollers.[100]

---

[97] Bertrand Leclair, *L'Industrie de la consolation: La Littérature face au 'cerveau globale'* (Paris: Verticales, 1998).

[98] Michel Waldberg, *La Parole putanisée* (Paris: La Différence, 2002), p. 39.

[99] Pierre Jourde, *La Littérature sans estomac* (Paris: L'Esprit des Péninsules, 2002).

[100] Eliane DalMolin and Roger Célestin, eds, 'Writing in French in the '90s: Novelists and Poets', *Contemporary French and Francophone Studies/Sites* (Part 1) 2/2 (1998), (Part 2) 3/1 (1999), and (Part 3) 3/2 (1999).

Meanwhile the advent of specialist literary websites, weblogs, and Internet communities such as *Fabula* (<http://www.fabula.org>) create new fora for discussion, offering the potential for shifting literary criticism away from the institutionalized power of the market and of academe. The change from monthly to quarterly publication of the *NRF* also points to a critical field increasingly dominated—and therefore arguably democratized—by newspaper book reviews and magazines with a broader cultural remit (and according to their detractors, a pop journalistic approach) such as *Art press*, *Technikart*, and *Les Inrockuptibles*. Indeed just as traditional organs appeared to be on the wane, the 1990s saw the launch of a cluster of literary reviews with manifestos aiming to promote innovation in prose fiction including *L'Animal*, *L'Atelier du contemporain*, *L'Atelier du roman*, *Les Cahiers de la Villa Gillet*, *Hespéris*, *Ligne de risque*, *Le Matricule des Anges*, *Nouvelle revue violente*, *Perpendiculaire*, *Prétexte*, *Quai Voltaire*, *La Revue de littérature générale*, *Scherzo*, and *Le Trait*. Whilst the inherently transient patterns of the field led to the demise of some titles, and *Perpendiculaire* was a casualty of the *affaire Houellebecq*, *L'Atelier du roman* and *Le Matricule des Anges* had become credible critical champions of French prose fiction by 2000, whilst *Prétexte* has transmuted into a publishing house. Rival websites dedicated to Houellebecq (*Les Amis de Michel Houellebecq* (<http://www.houellebecq.info>) and *L'Amicale des Ennemis des Amis de Michel Houellebecq* (<http://aeamh.free.fr>) are further testimony to the democratization of the critical field, although beset by acrimonious cyber-sniping in a virtual simulacrum of the *affaire Houellebecq*.

THE *CRISE DU ROMAN* AND THE RETURN TO CRISIS

As the twentieth century drew to a close, the perception was that no *grand écrivain* had emerged in the wake of Marguerite Duras, Georges Perec, or Michel Tournier (the most prominent of writers latterly considered as such, though many critics look back still more nostalgically to Sartre or Camus); and no self-declared or media constructed avant-gardes on the scale of the *nouveau roman* had emerged. Yet established literary figures writing since the 1960s and 1970s including Jean-Marie Le Clézio, Echenoz, Annie Ernaux, Patrick Modiano, and Érik Orsenna continued to produce contrasting, acclaimed work. Moreover, from the 1980s diverse writers including Pierre Michon, Marie Ndiaye, Daniel Pennac, Pascal Quignard, and Antoine Volodine have received serious critical attention. Others including Angot, Marie Darrieussecq, and Houellebecq have sparked renewed literary debate and violently diverging opinions. Indeed, if the defining features of the *fin de millénaire* French literary field are heterogeneity and competing crisis discourses, that of the critical field is contradiction.

Literary movements continue to be identified and to self-designate. 'L'École de Brive' comprises eight writers (Gilbert Bordes, Colette Laussac, Claude Michelet, Martine-Marie Muller, Michel Peyramaure, Denis Tillinac, Jean-Guy Soumy, and Yves Viollier) who in 1997, 1998, and 1999 all contributed a short story to a thematically based collection published by Robert Laffont for the annual Brive book fair. 'Les Moins que rien', a media-constructed grouping of writers of fictions exploring the intimate experiences of the everyday includes Pierre Autin-Grenier, François de Cornière, Philippe Delerm, Éric Holder, Gil Jouanard, and Jean-Pierre Ostende. 'La Nouvelle fiction', another self-elected group (Francis Berthelot, Georges-Olivier Châteaureynaud, François Coupry, Hubert Haddad, Jean Levi, Marc Petit, and Frédéric Tristan) privileges the imagination over realism.

The most frequently cited 'school' is 'minimalist', an umbrella term which, echoing that applied to the *nouveau roman,* is used to designate fictions published from the 1980s by Minuit (authors thus described include François Bon, Eric Chevillard, Patrick Deville, Echenoz, Marie Ndiaye, Pascal Quignard, Redonnet, Jean-Philippe Toussaint, and Antoine Volodine). Fieke Schoots describes writing categorized as 'minimalist' in terms of self-conscious brevity (of words, description, sentences, paragraphs, plots, protagonists, and indeed whole works): characteristics which constitute an exploration of the possibilities of language. For Schoots, the originality of fiction designated 'minimaliste' is 'sa façon de redécouvrir le récit tout en mettant en cause la représentation de la réalité par le langage'.[101] Yet the 'Jeunes auteurs autour de

[101] Fieke Schoots, *'Passer en douce à la douane': L'Écriture minimaliste de Minuit: Deville, Echenoz, Redonnet et Toussaint* (Amsterdam and Atlanta, GA: Rodopi, 1997), p. 58: 'the way [these fictions] simultaneously rediscover storytelling and bring the capacity of language to represent reality into question'.

Minuit'[102] do not recognize themselves as a group, and their literary projects contrast in ways that the label 'minimalist' occludes.

Another marked characteristic of the late twentieth-century French literary field is the proliferation of first-person narratives which intersect with the advent of reality television (examples include Hervé Guibert's *À l'Ami qui ne m'a pas sauvé la vie* (1990); Catherine Cusset's *Jouir* (1997); Angot's *L'Inceste* (1999); and Marie Nimier's *La Nouvelle pornographie* (2000).[103] Of course by the 1990s the crises of language and the self were common intellectual currency, and the hybrid 'genre' of *autofiction* was by no means new (Vincent Colonna argues that its first exponent dates back to AD2, but more frequently cited antecedents include Serge Doubrovsky and Annie Ernaux).[104] Marking a shift from Philippe Lejeune's description of the *pacte autobiographique* between reader and autobiographer,[105] Doubrovsky invented the term *autofiction* in 1977 to qualify a mode of writing which explores relationships between language, psychoanalysis, and the question of writing the self, and which he describes as: 'Fiction d'événements et de faits strictement réels; si l'on veut, *autofiction*, d'avoir confié le langage d'une aventure à l'aventure du langage.'[106] For Marion Sadoux *autofiction* is 'a resilient attempt to deal with notions of the self and subjectivity in writing in an age of multiple crisis'.[107] Laurent Flieder identifies the particularity of diverse French narratives categorized as *autofiction* as an introspection exemplified by narratives of the intimate details of daily life that afford new perspectives on the world and a new sensitivity in the narration of

[102] See Henk Hillenaar and Michèle Ammouche-Kremers, eds, *Jeunes Auteurs autour de Minuit* (Amsterdam and Atlanta, GA: Rodopi, 1994).

[103] Hervé Guibert, *À l'Ami qui ne m'a pas sauvé la vie* (Paris: Minuit, 1990); Catherine Cusset, *Jouir* (Paris: Gallimard, 1997); Christine Angot, *L'Inceste* (Paris: Fayard, 1999); Marie Nimier, *La Nouvelle pornographie* (Paris: Gallimard, 2000).

[104] Vincent Colonna, *Autofiction et autres mythomanes littéraires* (Paris: Editions Tristram, 2004).

[105] Philippe Lejeune, *Le Pacte autobiographique* (Paris: Seuil, 1975).

[106] Serge Doubrovsky, 'Autobiographie/Vérité/Psychanalyse', *L'Esprit Créateur*, 20 (1980), 86–98, at p. 90: 'A fiction made of real facts and events that are strictly real; or in other words, an *autofiction*, that entrusts the language of an adventure to the adventure of language.'

[107] Marion Sadoux, 'Christine Angot's *Autofictions*: Literature and/or Reality', in Gill Rye and Michael Worton, eds, *Women's Writing in Contemporary France: New Writers, New Literatures in the 1990s* (Manchester and New York: Manchester University Press, 2002), pp. 171–81, at p. 177.

the self. He identifies subcategories of 'autodiction' (the narration of experience exemplified by Annie Ernaux and Hervé Guibert); 'auto-scription' (the inscription of the self through biographical fiction exemplified by Pierre Bergounioux, Pierre Michon, and Jean Rouaud); and 'autofabulation' (synthetic fictions of the self exemplified by Philippe Sollers, Pascal Quignard, Gérard Macé, and Richard Millet).[108] Contrastingly, and it would seem like Flieder unaware of the irony of producing new labels, Marc Lambron dismisses such narratives as a market-driven '*narcisso-show*'.[109]

Such contradictions are symptomatic of the *fin de millénaire* literary field. Indeed this labelling dynamic—whether by journalists or academics—is itself inconsistent, with the same writers ascribed to different categories, or championed as major proponents of a trend in certain cases, but absent from descriptions of that trend in others. Whilst some writers are grouped by a perceived shared aesthetic, others are grouped by dint of ethnicity: *beur* and part-North African writers living in France (including Nina Bouraoui, Mehdi Belhaj Kacem, and Leïla Sebbar); or, in potentially neo-imperialist terms, as representative of *la francophonie* (North African writers such as Tahar Ben Jalloun, Rachïd Boujedra, Mohammed Dib, Assia Djebbar, and Albert Memmi; and *créole* Carribean writers including Patrick Chamoiseau, Maryse Condé, Raphaël Confiant, and Edouard Glissant). It is interesting to note that Belgian writers such as Amélie Nothomb and Jean-Philippe Toussaint are usually treated as French.

Sexual orientation provides another often falsely homogenizing label that leads to the bracketing of homosexual writers such as Renaud Camus, Guillaume Dustan, Tony Duvert, Hervé Guibert, and Guy Hocquenghem (the latter two featuring in a study of 'Sida-fiction').[110] And if at last women writers are becoming ever more present in the French literary field, where male writers are not classified by gender, writers as diverse as Angot, Nina Bouraoui, Paule Constant, Catherine Cusset, Marie Darrieussecq, Agnès Desarthe, Marie Dechesplin,

---

[108] Laurent Flieder, *Le Roman français contemporain* (Paris: Seuil, 1998).

[109] Claude Arnaud and Marc Lambron, 'Le "Piercing" littéraire', *La Revue des deux mondes* (2001), 9–14, at p. 10.

[110] Joseph Lévy and Alexis Nouss, *Sida-fiction: Essai d'anthropologie romanesque* (Lyon: Presses Universitaires de Lyon, 1994): 'AIDS-fiction'.

Virginie Despentes, Régine Detambel, Annie Ernaux, Anne Garréta, Sylvie Germain, Camille Laurens, Linda Lê, Marie Ndiaye, Marie Nimier, Lorette Nobécourt, Amélie Nothomb, Redonnet, Danièle Sallenave, Lydie Salvayre, and Leïla Sebbar are all too frequently grouped together in relation to anachronistic perceptions of difference feminism. In some cases, often homogenizing positive appraisals are countered by interpretations of the graphic but ambivalent exploration of female sexuality in Virginie Despentes's *Baise-moi* (1993); and Marie Darrieussecq's *Truismes* (1996) not as challenges to *fin de millénaire* misogyny, but as travesties of *écriture féminine*.[111] Of course, the best critical works which adopt a thematic approach or group together writers consider texts comparatively, but others parallel the commodifying dynamic of the market, constructing female, gay, or *beur* (writing) subjects as homogenized Others.[112]

Prose fictions apparently reflecting or inspired by the aesthetics of *reality shows* and crime reportage appear to corroborate a perceived colonization of the French field of cultural production by the American media, market economics, and litigation. In 2000 alone, a rash of such texts was brought into legal question for a perceived infringement of the privacy of the individual or the defamation of a person, company or brand. The Le Pen family attempted to block the publication of Mathieu Lindon's *Le Procès de Jean-Marie Le Pen* (2000). Publishers Calmann-Lévy withdrew Paul Smaïl's *Ali le magnifique* when the author refused to make amendments to the manuscript following the suicide of serial killer Sid Ahmed Rezala, model for the central protagonist, although Denoël subsequently published the text unchanged in

---

[111] Virginie Despentes, *Baise-moi* (Paris: Florent-Massot, 1993); Marie Darrieussecq, *Truismes* (Paris: P.O.L, 1996).
[112] Good studies reflecting the heterogeneity of writing by women include Shirley Ann Jordan, *Contemporary French Women's Writing: Women's Visions, Women's Voices, Women's Lives* (Bern: Lang, 2004); Catherine Rodgers and Nathalie Morello, eds, *Nouvelles écrivaines: Nouvelles voix?* (Amsterdam and Atlanta, GA: Rodopi, 2002); Gill Rye, ed., *Hybrid Voices, Hybrid Texts: Women's Writing at the Turn of the Millenium*, *Dalhousie French Studies*, 68 (Fall 2004); Rye, ed., *Contemporary Women's Writing in French*, *Journal of Romance Studies*, 2/1 (Spring 2002); Rye and Worton, eds, *Women's Writing in Contemporary France*; and Gill Rye and Carrie Tarr, eds, 'Focalizing the Body in Contemporary Women's Writing and Film-making in France', *Nottingham French Studies*, 45/3 (Autumn 2006); and Colette Sarrey-Strack, *Fictions contemporaines au féminin: Marie Darrieussecq, Marie Ndiaye, Marie Nimier, Marie Redonnet* (Paris: L'Harmattan, 2002).

2001. Jean-Louis Turquin (sentenced to twenty years for killing his son) attempted to block the publication of Marc Weitzmann's *Mariage mixte* (2000), a fictional reconstruction of the crime. Although Frédéric Beigbeder changed the name of his employer and client in *99 Francs* (2000), a novel based on his own experience as an advertising copy-writer, he was dismissed at the earliest opportunity.[113] If the scandals surrounding Houellebecq's *Les Particules élémentaires* (1998) and Angot's *L'Inceste* (1999) bring the question of the freedom of speech to the fore, so do legal proceedings brought against the fictions of Lindon, Smaïl, and Weitzmann.

Nonetheless, if both totalizing narratives and allegiance to theoretical paradigms are for the most part abandoned, the *fin de millénaire* literary field is not bereft of commitment. If intellectualism is eschewed, a concern for cultural heritage and the legacy of the past is evident, together with an intellectual engagement with social issues, and a socio-logically or anthropologically inflected concern for the detail of daily life. These strands are diversely and interconnectedly explored for example in the biographical fictions of Pierre Bergounioux and Pierre Michon; in the figuring of ghosts raising questions of personal and collective guilt by Marie Darrieussecq in *Naissance des fantômes* (1998), Lydie Salvayre in *La Compagnie des spectres* (1997), and Didier Van Cauwelaert in Goncout winning *Aller Simple* (1994);[114] in the implicitly investigative relationships between past and present, self and Other, agency and responsibility in the fictions of Patrick Modiano and Olivier Rolin, which intersect with and look beyond the fictional return to the legacy of the Second World War of the *mode rétro*; and in representations of the fabric and fractures of life in late twentieth-century France by Emmanuel Carrère, Vincent Ravalec, and Jacques Sérena.

Indeed scholarship on metropolitan French fiction in the 1990s examines a wide range of literary aesthetics and concerns. In successive bullish assessments of the contemporary French novel published by the Ministère des affaires étrangères in 1999 and 2000, Yves Mabin

---

[113] Mathieu Lindon, *Le Procès de Jean-Marie Le Pen* (Paris: P.O.L, 2000); Paul Smaïl, *Ali le magnifique* (Paris: Denoël, 2001); Marc Weitzmann, *Mariage mixte* (Paris: Stock, 2000); Frédéric Beigbeder, *99 Francs* (Paris: Grasset, 2000).

[114] Marie Darrieussecq, *Naissance des fantômes* (Paris: P.O.L, 1998); Lydie Salvayre, *La Compagnie des spectres* (Paris: Seuil, 1997); Didier Van Cauwelaert, *Aller Simple* (Paris: Albin Michel, 1994).

declared 'jamais le roman français n'a été aussi vivant'.[115] In 1990 Jean-Claude Lebrun and Claude Prevost identified twenty writers breaking new ground,[116] whilst Jean-Pierre Richard's surveys of 1990 and 1996 offer analyses of sixteen writers.[117] Laurent Flieder's 1999 survey of contemporary writing identifies multiple trends as heterogeneous testimony to the enduring of French literary production.[118] In 2001 Lakis Proguidis seeks to buck what he dismisses as the critical trend of reading novels as reflections of the contemporary world by reading predominantly little-known texts in terms of their 'artistic' value.[119]

Amongst this heterogeneity, a characteristic frequently identified by critics is the figure of the return. In *French Fiction in the Mitterrand Years: Memory, Narrative, Desire* Colin Davis and Elizabeth Fallaize discuss the phenomenon of 'returns' to memory, narrative, and desire in late twentieth-century French fiction (Marguerite Duras, Echenoz, Annie Ernaux, Hervé Guibert, Daniel Pennac, and Jorge Semprun are used as examples): 'However fractured, fictional, illusory, or elusive the subject might be, the questions of subjectivity, of the relationship between author and narrator, or author and text, were restored as valid topics for literary investigation, especially in relation to the central issues of identity, memory and desire.'[120] These returns were conceived by Dominique Viart as the 'retour au sujet, à l'histoire, et au discours'.[121] Returning to the subject does not reinstate a self-aware, self-identical entity providing (illusory) common ground and purpose for civilization. Instead it entails the notion of subjecthood as an impossible fantasy that nonetheless affords the potential for establishing

[115] Yves Mabin, ed., *Le Roman français contemporain* (Paris: Ministère des affaires étrangères, 1999 and 2002): 'the French novel has never been so vibrant'.

[116] Jean-Claude Lebrun and Claude Prevost, *Nouveaux territoires romanesques* (Paris: Messidor-Editions Sociales, 1990).

[117] Jean-Pierre Richard, *L'État des choses: Études sur huit écrivains d'aujourd'hui* (Paris: Gallimard, 1990); *Terrains de lecture* (Paris: Gallimard, 1996).

[118] Fleider, *Le Roman français contemporain*.

[119] Lakis Proguidis, *De L'Autre côté du brouillard: Essai sur le roman français contemporain* (Paris: Nota Bene, 2001).

[120] Colin Davis and Elizabeth Fallaize, *French Fiction in the Mitterrand Years: Memory, Narrative, Desire* (Oxford: Oxford University Press, 2000), p. 14.

[121] Dominique Viart, ed., *Écritures contemporaines 1: Mémoires du récit* (Paris and Caen: Lettres Modernes Minard, 1998); idem and Jan Baetans eds, *Écritures contemporaines 2: États du roman contemporaine* (Paris and Caen: Lettres Modernes Minard, 1999): 'the return to the subject, to history, and to narrative'.

a provisional identity. The return to the subject is interlinked with the influence of Bourdieusian sociology, the rise of *autofiction*, and with an exploration of memory such that the self cannot be conceived out of its socio-historical context. Thus the 'return to history' entails a quest rather than a linear narrative. A 'travail de mémoire' rather than a 'devoir de mémoire': a critical activity that may resist institutionalized discourses. Likewise, the return to narrative, or storytelling does not imply an unproblematized confidence in the trope of the turning point, but a self-reflexive mode of storytelling that brings both pleasure and the question of ethics back into the literary project. It implies accepting the need to tell stories to negotiate, if not to make sense of the world, and the possibility of enjoying language as a knowingly flawed tool.

Epitomizing the risk of the double bind of the recuperation of critical discourses, Viart's provisional taxonomy has been appropriated by critics anxious to categorize contemporary writing. Recognizing his own unwilling role in this neutralizing dynamic, Viart problematizes the transformation of conceptual frameworks into paradigms, and explains that the returns he identifies are conceived in the mode of interrogation and exploration, a 'retour à la question du...'.[122] What is more, he describes a network of interlinking, pro-visional questions, adding a perceived 'retour au réel' from the 1990s.[123] This he suggests is manifested in an acknowledgement of the impossibility of mimesis which informs a knowing return to the 'romanesque' that does not seek psychological realism, and often tells stories in a questioningly referential form. His examples include Fran-çois Bon, Didier Daeninckx, Annie Ernaux, Olivier Rolin, and Daniel Sallenave and span the provincially situated fictions of Pierre Michon and Pierre Bergounioux; those of Houellebecq and Frédéric Beigbeder which comment on the state of the social body and its practices; fictions using contemporary *faits divers*; and the 'kitsch' of Echenoz and Jean-Philippe Toussaint which tells 'une histoire à laquelle *nous avons plaisir à ne pas croire*'.[124]

---

[122] Viart, *Le Roman français au XXe siècle* (Paris: Hachette, 1999), p. 13: 'return to the question of...'.

[123] Ibid., p. 121: 'return to reality'.

[124] Ibid., p. 19: 'a story it is a pleasure *not to believe*'.

However, what Viart's analysis does not consider is how the return to the trope of crisis as a turning point and the intersection of that return with *fin de millénaire* crisis discourses and tangible crises is a culturally and temporally specific development of the French literary field. This study identifies in *fin de millénaire* prose fictions diverse representations and narrative strategies which, returning to the trope of the turning point, may be read as implicit critiques of the generation and manipulation of crisis by the mass media and global market economics. Foregrounding heterogeneity, and seeking to avoid the risk of imposing falsely homogenizing labels, it does not aim to add to the literature that surveys late twentieth-century French writing; to identify new 'schools' of French fiction; or to contribute to the specialist discussion of putative late twentieth-century literary trends.

Whilst this study focuses on contrasting *fin de millénaire* prose fictions of four writers, it invites readers to use these analyses and the loose critical framework of the *fin de millénaire* aesthetics of crisis as a springboard for analysing a wide range of other contemporary texts. As mentioned above, diverse writers reflect, engage with, seek to challenge, and perpetuate the aesthetics of the global market and the mass media. Amongst others Frédéric Beigbeder, Emmanuel Carrère, Catherine Cusset, Maurice G. Dantec, Mathieu Lindon, François Maspero, Vincent Ravalec, Jean Rolin, and Jacques Serena can all be read from this perspective. François Bon's writing revolves around *fait divers* and material derived from *ateliers d'écriture*, focusing on the experience of the exploited and the marginalized behind the corporate gloss of neoliberalism. Annie Ernaux's *fin de millénaire* prose fiction develops a dual perspective, on the one hand writing arguably *autofictional* narratives with a growingly explicit exploration of her sexual experiences, and on the other publishing quasi-ethnographic records of aspects of consumer culture she experiences in her daily life.[125] Jean-Philippe Toussaint's *La Télévision* (1997) operates as a critique of the ubiquity of television and its addictive but emasculating influence on the critical capacity of the subject.[126]

---

[125] Annie Ernaux, *Passion simple* (Paris: Gallimard, 1990); *La Honte* (Paris: Gallimard, 1997); *Journal du dehors* (Paris: Gallimard, 1993); *La Vie extérieure* (Paris: Gallimard, 2000).

[126] Jean-Philippe Toussaint, *La Télévision* (Paris: Minuit, 1997).

Although less overtly politically aligned than the *néo-polar*, *fin de millénaire* narratives harnessing the tropes of detective fiction and film offer critical perspectives on the global market and the mass media. Examples include Tonino Benacquista, Didier Daeninckx, and Daniel Pennac, whose six-novel Malussène series figures victims of late capitalist ideology in the counter-cultural melting pot of Paris's Belleville, exposing contemporary modes of cultural imperialism that seek to transform individuals and non-mainstream communities into homogenized products. The aforementioned true-crime inspired fictions may be intended as implicit critiques of the aesthetics of reality television. Marie Darrieussecq's 1996 bestseller *Truismes* tells the tale of the metamorphosis into a sow of a young woman whose job in a *parfumerie* is nothing short of prostitution, and who is exploited then discarded by her employer, partner, and a neo-fascist regime. Within a frame which links late capitalism and totalitarianism, the sexual politics of what appears to be an allegorical fable are provocatively ambiguous, and so the fiction re-opens the questions of sexual politics in an ostensibly post-feminist world. Marie Nimier's *La Nouvelle pornographie* (2000) explores and seeks to subvert the commodification of women (and female writers) sex objects, and that of the writer.

Of course, as discussed above, simply to assume that literary heterogeneity and the identification of a discreet phenomenon of the return to the trope of the turning point constitute evidence that *fin de millénaire* prose fiction comprehensively resists the aesthetics and ideology of the mass media and the global market is a naive oversight. Nonetheless, mindful of the contemporary double bind of recuperation and commodification, this study explores the relationship in the work of Angot, Echenoz, Houellebecq, and Redonnet between the inherent crises of language and the self and the production and manipulation of crisis by the global market and the mass media. Investigating the simultaneously problematic and problematizing status of the literary text, it gauges the aesthetic and critical potential of contrasting *fin de millénaire* prose fictions, identifying the ways that they reflect, negotiate, challenge, and perpetuate the contradictory *fin de millénaire* aesthetics of crisis.

2

Jean Echenoz: problematic patterns and symbolic violence

Jean Echenoz's literary reputation was established with his first four novels, often described in terms of their subversion of genres of popular fiction: the *roman d'aventures* in *Le Méridien de Greenwich* (1979) and *L'Équipée Malaise* (1986); the *roman noir* in *Cherokee* (1983); and the *roman d'espionnage* in *Lac* (1989). The texts, published by Minuit, were critically acclaimed for their acuity in the representation of contemporary culture, and in 1990 *Le Monde*'s Pierre Lepape described Echenoz as the foremost observer of his times: 's'il fallait raconter cette époque, c'est avec les livres d'Echenoz qu'on le ferait'.[1] *Nous trois* in 1992 marked a shift towards an exploration of the potential of representational practice in an increasingly globalized world. Echenoz's cultural equity in the literary marketplace was confirmed when *Je m'en vais* won the 1999 Prix Goncourt. Since the news of Echenoz's win came a week early to steal a march on other literary prizes, the announcement attracted considerable media attention, and generated allusions to selling out.[2] This contradicts evidence of the writer's perception of his own position in the literary field in his 2001 work *Jérôme Lindon*.[3] Ostensibly a tribute to his recently deceased publisher, the slim volume is at once an assessment of the commercial dynamics of the French literary field and an implicit claim that Lindon, his publishing house, and, by

---

[1] Pierre Lepape, 'Jean Echenoz: Pour raconter cette époque', *Le Monde*, 24 March 1990: 'if you wanted to tell the story of our times, Echenoz's novels would be the way to do it'.

[2] See, for example, Jean-Pierre Salgas, 'Défense et illustration de la prose française', in Yves Mabin, ed., *Le Roman français contemporain* (Paris: Ministère des affaires étrangères, 2002), pp. 73–127, at p. 78.

[3] Echenoz, *Jérôme Lindon* (Paris: Minuit, 2001).

association, Echenoz himself maintain a distance from market-driven writing.

Described by Yves Mabin as a 'classique vivant',[4] Echenoz features as a consecrated author in surveys of the *fin de millénaire* literary scene and receives mainstream press coverage. His fictions are the subject of numerous academic articles and several monographs. A special issue of *Romans 20–50* is devoted to three of his *fin de millénaire* fictions: *Les Grandes Blondes*, *Un An*, and *Je m'en vais*; and Echenoz was the subject of the first conference on his work in 2004. Papers examined intertextual links between Echenoz's novels and art, cinema, photography, and other writers (Flaubert, Balzac, Pierre Michon); style; representations of space; and intersections with Viart's concept of the 'retour au réel'. Participants added to those labels already ascribed to Echenoz's fiction: 'l'écriture de l'instabilité' (Viart); 'l'esthétique du bancal' (Jean-Bernard Vray); 'une poétique de l'équivoque' (Jérusalem); and 'l'écriture réversible' (Bruno Blanckeman).[5]

Whilst this labelling points to a commodifying dynamic, it also suggests that Echenoz's *fin de millénaire* fiction evades categorization and may indeed seek to establish a critical distance from the tropes of the mass media and the global market. However, uncertainty as to the nature of any intended challenge is also evidenced by the disagreement between commentators alluding to potentially critical perspectives in Echenoz's *fin de millénaire* prose fiction. Whilst some reject it as symptomatic of postmodern nihilism others consider it as a fictional encapsulation of Debord's spectacle or Baudrillard's hyperreal (*vide* Jérusalem: '[Echenoz] multiplie les portraits d'une société mise en spectacle';[6] and Blanckeman: 'Il établit les premiers portraits romanesques de la société-spectacle [. . .] un état de civilisation où le simulacre accapare le regard et embrouille les consciences').[7] This use of the

[4] Mabin, 'Introduction', in Christine Jérusalem, *Jean Echenoz* (Paris: Ministère des affaires etrangères, 2006), p. 9: 'a living classic'.

[5] See Jérusalem and Jean-Bernard Vray, eds, *Jean Echenoz: Une Tentative modeste de description du monde* (St Etienne: Publications de l'Université de St Etienne, 2006): 'writing the unstable'; 'the aesthetics of uncertainty'; 'a poetics of ambiguity'; 'interchangeable writing'.

[6] Ibid., 2006, pp. 58–9: '[Echenoz] provides multiple portraits of a society turned spectacle'.

[7] Blanckeman, *Les Récits indécidables: Jean Echenoz, Hervé Guibert, Pascal Quignard* (Paris: Presses Universitaires du Septentrion, 2000), p. 73: 'He provides the first portraits

vocabulary of Debord's spectacular and Baudrillard's hyperreal invites an investigation of the extent to which Echenoz avoids recuperation by media and marketing discourses; remains at some critical distance from them; harnesses them to creative or critical ends; or indeed perpetuates their manipulation and generation of crisis.

COUNTER AESTHETICS AND CRITICAL CONTRADICTIONS

Dramatizing the contradictions of the *fin de millénaire* literary and critical fields, the publication of *Nous trois* in 1992 precipitated a polemic. An article in the literary review *Esprit* signed by one Jean Martin (later revealed to be Jean-Philippe Domecq, the director of another review *Quai Voltaire*) rejected Echenoz's novel as symptomatic of post-modern relativism and of a perceived subjugation of authors, critics, and publishers to the dynamics of the market.[8] In a subsequent issue, Claude Habib responded that beneath its ludic surface Echenoz's writing aims not to elide or submit to neoliberal ideology, but instead to express the particular anxieties of contemporary life through 'un fond de désespoir feutré qui est comme la tonalité de l'époque'.[9] Meanwhile, Fieke Schoots identifies a problematization of both the aesthetics of consumer culture and of more than a century's literary questioning of the mimetic capacity of fiction: '*Nous trois* non seulement imite la superficialité contemporaine mais il la critique également. Au lieu de retourner au réalisme traditionnel ou de renier tout renvoi à la réalité, l'œuvre d'Echenoz met en cause la représentation de la réalité.'[10] Similarly, Lepape suggests

of spectacular society [...] a state of civilization where simulacra divert our gazes and confuse our minds.'

[8] Jean Martin, 'Critiques littéraires à la dérive [...] Lettre à la revue *Esprit*', *Esprit*, 190 (1993), 153–87, at p. 163. In 1994, in *Le Pari littéraire* (Paris: Éditions Esprit, 1994), Jean-Philippe Domecq confirmed that he was the author of the article. See p. 184.

[9] Claude Habib, 'Légèreté d'Echenoz', *Esprit*, 192 (1993), 163–7, at p. 164: 'a muffled tone of despair which is like the soundtrack to the time.'

[10] Fieke Schoots, *'Passer en douce à la douane': L'Écriture minimaliste de Minuit: Deville, Echenoz, Redonnet et Toussaint* (Amsterdam and Atlanta, GA: Rodopi, 1997), p. 181: 'Not only does *Nous trois* imitate the superficiality of our times, but it also critiques it. Instead of going back to traditional realism or rejecting all attempts to represent reality, Echenoz's writing brings the representation of reality into question.'

that *Les Grandes Blondes* reasserts the power of prose fiction to foreground questions of agency and of resisting commodification: 'À lire *Les Grandes Blondes,* il apparaît même que le romanesque, cette mise en présence de l'aléatoire, du libre-arbitre et de la nécessité, soit un des derniers espaces qui résistent à la vitrification de notre univers, une des dernières chances de l'irrégularité.'[11] Later, discussing *Je m'en vais,* Lepape suggests that Echenoz's fiction is not a postmodern celebration of perpetual crisis, but rather, a critical poetics with an implicitly ethical facet.[12] Colin Nettelbeck suggests that rather than embodying a postmodern resignation to crisis without end, Echenoz's prose fiction articulates his concern with the ethics of sense-making narratives, demonstrating 'that the quest for meaning and understanding cannot be divorced from the question of moral integrity'.[13] Eric Reinhardt goes as far as to identify an implicitly political critique in *Un An*: 'On sent dans cet ouvrage, en filigrane, une conscience politique aiguë, une inquiétude et des sentiments critiques à l'égard de notre époque.'[14] Olivier Bessard-Banquy perceives in Echenoz's *fin de millénaire* prose fictions a foregrounding of the question of the freedom of the individual—the possibility of engineering a turning point on a personal level.[15] Bessard-Banquy also identifies a preoccupation with a crisis in belief structures: 'L'œuvre d'Echenoz est donc une brûlure inextinguible de ce qui semble être la grande affaire de ce XXème siècle affairé—la disparition de Dieu sur la pointe des pieds.'[16]

Far from identifying his work as a deliberate critique of neoliberalism and the mass media or as an attempt to rehabilitate the sense-making

---

[11] Pierre Lepape, 'L'Irrégulier', *Le Monde,* 22 September 1995, p. 7: 'When you read *Les Grandes Blondes* you realize that because the novel can bring the arbitrary, free will, and necessity to the fore, it is one of the last ways of resisting the glazing over of our world, one of the last possibilities for irregularity.'

[12] Lepape, 'Petites nouvelles du coma', *Le Monde,* 17 September 1999.

[13] Colin W. Nettelbeck, 'The "Post-Literary" Novel: Echenoz, Pennac and Company', *French Cultural Studies,* 5 (1994), 113–38, at p. 137.

[14] Eric Reinhardt, 'Jean Echenoz: *Un An*', *Les Inrockuptibles,* 5–11 March 1997, <http://www.lesinrocks.com/DetailCritique.cfm?iditem=71039&idheading1=6> (accessed 22 March 2004): 'In this work you can sense a keen political conscience, concerned for and critical of our times.'

[15] Olivier Bessard-Banquy, 'Le Parti pris d'Echenoz', *Critique,* 595 (1996), 1056–73, at p. 1065.

[16] Ibid., 1073: 'So Echenoz's works keep burning onto our consciousnesses what seems to be the biggest issue of our frantic twentieth century: that God has tiptoed out of our lives.'

potential of the novel, Echenoz denies any such totalizing aims: 'Pour moi, la mécanique et l'esthétique sont plus importantes que les messages. Je ne suis pas fait pour ça, pour formuler des théories.'[17] He distances his writing from both putative postmodern and 'minimalist' aesthetics: 'La notion du minimalisme en littérature, me semble avoir à peu près autant de pertinence que celle de postmodernité: c'est-à-dire proche de zéro.'[18] Nonetheless, elucidating his decision to shift emphasis from the investigation and subversion of different genres of popular fiction, he articulates a keen awareness of the exploitation of crisis by the global market and the mass media, situating it at the centre of *Nous trois*:

> je n'avais plus envie d'écrire [...] à partir d'un modèle existant. Je voulais travailler sur des oppositions, des couples d'oppositions. L'intimisme et le spectaculaire. [...] La coexistence d'un risque naturel imprévisible [...] en opposition au risque hyper-sophistiqué culturellement que peut être, par exemple, une expédition spatiale. Ces deux phénomènes sont à la fois exceptionnels et quotidiens, se retrouvent à peu près tous les jours dans la presse.[19]

Also discussing *Nous trois* Echenoz draws particular attention to the impact of the mass media on the critical capacity of the subject: 'Dans mon esprit, cela devait aussi être un peu, discrètement, un roman sur l'information. Sur l'effet de l'indifférenciation de l'information, quand se succèdent une multitude d'événements, du plus tragiques aux plus dérisoires, qui arrivent tous également refroidis sur l'écran de la télévision.'[20]

---

[17] Echenoz in Geneviève Winter, 'Dans l'atelier de l'écrivain: Entretien réalisé par Geneviève Winter et al.', in Jean Echenoz, *Je m'en vais* (Paris: Minuit, Collection 'double', 2001), p. 242: 'For me, aesthetics and form are more important than any message. Theories aren't what I'm about.'

[18] Echenoz in Argand and Montremy, 'Entretien: Jean Echenoz', *Lire*, September 1992, p. 5: 'The ideal of literary minimalism seems to me to be about as relevant as postmodernism, that is to say devoid of relevance.'

[19] Echenoz in Claude Murcia, 'Jean Echenoz: Entretien avec Claude Murcia: Décalage et hors champs', *Art Press*, 175 (1992), 57–8, at p. 57: 'I didn't want to carry on [...] using existing forms. I wanted to work with oppositions, with pairs of oppositions. The intimate and the spectacular [...]. Putting unpredictable natural disaster [...] alongside hyper-sophisticated manmade dangers, such as a space mission. Both phenomena are at once exceptional and part of everyday life that you find almost daily in the newspapers.'

[20] Ibid., 58: 'In my mind, the novel was also, in a quiet way, meant to be about the news media. About the effects of the homogenization of news stories, the way that whole floods of events ranging from the most tragic to the most trivial are all channelled in exactly the same neutralized way onto television screens.'

Echenoz's comments on *Les Grandes Blondes* suggest that he seeks to put into practice his description of his writing project as an exploration of a counter-aesthetic to the audiovisual media: 'L'audiovisuel est un univers rigide, codé, lourd. Les images ne sont pas libres. Le roman, lui, n'est pas contrôlable, il laisse encore quelques espaces de liberté, quelques marges. J'y suis, j'y reste.'[21] Likewise a self-reflexive investigation of the crises and crisis discourses of turn-of-the-millennium France and their implications for the potential of prose fiction are inscribed in Echenoz's comments on *Un An*: 'ce livre est lié au moins autant à l'idée de l'incertitude romanesque qu'à celle de la fragilité sociale.'[22] This invites an investigation of whether Echenoz's *fin de millénaire* prose fictions harness the counter-cultural potential of literature, and of the extent to which they outstrip the perpetual crisis associated with post-modernism and the discourses of the mass media and the global market.

TELEVISION, REALITY, AND CRITICAL DEBATES

The representation of television in Echenoz's *fin de millénaire* prose fictions foregrounds the influence of the audiovisual media on cultural products, on cultural producers, and on consumers. In *Je m'en vais*, television replaces the windows in every other apartment in the block opposite Ferrer's gallery, a worldview filled with refracted images of alienation: 'quand le soleil était présent, ces paraboles devaient l'empê-cher d'entrer, accueillant à sa place les images destinées au téléviseur qui remplaçait ainsi la fenêtre' (JMV, 219).[23] Here, Echenoz's representa-tion of the ubiquitous small screen intersects with Marc Augé's descrip-tion of the experience of *non-lieux*, the hollow non-spaces (physical and

[21] Echenoz in Argand and Montremy, 'Entretien: Jean Echenoz', *Lire*, September 1992, pp. 22–6, at p. 26: 'The audiovisual universe is rigid, heavy, and codified. Images do not circulate freely. Novels, however, escape control, they still retain some freedom, some room for manoeuvre. That's my world, and that's where I'm going to stay.'

[22] Bessard-Banquy, 'Il se passé quelque chose avec le jazz', *Europe*, 820–1, August 1997, 195–202: at p. 196. 'this novel is as much about the notion of literary uncertainty as it is about the problems of our society.'

[23] 'When the sun did shine, the satellite disk must block it out, instead beaming images to the television set that thus replaced the window.'

virtual) of *surmodernité*.[24] Earlier, the black humour of drug addict Le Flétan's response to Delahaye/Baumgartner's murderous threats evokes the institutionalization of symbolic and physical violence by the audiovisual media: 'On tue les gens comme ça dans tous les téléfilms, ça n'a vraiment rien d'original' (JMV, 152).[25]

Similarly *Nous trois* opens with a *mise en scène* of how the manipulation of crisis by the mass media emasculates empathy and critical capacity, as Meyer relates to a motorway pile-up as though it were a television news report. The earthquake and tsunami which destroy Marseilles also foreground the homogenization of tangible crises by the media, as exemplified by the codification of horror into trivializing, distorted news bulletins which are not considered incongruous by a protagonist who has just escaped from the jaws of death: 'Cela semble être quelque programme de variétés, l'image n'est pas arrangée ni le son. Sous le défilement qui gonfle sa mâchoire en outre et lui taille les oreilles en pointe, ce n'est pas si facile pour le pitre d'exposer que, malgré le drame de Marseille qui nous touche tous, le spectacle doit continuer' (NT, 99).[26]

By offering a new perspective on media images which intersects with and diverges from Debord's spectacle and Baudrillard's hyperreal, Echenoz draws attention to the conversion of trauma into tropes such that protagonists can neither respond critically to real crises they experience, nor to their extremely troubling ramifications. If the Lisbon earthquake of 1755 was a contributing factor in precipitating the Enlightenment questioning of extant belief systems, here no so such questioning of consumer ideology occurs. Moreover, a link between television and the very real threat of ecological disaster is implied by the juxtaposition of impassive responses to the earthquake and tsunami which, like the transformation of the galaxies into an astrological dumping ground by commercialized space travel, bespeak the tangible results of the mismanagement of the planet.

[24] Marc Augé, *Non-lieux: Introduction à une anthropologie de la surmodernité* (Paris: Seuil, 1992), p. 102.

[25] 'People get killed like that all the time in television dramas, there's absolutely nothing original about it.'

[26] 'It seems to be some kind of entertainment show, but both the sound and the image are distorted. Since the picture is stretching out his chin and giving him pointed ears it's quite hard for the clown to get it across that, in spite of the drama in Marseilles, which of course, touches all of us, the spectacle must go on.'

Nous trois and *Les Grandes Blondes* both harness cinematographic techniques and feature filmic intertexts, but in the latter text television provides the fulcrum. It was published in 1995, when reality television formats had already spread across French television programming and the year before the publication of *Sur la Télévision*, Bourdieu's polemical pamphlet foregrounding the extent to which the mass media in general and television in particular corrode potential for the agency of the intellectual.[27] The 'hero' and 'heroine' of *Les Grandes Blondes* are Salvador, an anxiety-ridden television producer and Gloire, a one-time television star who the former is pursuing to feature in a *reality show* that is a pastiche of the then most influential French example of the genre, TF1's *Perdu de vue* (Salvador is also working on the concept for *Les Plus belles filles de la plage*). Here it seems Echenoz provides an implicitly critical perspective by appropriating the tropes of reality television in a fictional example of Baudrillard's hyperreal, where 'maps' of reality, such as television and film, are considered to be more real than the experience of life. However, since there is no critical meta-discourse and television and film play key roles in the narrative, such representations invite the question of the extent to which Echenoz's fiction itself escapes the double bind of commodification.

Updating the Foucauldian image of the Panopticon as a self-perpetuating mode of surveillance, Echenoz underpins how the ubiquitous small screen is synonymous with symbolic incarceration for those both within and without the star system:

longtemps qu'elle ne s'était plus vue sur un écran. Gloire ne s'y était pas regardée souvent de toute façon, le temps de sa petite célébrité instantanée, couchée comme un soleil à peine levé [. . .]. Ne s'y était jamais revue que dans les zones électroménagères des grandes surfaces, sur les écrans de matériel vidéo en démonstration pour les particuliers, ou dans le métro, juste avant son départ de Paris, sur les écrans témoins. (LGB, 86–7)[28]

---

[27] Pierre Bourdieu, *Sur la Télévision; suivi de L'Emprise du journalisme* (Paris: Raisons d'agir, 1996).

[28] 'it was ages since she had seen herself on screen. In any case, Gloire had rarely watched herself when she was momentarily famous, a time in the sun that set almost as quickly as it had risen [...]. Since then, she had only ever seen herself on the screens of supermarket electronics department audiovisual demonstration models, or in the Métro on CCTV screens, just before she left Paris.'

Meanwhile, Gloire's flight from Salvador is prefigured by her rejection of the anaesthetizing power of television: 'sans qu'en elle rien ne les retienne, les images la traversent comme des rayons X, comme un vent électronique indifférencié, monochrome et lisse, tiède et sourd. Gloire trouve la force d'éteindre l'appareil avant l'hypnose' (LGB, 40–1).[29] This implicit reference to the enduring agency of the subject to resist the images imposed by the audiovisual media is inversely underpinned by the pathetic figure of Geneviève Jouve, pacified into miserable inertia by 'séries produites outre-Atlantique et outre-Rhin' (LGB, 201).[30] A link between the erosion of collective responsibility and the intrusive nature of reality television is also made:

Les projets d'émissions de Salvador en appellent d'habitude à la mémoire collective. Que sont-ils devenus? [. . .] Quelqu'un dont on se souvient si peu qu'on ne se rappelait même plus l'avoir oublié mais qui est là: rangé comme les autres au fond d'un placard, dans les plus vieux cartons de la mémoire. [. . .] Les émissions de Salvador consistent à [. . .] rafraîchir la mémoire et rouvrir les cartons. (LGB, 29–30)[31]

If the programmes Salvador produces appear to be anodyne, they at once exploit their subjects and lure their audience into passivity. What is more, the reference to collective memory brings to the fore the mass media homogenization of the traumas of the past whilst exemplifying Debord's contention that spectacular society strives to create an eternal present. An eternal present which, with its own artificially manufactured past, obviates the need and indeed the capacity for critical thought. So whilst this description of Salvador's professional activities appears to describe their cultural function, it establishes a pattern of symbolic violence which is inextricable from the patterns of physical violence that recur throughout the novel.

---

[29] 'without anything in her taking any of them in, the images pass through her like X-rays, like a calm electronic breeze, black and white and smooth, warm and dull. Gloire summons the strength to switch off the set before she is hypnotized by it.'

[30] 'series from the other side of the Atlantic and the Rhine'.

[31] 'Salvador's programme concepts usually appeal to a sense of collective memory. Where are they now? [...] Someone who you remember so hazily that you haven't even realized you'd forgotten them but who is nonetheless there, with all the others, stashed in the bottom of a cupboard, in the oldest boxes of your memory. [...] Salvador's programmes are about [...] refreshing your memory and opening up those boxes again.'

Throughout *Les Grandes Blondes* the ambivalence of Gloire's relationship with the mass media is represented in her violent reactions to and flight from the symbolic violence that goes hand-in-hand with television celebrity. Gloire fails to escape its grip (and her co-implication in it), submitting to the media hegemony by her return to the televisual spotlight. The success of her appearance is judged in commercial terms, recalling the tyranny of audience ratings described by Bourdieu. Yet Gloire's experience can be better measured in terms of symbolic violence as she is once again incorporated into the pattern of institutionalized sexual exploitation:

Diffusée en prime time, avec une moyenne de 16,2 points Médiamat et 35,6% de parts de marché, la série de Salvador a recueilli un vif succès. [. . .] Autre conséquence de cette diffusion, Gloire a dû faire les frais d'une popularité nouvelle. [. . .] Après qu'elle a pu s'amuser quelques heures de cette situation, rapidement elle a recommencé à vouloir se cacher. (LGB, 245–6)[32]

Thus Echenoz depicts how the mass media package, promote, and then drop ephemeral stars. Just as the market produces crises to generate purchases, so celebrity culture generates the desire for fame, but never satisfies it, discarding the momentarily famous, inexorably moving onto the next short-lived novelty.

As well as illustrating how television follows the *fin de milllénaire* product cycle, this representation operates as a microcosm for the organization of the field of cultural production around the generation, manipulation, and consumption of crisis. Likewise, when Gloire defenestrates her abusive agent her crime brings her exposure across the broader media spectrum, like a commodity she is moved from rubric to rubric until her newsworthiness is exhausted: 'ayant occupé le terrain dans les mensuels de teenagers, puis dans la presse hebdomadaire du cœur, s'étant fait sa petite place dans les rubriques Arts et spectacles des quotidiens, c'est d'en plus en plus noir sur blanc qu'ensuite on l'a transférée des colonnes Faits divers aux colonnes Justice avant qu'elle

---

[32] 'Broadcast in prime time and scoring ratings of 16.2 and a 35.6 per cent market share, Salvador's series has been resoundingly successful. [...] Another result of the broadcast is that Gloire has had to pay the price of renewed fame. [...] She enjoyed it all for a few hours, but it wasn't long before she wanted to hide away again.'

sombre dans la profonde colonne Oubli' (LGB, 31).[33] A loss of ethical bearings is also foregrounded. Gloire's criminal past is recorded as sanguinely as the minor successes of her career. Indeed, her crime is momentarily 'rewarded' with coverage in the quality press. The justice system is subordinate to the media, so Gloire's punishment is short, and her rehabilitation is swift once she capitulates to *fin de millénaire* patterns of consumption. Thus contrary to descriptions of Echenoz as a postmodern nihilist, his treatment of the news media—both audiovisual and print—implicitly opens up critical perspectives.

However, Gloire is at once victim and villain. On the one hand, her brief trajectory through media celebrity to murder is a story of sexual exploitation. Men attempt to consume Gloire as a sex object, whether teen star manipulated by her lascivious agent, accosted as she crosses the Sydney Harbour Bridge, or disguised as a simple country girl. On the one hand, Gloire's crimes appear to have some justification, the inference being that she disposes of her pursuers as a response to sexual exploitation. On the other, by meeting violence with violence, Gloire perpetuates the cycle she wishes to break. She disposes of her victims by pushing them into the void, just as the mass media serially replaces ephemeral stars, pushing them off the pinnacle of fame into the abyss of obscurity. So Echenoz supplements Bourdieu's critique of the responsibility of the cultural producer with an emphasis on that of the cultural product (here Gloire) and of the consumer. Thus he exposes the role of the audiovisual media in generating symbolic and material violence and creating complicit victims: cultural producers, cultural products, and consumers alike.

The same pattern is foregrounded in *Je m'en vais* in the corruption of trend-following artists, art dealers, and collectors (which can in turn be interpreted as a wink to the successive, short-lived avant-gardes of recent literary history). The ethical bankruptcy of the market is encapsulated in the 'stand-off' staged at the end of the novel between Ferrer and Delahaye/Baumgartner, both of whom have used dishonest means to acquire disputed artefacts. Since neither has the higher moral ground,

[33] 'having featured in teenage monthlies, then in weekly gossip mags and having even managed a few column inches in the Arts sections of the dailies, she appeared increasingly in black and white, moving from the News section to the Legal column before ending up in the bottomless column of Oblivion.'

the argument is resolved in a transaction from which Ferrer emerges victorious by dint of his financial superiority. Delahaye/Baumgartner exploits Le Flétan's heroin addiction as mercilessly as would a dealer and Ferrer's traffic is as corrupt as that of the narcotics smugglers who provide a useful diversion as he clears customs with his cache of Iguluk artefacts. Given that both are dealers in the art world, Echenoz suggests that its business is run on the same criminally exploitative lines as the illegal drug trade.

In *Les Grandes Blondes* an international criminal ring manipulates impoverished Indians by rendering them drug dependent, and uses Gloire as a mule. Salvador is dependent on sleeping pills and the 'gels euphorisants'[34] dispensed in *Nous trois* boost the astronauts' performance on television link-ups, no doubt a wink to the notion of the media as an opiate for the masses. These narcotics are represented as the inevitable outcome of the need to perpetuate the demand of both the legitimate and parallel economies, at once in order to generate markets and to produce an artificial but lucrative way of detracting from the dissatisfaction inherent in the process. Thus the recurrent presence of drugs underpins the institutionalized exploitation of crisis—mental, symbolic, physical, and financial.

GLOBAL PERSPECTIVES, CRISIS PATTERNS, AND COMMITMENT

From microcosms ranging from television, the art market, space travel, and drug cartels to tropes of contemporary cultural production, Echenoz extrapolates a model that, mapping onto neoliberal ideology, operates on a global scale. Indeed the production and manipulation of crisis by the global market and the mass media emerges far more clearly as the 'subject' of the *Les Grandes Blondes* than its ostensible plot involving a television producer who seeks to trace an erstwhile star of the small screen. The same pattern recurs with objects, employees, partners, and travel, and its effects are revealed to be ubiquitous, affecting the individual and the local, the national, and the global. Through Gloire's

[34] 'pep pills'.

involvement with Moopanar's Bombay-based criminal ring Echenoz exposes the existence of a parallel crisis-generating economy underlying the legitimate face of the global market. This intersects at once with Debord's notion of the predominance of Mafia-type activities in integrated spectacular society and the structural corruption deplored by Bourdieu. The extent to which such financially motivated manipulation of crisis permeates the socio-political infrastructure worldwide is exemplified by the description of Moopanar's activities. Here the exploitation of the object has been superseded by the multifaceted exploitation of the commodified human: 'Puis de nouveaux secteurs [...] paraissaient en pleine expansion. Les organes humains, par exemple— reins et cornées prélevés sur les champs de bataille d'Europe de l'Est— [...] détournements de subventions au développement, distraction de l'aide internationale ou des fonds communautaires, [...] fraudes à la politique agricole commune, bref tout un monde' (LGB, 179–80).[35] So *Les Grandes Blondes* moves beyond television, and beyond the critiques of Bourdieu, Debord, and Baudrillard to an implicitly critical exposé of the global market.

By casting the head of the global Mafia in *Les Grandes Blondes* as an Indian with Europeans in his thrall, Echenoz suggests that power is no longer concentrated by nationality, but by capital: those with economic equity exploit the weak and vulnerable. Thus, unlike many of his contemporaries Echenoz does not follow the pattern of bemoaning the 'McDonaldsization' of the world, a stance that can be criticized for eliding personal or national responsibility by holding the United States solely responsible. Instead, he foregrounds not only individual but also collective responsibility, underpinning that of Western Europe.

Echenoz links the commercial face of European colonial exploitation to one of its contemporary incarnations—Western tourism—a facet of *fin de millénaire* neo-imperialism that continues to produce crisis in the developing world. Customers of international hotels meet, drink, sleep with, and then discard one another. Their only contact with indigenous

---

[35] 'And then new sectors [...] looked like they had real growth potential. Human organs, for example, kidneys and corneas, harvested from the battlefields of Eastern Europe, [...] embezzling development subsidies, misappropriation of international aid and EU funding, [...] fraudulent claims to the Common Agricultural Policy. In short, a wealth of opportunities.'

populations is to exploit market opportunities. These neo-imperialist tourists find for conversational common ground topics which underpin the tangible ecological crises produced by global market economics, from the hole in the ozone layer to the culling of seal cubs: 'pour qu'on fabrique avec leur peau des pantoufles et des porte-clefs, mais surtout de petits jouets articulés en forme de phoque du Labrador' (LGB, 113).[36] This echoes the inferred contribution of global market economics to the earthquake and tsunami of *Nous trois*. Meanwhile, the image of a contemporary *mission anti-civilisatrice* recurs in *Je m'en vais*, when Ferrer visits Labrador in search of ethnic art to sell in Paris at vastly inflated prices and sees villages abandoned due to the effects of Western consumerism.

Just as the media dispenses with its stars, tourist-cum-cultural-imperialists derive no satisfaction from the potential for embracing alterity and for the cultural exchange that travel offers, able only to produce (and then close their eyes and minds to) the crisis of those marginalized and exploited by global market economics. Gloire's well-being on arrival at each destination turns to boredom. There is nothing cosmopolitan about the Club Cosmopolite; privilege still reigns at the Taj; and the Intercontinental eradicates rather than promotes cultural exchange. Tourist consumption patterns are the same the world over, and the tourist trade does not fulfil the desire it creates. Moreover, *Nous trois*, *Les Grandes Blondes*, and *Je m'en vais* reference colonial and postcolonial exploitation in French Guyana, India, and Labrador respectively. If Iguluk people of *Je m'en vais* attempt to harpoon Ferrer's Western wealth by offering him a virgin bride, these texts demonstrate how the colonial exploitation of the past has been replaced by the cross-national exploitation of communities and individuals, ex-colonizers and ex-colonized alike. Likewise in *Les Grandes Blondes* as Moopanar pulls his invisible strings worldwide and generates lucrative heroin addiction in his own compatriots, he exploits Gloire, who in turn is exploited by Salvador. All are stateless cogs in the wheels of global capitalism.

To what extent then, do these novels contribute to the ethical questioning of cultural and economic neo-imperialism in the postcolonial moment? Although Echenoz puts an Indian at the helm of a worldwide

---

[36] 'using their fur to make slippers and keyrings, or more often than not, Labrador seal-shaped soft toys'.

organization, that organization follows the patterns of the global market economy. His use of India to figure the proliferation of exploitative patterns also perpetuates negative stereotypes of an overcrowded subcontinent that mimics the West. Representations of Moopanar as arch criminal, and of the heroin addiction enforced upon Gloire's Indian rickshaw driver both reinforce what Said describes as an Orientalist stereotype of a perceived degenerate nature of the Indian.[37] Moreover, whilst Moopanar is cast is the same exploitative role as his Western counterparts, he corresponds to Homi K. Bhabha's critique of the postcolonial subject's mimicry of the colonizer's behavioural patterns.[38] Echenoz may intend the recruitment and exploitation of a rickshaw driver as drug consumer to illicit critical comparison with the activities of multinational pharmaceutical companies seeking to create and exploit new markets in the developing world. However, the unfortunate man's passivity and acceptance of his role as consumer reinforces what Spivak calls the postcolonial position of subaltern, here in relation to Western patterns of consumption.[39] Meanwhile, as is often the case in both colonial representations of the East and postcolonial critiques of them, women in Echenoz's developing world are absent. Whilst these shortcomings are clearly unintentional, they map uneasily onto the cultural exceptionalism that seems to underlie the failure of French intellectuals to embrace the insights of postcolonial thinkers.[40]

Nonetheless, it seems that Echenoz's implicit intention is to bring into question these exploitative patterns rather than to perpetuate them. For in addition to evoking the global implications of the unquestioned acceptance of the discourses of the media and the market, these novels foreground issues of collective responsibility. If Debord's critical descriptions of the spectacular have been appropriated and commodified, recalling Nora's attempts to protect collective memory in *Lieux de mémoire*, Echenoz appears to seek to resist the commodification of the past and that of the critical voices which aim to counter reifying

[37] Edward W. Said, *Orientalism* (London: Penguin, 1978).
[38] Homi K. Bhabha, *The Location of Culture* (London: Routledge, 1994).
[39] Gayatri Chakravorty Spivak, 'Can the Subaltern Speak?' in *Colonial Discourse* (London and New York: Harvester Wheatsheaf, 1993), pp. 66–111.
[40] Bhabha's *The Location of Culture* was not published in translation in France until 2007.

discourses. Apparent 'asides' which draw attention to the dehistoricizing dynamic of the *fin de millénaire* are embedded in representations of contemporary consumer culture. For example in *Je m'en vais* a description of the rue 4-septembre in Paris with its banks, travel agents, and launderettes ends with a citation from a commemorative plaque that (at least by association) underpins the ethical responsibility of the reader: 'un champion du monde de coiffure et la plaque commémorative d'un F.F.I. mort pour la France à dix-neuf ans (Souvenez vous)' (JMV, 158).[41] Whilst coinciding with the return to history discussed above, this juxtaposition of past and present recalls Debord's vision of collective unconsciousness replaced by inertia and a cult of the ephemeral, inviting the question of the extent to which Echenoz's *fin de millénaire* fiction constitutes an implicit return to the question of the enduring potential for the political commitment of literature.

This question is most conspicuously raised in *Un An*, where exceptionally Echenoz chooses an overtly politically contentious context: the descent of protagonist Victoire into homelessness. In contrast with the co-implication of Echenoz's protagonists in the global cycle of corruption, Victoire and her disenfranchised SDF companions steal only according to their needs for survival. Authorial intervention adds to the use of destabilizing juxtapositions and the repetition of patterns to foreground symbolic and physical violence: 'Donc nombre de maires conçurent d'ingénieux arrêtés prohibant la mendicité, la station allongée dans les espaces publics, le regroupement de chiens sans muselière ou la vente de journaux à la criée, sous peine d'amende de mise en fourrière suivie de frais de fourrière. Bref on entreprit d'inciter les gueux à courir se faire pendre ou simplement se pendre ailleurs'(UA, 76).[42] Moreover, this exceptional narratorial *prise de position* foregrounds the question of collective responsibility—and by extension that both of cultural producer and consumer—for the institutionalized exploitation and

---

[41] 'A world champion hairdresser and a plaque commemorating a F.F.I. fighter who died for his country at the age of nineteen (We shall remember them).'

[42] 'So several mayors came up with the ingenious idea of passing bye-laws against begging, sleeping in public places, dogs without muzzles, or selling street newspapers, punishable by a fine and the pound, then charging for release. In short, the aim was to encourage the poor bastards to go hang themsleves, or indeed, to go hang themselves somewhere else.'

dissimulation of crisis. Thus, like the boxes Salvador opens in *Les Grandes Blondes* Echenoz opens ethical questions, from the local in *Un An* to the global in *Les Grandes Blondes* and *Je m'en vais* and indeed to the planetary in *Nous trois*.

IDEALIZED IMAGES AND IDENTITY CRISES

Some of Echenoz's critics describe his prose fictions as dramatizations of the postmodern, the hyperreal, or the spectacular. However, whilst for Debord spectacular society is organized around quashing subjectivity by producing spectacle, and in Baudrillard's realm of the hyperreal, commodified images have become more real than individual subjectivities, Echenoz's emphasis is on the crises precipitated by the symbolic violence inherent in the *imposition* of idealized images by media and marketing discourses. His *fin de millénaire* fictions at once foreground the constructedness of the fictional protagonist and of the self, and the production of additional identity crises by the global market and the mass media. The imposition of images leads protagonists to lose not only critical capacity, but also the capacity to deal with emotions, and to perceive love as a potential turning point. In *Les Grandes Blondes* both television producer Salvador and detective Personnettaz live a life of solitude as it involves less risk than attempting to grapple with the uncertainty of intimacy. Yet they are nonetheless consumed by their failure to live up to media-imposed images and by their inability to expose themselves to those, idealized, they have of the Other. Satisfaction of desire is impossible, yet striving for commodified ideals of love is constantly promoted.

Inexorably, protagonists fall short of market-driven stereotypes. Gloire, product and victim of the media, discovers that she cannot escape the image that has been created for her. Geneviève Jouve, consumer and victim, incessantly watches romantic dramas and is depressed because she cannot live up to their images of unattainable perfection. Salvador, agent and victim, lives, drinks, and attempts to sleep his work, at once producing, attempting to dissimulate, and suffering from the crisis of confidence of the *fin de millénaire* subject. In *Nous trois* the identity crisis beneath the media image imposed upon De Milo is emphasized as the novel opens with the question 'Vous vous êtes vu?' (NT, 8),[43] as he contemplates a portrait of himself painted from an old promotional photograph. De Milo's belief in the cultivation of his 'playboy' image cannot obscure the loneliness resulting from his failure to progress beyond the superficial in a series of ephemeral relationships based on external criteria alone. In *Un An* symbolic violence has material consequences as Victoire's clothes deteriorate by dint of her progressive marginalization. She becomes more and more disenfranchized both as result of her financial situation and of others' judgement of her appearance.

Echenoz also appropriates the specular image, but departs from psychoanalytical frameworks and the use of the mirror as a literary motif for the constitution of identity. Instead, mirrors reflect how protagonists fail in their unsuccessful attempts to mitigate the imposition of unattainable stereotypes. After escaping the devastation of Marseilles and hearing news reports banalizing the horror of his experience, *Nous trois*'s Meyer catches his reflection in the mirror of his hotel room, and unable to maintain the sanguine image required of him, he faints. Resuming the pressure of keeping up appearances, he hides this incident from Mercedes. In *Les Grandes Blondes* the specular image foregrounds the question of co-implication and of the enduring possibility of free will. By avoiding mirrors, Personnettaz avoids responsibility for his own destiny. Just as this self-protective fiction fails the protagonists, so in Echenoz's novels legitimizing discourses fail to dissimulate their manipulation of crisis.

Nonetheless, Gloire appears to challenge the mirror by producing a wilfully unattractive image: 'Ainsi peinturlurée, comme elle détaille son visage dans le miroir jusqu'à ce qu'une envie de vomir lui vienne, en effet la voilà très contente et qui s'exalte' (LGB, 54).[44] She also attempts to resist the imposition of idealized stereotypes by deliberately allowing her image to be constructed by her hiding place: 'Gloire n'y a rien changé, préférant ne plus manifester aucun de ses goûts, qu'elle abdiquait. C'est au contraire elle-même, sa propre personne qu'elle a tâché d'y conformer, se laissant imprégner, remodeler par ce

---

[43] 'Did you see yourself?'.
[44] 'Daubed with make up, staring at her face in the mirror until it turns her stomach, she feels a surge of joy and triumph.'

petit logement mal éclairé' (LGB, 69).[45] Here, Gloire's exercizing of
free will momentarily resists symbolic violence (and at the same time
inverts Baudrillard's notion of the primacy of the object). Yet there is
no turning point, and Gloire resumes the image she earlier sought to
flee in an eloquent example of the recuperation of voices of dissent.
The failure of Gloire's attempt to escape the exploitative cycles of the
mass media and the global market is ironically underpinned by her
attempt to convince herself that resuming her 'grande blonde' image
will enable her to assume a new identity in Australia. Yet predictably,
the cycle of symbolic and physical violence continues. Likewise, in *Je
m'en vais* Delahaye/Baumgartner manipulates his image in order to
defraud Ferrer, but finds himself trapped in the identity he has
assumed for commercially exploitative purposes, and is consequently
condemned to a life of exile.

Thus instead of operating as a mode of self-constitution, Echenoz's
protagonists' reactions to their reflections serve to magnify the results of
attempting to live in accordance with the dynamics of the market.
Gloire still dreams of breaking out of this cycle: 'Se représentant au
bout de ce bas monde une retraite introuvable, inviolable, hors d'at-
teinte. Une poche de marsupial au fond de quoi se blottir et puis hop,
hop toujours plus loin vers l'horizon meilleur pour oublier jusqu'à son
nom, tous ses noms' (LGB, 92).[46] Echenoz, however, dramatizes this
self-delusion by immediately revealing its futility, for the final paragraph of Chapter 11 quoted above is immediately followed by the
dismissive opening of the following chapter: 'Il n'en serait rien' (LGB,
93).[47] Indeed, Gloire's attempted evasions operate as a paradoxical
counterpoint to her ever-deeper embroilment in cycles of physical and
symbolic violence. Just as murdering her agent Flon brings incarceration and flight, and killing Salvador's detective Kastner, renewed pursuit

[45] 'Gloire made no changes, instead choosing not to show her taste at all any more: she
had given up having tastes. Instead she took herself, her own self and tried to make it blend
into her surroundings, to fit in, to let herself be absorbed and reinvented by this dingy little
place.'
[46] 'She imagined that at the back of beyond down under, there was somewhere no one
would find her, where no one would attack or violate her. The pocket of a marsupial to
hide in, then go hop, hop, hopping off to a better place further and further away where
she could forget her name, all her names.'
[47] 'It was out of the question.'

and flight, the murder of a predatory Australian causes her to flee to India. Here, the short-term benefit is a brief respite of idle luxury, but this is short-lived, and earned at the price of being blackmailed by Moopanar into drug running. Acting on the questionable guidance of Béliard, her self-obsessed 'guardian angel', Gloire persuades herself that a return to the spotlight is a means of re-integration. Yet she swiftly learns that she cannot play a second burst of fame by her own terms, that she must once again become a product, commodified for public consumption. Although Gloire intuits that fame is ephemeral and constructed to create ongoing demand rather than bring satisfaction, she nevertheless, with trademark blonde hair, submits to the dictates of the media and the market.

Nonetheless, Echenoz parallels what may seem to be a foregone conclusion with an emphasis on how this outcome depends, at least to some extent, on the choices Gloire makes. Complicity in symbolic violence is also foregrounded by the way that whilst Victoire in *Un An* appears to be a victim, her disenfranchisement is the result of a series of decisions. This is not a neo-conservative representation of a failure of self-determination. Rather, the implicit question is whether, in spite of the symbolic violence generated by the mass media and the global market, freedom of choice and thus agency and potential for resistance may still exist. Both Victoire and Gloire sense that they are victims, so are co-implicated in their assuming of that stereotype, and each fails to adopt an actively critical perspective. Echenoz, on the other hand, attempts to avoid inscription of his narrative in the symbolic order by foregrounding his protagonists' negative choices, thus inviting the question of individual responsibility in exploitative patterns and identity crises. So whilst Debord's figuring of the integrated spectacle and Baudrillard's of the loss of the real do not allow for the responsibility of the subject, here evidence of the potential to exercise free will is reflected in the attention that Echenoz draws at once to how protagonists effectively choose not to have agency and to the power of the mass media and the global market to negatively inflect their choices.

SYMBOLIC VIOLENCE AND
MISOGYNIST STEREOTYPES

If Echenoz's representations seek to avoid co-implication and recuperation into the vocabulary of the hyperreal and the spectacle, the absence
of an explicitly critical stance in these novels is nonetheless problematic.
Although implied criticism is signalled by the recurrence of negative
choices, by the use of humour, and by the interjections of the narrator,
Echenoz's representations run the risk of operating as *mises en abyme*
that perpetuate rather than challenge market-driven images. In particular, presumably implicitly critical representations of multi-faceted and
ethically bankrupt (and bankrupting) modes of exploitation do not
establish a critical distance from the misogyny of these processes.
Indeed, all Echenoz's novels foreground the imposition of stereotypical
images on women, but do not overtly problematize them. This begs the
question of the extent to which they perpetuate misogyny.

Like their male counterparts, Echenoz's female protagonists strive to
fashion themselves into over-determined images, but they are also
subjected to and subject themselves to mass-mediatized misogynist
stereotyping. Whilst idealized female sexuality is an age-old form of
oppression, late capitalism constantly renews ever more widely diffused
unattainable misogynist stereotypes. This symbolic bombardment aims
to lead women into a perpetual cycle of consumption in a futile attempt
to live up to constantly updated images. Simultaneously, male sexual
desire for these ever-changing ideals is generated. Salvador's unsuccessful attempts to define the 'grandes blondes' can be read as an implicitly
critical reference to the misogynist generation of celluloid images of
women. Salvador is determined to commodify the subjects of his series,
conflating women with consumer products: 'quelques mots étaient
tracés d'une main mal assurée: les adjectifs *brunes* et *blondes* l'un au-
dessus de l'autre, puis les substantifs *cigarettes* et *bières*' (LGB, 171–2).[48]
Meanwhile, following in a long line of misogynist stereotypes, Salvador
identifies 'grandes blondes chaudes et grandes blondes froides' (LGB,

---

[48] 'there were a couple of words scribbled in a shaky hand: the adjectives *dark* and
blond above one another, then the nouns *cigarettes* and *beer*'.

96).[49] His hot blondes are intimidating in their excess of sexual promise, whilst the cold blondes intimidate by their power to withhold their
sexual favours.

Here Echenoz repackages the virgin/whore dichotomy, a recurrent
feature of nineteenth-century cultural production whereby writers such
as Baudelaire sublimated the threat of powerful female sexuality betrayed by images of women as simultaneously seductive and cruel:
'Certaines grandes blondes incandescentes s'élancent au bras ouverts
au-devant du monde. [. . .] Elles regardent fièrement le monde, elles lui
adressent des sourires terribles et généreux. Parfois le monde se trouble à
leur vue, parfois il est intimidé par cette façon sûre, certaine et décolletée
de s'élancer vers lui, vers vous, bras grand ouverts en direction des
vôtres' (LGB, 96).[50] Salvador favours the hot blondes, and to justify
his process of selection his thoughts take a turn reminiscent of fascist
propaganda, potentially all the more powerful in the mass mediascape, a
'final solution', based on the pigmentation of skin: 'le soleil bronze
ou brûle, il vous tanne ou vous tue. S'il cuivre généreusement les grandes
blondes chaudes et conquérantes, il calcine sans miséricorde les grandes blondes chlorotiques réfrigérées. [. . .] Restent les conquérantes,
[. . .] leur épiderme plus dense, leur carnation plus résistante accueillent
en héros les ultraviolets' (LGB, 237–8).[51] Blind to the misogynist
symbolic violence that his work perpetrates and perpetuates, and faith-
ful in the power of the market to commodify nature itself, Salvador
fantasizes about the ultimate commodification of women—a 'super-
product' combining the warmth of the sun and the idealized sexual
availability of the hot blonde: 'les grandes blondes conquérantes pren-
nent le soleil, l'absorbent, l'assimilent puis l'arborent. Sous forme de
pigments. Ainsi les soirs d'été, dans les night-clubs, croisant leurs jambes
interminables sur de hauts tabourets, rayonnent-elles comme des soleils

---

[49] 'big hot blondes and big cold blondes'.
[50] 'Some white-hot big blondes greet the world with open arms. [...] They survey it
boldly, bestowing devastating wide smiles on it. Sometimes the world is flustered at the
sight of them, feeling threatened by the brashness, confidence, and cleavage thrusting
towards it, towards you, arms wide open, bearing down on you.'
[51] 'the sun tans or burns, it bronzes you or obliterates you. If it gives the hot
indomitable big blondes a healthy glow, it systematically burns the downbeat sickly
big blondes to a crisp. [...] So that leaves the indomitable big blondes [...] their skin is
thicker, its denser pigmentation laps up those ultraviolet rays.'

portatifs' (LGB, 241).[52] To what extent, then does Echenoz acknowledge or seek to counter the risk of the recuperation of his protagonists'
misogyny?

Certainly, the misogyny inscribed in Salvador's attempt to define the
'grandes blondes' bespeaks a society based on the suppression of feminine difference in favour of a male fantasy version of woman-as-object,
and the production of an idealized female homogeneity and availability.
This representation can, of course, be read as implicitly critical, and is
perhaps intended to be so. Salvador's attempts to classify women in
terms of blondeness elude him, so women defy the reifying man. It is
also perhaps Echenoz's intention to mock the misogyny of the 'blonde
joke'. However, if Echenoz seeks to portray structural misogyny critically, he perhaps unwittingly contributes to it at once by failing to
overtly problematize it and by drawing attention to it through humour
and so eliciting readers' complicity. Thus he provides a sobering example of how literature too can create and perpetuate misogynist tropes,
compounding those churned out by the mass media.

A neutralizing of female power is another troubling feature of Echenoz's fiction. If Gloire is categorized by Salvador in terms of media
images of perfection, her sexuality is elsewhere described as at once
threatening and fascinating: 'Hache à la main, visage de méduse, dans
l'ombre elle paraît surgir d'un panthéon barbare, d'un tableau symbo-
liste ou d'un film d'horreur' (LGB, 73).[53] Echenoz's recurrent evocation
of the virgin/whore dichotomy recalls both the misogyny of literary
history and the commodified images of the Hollywood horror movie.
The enduring deployment of misogynist literary tropes is reflected in
the way that Gloire and Donatienne also evoke and troublingly update
the twentieth-century literary and filmic stereotype of the femme fatale.
Arguably, Echenoz attempts to subvert the image of the simultaneously
sexually threatening and fascinating femme fatale by implying that these
women are superior to the male protagonists. However, whilst Gloire
and Donatienne are far more resourceful than the men surrounding

[52] 'indomitable big blondes take the sun, absorb it, assimilate it then show it off in the
form of their tans. So on summer evenings in night clubs as they sit on bar stools and
cross their never-ending legs, they shine like portable suns.'
[53] 'Wielding an axe, with a face like Medusa, in the shadows she looked like
something straight out of a horde of barbarian gods, a symbolist painting, or a horror
movie.'

them, both are portrayed as manipulative and sexually incontinent (Gloire assuages her frustration with a black army officer on her flight to Australia; Donatienne with an Indian taxi driver as she waits for Personnettaz, whom she then coerces into a relationship). Yet their power is ephemeral and confined to the personal sphere, for both women are pawns.

Gloire and Donatienne may demonstrate strength, but their subjugation to the patriarchal order speaks volumes of the limits of ostensible female emancipation at the *fin de millénaire*. If the implied affair between Gloire and Rachel, irrelevant in terms of the plot, is an attempt to assert female sexuality, it also feeds the male fantasy of lesbian sex. The formidable Donatienne is described as the idealized embodiment of sexual availability: '95–60–93, en toute saison Donatienne se distingue par le port de vêtements surnaturellement courts et miraculeusement décolletés, quelquefois en même temps si courts et décolletés qu'entre ces adjectifs ne demeure presque plus rien de vrai tissu' (LGB, 28).[54] Similarly, the description of the receptionists at Salvador's production company, presumably intended to represent the institutional misogyny of the mass media, embodies a media-generated male fantasy: 'A droite un rang d'exceptionnelles réceptionnistes tout ongles, cils et seins' (LGB, 26).[55] Gloire's return to fame is corroborated in terms of offers to pose nude, and such depictions of Donatienne and Gloire may aim to draw attention to misogyny, yet they do not bring themselves into question.

The ambivalence of the narrator's questioning of Gloire's deliberate subversion of idealized femininity in *Les Grandes Blondes* also begs the question of the ambivalence of Echenoz's stance: 'Quand même, que ne s'arrange-t-elle un peu? On comprend qu'elle ait ses raisons mais elle pourrait peut-être s'acheter un vêtement de temps en temps, qui pourrait la mettre en valeur, non?' (LGB, 67).[56] Whilst Echenoz may seek to foreground a critical intention by using his narrator to address readers,

---

[54] '38–24–36, year round Donatienne is remarkable for her uncannily short and miraculously low-cut clothes, sometimes so short and so low-cut that between the two adjectives, there is hardly any material at all.'

[55] 'To the right, a bank of extraordinary receptionists, all nails, eyelashes, and breasts.'

[56] 'For heaven's sake, she could make an effort, couldn't she? Fair enough, you can understand where she's coming from, but couldn't she buy some new clothes occasionally, make the best of herself?'.

the text presents in *Gloire* a succession of misogynist stereotypes that, if intended as a challenge to such clichés, nevertheless serves to perpetuate them. Moreover, the narrator frequently revels in verbal humour. So, as readers laugh, they join with Echenoz in perpetuating market-led misogyny.

Following in a long literary tradition Echenoz confers first names on female characters and surnames on male characters in *Les Grandes Blondes* and *Je m'en vais*, thus underpinning patriarchal power relations. In *Nous trois* men are designated by their surnames, and Mercedes/Dr Blanche/Lucie is named according to the narrator's assessment of her sexual availability. Meanwhile, the sexually unavailable test engineer Danièle is dubbed a dragon and an iceberg. In *Un An* only Victoire's first name is used, reflecting her exclusion from both the consumer and sexual economies. In *Je m'en vais* Ferrer describes his ex-wife as a cave-dwelling monster, and his serial conquests constitute a parade of misogynist stereotypes ranging from ice maiden to subservient lover, sex-starved single mother, and voracious mistress. Inversely, but equally phallocentrically, in *Un An* Victoire is doubly disenfranchised for once her financial problems lead to a degeneration of her physical appearance so she loses her status in both financial and sexual terms.

The responsibility of the cultural producer to negotiate the *fin de millénaire* double bind of commodification and misogyny is no doubt unwittingly but nonetheless ironically underpinned in *Je m'en vais* in the sanguine, financially driven exchange between Ferrer and his client Réparaz over an artwork comprising a graphic rape scene set in a frame of barbed wire: 'Attendez une seconde, dit Ferrer, vous avez vu que l'image est un petit peu violente, quand même, vous convenez que c'est un petit peu brutal. Ce cadre, l'artiste l'a justement fait faire spéciale-ment pour ça, n'est-ce pas, parce que ça fait partie du truc. [...] Je vais réfléchir, dit Réparaz, je vais en parler à ma femme' (JMV, 181–2).[57] Another artwork involves a giant bra, so Echenoz presumably intends an ironic representation of the commercialization of misogyny.

---

[57] 'Hang on a second, says Ferrer, you've noticed how the picture is just a little violent, haven't you, you know, that it's just a little harsh. Well the artist made the frame precisely to go with the picture, it's all part of the concept. [...] I'll have to think about it, says Réparaz, I'll discuss it with my wife.'

However, if these texts seek to implicitly critique misogyny, by reproducing stereotypes and by using humour without problematizing such discourses, Echenoz—like Ferrer and Réparaz—provides a *mise en abyme* of the risk of prose fiction perpetuating structural misogyny. From this perspective, his novels chime uncomfortably with Christine Delphy's description of the *fin de millénaire* political economy. She argues that patriarchy and its systemic oppression of women is perpetuated through contradictory manipulation of crisis discourses by the mass media, on the one hand producing false claims of 'l'égalité déjà là',[58] and on the other producing an anti-feminist backlash via the negative stereotyping of feminist political activism. So although it is surely not his avowed intention, for want of overt problematization of misogynist tropes Echenoz's female protagonists are doubly commodified. Thus what may be an attempt to subvert misogynist stereotypes is caught in a redoubled double bind: that of perpetuating stereotypes— simultaneously anachronistic and contemporary—of the female subject.

PROBLEMATIZING THE AESTHETICS OF CRISIS

Whilst Echenoz's avoidance of overt criticism of consumer culture leads to the potential of perpetuating its misogyny, his fiction is more thoroughgoing in underpinning the ramifications of the manipulation of crisis tropes by the market and by the media on a local and a global scale. Indeed these patterns are subverted in the texts' own narrative economies. Each brings into question the relationship of its title with the structure of the narrative. The title of *Un An* undercuts rather than validates reassuring temporal fictions since the novel's time frame is just under a year. *Je m'en vais* opens and closes with the assertion, 'J/je m'en vais' (JMV, 7 and 253),[59] yet highlights Ferrer's failure to escape market-driven cycles which take him back to where he began. In *Les Grande Blondes* the attempt to make a television programme about blonde stars of the screen is not central to the plot, and the experiences of the text's reluctant bottle blonde do not map onto those of the classic

---

[58] Christine Delphy, *L'Ennemi principal: Économie politique du patriarcat* (Paris: Syllepse, 1998): 'already achieved equality'.
[59] ' "I'm off." '

Hitchcockian blonde heroine. Instead, the novel reveals the symbolic violence inherent in *fin de millénaire* cultural production. Whilst nominally structured as a love triangle, *Nous trois* gestures far beyond three protagonists to the potentially radical implications for the human race of the expansion of global market economics. Ignoring both warning signs and their first-hand experience of natural catastrophes, Meyer and Mercedes fail to question the implications of events which point to an apocalyptic outcome for the planet. Hence one of the possible interpretations of the title of *Nous trois*: that the responsibility for the future of the world hangs in the balance of writer, narrator, and reader.

Things in Echenoz's fiction therefore, are not as clear, or as impassive, as they might initially seem. Of course the ambiguous ending is a familiar trope of twentieth-century French fiction, drawing attention to the aesthetics of crisis of fiction, to the impossibility of using language to mirror reality, and to that of constructing a stable self. However, the strategic absence of closure in Echenoz's novels also brings into question the tropes of crisis resolution falsely premised—and promised—by the mass media and the global market. *Les Grandes Blondes* concludes with a play on the happy ending of a 'feel-good' movie, which, offset by staged ambiguity, leaves readers like the protagonists in a state of suspended animation. When Gloire finally embraces Salvador, dangling over an abyss in a cable car, the narrative is imbued with a sense of the provisional. Echenoz closes the novel as he began it, with his narrator addressing readers directly and thus implicitly prompting them to question the narrative perspective: 'Vous prévoyez le pire, on vous comprend' (LGB, 250).[60]

This undermining of the idealized 'happy ending' also undermines media images of crisis resolution. Whilst market-driven cultural products provide slick conclusions, Echenoz leaves his fictions open-ended, perhaps with the intention of leaving readers to consider their own co-implication in the patterns exposed. The relationship between Personnettaz and Donatienne is described in terms of the material improvement of the former's standard of living rather than in terms of emotional development. It founders according to the pattern established in *Nous trois* where both Meyer and De Milo expect their

---

[60] 'You're thinking the worst, and that's perfectly understandable.'

ephemeral couplings to follow the inexorable cycle of attraction, desire, frustration, and loss of interest. This same pattern is repeated across *Un An* and *Je m'en vais*, as Félix/Ferrer's serial romantic failures punctuate both narratives. Nonetheless the potential for recognizing an urgent need to break out of these cycles of market-driven failure—and readers' and the writers' co-implication in them—is underpinned by the narrator's direct questioning as *Les Grandes Blondes* moves towards its questionably romantic dénouement: 'Bref, les choses ont vogué de telle sorte qu'à ce point de notre affaire nous nous retrouvons avec deux hommes épris de deux femmes extrêmement différentes sur les bras. Que vont-ils entreprendre? Qu'allons-nous devenir?' (LGB, 242).[61] This jarring conclusion simultaneously foregrounds the turning point as a knowingly flawed trope in the text and invites the question of its enduring potential, and includes readers in these questions.

Although Echenoz's protagonists do not subscribe to any belief system beyond their unthinking co-implication in the ideology of the market, the trope of apocalypse and the manipulation of other biblical references are emphatically present in his *fin de millénaire* prose fictions. Echenoz has co-translated the Book of Samuel for the new Bayard translation of the Bible (contemporary writers Pierre Alferi, François Bon, Olivier Cadiot, and Jacques Roubaud are also involved).[62] However, biblical and apocalyptic references are neither a *profession de foi* nor a ludic *clin d'oeil* to the death of God in a postmodern world. In *Un An* corrupt Louis-Philippe is the opposite of the Good Samaritan, evoking the commodification of religion. In *Je m'en vais* Ferrer is a *faux* Lazarus, a medical anomaly who rises again to exploit indigenous art. In *Je m'en vais* Echenoz describes an ecumenical spiritual centre at Roissy. Here, the commodification of major world religions is underpinned, in the barely distinguishable 'microsynagogue', 'microchapelle', 'micromosquée', and 'Multistore'. The description also suggests the terror of the postcolonial subject seeking comfort in colonially imposed belief systems that have been superceded by the neo-imperialist

---

[61] 'So, things have drifted along so that we now have two men who have two wildly different women they've fallen for to contend with. What are they going to do next? What will become of us?'

[62] *La Bible—Samuel*, trans. Pierre Debergé and Echenoz (Paris: Bayard; Montreal: Médiapauls, 2001).

market: 'un petit jeune homme frêle et barbu, au physique éthiopien—
ses yeux rouges exprimant l'horreur du vide, la peur du mal de l'air,
avant d'embarquer il souhaitait recevoir le sacrement d'un prêtre qu'à
contre-cœur Ferrer dut convenir n'être pas' (JMV, 112).[63] Thus, highlighting a loss of capacity to 'read' the world, Echenoz points to the
appropriation and commodification of religious sense-making narratives (it is surely not by chance that his 2003 prose fiction *Au Piano*
figures the commodification of heaven and hell, complete with celebrity
guardian angels).

Nous trois links disaster with the failure of the trope of apocalypse.
Warning signs are neither decoded nor interpreted after the event. So
not only do secular crisis discourses fail to create viable sense-making
fictions, but there is also a suggestion that they render subjects blind
to threats of a potentially irrevocable—and implicitly man-made—
planetary apocalypse. This representation of the denial of crisis resonates with some of the tangible crises facing France. Published shortly
after the fall of the Berlin Wall, at a time when Cold War fears of
nuclear war were fresh in the mind, it is surely not by chance that the
scenes of destruction in *Nous trois* evoke images of post-nuclear devastation whilst presaging the tangible crisis of global warming. Earlier
in the novel the description of the explosion of Mercedes's car is
juxtaposed with that of a nuclear power station: 'Derrière la Mercedes
brûlée, au-delà d'une ligne de tilleuls, la centrale nucléaire est un
bâtiment plat flanqué de constructions cylindriques courtes sur pattes,
coiffées de coupoles, un long bâtiment plat que dominent trois chemi-
nées géantes, profilées cathédrale, évasées château d'eau' (NT, 28).[64]
The represention of a nuclear plant as a cathedral encapsulates how
religious belief has been superceded by the worship of power (both
literally and in terms of capital). Moreover, by describing the nuclear
reactor immediately after a violent explosion, with its connotations of
mortal danger, nuclear power provides a metaphor for the potential

---

[63] 'a frail little bearded young man, Ethopian looking, with red eyes bespeaking the
terror of the void and the fear of airsickness, and who, before boarding his plane, had
come to be blessed by a priest, that, reluctantly, Ferrer had to admit he wasn't.'

[64] 'Behind the burnt-out Mercedes, beyond a row of lime trees, is a nuclear power
station, a low building flanked by squat, cylindrical constructions topped with domes, a
long low building with three massive chimneys like a sort of cathedral-cum-watertower.'

outcome for a world where the market and the media elide the tangible crises threatening the planet.

The juxtaposition of representations of tangible crises and apocalyptic discourses and the writer's own manipulation of crisis tropes in these novels also operates self-reflexively. The description of the earthquake in *Nous trois* has a grimly poetic quality: 'La façade entière [. . .] se fissure de lézardes rapides, instantanées, vives comme des plumes en train d'écrire l'apocalypse à toute allure' (NT, 64).[65] Simultaneously Echenoz draws attention to the use of the trope of apocalypse in the writing process, and to the crisis of language and of all representational practices including fiction, underscoring their inevitable failure to encapsulate human experience. The narrator appeals to readers encourage questioning, such as those which conclude Chapter 9: 'Et notez bien que depuis que les choses ont commencé de trembler, neuf secondes seulement se sont écoulées. Notez' (NT, 66);[66] and open Chapter 10: 'Puis souvenez-vous que la détresse, l'effroi déforment notre conscience de la durée, que l'affolement ralentit le temps. Imaginez l'ambiance dans la cabine de l'ascenseur' (NT, 67).[67] However, this does not imply that Echenoz rejects the critical potential of fiction. Nor does it represent a surrender to the privileging of the audiovisual image. Rather, these descriptions evoke disaster movies, and such pastiche—like that of reality television in *Les Grandes Blondes*—implies that Echenoz invites the comparison of his provisional, problematized narratives with the imposition of unproblematized crisis tropes by the audiovisual media. As do the opening pages of *Nous trois* where readers experience at first hand difficulties in distinguishing between fiction and reality as the descriptions of a simulated rocket take-off seems more 'real' than the 'real' launch.

Echenoz also goes beyond Baudrillard's argument that the images generated by the mass media have become completely detached from the reality they represent. Rather than simply comparing the representational potential of two different cultural products, *Les Grandes Blondes*

---

[65] 'The whole facade [...] is covered with sudden streaks of cracks, like quill pens dashing off the apocalypse at break-neck speed.'

[66] 'And note that within nine seconds of the beginning of the quake, everything had collapsed. Take note.'

[67] 'And remember that terror and distress distort our sense of time, panic slows everything down. Imagine how it felt in that lift.'

demonstrates that the images produced by the mass media are as much a fiction as is the literary text. A potentially violent fiction which compromises the subjectivity of audiences as they attempt to create of their selves fictional constructs which comply with market-driven stereotypes. On the one hand, the fantastic figure of Béliard (who is either Gloire's often malevolent guardian angel or an equally malevolent figment of her imagination) references the loss of the distinction between fiction and reality evoked by Debord and Baudrillard. On the other, Béliard's awareness of the blurring of fiction and reality suggests that the self-reflexive manipulation of sense-making tropes retains some critical potential.

When Béliard saves Personnettaz and Donatienne, the two process the event as consumers of a spectacle rather than as participants, no longer able to make the distinction between media construct and experience: 'On était légèrement engourdis comme à l'issue d'un match ou d'une première, quand on se remet de son effort dans les vestiaires ou dans sa loge' (LGB, 225).[68] Gloire's perception of Béliard mirrors her pursuers' inability to differentiate between the real and the media image of the real: 'Elle se méfie toujours un peu, d'ailleurs, de la réalité quand Béliard condescend à s'en mêler' (LGB, 227).[69] What is more, Béliard contrasts with both the mimetic tradition of the novel and the commodification of crisis into narratives by the mass media. An overtly fantastic and unreliable narrator, Béliard allows Echenoz to draw attention to the intrinsic unreliability and artificiality of all the discourses staged in *Les Grandes Blondes*. He is also a means of foregrounding the manipulation of crisis by the mass media, including reality television and 'factual' programming such as news reporting:

Au mieux, Béliard est une illusion. Au mieux il est une hallucination forgée par l'esprit déréglé de la jeune femme. Au pire il est une espèce d'ange gardien, du moins peut-il s'apparenter à cette congrégation. Envisageons le pire.

S'il en est vraiment un, né trop moche et trop petit pour être officiellement reconnu par une confrérie soucieuse de son physique de cinéma, tout de suite on l'a placé à l'Assistance. [...] Toujours plutôt préoccupé de lui-même, pas

---

[68] 'They had that slightly numb feeling you get after a match or a première, when you're coming down in the changing rooms or in your dressing room.'

[69] 'In fact she is already rather wary of reality when Béliard deigns to get involved.'

trop regardant sur les principes, souvent d'assez mauvaise humeur [. . .] il est assez irrégulier. (LGB, 36–7)[70]

By subverting the stereotype of the guardian angel, Echenoz implicitly mocks belief in transcendence through consumption. Here in particular he suggests that on the altar of consumerism not only the aesthetic, but also the ethical and the metaphysical are sacrificed to market forces, whilst the notion of agency is superseded by a credo of pragmatic self-interest. Thus Béliard brings both literary practice and the market's generation of idealized fictions into question.

Moreover, whether a hallucinatory alter ego or a guardian angel, Béliard also fails to live up to impossible stereotypes, and is subject to the same identity crises that beset Echenoz's other equally fictional protagonists. Béliard does not toe any psychoanalytical interpretative line. Swinging from the elated to the depressive via delusions of grandeur, he simultaneously performs the arbitrary but constructed nature of fiction and the necessary unreliability of the writer who on one hand strives to produce a narrative that offers an apparently cohesive meaning, but on the other hand is constantly grappling with the impossibility of making sense.[71]

Echenoz has suggested that both Salvador and Béliard are in some way his proxies in the text, and here it seems that Béliard is used to demonstrate his creator's awareness of how prose fiction is a construct that seeks to make sense of a contingent world.[72] Hence Echenoz implicitly situates his text within twentieth-century debates about signifying and representational practices, the perceived failure to develop new sense-making paradigms, and the influence of the dynamics of the market economy on literary production. Moreover, drawing attention to the problematic of the distinction between fiction and reality in a self-

---

[70] 'At best Béliard is an illusion. At best he is a hallucination, a figment of the young woman's unhinged imagination. At worst, he is some sort of guardian angel, or at least he might bear some relation to that holy host. Let's assume the worst-case scenario.
If he really is a guardian angel, he was born too ugly and too small to be officially recognized by a brotherhood very conscious of their film-star looks, and was immediately left to social services. [...] Constantly self-absorbed, sketchy when it comes to rules, and often in a bad mood [...] he is pretty erratic.'

[71] An enigmatic character named Béliard also features in Echenoz's *Au Piano* (Paris: Minuit, 2003).

[72] See Pascale Bouhénie, *L'Atelier d'écriture de Jean Echenoz: Film de Pascale Bouhénie* (Paris: Centre national d'art et de culture Georges Pompidou, 1998).

consciously fictional form, Echenoz leads readers to question their own criteria for judging information, whether overtly 'fiction' or 'fact'. By raising such questions, and by underpinning their own artificial status, Echenoz's *fin de millénaire* prose fictions do not simply reproduce the loss of reality theorized by Baudrillard and Debord. Instead, they draw attention to the idealized images and unrealizable happy endings generated by the mass media and the global market.

INTERTEXTS AND AESTHETIC QUESTIONS

Although Echenoz's *fin de millénaire* prose fictions lend themselves less than his earlier novels to being categorized in terms of a reworking or subversion of genres of popular fiction, he continues to draw both on (para) literary genres and on the tropes and techniques of cinema. The narrator shifts attention from the earthquake to the tsunami in *Nous trois* by evoking a 'contre-champ sur la mer' (NT, 71).[73] It is in cinematic terms that Echenoz compares *Les Grandes Blondes* and *Un An*: 'J'ai le sentiment que l'avant-dernier [*Les Grandes Blondes*], je l'avais tourné en "scope" couleurs, avec son dolby, alors qu'*Un An*, j'ai l'impression de l'avoir fait en 16mm gonflé noir et blanc.'[74] In *Les Grandes Blondes* Echenoz plays on tropes from *roman* and *film noir*, exploiting and bringing into question their artificial structures whereby a rational investigation, although punctuated by misleading avenues of enquiry, progresses to a conclusion usually marked by the triumph of good over evil. Thus a self-reflexive questioning of different genres and media is intertwined with a foregrounding of the production and manipulation of crisis tropes. In parallel, intertextual play appropriates the creative potential of the tropes of both high and low culture (literary and audiovisual) with an implicitly critical edge that sets these prose fictions apart from the language games associated with postmodernism.

Les Grandes Blondes reveals how the mass media's manufacturing of manageable suspense and neat resolutions obscures difference, sup-

[73] 'a reverse shot of the sea'.
[74] 'I felt as though I filmed my penultimate novel in colour with cinemascope and Dolby sound, whereas *Un An* feels as though I shot it on distorted 16mm black and white film.'

presses dissent, and dissimulates the symbolic violence inherent in these processes. As the text opens, private investigator Kastner experiences cold sweats just before being pushed off a cliff by Gloire. Here French lovers of the *film noir* may identify a reference to *Sueurs Froides*, the French title for Alfred Hitchcock's *Vertigo* (1958), with its male lead suffering from vertigo, hapless attempts at detection, cases of mistaken identity, and an alternately blonde and brunette *femme fatale*. *Sueurs Froides* in turn may refer *roman noir* enthusiasts to the Boileau-Narcejac novel, *D'Entre les Morts* (1954) on which Hitchcock's film was based;[75] to Denoël's 'hard-boiled' detective series 'Sueurs Froides'; and to Erich Kästner, author of *Emil and the Detectives* (1929).[76] On the one hand, the title *Les Grandes Blondes* operates as an 'in-joke' for Hitchcock fans (although Echenoz unfortunately matches Salvador's misogynist concept for his television series with Hitchcock's unsavoury predilection for blonde actresses). On the other, film is used as a creative springboard, and with apparently critical intention.

Of course, the witty *clin d'œils* to *Vertigo* (and to a range of other texts spanning the cultural spectrum) are all part of the fun. However, at once inverting the familiar mass-market turning of novels into blockbusting films, and writing in the wake of the *grands écrivains* of the nineteenth and twentieth centuries, Echenoz uses intertextual references to other forms of cultural production (past and present) to seek new ways of bringing the possibility of mimesis—the claim of language to mirror the world—into question. Situating this pivotal development of Western aesthetics in a specifically *fin de millénaire* context, by appropriating and foregrounding the tropes of cinema, alongside those of television, the *roman noir*, and conventional prose fiction, *Les Grandes Blondes* not only draws attention to the artificiality of all fictional representations of 'reality', but also invites the question of their relative potential for promoting or repressing critical capacity.

Whilst Gloire's serial killing recalls Anthony Perkins in *Psycho* (1960), the impossibility of any attempt to fix meaning is brought into relief by Salvador's incongruous classification of Kim Novak, the

---

[75] Pierre Boileau and Thomas Narcejac, *D'Entre les Morts* (Paris: Denoël, 1954). After the release of *Vertigo*, reprints of the novel were entitled *Sueurs froides*, the French title of the Hitchcock film.

[76] Erich Kästner, *Emil and the Detectives* (London: Jonathan Cape, 1931).

actress who plays calculating Judy/Madeleine in *Vertigo* as exemplary of the 'redoutable gaieté de ces grandes blondes solaires' (LGB, 96).[77] Despite Gloire's habit of disposing of male pursuers from a great height—a trait that implies anything but a sunny disposition—Salvador decides she is his ideal woman and falls into her arms as they dangle over an abyss at the end of the novel: 'Comme elle est contre lui, ses lèvres sur son cou, Salvador ouvre un œil et, par-dessus l'épaule de Gloire, il voit distinctement l'abîme. Or, miracle numéro un, nul vertige ne le prend' (LGB, 250).[78] This is an intertextual reference to the end of *Vertigo* when Scottie finds himself cured of his fear of heights having been tricked by appearance-changing 'grande blonde' Judy/Madeleine. It also intersects with Slavoj Žižek's 1991 study *Looking Awry*.[79]

Žižek uses *Vertigo* to dramatize Lacan's theory of the function of the symbolic order in protecting the subject from psychosis. From Žižek's Lacanian perspective, Echenoz's intertextual references to *Vertigo* and to the physical/psychological condition in *Les Grandes Blondes* may be read as an expression of the protagonists' distress when confronting the Real of desire. Given that Echenoz professes to reject psychoanalytical motifs and psychological realism in favour of his own take on the behaviourist tradition of the *noir* narrative, it is unlikely that he is deliberately referencing Žižek. Nevertheless, his description of his own narrative style suggests that his writing may be considered as a means of 'looking awry', of adopting a perspective that opens up new possibilities: 'Je ne cherche pas à faire le malin, mais j'aime chercher l'angle, l'ouverture par laquelle on va pouvoir désigner un élément (personnage ou décor), dans un souci de relief.'[80] To use the Lacanian terms employed by Žižek, then, the intertext in Echenoz's narrative economy may be read as phallic. It is the element which 'sticks out' in an apparently linear

---

[77] 'the terrifyingly jolly nature of those sunny big blondes'.

[78] 'Since she is snuggled up against him, nuzzling into his neck, Salvador opens one eye and over Gloire's shoulder he catches sight of the abyss. Well, miracle number one, no vertigo at all.'

[79] Slavoj Žižek, *Looking Awry: An Introduction to Jacques Lacan through Popular Culture* (Cambridge, MA, and London: MIT Press, 1991).

[80] Echenoz in Sylvain Bourmeau and Marc Weitzmann, 'Jean Echenoz: "*Les Grandes Blondes*: On peut aussi imaginer un film de Lautner avec Mireille Darc"', *Les Inrockuptibles*, 11–17 October 1995, 60–5, at p. 63: 'I'm not trying to be clever, but I do like seeking out that angle, the chink that enables me to bring something to the fore, be it a character or in the background.'

narrative, drawing attention to the manipulation of crisis tropes by different forms of cultural production.

The first intertext to *Vertigo* recalls Scottie's dream of falling into the void: 'Rêve classique de vertige: Kastner s'agrippe de toutes ses forces au sommet d'un montage vertical fait de poutrelles disjointes et croisillons rouillés, surplombant un abîme' (LGB, 14).[81] Whilst Žižek might offer a Lacanian interpretation of this dream—vertigo exemplifying the terrified reaction of the subject to the dizzying abyss of the Real of desire—this would belie the multi-faceted nature of the filmic intertexts in *Les Grandes Blondes*. This dream sequence is also part of a self-reflexive exploration of the materiality of language and the sense-making potential of fiction, intersecting with poststructuralist thought. The dream appears as a fictional and psychoanalytical cliché, and thus brings into question not only the aim of *vraisemblance*, but also the ethos of the avant-garde, with its belief in achieving a complete break from the past. When a disheartened Salvador suffers an attack of vertigo, the symptoms are represented not in psychoanalytical terms, but with a reference to the nausea Sartre evokes as a reaction to the apprehension of the terrifying burden of existential freedom: 'l'idée de se retrouver trente mètres cinquante au-dessus du sol, à la place de Philippe Auguste, a brutalement fait resurgir son vertige. Le voici non loin de la nausée' (LGB, 199).[82] These intertexts 'stick out' to demonstrate how fiction is necessarily a process of recycling of words and images, a process that is at once regenerative and articulates its own intrinsic failure.

An earlier attack of vertigo and nausea also exceeds a psychoanalytical interpretation: 'On possédait plusieurs photogrammes de la scène du clocher dans *Vertigo*, parmi lesquels un plan vertical de la cage d'escalier (combinaison de travelling arrière et de zoom avant), mais Salvador est lui-même très sensible au vertige, à ce point sensible que le moindre cliché d'à-pic en plongée lui donne la nausée' (LGB, 96–7).[83] Žižek might interpret

---

[81] 'It was the classic vertigo dream: Kastner clung on with all his might to the top of a vertical structure made of uneven planks and rusty nails, the void below him.'

[82] 'the idea of being buried thirty-five metres underground like Philippe Auguste suddenly brings on another attack of vertigo. He thinks he's going to throw up.'

[83] 'There were several stills of the clock tower scene from *Vertigo*, including a vertical shot of the staircase (a dolly back/zoom forwards combination), but Salvador himself suffers badly from vertigo, so badly in fact, that even a sheer high angle shot turns his stomach.'

Salvador's morbid fear of heights as the fear of encountering the Real of desire, whilst Sartre would figure it as a reaction to the apprehension of freedom. However, in Echenoz's texts it seems to be motivated by the panic invoked by his protagonist's failure to live up to the images produced by the system he actively perpetuates. This intertext also operates as a *mise en abyme*, emphasizing the technical composition of the film to invite readers to reflect on the equally artificial use of such references in prose fiction. Here the aesthetics of the global market and the mass media are harnessed with those of all signifying practice to emphasize the artifice of television, film, and prose fiction. An artifice that is at once an inescapable condition of all cultural production and, if self-reflexively harnessed, the medium for its necessarily limited critical and sense-making potential.

The artificiality of the fictionalized representation of 'reality' is further underpinned in a *clin d'œil* to the bell-tower scene of *Vertigo* when in a pastiche of Scottie's pursuit of Judy/Madeleine, Personnettaz and Donatienne chase Gloire as she lures them up a lighthouse. This cinematic reference foregrounds the constructedness of the more convincing and thus all the more artificial scene in Hitchcock's film. Both the unprepossessing lighthouse and the more 'realistic' structure in *Vertigo* appear as constructions that contribute to the illusory totality of meaning of both narratives: 'On l'a dit, ce n'est pas un grand phare, on dirait presque un jouet, un élément de décor pour film à petit budget' (LGB, 223).[84] Moreover, the suggestion is that audiovisual representations have become benchmarks for the apprehension of reality.

By overtly or implicitly casting protagonists in the role of screen actors Echenoz at once foregrounds the symbolic violence inherent in the production and assumption of stereotypical images and exposes the double bind of fiction whereby images are necessarily employed to impose an artificial totality of meaning on the radical contingency of language. Moreover, if all Echenoz's *fin de millénaire* fictions point to their own artifice, they also expose how other forms of cultural production do likewise, but often to commercial ends. In *Les Grandes Blondes* it is inferred that the commodification embodied by the 'grande blonde' stereotype is also a feature of the art market, as Salvador ponders a reproduction of a Jim Dine canvas 'intitulée *The blond girls* (huile,

---

[84] 'They'd already remarked that it wasn't a big lighthouse. It looked almost like a toy, something from the set of a low-budget movie.'

fusain, corde, 1960)' (LGB, 134).[85] In *Je m'en vais* the plastic arts are subjugated to the dictates of market economics, as Ferrer admonishes one of his artists for moving away from money-spinning forms of art, whilst another shows how tapping into lucrative trends eats away at creative and critical potential: '"Cette fois, au lieu d'accrocher un tableau sur un mur, il s'agit de ronger à l'acide, à la place du tableau, le mur du collectionneur [...] Je développe l'idée de l'œuvre en négatif"' (JMV, 143).[86] Intertextual references to contemporary cultural production are juxtaposed with references to contrasting monuments of modern French literature: Flaubert's *L'Éducation sentimentale*, Jarry's *Ubu Roi*, and Beckett's *Murphy* (JMV, 196, 210, and 236 respectively). These references are not only to Echenoz's avowed literary preferences, but are also examples of avant-gardes that sought to bring into question the sense-making capacity of language and the ethics of contemporary society.[87] On the one hand, this intertextuality foregrounds the poststructuralist concept of linguistic usage as always already inscribed in a tissue of texts. On the other, it also implies some confidence in the enduring capacity of fiction as a provisional means of bringing into question dominant aesthetics, and, by implication, ethics.

Echenoz also sets up a self-reflexive intertextual game between *Un An* and *Je m'en vais*, developing the potential for critical perspectives by connecting two ostensibly independent plots via the appearance in each of three characters: Victoire, Félix/Ferrer, and Louis-Philippe/Delahaye/Baumgartner. In *Un An* 'Félix' appears briefly as Victoire's lover, who suffers what seems to be fatal heart attack, precipitating her flight from Paris. Later, homeless Victoire flags down a car driven by 'Louis-Philippe', an acquaintance of 'Félix' who feigns not to recognize her, but whose own death, she learns on her return to Paris, apparently took place before this encounter. In *Je m'en vais* Victoire makes a fleeting appearance on her first night back in Paris in a bar, surprised to see 'Félix Ferrer' just out of hospital after treatment for heart problems, and very much alive. 'Ferrer' is an art dealer who has smuggled polar

---

[85] 'Entitled *The blond girls* (oils, charcoal, rope, 1960)'.

[86] '"This time, instead of hanging the canvas on a wall, I'm going to use acid to eat into the collector's wall where the canvas would normally hang [...] I'm working on the idea of the work of art in negative."'

[87] Echenoz discusses his filial relationship with Flaubert in an interview with Pierre-Marc Biasi, *Magazine Littéraire*, 401, September 2001, 53–6.

artefacts into Paris to sell, only to be defrauded by his 'assistant', 'Louis-Philippe Delahaye', who, disguised as 'Baumgartner', has faked his death to defraud Ferrer and is on the run when he encounters Victoire (an encounter described in *Un An* but not in *Je m'en vais*). Once the connections are identified, readers' original interpretations of both novels are destabilized. This fictional return of the non-dead intersects with Derrida's the discussion of the *revenant* in *Spectres de Marx* as an uncertain symptom of the disjunction of past and present.[88] However, instead of ethical potential, here, engaged in corrupt commercial wrangling, the returns of the still living spectres draw attention to the exploitative dynamics of the global market.

Indeed this is more than a game for the attentive reader. By shedding a retrospective light on the events and characters of *Un An* Echenoz leads readers of *Je m'en vais* to reassess their understanding of the 'ends' of both and the causality of their 'plots', laying emphasis on the processes of the construction and interpretation of fictional narratives. The reappearance of the characters also underpins the corrupt motivations of Félix/Ferrer and Louis-Philippe/Delahaye/Baumgartner, suggesting through the repetition of patterns of exploitation and falsification across the two novels that they are symptomatic of the aesthetics of the mass media and the global market.

There is, of course, an element of fun, such as when Echenoz lets the canny reader in on the joke when he toys with blowing his own cover in *Je m'en vais*: 'Nous n'avons pas pris le temps, depuis presque *un an* pourtant que nous le fréquentons, de décrire Ferrer physiquement. Comme cette scène un peu vive ne se prête pas à une longue digression, ne nous y éternisons pas: disons rapidement qu'il est un assez grand quinquagénaire brun aux yeux verts, ou gris selon le temps' (JMV, 234, emphasis added).[89] However, by referring at once to the temporal scheme and title of his previous novel Echenoz also foregrounds the artifice of the contruction of a protagonist and of the author seeking to

---

[88] Jacques Derrida, *Spectres de Marx: l'État de la dette, le travail du deuil et la nouvelle Internationale* (Paris: Galilée, 1993), p. 162.

[89] 'It's nigh on *one year* that he's been around so it's about time to describe what Ferrer looks like. Since this pretty lively scene doesn't really lend itself to a long digression, we won't spend too long, but suffice to say that he's a quite tall fifty-year-old with brown hair and eyes which are green or grey, depending on the weather' (emphasis added).

achieve *vraisemblance*. Thus, from their titles to their ambiguous conclusions; from their intertextuality to their self-reflexive games; and in the cases of *Un An* and *Je m'en vais* in deliberately open-ended dialogue with one another; Echenoz's *fin de millénaire* fictions simultaneously bring into question the manipulation of crisis and the sense-making potential of the fictional process whilst also foregrounding the need to bring critical perspectives to bear on the same mechanisms in a range of modes of contemporary cultural production.

LANGUAGE GAMES AND IMPLICIT CRITICISM

Destabilizing narrative perspectives and linguistic play are also strategies used by Echenoz to draw attention to the artificiality of fictional attempts to represent reality. *Nous trois* surprises readers familiar with Echenoz's fiction by appearing to have a first-person narrator. Yet in the course of the text, the narrative perspective moves between the first person singular 'je', an implied first person plural 'nous', and a third-person omniscient narrator. In all four of Echenoz's *fin de millénaire* prose fictions the omniscience of the narrator is persistently brought into question by interjections and interpellations, addressing readers directly and so inviting them to put themselves in the place of a protagonist. With a wink to Minuit stable-mate Michel Butor's *La Modification*,[90] the opening line of *Les Grandes Blondes* establishes from the outset the reader's co-implication in the patterns foregrounded in the narrative: 'Vous êtes Paul Salvador et vous cherchez quelqu'un' (LGB, 7).[91] Elsewhere Salvador's attempt to impose order on contingency is underpinned by the author's wry nod to his own imposition of order in the construction of his novel: 'Restent les conquérantes, telles qu'au chapitre onze nous avons tenté d'en esquisser le portrait' (LGB, 238).[92] Narratorial interjections also draw attention to the outdated cliché of literary alchemy by humorously exposing how the imposition of the trope of the turning point transforms the arbitrary nature of life into a linear narrative. Hence in *Je m'en vais*:

---

[90] Michel Butor, *La Modification* (Paris: Minuit, 1957).
[91] 'You are Paul Salvador and you are looking for someone.'
[92] 'That leaves the indomitable ones, the ones I tried to describe in Chapter Eleven.'

Car c'est ainsi, dit-on, que naissent les grandes inventions: par le contact inopiné de deux produits posés par hasard, l'un à côté de l'autre, sur une paillasse de laboratoire [. . .]. Et puis un jour, un faux mouvement, on bouscule deux objets qui traînaient depuis des mois sur la paillasse [. . .] et aussitôt se produit la réaction qu'on espérait depuis plusieurs années [. . .]. Mais nous ne pouvons, dans l'immédiat, développer ce point vu qu'une actualité plus urgente nous mobilise: nous apprenons à l'instant, en effet, la disparition tragique de Delahaye. (JMV, 61–2)[93]

The narrator also comically flaunts his power over the fate of his protagonists: 'Personnellement, je commence à en avoir un peu assez, de Baumgartner' (JMV, 189).[94] Likewise in *Nous trois*, whilst also drawing attention to protagonists' names: 'D'accord, appelons-la Mercedes et n'en parlons plus' (NT, 30).[95] Mercedes is not, of course, Lucie/Dr Blanche's 'real' name, but by describing her in terms of her car, Echenoz encapsulates (and for want of overt criticism perpetuates) the misogynist commodification of her by Meyer. Salvador, far from a saviour, perpetrates symbolic violence in *Les Grandes Blondes*. Gloire's career is less than glorious, and it is surely not by chance that her surname Abgrall is the same as that of the detective who identified the serial killer who struck in 1989 in Brittany where Gloire takes refuge and then kills Kastner. In *Un An* homeless Gore-tex neither has access to expensive consumer goods nor to protection from the elements, and Victoire's passive co-implication in her disenfranchisement makes her far short of victorious (and another misogynist cliché). Other proper nouns are 'real' names (for example the Iguluk settlement of Port Radium), or are linguistically striking but offer up no meaning (such as Personnettaz and Réparaz). Thus this onomastic play draws readers' attention at once to the simultaneously artificial and arbitrary nature of signifying practice in general, and of prose fiction in particular.

---

[93] 'That's how, or so they say, great inventions come about, when, by chance two materials are unintentionally brought into contact next to one another on a laboratory bench [...]. And then one day, one little slip, and two elements that have been there on the bench for months get mixed up [...] and suddenly the reaction researchers have been seeking for years happens [...]. But right now we're going to have to leave all that because breaking news is the tragic loss of Delahaye.'

[94] 'To be honest, I'm beginning to get a bit tired of Baumgartner.'

[95] 'OK, let's call her Mercedes, and be done with it.'

Meanwhile, an awareness of the poststructuralist notion of the literary work as always already part of an intertextual weave of linguistic traces is inscribed in names. Fraudster Louis-Philippe/Delahaye's alias Baumgartner recalls Alexander Gottlieb Baumgarten, a disciple of Leibniz who invented the term aesthetics in *Aesthetica* (1750). Desultory detective Supin in *Je m'en vais* evokes this character's less than energetic enquiries and contrasts with Dupin, the perspicacious mystery-solver in Edgar Allen Poe's 1841 prototype for the detective novel, *The Purloined Letter*.[96] Thus the aesthetics of crisis inherent in all linguistic usage—the failure always already inscribed in representational practice—is underpinned. Yet Echenoz's enjoyment of language is palpable, and far from being a pessimistic indictment of the impossibility of mimesis, or a postmodern celebration of radical relativity, his *fin de millénaire* prose fictions at once celebrate the materiality of language and self-reflexively point to its inherent crisis.

Nonetheless, Echenoz also underpins the particular dangers of the manipulation of language and the compromising of linguistic ability. Direct narratorial intervention underpins how readers (and therefore consumers) like cultural producers (here the writer) are implicated in exploitative patterns and inequities. Accordingly in *Je m'en vais*: 'C'est qu'une des plus ingénieuses ruses des riches consiste à faire croire qu'ils s'ennuient dans leurs quartiers, au point qu'on en viendrait presque à s'apitoyer, les plaindre et compatir à leur fortune comme si c'était un handicap, comme si elle imposait un mode de vie déprimant. Tu parles. On a tout à fait tort' (JMV, 101–2).[97] Contrastingly, performing the inbuilt obsolescence of relationships which mirror those of media stars and consumer products, the use of truncated sentences to express the tongue-tied prelude to sex in *Nous trois* at once provides comedy and draws attention to the serial failure of relationships in the novel: 'Pourquoi vous ne me, pourquoi vous faites comme si je ne, comme si on se? [*sic*]' (NT, 180).[98] *Je m'en vais* also foregrounds a symptomatic

---

[96] See Edgar Allen Poe, 'The Purloined Letter', in *The Fall of the House of Usher and Other Tales* (London: Penguin, 1956).

[97] 'One of the most ingenious tricks the rich play is to make out that they are bored to tears out there in their enclaves, so you almost start to feel sorry for them, to think that their fortune is a handicap that makes their lives depressing. You must be joking. It's absolutely not the case.'

[98] 'Why don't you, why are you behaving as though I don't, as though we? [*sic*]'.

failure of communication: 'Mais les paroles, une fois émises, sonnaient trop brièvement avant de se solidifier: comme elles restaient un instant gelées au milieu de l'air, il suffisait de tendre ensuite une main pour qu'y retombent, en vrac, des mots qui venaient doucement fondre entre vos doigts avant de s'éteindre en chuchotant' (JMV, 54).[99] The incongruously poetic emphasis on the immanent failure of language is juxtaposed with a comic adherence to rigid linguistic codes, underpinning a crisis of creative and critical capacity in a media-saturated world. *Mises en scène* of the emasculation of self-expression are also staged at times of tangible crisis, for example in Meyer's sustained politeness as he guides Mercedes out of the horrific devastation in *Nous trois*. In *Un An* Victoire's fear of the judgement of others is manifested in an extreme reticence to participate in social discourse and is one of the factors that determine the process of social exclusion which results in her symbolic erasure.

In *Les Grandes Blondes* an overt play on the word 'blond' evokes the role of the market in creating new forms of commodification:

Et d'abord, qu'appelle-t-on blondeur? Les encyclopédies françaises, qui s'accordent à la définir comme la couleur moyenne entre châtain clair et doré, ne mentionnent ensuite que deux ou trois nuances, le vénitien, le cendré, que sais-je. Les américaines établissent une typologie plus fine, distinguant le blond sable du blond cuivre et le blond platine du blond miel, sans oublier le blond sale (*dirty blond*). D'autres encore. Bien. Poursuivons. (LGB, 219)[100]

Moreover this language game unintentionally draws attention to the danger of fun turning into complicity, as a range of the misogynist stereotypes available on the global market are introduced. Thus simultaneously, if unintentionally, these fictions underpin the risk of falling into the double bind of co-implication. Nonetheless, Echenoz's manipulation of language works against a completely negative prognosis, for irony, comedy, intertextuality, word play, and narratorial interjections

[99] 'But once they'd been uttered, the words sounded all too briefly before solidifying, as though frozen in the air, all you needed to do was put your hand out and they'd all fall into, words whispering softly, melting between your fingers.'

[100] 'For a start, what do we mean by blond? French enyclopedias describe it as the colour between light brown and gold, and only give a couple of variations, ash blond, titian and what have you. Americans have lots more categories, distinguishing between sandy and strawberry blond, and platinum blond and honey blond, not forgetting, of course, *dirty blond*. And there are plenty of others. Anyway, let's carry on.'

destabilize the homogenized, idealized images imposed by the mass media and the global market, and suggest an implicitly critical potential.

Thus through their linguistic virtuosity and representations of comtemporary culture Echenoz's *fin de millénaire* prose fictions offer readerly pleasure and contradict those critics who classify them as symptoms of Baudrillard's hyperreal or Debord's spectacular society. These texts reveal multiple, worldwide patterns of exploitation whilst foregrounding the dangerous ramifications of them. Thus it seems that Echenoz's objective is not simply to expose the mass media and the global market as the agents of oppression; or to draw on their crisis discourses in a pastiche; or to offer a celebration of postmodern relativity. Rather, these texts attempt to develop an implicitly critical poetics that draws on the aesthetics of crisis inherent in all linguistic usage to expose the dependency of cultural production on falsely reassuring crisis narratives and discourses that falsely promise crisis resolution. At the same time Echenoz seeks to counter these by re-introducing perspectives of the unpredictable, of the relative, and of free will. This implicitly advocates a move from the passive consumption of images, stereotypes, and crisis narratives to an interrogation of them. Witness *Nous trois* in what might at a first glance be an example of what many critics describe as Echenoz's ethnographic representation of contemporary life:

Les voitures garées dans l'impasse ont l'air vides mais on aperçoit, sur leur plage arrière, quelques journaux pliés, des cartes et guides routiers, parapluies et catalogues, boîtes de Kleenex et petits ventilateurs ou par exemple une peluche décorative décolorée, un chapeau vert, un gant vert, un listing d'ordinateur, l'édition de poche d'un roman d'Annabel Buffet, rarement plus d'une ou deux de ces choses en même temps. (NT, 16)[101]

This tableau in which maps, newspapers, consumer goods, and computer print-outs are abandoned along with a novel implicitly brings into question the artificial sense-making capacity of consumer products and prose fiction alike. Indeed fiction and market-driven forms of cultural production—from *reality shows*, news reporting, and film, to

[101] 'All the cars parked on the one-way street seem empty, but on the back shelf there are old newspapers, maps and road atlases, umbrellas and catalogues; tissue boxes and mini fans or, maybe a faded soft toy mascot, a green hat, a green glove, a computer printout, an Annabel Buffet novel in paperback, but rarely more than a couple of these things at any one time.'

the art market, tourism, and space travel—are as much the subject of these texts as are their protagonists. Nonetheless, Echenoz's prose fictions do not precipitate turning points. By adopting a stance of implied criticism, but by failing to problematize the risk of co-implication, Echenoz does not challenge the status quo. Rather his representations perpetuate structural misogyny. However, from the local to the global, by foregrounding patterns of exploitation and corruption, and by contrasting the false promises of crisis resolution of consumer culture with the at once artificial and arbitrary nature of representational practice, these fictions bring the extent of the institutionalized patterns of manipulation of crisis to the fore. Both deliberately and unintentionally, then, Echenoz draws on and draws attention to the simultaneously homogenizing and critical potential of different fictional constructions of reality. Thus his *fin de millénaire* prose fictions lead readers to question not only the tropes of the mass media and the global market, but also their own responsibility in representing, challenging, or perpetuating symbolic violence.

3

Michel Houellebecq: ideological challenge and precipitating crisis

In 1994 Michel Houellebecq was already known in literary circles as a poet and essayist, but his début prose fiction *Extension du domaine de la lutte* developed a cult status, and despite the absence of marketing expenditure, sold an impressive 16,000 copies. Houellebecq joined the editorial board of *Perpendiculaire*, a left-wing literary review, and published two volumes of poetry, *Le Sens du combat* (1996) and *Rester vivant suivi de La Poursuite du bonheur* (1997).[1] Articles and interviews written 1992 to 1997 were published in *Interventions* in 1998 soon after *Les Particules élémentaires*, the text that shot Houellebecq to fame.[2] *Interventions* supplements *Rester vivant* and Houellebecq's 1991 study of American science-fiction writer Lovecraft[3] in articulating what transpire to be Houellebecq's often-contradictory stances with regard to his own writing project and the *fin de millénaire* field of cultural production. Whilst the polarized critical responses to Echenoz's *Nous trois* are symptomatic of the contradictory discourses of the *crise du roman* in the 1990s, and Angot has attracted polemics since *L'Inceste* came out in 1999, the scandal surrounding Houellebecq's second novel was unprecedented. Indeed, the 1998 *affaire Houellebecq* is resoundingly the most prominent of French literary scandals of the late twentieth century, and sets the tone for the media feeding frenzies around Houellebecq's next two novels, *Plateforme* (2001) and *La Possibilité d'une île* in 2006. What

---

[1] *Extension du domaine de la lutte* (Paris: Maurice Nadeau, 1994; Paris: J'ai lu, 1997), here all references are to the latter; *Le Sens du combat* (Paris: Flammarion, 1996); and *Rester vivant suivi de La Poursuite du bonheur* (Paris: Flammarion, 1997).

[2] *Les Particules élémentaires* (Paris: Flammarion, 1998); *Interventions* (Paris: Flammarion, 1998). *Renaissance* (Paris: Flammarion, 1999), a further volume of poetry followed.

[3] *H.P. Lovecraft: Contre le monde, contre la vie* (Paris: Éditions du Rocher, 1991).

then, beyond the media manipulation of crisis discourses, the contra-dictory claims of the *crise du roman*, and the provocative and ambiguous rhetoric of the author, are the crisis manipulating, challenging, provoking, and perpetuating characteristics of Houellebecq's *fin de millénaire* prose fiction?[4]

CRISIS, CRITICISM, AND *L'AFFAIRE HOUELLEBECQ*

Les Particules was the subject of legal proceedings even before it was published. In August 1998 L'Espace du Possible, the 'New-Age' holiday centre caricatured in the text took out an injunction to block distribu-tion. As a result of this paradoxical attempt to curtail freedom of speech by an organization professing the most liberal of values Houellebecq was forced to change the name to Le Lieu du Changement.[5] All the more paradoxically (or perhaps premeditatedly) this generated considerable publicity for the aggrieved party and even broader coverage of Houelle-becq's text, with writers and critics including Noguez, Weitzmann, and Beigbeder springing to defend the Houellebecq's right to freedom of speech. Contemporaneously, *Perpendiculaire* dismissed Houellebecq from its editorial board for ideological differences. What began as a literary spat soon escalated when the interview that preceded Houelle-becq's sacking was reproduced by *L'Événement de jeudi* and *Le Monde* provided *Perpendiculaire*'s board with a forum to defend their actions.[6] Noting that the journal had previously published Houellebecq's work in which similar positions were expressed, the right-wing press decried this

---

[4] *Lanzarote*, a novella set in Tenerife and accompanied by Houellebecq's photo-graphs, was precipitously published by Flammarion in 2000 but did not make the splash the publisher and author no doubt intended. As Houellebecq pairs it with *Plateforme* under the title 'Au milieu du monde' and the rather thin tale's major component—the sexual politics of tourism and a critical view of a religious cult—are extensively reworked in *Plateforme* (Paris: Flammarion, 2001) and *La Possibilité d'une île* (Paris: Fayard, 2006), *Lanzarote* is not addressed in detail here. In 2008 Flammarion brought out an augmented volume of previously published essays, *Interventions 2* (Paris: Flammarion, 2008).

[5] From 'The Space of Possibility' to 'The Place of Change'.

[6] Olivier Wicker, '*L'Affaire Houellebecq*: Une Interview à couteaux tirés', *L'Événement de jeudi*, 17–23 September 1998, p. 5; and Jean-Luc Douin, 'Michel Houellebecq débarqué', *Le Monde*, 11 September 1998.

dismissal as a Stalinist show trial, whilst the left argued for freedom of speech. Neither camp investigated in any depth the implications of the manipulation of crisis discourses staged in the text or the crisis rhetoric surrounding it. Thus a precedent was set whereby commentary on *Les Particules* often rehearses the contradictory discourses of the *crise du roman* whilst avoiding a reading of the text itself. Meanwhile, Flammarion, both Houellebecq's and *Perpendiculaire*'s publishers, broke its contract with the latter. A commercially motivated pragmatism also adopted by members of the literary community who so vociferously defended Houellebecq's right to use a brand name, but failed to champion the cause of the minority critical review.

The controversy surrounding *Les Particules* dominated the 1998 *rentrée littéraire*. Flammarion released proofs in May, and by the summer interviews, features, and front covers of *Les Inrockuptibles* and *Lire* had been secured, together with a modest spread of reviews in the book pages of national dailies and weeklies, and one television appearance. However with the Espace du Possible and *Perpendiculaire* 'trials', and with Houellebecq's often contradictory and provocative interviews proving him to be the sure market value of the moment, coverage quickly spread across the print, audiovisual, and on-line media. The mainstream press dominated the debate, with *Le Monde* playing ringmaster; coining the phrase *l'affaire Houellebecq*; making it front-page news five times that autumn; publishing conflicting analyses; and providing platforms for critical clashes. All of this whilst assuming a position of editorial impartiality in a prime example of the manipulation of crisis by the media. In an overview of the *affaire*, Marion van Renterghem notes that detractors judged the text reactionary in its analysis of the outcome of 1968; ideologically questionable in its instances of misogyny and racism; and dangerous for its conclusion offering an apparently unproblematized 'final solution' to human suffering.[7] Meanwhile Pierre Lepape hails Houellebecq as 'une vraie bête de scène littéraire comme nous n'en avions pas eu depuis longtemps'.[8] Whilst pointing to the importance of the text, this typifies a nostalgic critical attachment to the notions of the *grand écrivain* and the

---

[7] Marion van Renterghem, 'Le Procès Houellebecq', *Le Monde*, 9 November 1998.

[8] Pierre Lepape, 'Dernière station avant le désert', *Le Monde*, 28 August 1998: 'a genuine literary animal, the likes of which we have not seen in ages'.

avant-garde that has also generated a range of commodifying labels to designate the harbinger of a new literary movement.

The trend in the mainstream press is to acknowledge *Les Particules* as important, but then to evade textual analysis by reporting coverage-worthy reactions to Houellebecq's contradictory television and press interviews. Many critics note aspects of the work judged to be politically incorrect, but do not go on to interrogate how these function in the narrative economy or any ideological challenge they might imply (let alone to interrogate the notion of political correctness itself). As van Renterghem comments, press reception falls into polarized apocalyptic rhetoric: 'Ne sachant quoi penser du roman, on se rabat sur les discours.'[9] The comment foregrounds the relativism of a critical field that appears to avoid tackling the aspects of the text that challenge the intellectual—and commercial—status quo. Likewise *Le Monde*'s account of the different strands of the trial by media and its *mise en scène* of talking heads points on the one hand to the commercial production of crisis, and on the other to a manipulation of crisis narratives as a means of not engaging with the text itself. Yet critical obfuscation and the intensity of the debate precipitated by *Les Particules* indicate that the text has a profound impact. An impact that the discourses of its critical reception simultaneously evoke and avoid. Clearly there is more at stake here than a media construct or an embodiment of the contradictory discourses of the *crise du roman*.

Whilst less overtly than the mainstream press, the French critical field also tends to fall back into paradigmatic frames of reference. Debate in reviews representative of the 1990s diversification of the critical field such as *Art press*, *Ligne de risque*, and *L'Atelier du roman* are beset by polarization, reading *Les Particules* on the one hand as a symptom of insidious postmodern relativism, and on the other as the saviour of French fiction. *L'Atelier du roman* has continually championed Houellebecq, and its June 1999 edition ran nine articles on *Les Particules* variously in praise or defence of the text. In diametric opposition, a dossier in the March 1999 edition of *Art press*, 'Littérature: Le Nihilisme en habits neufs', features critiques whose titles alone—'La Barbarie postmoderne' (by Redonnet) and 'Le Roman, le rien' (by Philippe

---

[9] van Renterghem, 'Le Procès Houellebecq': 'Because they don't know what to make of it, people are falling back on rhetoric.'

Forrest)[10]—articulate their stance with regard to Houellebecq's fiction. Meanwhile, the Internet provides a lively forum for discussion, indicating its potential as a challenge to the mainstream media. Nonetheless, endemic polarization is exemplified in rival websites dedicated to Houellebecq. The first, *Les Amis de Michel Houellebecq* (<http://www.houellebecq.info>) was intended as a forum for literary debate but gave rise to a cyber-spat over the allegedly racist content of Renaud Camus's *La Campagne de France*. Following accusations of censorship on the message board, a rival site, *L'Amicale des Ennemis des Amis de Michel Houellebecq* (<http://aeamh.free.fr>) was created, and vicious sniping between the two has ensued.[11]

If the critical community appears to avoid the challenge inscribed in *Les Particules*, the author himself freely comments upon his writing project. Indeed, Houellebecq's often contradictory and troubling contributions to the *affaire* not only indicate the author's uncanny ability to manipulate the media, but also add to the difficulties of textual analysis. The pattern established by *Les Particules* continues to inflect and deflect readings of Houellebecq. Indeed even greater critical and media crisis discourses surround *Plateforme*, published in 2001. Here there are more evident legal, socio-political, and indeed democratic issues at stake. In juxtaposition with a doomed love story, the novel features what many critics read as an apology for sex tourism and a critique of Islam. In an interview published in *Lire* in September 2001, the author launched an overt attack on the religion, which was exacerbated by the grim prescience of the novel's intersection with the terrorist attacks on the United States of September 11 2001, and later, the Bali bombing of July 2002. Houellebecq was taken to court by France's Islamic League, the International Islamic League, the Grand Mosque of Lyons, and the French League of Human Rights and was tried for 'provocation à la haine raciale et injure raciale en raison d'une appartenance religieuse'.[12] Yet as Houellebecq argued in court, to attack

---

[10] 'Literature: Nihilism dressed up in new clothes'; 'Postmodern barbarism'; 'Novels and nothingness'.

[11] Renaud Camus, *La Campagne de France* (Paris: Fayard, 2000). For a detailed discussion see Ruth Cruickshank *'L'Affaire Houellebecq*: Ideological Crime and *Fin de millénaire* Literary Scandal', *French Cultural Studies*, 40 (2003), 101–16.

[12] See Jean-Georges Fredet, 'L'Affaire Houellebecq', *Le Nouvel Observateur*, 13 September 2001, 98–110 and Salman Rushdie, 'A Platform for Closed Minds', *The Guardian*, 28 September 2002: 'incitement to religious and racial hatred and making religious insults'.

ideologies or belief systems is not to attack those who subscribe to them, so if democratic freedom of speech and thought is to be preserved, ideas, beliefs, and attitudes themselves cannot be outlawed. From this perspective, this *affaire* raises urgent ethical questions about the protection of individual freedom, and about the autonomy of the literary text and the freedom of the writer to represent characters or ideologies that readers may find odious. Houellebecq was acquitted, going on to further fan flames of controversy with ongoing politically ambivalent media interjections, epitomized at once by his use of rhetoric reminiscent of the far right and by his support for Jean-Pierre Chevènement in the 2002 presidential elections. So, the ambivalence and prescience of Houellebecq's fiction and the crisis discourses it manipulates and generates intersect with contemporary intellectual concerns about the mass media and the global market and ethics of bearing witness to the Holocaust, and to subsequent atrocities.

It is hardly surprising, then, that Houellebecq's 2006 novel *La Possibilité d'une île* also attracted huge pre-emptive media attention. However, this was arguably for the author's lucrative 'transfer' from Flammarion to Fayard. Fayard's plans for the promotion of *La Possibilité* accorded exclusive advance copies to *Les Inrockuptibles*, *Le Nouvel observateur*, and *Le Monde*, tacitly acknowledging that the latest 'Houellebecq' would generate the kind of media coverage that cannot be planned or bought (although the novel sold less well than Fayard anticipated). Indeed the post-apocalyptic portrayal of the potential effects of global warming has evoked less mediatized debate than its treatment of eugenics and a commercially driven religious cult. In 2008, if Houellebecq remained uncharacteristically and perhaps strategically tight-lipped on the publication of *L'Innocente*,[13] his mother's vituperative response to his putative fictional representation of her in *Les Particules*, he returned to the media-intellectual fray in an unlikely partnership with Bernard-Henri Lévy in *Ennemis publics*.[14] This epistolary and questionably autofictional exchange revisits (and arguably rewrites) childhood experiences, perspectives on historical events, and the ostensible manipulation of both men by the media (also reflecting, perhaps unwittingly, their own manipulation of it).

[13] Lucie Ceccaldi, *L'Innocente* (Paris: Scali, 2008).

[14] Houellebecq and Bernard-Henri Lévy, *Ennemis publics: Correspondance entre Michel Houellebecq et Bernard-Henri Lévy* (Paris: Flammarion and Grasset, 2008).

Following the 1998 and 2001 *affaires Houellebecq* extensive press coverage and television appearances have been paralleled by the harnessing of the author by a veritable Houellebecq industry. A succession of often swiftly executed polemical pamphlets and volumes has followed,[15] countered by predominantly positive volumes by Fernando Arrabal, Olivier Bardolle, and Dominique Noguez.[16] Meanwhile there is a pragmatic tendency in the French academy to take refuge behind canonical literary conventions, with surveyors of contemporary fiction such as Patrick Brunel, Dominique Rabaté, and Dominique Viart adopting solutions of more or less dismissive facility.[17] Nevertheless, *Les Particules* also appears to precipitate a new vein of literary *états des lieux* in which Houellebecq takes centre stage (often in the relative absence of his texts). These include Michel Crépu's *La Confusion des lettres* which describes the *affaire* as a contemporary quarrel of Ancients and Moderns; Pierre Jourde's idiosyncratic lambasting of most of the *fin de millénaire* literary field in *La Littérature sans estomac*;[18] and Michel Waldberg's *La Parole putanisée*.[19] Whilst Waldberg praises *Extension*, he slams *Les Particules* as a clumsy, self-indulgent sell-out:

un gros livre prétentieux, inutilement provocateur, où l'auteur récapitulait les ignominies—de façon critique, croyait-il, mais complice, en réalité—les errements de l'époque; imaginait à l'humanité le mol avenir d'une régénération par la 'science' et les biotechnologies. [. . .] le livre se signalait par une complaisance systématique dans le sordide, l'obscène, le graveleux [. . .]. Houellebecq y développait, sous couleur de 'réalisme', les plus ineptes dialogues, les plus abjectes descriptions.[20]

---

[15] See for example Denis Demonpion, *Houellebecq non autorisé: Enquête sur un phénomène* (Paris: Maren Sell Éditeurs, 2005); and Éric Naulleau, *Au secours, Houellebecq revient!* (Paris: Chiflet & Cie, 2005).

[16] Fernando Arrabal, *Houellebecq* (Paris: Le Cherche Midi, 2005); Olivier Bardolle, *La Littérature à vif: Le cas Houellebecq* (Paris: Esprit des Péninsules, 2003); and Dominique Noguez, *Houellebecq, en fait* (Paris: Fayard, 2003).

[17] Patrick Brunel, *La Littérature français du XXe siècle* (Paris: Nathan, 2002); Dominique Rabaté, *Le Roman français depuis 1900* (Paris: Presses Universitaires de France, 1998); Dominique Viart, *Le Roman français au XXe siècle* (Paris: Hachette, 1999).

[18] Michel Crépu, *La Confusion des lettres* (Paris: Grasset, 1999); Pierre Jourde, *La Littérature sans estomac* (Paris: L'Esprit des Péninsules, 2002).

[19] Michel Waldberg, *La Parole putanisée* (Paris: La Différence, 2002),

[20] Ibid., p. 39: 'a big pretentious book, spuriously provocative, wherein the author rehearses the ignominies and wrong turns of his time—in a critical way, or so he believes—but in fact he is complicit. He dreams up a limp future for humanity,

A swiftly growing corpus of academic edited volumes and articles are now devoted to the author. Meanwhile, testimony to Houellebecq's international cultural equity ranges from mainstream press coverage, Adam Gopnik's article on *Les Particules* in the *New York Review of Books*,[21] a 2002 BBC4 documentary *The Trouble With Michel*; and *Atomized*, a 2006 German-produced film version of *Les Particules* (*Elementarteilchen* directed by Oskar Roehler);[22] to the first international conference on Houellebecq in Edinburgh's Scottish Poetry Library in 2005, covered by BBC2's *The Culture Show*.

The following references to Houellebecq's comments on the *fin de millénaire* conditions of cultural production and on his own work are particularly mindful of the problematic of extra-textual influences on interpretation, and of that of making assumptions of authorial intention. In *Interventions* Houellebecq singles out political correctness as a scourge of the late twentieth century: 'Minés par la lâche hantise du *politically correct*, éberlués par un flot de pseudo-informations [. . .] les Occidentaux contemporains ne parviennent plus à être des lecteurs [. . .], pensant et ressentant par eux-mêmes' (INV, 75).[23] Houellebecq's conception of the discourse of the politically correct both intersects with and diverges from the negative use of the phrase by right-wing French commentators who use it to designate a censure of the freedom of the individual by the moral majority. Houellebecq uses *politically correct* to identify his perception of the compromising of the critical capacity of the subject, and, in particular, the reader. If taken at face value (an ill-advised move given his provocative proffering and withdrawal of clashing ideological positions), Houellebecq appears to elevate politically correct, market-driven relativism to the status of the dominant *fin de millénaire* discourse. His comments suggest that the intersection of

regenerated by science and biotechnology. [. . .] the book is remarkable for its conniving in the sordid, the obscene, smut [. . .]. Under cover of "realism" Houellebecq writes the most inept of dialogues, the most abject of descriptions.'

[21] Adam Gopnik, 'Noël Contendere', *The New York Review of Books*, 28 December 1998.

[22] A film adaptation of *Extension* directed by Philippe Harel with Houellebecq's collaboration was released in 1998 to little critical acclaim, and Houellebecq's own film adaptation of *La Possibilité d'une île* was a flop in 2008.

[23] 'Undermined by spineless political correctness, stunned by a stream of so-called news stories [. . .] Westerners today can no longer manage to read [. . .], to think or feel for themselves.'

political correctness with the mass media and the global market negates the potential agency of other discourses.

Yet Houellebecq evinces faith in the capacity of literature to make sense of this situation, and, what is more, claims that it is still possible to adopt a challenging stance to precipitate a critical turning point: 'Chaque individu est cependant en mesure de produire en lui-même une sorte de *révolution froide*, en se plaçant pour un instant en dehors du flux informatif-publicitaire [. . .] il suffit de faire un pas de côté' (INV, 80, Houellebecq's emphasis).[24] To what extent, then, is this *profession de foi* in the enduring potential of the trope of the turning point as both a sense-making structure and an agent of change borne out in Houellebecq's *fin de millénaire* prose fiction? And given his contradictory manipulation of crisis discourses in his fictions and in the media, to what extent does Houellebecq—France's most famous living literary product worldwide—escape the double bind of commodification and appropriation by the exploitative structures he appears to seek to challenge?

A *FIN DE MILLÉNAIRE* TOTALIZING THEORY

For Houellebecq, ostensibly politically correct discourses dissimulate and legitimize what he represents as the dual economies of neoliberalism. In parallel with the production of consumer desire conventionally associated with late capitalism, he identifies the production of unrealizable sexual desire, an economy based on a competitive hierarchy of attractiveness and wealth: 'Actuellement, nous nous déplaçons dans un système à deux dimensions: l'attractivité érotique et l'argent. Le reste, le bonheur et le malheur des gens, en découle' (INV, 41).[25] Houellebecq also states that a failure to change this neoliberal worldview will lead to terminal crisis: 'Nous avançons vers le désastre [. . .]. Tant que nous demeurerons dans une vision mécaniste et individualiste du monde,

---

[24] 'Each individual nonetheless has the enduring capacity to create from within themselves a kind of *cold revolution* by escaping the streams of news and advertising for a moment [. . .] it is simply a matter of taking a step aside.'
[25] 'Currently we live in a system governed by two parameters: sex appeal and money. Everything else, everyone's happiness or misery is determined by it.'

nous mourrons' (INV, 48).[26] In his own problematized and problematic return to the Marxist dialectic—the 'struggle' referenced in the title *Extension du domaine de la lutte*—Houellebecq's fiction develops a totalizing theory that simultaneously operates as a *mise en scène* and a diagnosis of what it portrays as the defining *fin de millénaire* crisis.

Corroborating its title, the narrator of *Extension* lays out this thesis explicitly. He states that the production of consumer desire is doubled by a parallel economy producing sexual desire, thus extending the realm of competition—and therefore of crisis production—into every aspect of life:

En système économique parfaitement libéral, certains accumulent des fortunes considérables; d'autres croupissent dans le chômage et la misère. En système sexuel parfaitement libéral, certains ont une vie érotique variée et excitante; d'autres sont réduits à la masturbation et la solitude. Le libéralisme économique, c'est l'extension du domaine de la lutte, son extension à tous les âges de la vie et à toutes les classes de la société. (EDL, 100)[27]

The narrator also writes animal stories, the second of which is a pretext for the exposition of the supporting claim for the totalizing theory set out and exemplified in the text (and subsequently variously embodied in *Les Particules*, *Plateforme*, and *La Possibilité*): '*La sexualité est un système de hiérarchie sociale*' (EDL, 93, Houellebecq's emphasis).[28] The narrator's argument is that adolescent desire is not simply a biological function, but is overlaid with socially constructed competition predicated on unrealizable promises of freedom and individuality. This construct of desire is situated within a specific socio-historical context, and at an identifiable turning point. For the '*génération sacrifiée*' (EDL, 114)[29] of the 1960s and 1970s, sexual liberation introduced an additional condition of production, adding the private crisis of failure in sexual competition to the public struggle of neoliberal economic competition.

[26] 'We are heading for disaster [. . .]. If we keep on seeing the world in this mechanistic individualistic way, we shall die.'

[27] 'In a completely liberal economy, some people accumulate large fortunes, whilst others grovel in unemployment and poverty. In a completely liberal sexual economy, some people have varied and exciting sex lives whilst others are reduced to masturbation and loneliness. Liberal market economics means the extension of the struggle, to all life stages and to all social classes.'

[28] Houellebecq's emphasis: '*Sexuality is a social hierarchy.*'

[29] Houellebecq's emphasis: '*the lost generation*'.

Les Particules builds on the theorizing of the narrator of *Extension* with the description of three 'mutations métaphysiques'.[30] Posited as irrevocable turning points in Western civilization, these are the advent of Christianity; its displacement by the development of the physical sciences and materialism; and the radical change described at the end of the text: humanity's engineering of its own replacement by a cloned desire-free race. Recalling the end of the human race, the narrator (one of the post-human clones) outlines the ramifications of the third metaphysical revolution that began at the turn of the third millennium. At this turning point, procreating to guarantee survival and earning enough to subsist are no longer imperatives. Rather than becoming obsolete or pure sources of pleasure, individualistic quests for sex and money have been turned into narcissistic differentiating factors, creating a sexual hierarchy based on youth, attractiveness, and wealth. As argued by protagonist Michel, society is founded on the erroneous belief generated by neoliberal ideology that individual desire may be satisfied through material and sexual consumption: '"la société érotique-publicitaire où nous vivons s'attache à organiser le désir, à développer le désir dans des proportions inouïes [. . .]. Pour que la société fonctionne, pour que la compétition continue, il faut que le désir croisse, s'étende et dévore la vie des hommes"' (PE, 200).[31] Mapping onto the development of neoliberalism, this interpretation of post-1945 socio-economics ostensibly determines the destinies of Michel and Bruno, the half-brother protagonists abandoned by their free-love seeking mother to their respective paternal grandmothers.

Les Particules presents a selection of microcosms dramatizing the discourses portrayed as having both produced this utopian promise and dissimulated its dystopian consequences. The unattainable ideal of sexual liberation is played out in the sexual microcosms of gangbangs in the dunes of Cap d'Agde, *clubs échangistes*, and the Espace du Possible/Lieu du Changement (ironically dubbed 'une utopie concrète'

---

[30] 'metaphysical revolutions'. The theory is further developed in *Plateforme* (to sex tourism on a global scale), and in *Possibilité* which provides a different perspective on how individualism, science, and marketing usher in a post-human race.

[31] '"in the sex- and marketing-led society we live in, everything revolves around desire, around generating desire in untold proportions [. . .]. For society to function, to keep priming the pump of competition, desire must grow, infusing everything until it consumes human life."'

(PE, 121)).[32] Here in theory the ethos of free love extends to the old and the physically unattractive, but in practice affords them only the freedom to look on. Meanwhile, the narrative exposes the sublimation of sexual frustration in material acquisition, gastronomy, social activism, and therapy: activities that at once institutionalize and dissimulate the crises generated by the dual economies of material and sexual desire.[33] In *Extension* Houellebecq provides an illustration of 'Le monde comme supermarché et comme dérision' (INV, 71).[34] The unattractive are left on the shelf, watching the desirable enter into transactions denied them. Twenty-eight-year-old virgin Tisserand expresses this with pathos: ' "J'ai l'impression d'être une cuisse de poulet sous cellophane dans un rayon de supermarché" ' (EDL, 99).[35] Indeed the leitmotif of the supermarket runs through Houellebecq's work. In *Interventions* it is the model for the pathology of the desiring subject, taken up by the media to generate multiple, unrealizable *purchase-crises* that legitimize and conceal the operation of the dual neoliberal economies:

La logique du supermarché induit nécessairement un éparpillement des désirs [. . .]. D'où une certaine dépression du vouloir chez l'homme contemporain; non que les individus désirent moins, ils désirent au contraire de plus en plus; mais leurs désirs ont acquis quelque chose d'un peu criard et piaillant: sans être de purs simulacres, ils sont pour une large part le produit de déterminations externes—nous dirons *publicitaires* au sens large. (INV, 72)[36]

For Houellebecq, the consumer product itself is not a simulacrum. Rather it is consumer desire that is the copy without an original, a corollary of the production of sexual desire. This consumer desire at once masks and offers a futile means for the sublimation of sexual desire. In *Extension* the narrator witnesses a death in Nouvelles Galéries where-

---

[32] 'a real utopia'.

[33] For a detailed discussion of the links between sex, consumption, and psychoanalysis see Ruth Cruickshank, 'Sex, Shopping and Psychoanalysis: Houellebecq and Therapy', in Gavin Bowd, ed., *Le Monde de Houellebecq* (Glasgow: University of Glasgow French and German Publications, 2006), pp. 199–212.

[34] 'A mockery of a world made supermarket'.

[35] ' "I feel like a shrink-wrapped chicken leg on a supermarket shelf" '.

[36] 'The logic of the supermarket necessarily leads to a dissipation of desires [. . .]. Hence a certain weakening of the will in our contemporaries. It is not that people have fewer desires, in fact they have more and more. But their desires have become rather strident and whiny, and whilst they are not exactly pure simulacra, they are the products of external stimuli, which are to all intents and purposes *advertising*.'

by the corpse is bundled out like an obsolete commodity: 'Déjà ce n'était plus un homme, mais un colis' (EDL, 67).[37] This also implies that attempts to sublimate sexual desire through material consumption may have potentially fatal consequences. Other examples include the death of Tisserand (potentially a suicide) and the suicide of another unattractive colleague, who can afford a double bed but whose sexual penury indicates that he only requires a single. The hollow creed of consumerism is also undermined in the description of shoppers in the centre of Rouen: 'tous communient dans la certitude de passer un agréable après-midi, essentiellement dévolu à la consommation, et par là même de contribuer au raffermissement de leur être' (EDL, 70).[38]

Indeed it is the production of sexual desire rather than material desire that is the focus of *Les Particules* and *Extension*. Even those sexual microcosms offering the utopian promise of release from the struggle still operate as competitive markets. Sexual equity cannot be bought at any price, and the subject is trapped in the simulated 'meaning' that media-generated desire lends to everyday life: 'Michel vivait dans un monde précis, historiquement faible, mais cependant rythmé par certaines cérémonies commerciales—le tournoi de Roland-Garros, Noël, le 31 décembre, le rendez-vous bisannuel des catalogues 3 Suisses [*sic*]. [. . .] Consommateur sans caractéristiques, il accueillait cependant avec joie le retour des quinzaines italiennes dans son Monoprix de quartier' (PE, 152).[39] Thus whilst Houellebecq's *fin de millénaire* prose fictions depict life lived to the rhythm of consumption, material objects are not in themselves generators of alienation or aspiration. Instead they are portrayed as smoke screens for the production and sublimation of sexual desire. If the early Baudrillard sees consumption replacing the Marxist mode of production as the basis of social order, Houellebecq replaces the notion of sign-value with sexual equity. For Houellebecq the conditions of production of social life are organized by the system of needs

---

[37] 'Already it was no longer a man, it was a package'.

[38] 'all communing in the certainty of spending a pleasant afternoon, largely devoted to consumption, and so to shoring up their selves'.

[39] 'Michel lived in a precisely regulated world, of little historical interest yet punctuated by certain commercial events: Roland-Garros, Christmas, New Year's Eve, and the twice-yearly 3 Suisses catalogue [*sic*]. [. . .] Although nothing really marked him out from other consumers, Michel always looked forward to the Italian fortnights at his local Monoprix.'

created by sexual desire. Objects do not take over the world in their excess as in Baudrillard's later fatal theories; rather, they operate as an inadequate means for the sublimation of sexual frustration. In their unsatisfying but pervasive presence, ephemeral objects demonstrate not only the crises created by consumerism, but also indicate that no amount of material acquisition or wealth can guarantee fulfilment in the sexual economy. Accordingly, in *Extension* and *Les Particules*, the consumer object does not feature in a critique of bourgeois ideology as in Barthes's *Mythologies*.[40] Neither does it fit the contemporary intellectual shorthand of the spectacular, the simulacrum, the hyperreal, or the *ère du vide*.

In *Les Particules* consumer objects are often described as though directly imported from a price catalogue. Presenting the world in its familiar packaging, this technique anchors the narrative in tawdry consumerist reality: 'Les histoires d'argent et de rapport qualité-prix intéressent toujours beaucoup les hommes, c'est chez eux un trait caractéristique' (PE, 317).[41] It also draws attention to the inherent failure of attempts to assuage sexual desire through consumption. When Michel takes a photograph before visiting his estranged mother on her deathbed, the object does not connect him with her or the world. Rather, it further underpins his dislocation: 'Avant d'entrer, Michel sortit de sa poche un appareil photo *Canon Prima Mini* (zoom rétractable 38–105mm, 1 290 F à la FNAC)' (PE, 318).[42] The tent purchased by Bruno exceeds its functional purpose as a poignant reminder of his unsuccessful quest for sexual fulfilment: 'Juste avant de partir il avait acheté une tente igloo à La Samaritaine (fabriquée en Chine populaire, 2 à 3 places, 449 F)' (PE, 123).[43] Other purchases are simultaneously substitutes for social integration and attempts to sublimate frustrated sexual desire: 'Après quelques années de travail le désir sexuel disparaît, les gens se recentrent sur la gastronomie et les vins [. . .]. Tel n'était pas le cas de Bruno, qui n'avait fait aucune remarque sur le vin—du Vieux

---

[40] Roland Barthes, *Mythologies* (Paris: Seuil, 1957).
[41] 'Men are always particularly interested in financial issues and in getting value for money, it's one of their defining characteristics.'
[42] 'Before going in Michel took out of his pocket a *Canon Prima Mini* camera (38–105mm retractable zoom lens, 1,290 francs at the FNAC).'
[43] 'Just before setting off he had bought an igloo tent (2–3 man, made in China, 449 francs).'

Papes à 11,95 F' (PE, 220–1).[44] Thus objects with price points in Houellebecq's fiction symbolize how the discourses of the mass media and the global market generate and legitimize material and sexual consumption.

Brands also play an important role. Far from being aspirational or providing any material satisfaction, they are indicative of the impossibility of escaping from the crises produced by the dual economies of desire: 'Il avala trois Xanax. C'est ainsi que se termina sa première soirée de liberté' (PE, 21).[45] Bruno owns a Peugeot 305; Tisserand a 205, but whilst both protagonists enjoy the disposable income that such cars suggest, neither has commensurate currency on the sexual market. So material possessions are a gauge of position in the economic hierarchy, but at the same time emphasize that such trappings of material wealth are not guarantors of rank in the sexual economy. In *Extension* Houellebecq recalls and updates the aspirational lure of material acquisition as featured in Perec's critique of nascent consumerism in *Les Choses*:[46]

Dans une brochure éditée par les Galeries Lafayette j'ai trouvé une intéressante description d'êtres humaines, sous le titre 'Les actuels':

> '*Après une journée bien remplie, ils s'installent dans un profond canapé aux lignes sobres* (Steiner, Roset, Cinna). *Sur un air de jazz, ils apprécient le graphisme de leurs tapis Dhurries, la gaieté de leurs murs tapissés* (Patrick Frey). *Prêtes à partir pour un set endiablé, des serviettes de toilette les attendent dans la salle de bains* (Yves Saint-Laurent, Ted Lapidus). *Et c'est devant un dîner entre copains et dans leurs cuisines mises en scène par* Daniel Hechter *ou* Primrose Bordier *qu'ils referont le monde*'. (EDL, 123–4, Houellebecq's emphasis)[47]

---

[44] 'After a few years of work, sexual desire disappears, and people fall back on gastronomy and wine [. . .]. This however, was not the case with Bruno, who had not commented on the wine—a 11.95 franc Vieux Papes bottle of plonk.'

[45] 'He took three Xanax. And so ended his first night of freedom.'

[46] Georges Perec, *Les Choses* (Paris: Juillard, 1965).

[47] 'In a Galeries Lafayette brochure I found an interesting description of human beings, entitled "The In-crowd":

"*After a busy day, they sink deep into a classic sofa* (Steiner, Roset, Cinna). *Jazz playing in the background, they admire the patterns on their Dhurries rugs, and their beautifully decorated walls* (Patrick Frey). *In case they fancy a quick game of tennis, there are towels waiting in the bathroom* (Yves Saint-Laurent, Ted Lapidus). *And over dinner with friends in kitchens designed by* Daniel Hechter *or* Primrose Bordier, *they'll put the world to rights.*"'

In Perec's Barthesian representation of consumer culture of the 1960s, Jérôme and Sylvie and their faceless contemporaries dream of a life lived through consumption, conceptualized through a few over determined brands and narrated in the imperfect and the conditional tenses that perform the inevitable failure of consumer goods to fulfil their desires. Here the consumer has acceded to a wide range of prestigious brands in the present, which for all their superficial prestige are ubiquitous, so their value is negative. Where Perec's 1960s *jeunes cadres*[48] buy into the political positioning *du jour* and tentatively participate in political demonstrations as status symbols, the inertia of Houellebecq's *fin de millénaire* consumers reduces them to putting the world to rights over a well-lubricated meal.

In *Les Particules* the production of sexual desire alongside consumer desire has radical consequences for the human race. This is exemplified by a *Trois Suisses* catalogue which performs a number of narrative functions. As the support for Michel's perfunctory masturbation it underpins with grim humour the isolation of his existence and the link between crisis generation, unfulfilled sexual desire, and marketing. More sinisterly, it guides Michel's thoughts towards the turning point in his research that will enable the orchestration of the end of the human race: 'Le catalogue 3 Suisses [*sic*], pour sa part, semblait faire une lecture plus historique du malaise européen. [...] Michel médita plusieurs heures sur le message [...] "Optimisme, générosité, complicité, harmonie font avancer le monde. DEMAIN SERA FÉMININ"' (PE, 153).[49] The same slogan is subsequently used by Michel's disciple Hubczejak in the manipulation of promotional techniques and of unproblematized faith in technological advance which engineers public acceptance of the end of the human race with 'l'appel à un gouvernement mondial basé sur une "nouvelle alliance" au slogan quasi publicitaire: "DEMAIN SERA FÉMININ"' (PE, 388).[50] The slogan

---

[48] 'young professionals'.

[49] 'The 3 Suisses catalogue [*sic*], however [...] seemed to offer a more historically inflected insight into Europe's current malaise. [...] Michel mulled over the strap-line of the collection for several hours [...] "Optimism, generosity, complicity, and harmony make the world go round. THE FUTURE IS FEMALE".'

[50] 'the appeal for world government based on a "new alliance", complete with a slogan that could have come straight out of an advertising campaign: "THE FUTURE IS FEMALE".'

recalls Lefebvre's 1961 assertion 'L'homme sera quotidien ou ne sera pas'.[51] If Lefebvre warns against the alienation of the subject in 1960s consumer society from the potential nourishment of individual everyday activity, for Houellebecq the discourses of the mass media and the global market threaten more than alienation, for they harness scientific advance and the inertia of the populace to engineer the end of the human race. The slogan is also a commodification of feminist discourses and thus perhaps unwittingly points to the misogyny of the writer, and certainly dramatizes institutional misogyny.

In *Les Particules* the mass media not only precipitate actions that lead to the end of the human race, but they are also portrayed as agents of the text's reductive and arguably reactionary account of the importation of American models of the market economy and sexual liberation to France. Houellebecq adds emphasis to this coupling through the seemingly incongruous pairing of teenage girls' magazines and the nascent libertarian press: 'Le conflit idéologique, latent tout au long des années 60, éclata au début des années 70 dans *Mademoiselle Âge tendre* et dans *20 Ans* [. . .]. Ces mêmes années, l'option hédoniste-libidinale d'origine nord-américaine reçut un appui puissant de la part d'organes de presse d'inspiration libertaire' (PE, 70–1).[52] As a teenager, Annabelle's reading of *Stéphanie* leads her to break off her unconsummated relationship with Michel in search of the 'normal' sexual experiences dictated by the new terms of the economy of desire. Film of the 1970s is portrayed as having a similarly detrimental potential, promoting 'une culture "jeune", essentiellement basée sur le sexe et la violence' (PE, 88–9).[53] Indeed, the 1970s are described in reactionary terms as a time of negative social and ideological change, with the establishment of Vitatop gyms, the legalisation of adultery, the lowering of the voting age to eighteen, and the *loi Veil* legalizing abortion cited as examples of the subversion of Judeo-Christian values by consumerism. The consequences of the yoking of neoliberalism and libertarian values in the

[51] Henri Lefebvre, *Critique de la vie quotidienne*, vol. 1 (Paris: L'Arche, 1961), p. 140: 'Man will live on a daily basis or will not live at all.'

[52] 'The ideological conflict which had been bubbling under throughout the Sixties, exploded in the early Seventies in magazines like *Mademoiselle Âge tendre* and *20 Ans* [. . .]. At the same time the North American notion of free-love received considerable support from the liberal press.'

[53] 'a "youth culture", effectively revolving around sex and violence'.

exponential production of desire are graphically evoked in the account of the gruesome sex-crimes of David di Méola. Yet once again, in reactionary terms, they are accounted for by the neo-conservative defence of di Méola: ' "la destruction progressive des valeurs morales au cours des années 60, 70, 80 puis 90 était un processus logique et inéluctable. Après avoir épuisé les jouissances sexuelles, il était normal que les individus libérés des contraintes morales ordinaires se tournent vers les jouissances plus larges de la cruauté" ' (PE, 260–1).[54] Here Di Méola's snuff movie atrocities are described as the product of the coupling of economic and sexual competition. The inference is that beneath the neoliberal narrative of progress is not just economic marginalization of the 'have nots', but also a potentially fatal generation of sexual desire. Thus it seems that *Les Particules* incorporates a warning. A warning that crystallizes around the depiction of the agency of the mass media and neoliberalism in the parallel sexual and material economies, and in particular their potential for harnessing recent scientific and technological advance. And so around the failure not only of the individual, but also of the intellectual field to recognize that threat, and thus avert what is represented as the final crisis of the human race.

PSYCHOANALYSIS AND CRISIS: LEGITIMIZING THE ECONOMY OF DESIRE

In *Interventions* Houellebecq suggests that advertising is the *fin de millénaire* credo. Not only does it over-ride Christianity and subsequent secular Western belief systems, but it also produces irresolvable mental crises:

La mort de Dieu en Occident a constitué le prélude d'un formidable feuilleton métaphysique, qui se poursuit jusqu'à nos jours. [. . .] Toutes ces tentatives, jusqu'à présent, ont échoué, et le malheur a continué à s'étendre.

---

[54] ' "the systematic destruction of moral values during the '60s, the '70s, the '80s, and the '90s was a logical and inexorable process. Having got everything they could out of sexual pleasures, and freed from traditional codes of values, it followed that people would turn to the broader spectrum of kicks to be got out of cruelty".'

La publicité constitue la dernière en date. [...] La publicité échoue, les dépressions se multiplient, le désarroi s'accentue; la publicité continue cependant à bâtir les infrastructures de réception de ses messages. (INV, 75–6)[55]

The *sciences humaines* are represented as failing to gain a critical purchase on hard scientific advance and the discourses of neoliberalism (it is not by chance that Hubczejak's second slogan harnesses marketing discourses and hard science: 'LA MUTATION NE SERA PAS MENTALE, MAIS GÉNÉTIQUE' [PE, 392]).[56] However, psychoanalysis is represented in a particularly critical light, colluding not only with the production of desire, but also with the dissimulation of its consequences. If belief in advertising produces depression, psychoanalysis is portrayed in both *Extension* and *Les Particules* as a mode of legitimizing market-driven mental health crises, and of institutionalizing sexual frustration rather than operating as a therapeutic mode of crisis resolution.[57]

In *Extension* analysis is portrayed as destroying the elusive capacity to love: 'les psychanalystes [...] anéantissent définitivement chez leurs soi-disant patientes toute aptitude à l'amour' (EDL, 103).[58] The narrator's experience of analysis solicits readers' compassion (and arguably their identification). Indeed his hospitalization (like that of Bruno in *Les Particules*) and references to a considerable number of depressive collegues underpin the ubiquity of psychological crisis. Houellebecq also represents mental illness being positioned by the psychiatric institution as a dysfunction of the operation of desire in the individual rather than as a result of the dual material and sexual economies generating desire but failing to fulfil it. In *Extension* the analyst rejects as abstractions the links made by narrator between mental illness and the sexual economy, imposing instead an interpretation that it is rooted in the individual

---

[55] 'The death of God in the West was the prelude to an extraordinary metaphysical soap opera, and one that's still running today. [...] To date, all these attempts to make sense of the world have failed, and unhappiness keeps on spreading.
Advertising is the latest in a long line of such attempts. [...] Advertising fails us, so more and more of us are becoming depressed. We feel increasingly helpless, yet the advertising industry keeps on developing new ways of getting its messages across.'

[56] 'THE REVOLUTION WILL NOT BE MENTAL, IT WILL BE GENETIC.'

[57] For a fuller discussion of the relationship between psychoanalysis and consumerism in Houellebecq's four novels see Cruickshank, 'Sex, Shopping and Psychoanalysis'.

[58] 'psychoanalysts completely destroy the capacity to love in their so-called patients.'

psyche. In *Les Particules* psychiatrists are described as dismissing writing as a purely diversionary activity: 'La plupart des psychiatres voient d'un bon œil les griffonnages de leurs patients. Non qu'ils leur attribuent une quelconque valeur thérapeutique' (PE, 322).[59] Yet as also suggested in *Extension*, the mental health-prejudicing production of desire is a structural necessity of the market. Indeed the analyst suggests that the purpose of psychoanalysis is to rehabilitate analysands in order to reinstate them into the sexual economy: '"En tant que psychologue, mon rôle est de vous remettre en état d'entamer des procédures de séduction afin que vous puissiez, de nouveau, avoir des relations normales avec des jeunes femmes"' (EDL, 149).[60] Thus Houellebecq depicts therapy as both a legitimizing discourse and a symptom of the production of unrealizable desire.

What is more, the inference is that the psychoanalytic process has led to the commodification of mental illness and the marginalization of its sufferers. A Minitel service makes arranging therapy as simple as ordering a pizza, and the resulting 'dial-an-analyst' diagnosis is a mass-produced cliché: 'Tous mes déplacements, généralise-t-il avec audace, sont autant de "quêtes d'identité"' (EDL, 132).[61] Diagnosis may also lead to social and professional exclusion, as the narrator's breakdown at work signals the end of his career: 'Mort d'un cadre' (EDL, 134).[62] So whilst patients might derive some comfort from articulating their distress, or from the seductive implication that their feelings might be accounted for in a sense-making structure, there is no turning point. Any sense of relief is at the cost of submitting to the terms of an order that perpetuates and promotes mental illness, dissimulating crisis with a detrimental rather than a therapeutic agency.

In addition to this implicitly critical manipulation of psychoanalytical tropes, Houellebecq suggests that the same tropes are appropriated in the commercial generation of desire and the dissimulation of its consequences. Reflecting the vernacularization of psychoanalytical

---

[59] 'Most psychiatrists are quite happy to let their patients write. Not that they see any therapeutic value whatsoever in their scribbling.'

[60] '"As a therapist, my role is to get to the stage when you are able to go back into the process of seduction, so that you can have normal relationships with girls again."'

[61] 'The fact that I have moved around a lot, he says, with the most sweeping of generalizations, demonstrates I've been following a succession of "quests for identity".'

[62] 'Death of an executive'.

discourses by reality television when the narrator of *Extension* witnesses a death in Nouvelles Galeries, the store's jingle marries popular psychology with advertising, an implicitly fatal *fin de millénaire* soundtrack: ' "*Nouvelles Galeries, aujourd'huiii . . . [sic] Chaque jour est un nouveau jour . . .* "'(EDL, 67).[63] This resonates with a similar juxtaposition of cod psychology and the promotion of consumer desire in *Les Particules* when Bruno attempts to break out of the binge eating cycle that results from his failure to sublimate his frustration: ' "Aujourd'hui est le premier jour du reste de ta vie"' (PE, 189).[64] The title of the penultimate chapter of *Extension*, 'Vénus et Mars', mirrors *Men are from Mars, Women are from Venus*, a best-selling 1990s American 'self-help' manual, claiming to provide the key to a successful relationship through an understanding of the differences between men and women.[65] The narrator's diagnosis, however, is profoundly negative: 'Il y a un système basé sur la domination, l'argent et la peur—un système plutôt masculin, appelons-le Mars; il y a un système féminin basé sur la séduction et le sexe, appelons-le Vénus. Et c'est tout. Est-il vraiment possible de vivre et de croire qu'il n'y a rien d'autre?' (EDL, 147).[66] Yet the analyst legitimates this market-driven phenomenon, describing it as a biological given: ' "Tout être humain normal accepte les deux systèmes dont vous parlez"' (EDL, 147).[67]

Elsewhere dream work is evoked, not only to subvert psychoanalytic motifs, but also to exemplify market-led interpretations. On the first night of Michel's sabbatical, castration and consumerism intertwine in his dream: 'il rêva de poubelles gigantesques, remplies de filtres à café, de raviolis en sauce et d'organes sexuels tranchés' (PE, 20).[68] In *Extension* horror and desire merge in a dream that culminates in a castration fantasy: 'Il y a des ciseaux sur la table près de mon lit. L'idée s'impose:

---

[63] ' "*Nouvelles Galeries, here todayayay . . . Today is a brand new day . . .* ".'

[64] ' "Today is the first day of the rest of your life."'

[65] John Gray, *Men are from Mars, Women are from Venus* (New York: Harper Collins, 1992).

[66] 'There's a system based on domination, money, and fear; a system that's quite masculine, let's call it Mars. And there's a feminine system based on seduction and sex, let's call it Venus. And that's all. Is it really possible to live believing that there's anything else to it?'.

[67] ' "Any normal human being accepts the two systems you are talking about."'.

[68] 'he dreamt of giant dustbins, filled with coffee filters, tinned ravioli, and sliced-off genitalia'.

trancher mon sexe. Je m'imagine la paire de ciseaux à la main, la brève résistance des chairs, et soudain le moignon sanguinolent, l'évanouissement probable' (EDL, 143).[69] Both the Oedipal motifs and the drugs that provide the backbone of contemporary mental health care are present here, and Houellebecq harnesses them to underpin the co-implication of psychoanalysis and mental health services in legitimizing and dissimulating the crises provoked by the dual material and sexual economies. The narrator of *Extension* derides his analyst's alacrity to note the motif of the mirror: '"C'est intéressant, le miroir..." Elle devait avoir lu quelque chose dans Freud, ou dans *Mickey-Parade*' (EDL, 147).[70] Yet there is more here than an ironic reference to the specular image as an example of the commodification of potentially critical discourses. Whilst the reference may evoke Baudrillard's description of Disneyland as the epitome of the hyperreal, this also implies that psychoanalysis is commercially driven, and by association recuperated as a tool to legitimize the manipulation of crisis by the global market and the mass media. And, moreover, to guard against the development of modes of thinking that might challenge that contradictory process. Houellebecq also uses a mirror as a narrative function that precipitates a decisive turning point in Michel's thought: 'alors qu'un miroir ne renvoie jour après jour que la même désespérante image, deux miroirs parallèles élaborent et construisent un réseau net et dense, qui entraîne l'œil humain dans une trajectoire infinie [...] au-delà des souffrances et du monde' (PE, 207).[71] Recurring specular images operate as intertexts to the mirror phase of the constitution of the self, but here the suggestion is that the privileging of individualism rather than the fragmentation of the subject or lack is the source of suffering.

In both *Extension* and *Les Particules* the reader 'sits in' on protagonists' analysis. Bruno's fascination with his mother's ageing vagina and sense of

[69] 'There is a pair of scissors on the table near my bed. The idea comes into my head: cut off my penis. I imagine myself with the pair of scissors in my hand, the slight resistance of the flesh, and suddenly the bloody stump, the dizzy brink of passing out.'
[70] '"That's interesting, the mirror..." She must have read something in Freud, or in *The Mickey Mouse Annual.*'
[71] 'whilst day in, day out, a single mirror a reflects back the same depressing image, two mirrors facing one another create a dense, intricate network of images, creating a perspective reaching as far as the human eye can see [...] extending beyond suffering and the world.'

exclusion from the sexual economy marks his initiation into the hierarchy of desire. Whereas in Freudian and Lacanian terms, this trauma would manifest itself by substitution or condensation, here the image recurs— with provocative misogyny—as a marker for the fate of the old and unattractive. Bruno assesses the vaginas of the female holidaymakers at the Lieu du Changement and those of his mother and lover Christiane: 'L'espace d'un instant il revit la vulve, maigre et ridée, de sa mère' (PE, 176).[72] Whilst figured by Keith Reader as a manifestation of male abjection, this pathological obsession with sexual decline is not an exclusively male symptom.[73] The effect of ageing is equally a preoccupation of Christiane: '"J'ai bien vu tout à l'heure que tu n'étais pas vraiment attiré par ma chatte; c'est déjà un peu la chatte d'une vieille femme"' (PE, 177).[74] Meanwhile the psychiatrist approves of details in Bruno's story that fit the Oedipal paradigm, but not those which risk revealing contradictions: 'Le psychiatre appréciait moins la partie suivante du récit, mais Bruno y tenait beaucoup [...]. Après tout ce connard était là pour écouter, c'était un employé, non?' (PE, 94).[75] Once again, the commercial and the therapeutic are inseparable.

Bruno's mother's concern for her son's sexual initiation is couched in terms appropriated from structuralist anthropology and the sexual liberation movement of the 1960s and 1970s, no doubt intended to subvert or expose the limitations of the dominance of psychoanalysis in contemporary intellectual discourses: '"Dans beaucoup de sociétés primitives l'initiation se faisait naturellement, au début de l'adolescence [...]. Cependant, ajouta-t-elle, l'initiation se fait toujours en dehors du système familial directe"' (PE, 92).[76] However, whilst Houellebecq may aim to use the incest taboo to corroborate the totalizing theory of his fictions and illustrate his perspective on *fin de millénaire* sexual pragmatics, his appropriation of it is symptomatic of a pernicious misogynist textual pragmatics.

[72] 'Just for a second he had a flashback of his mother's skinny, wrinkled vulva.'

[73] For a discussion of castration motifs and phallic abjection in Houellebecq see Keith Reader, *The Abject Object: Avatars of the Phallus in Contemporary French Theory, Literature and Film* (Amsterdam and New York: Rodopi, 2006).

[74] '"I couldn't help noticing earlier on that you weren't really turned on by my pussy. It's already a bit like an old lady's pussy."'

[75] 'The psychiatrist was less keen on the next part of the story, but Bruno enjoyed telling it [...]. After all, he was paying the bastard to listen to him, wasn't he?'

[76] '"In many primitive societies sexual initiation used to take place in early adolescence as a matter of course [...]. Always, however, outside the immediate family circle."'

Certain passages which use Freudian and Lacanian motifs appear more clearly as intentionally ironic critiques. If for Lacan the unconscious is structured like a language, Houellebecq has Bruno consciously manipulate psychoanalytic language. Bruno shapes his story of incestuous desire to anticipate the analyst's reactions and interpretations: 'il devait y revenir à de nombreuses reprises, modifiant tel ou tel détail—le psychiatre, en fait, semblait apprécier énormément ce récit "[. . .] Je me suis agenouillé devant sa vulve. J'ai approché ma main à quelques centimètres, mais je n'ai pas osé la toucher. Je suis ressorti pour me branler"' (PE, 90–1).[77] This in turn—and perhaps unconsciously on Houellebecq's part—highlights the artificial sense-making activity of literary criticism, which like Bruno's own shaping of his personal crisis can involve the manipulation of tropes to fit interpretative grids. It may also be a pre-emptive strike by Houellebecq at critical attempts to psychoanalyse him through his fiction. Indeed, whilst some reported details of his life may seem to correspond to his own fictional representations (notably Houellebecq's abandonment by his mother at an early age and subsequent upbringing by his grandmother), to read Houellebecq's narrators or protagonists as autobiographical projections is an extremely problematic secondary revision.

Houellebecq's appropriation and subversion of psychoanalytical motifs culminates in the credulity-stretching conclusion of *Les Particules*, which castrates the human race to replace it by cloned beings modelled on female attributes and deriving sexual pleasure from contact with the skin. Psychiatrist François Lelord reads the novel's dream sequences and conclusion as literally advocating globalized castration as a radical solution to the suffering of the sexual economy: 'Pour en finir avec le désir, l'auteur propose alors une castration généralisée.'[78] Arguably this misogyny compounds that inherent in Freud and Lacan, and the narrative pragmatics mentioned above undermine Houellebecq's

---

[77] 'he must have come back to the story several times, changing odd details—in fact the psychiatrist seemed to be very keen on the narrative "[. . .] I knelt down in front of her vulva. I stretched my hand out, just inches away, but I didn't dare touch it. I went outside to jerk off".'

[78] Quoted in François Busnel, 'Le Fabuleux destin de Michel H.', *L'Express*, 30 August 2001, <http://livres.lexpress.fr/dossiers.asp/idC=2531/idTC=30/idR=4/idG=3> (accessed 22 May 2009): 'To get rid of the problem of desire, the author suggests universal castration.'

fictional totalizing theory.[79] Redonnet exemplifies criticism of the harnessing of psychoanalysis in *Les Particules* by describing it as a vulgarizing strategy that perpetuates the very commodification it seeks to critique: 'L'explication sociologique se double d'une explication psychanalytique de bazar, censée ridiculiser la pensée et la pratique-freudolacaniennes'.[80] Nonetheless the emphasis on how psychoanalysis seems to legitimize the dual neoliberal sexual and material economies highlights the question of the putative failure of the *sciences humaines* to challenge the commercial appropriation of scientific discourses which Houellebecq depicts as providing the means of engineering the radically challenging outcome of *Les Particules*. Such, perhaps is Houellebecq's conscious intention. Certainly, and perhaps unwittingly, his manipulation of the tropes of psychoanalysis, marketing, and the mass media draws attention to the textual unconscious that always already exceeds authorial intention. And to the inherent aesthetics of crisis of language and literature: the fallibility of all interpretative grids.

SCIENCE, TECHNOLOGY, AND INTELLECTUAL FAILURE

In his forward to the proceedings of a 2001 Cerisy-la-Salle conference on Auguste Comte Houellebecq asserts that contrary to Comte's predictions, humanity has not entered a post-metaphysical age. Instead he argues that Newtonian physics and quantum mechanics are being harnessed to support Cartesian ontology and the notion of the independent subject.[81] However in *Les Particules* the discourses of Michel, of other scientists, and of the clone-narrator (the product of science) play key roles in engineering the conclusion. The narrator explains that the suffering portrayed is a result of the destruction of any positive

---

[79] See Jeffrey Moussaieff Masson, *The Assault on Truth: Freud's Suppression of the Seduction Theory* (New York: Farrar Strauss, 1984).

[80] Marie Redonnet, 'La Barbarie postmoderne', *Art Press*, 244 (March 1999), 60–4, at p. 64: 'The sociological theorizing is matched with cod psychology, which is supposed to make Freudian and Lacanian thought and practices look ridiculous.'

[81] Houellebecq: 'Préliminaires au positivisme', in *Auguste Comte Aujourd'hui*, eds. Michel Bourdeau, Jean-François Braunstein, and Anne Petit (Paris: Kimé, 2003), pp. 7–12.

values of Christianity by materialism and the physical sciences: 'la mutation métaphysique opérée par la science moderne entraîne à sa suite l'individuation, la vanité, la haine et le désir' (PE, 200).[82] Houellebecq's representation of Michel's breakthrough intersects with Thomas Kuhn's figuring of scientific paradigm shifts as precipitated by a very small number of scientists at times of crisis whereby new theories emerge only after a radical failure of contemporary problem-solving frameworks.[83] Yet scientific breakthrough is also linked to intellectual failure. The clone-narrator opines 'aucune société n'est viable sans l'axe fédérateur d'une religion quelconque' (PE, 388).[84] According to this argument, crisis is caused by the Western eschewing of cohesive narratives of regeneration, and by investing instead in commercially motivated individualism, creating the fiction of space. If this also appears to resonate not only with the discourses of neoliberalism but also with the notion of a postmodern perpetual crisis, *Les Particules* nonetheless gestures towards the enduring possibility of non-scientific and non-commercial turning points. Michel's solution to eradicate desire from the human genome is motivated by the hope that it will: 'redonner un sens à la fraternité, la sympathie et l'amour' (PE, 372).[85] This hope and representations of the potential agency of love are strategically juxtaposed not only with hard science, but also with marketing and media discourses which may promise redemption and regeneration, but in fact create unrealizable desire. Discourses that occlude tangible crises and palpable turning points, with potentially radical implications for the future of humankind.

Michel and his colleagues Desplechin and Walcott embody the dangers of the intellectual failure to apprehend the implications of scientific advance: '"un tout petit groupe d'hommes [...] sont la puissance la plus importante du monde [...] ils détiennent les clefs de la certitude rationnelle. [...] À ce besoin de certitude rationnelle, l'Occident aura finalement tout sacrifié: sa religion, son bonheur, ses

---

[82] 'the metaphysical revolution brought about by modern science has ushered in individualism, vanity, hatred, and desire.'

[83] Thomas Kuhn, *The Structure of Scientific Revolutions* (Chicago: University of Chicago Press, 1962).

[84] 'no society can survive without the unifying structure of some religion or another.'

[85] 'to bring back some meaning to brotherhood, compassion, and love'.

espoirs, et en définitive sa vie"' (PE, 334–5).[86] Here once again resonat-
ing with Kuhn, Walcott's words also echo Houellebecq in *Interventions*:
'Une poignée de techniciens [...] ont en charge la définition des
protocoles et la réalisation des appareillages devant permettre dans les
prochaines décennies le transport instantané à l'échelle mondiale de
toute catégorie d'information' (INV, 44).[87] Indeed the threat Houellebecq perceives in the unproblematized faith in scientific and technological progress is encapsulated in Michel's disciple Hubczejak, who
harnesses science and media and marketing techniques to engineer the
end of the human race. Thus an intellectual failure to perceive the
magnitude of this turning point is foregrounded.

Elsewhere dark humour brings the role of the intellectual into question.
Janine dances with Sartre, but finds him too ugly to be a potential partner;
Deleuze supplies Bruno's father's porn actress mistress with 'des justifications intellectuelles du porno' (PE, 100);[88] and the suicides of Deleuze and
Debord are attributed to their fear of ageing. However the narrator also
recurrently notes what he presents as the failure of contemporary thinkers
to recognize the radical ramifications of the appropriation of break-
throughs in the physical sciences by the media and global market economics. Thus in the epilogue, the work of some of France's foremost
contemporary thinkers together with the whole Enlightenment tradition
are dismissed for failing to make sense of a changing world and allowing
the third metaphysical mutation to take place:

Le ridicule global dans lequel avaient subitement sombré, après des décennies de
surestimation insensée, les travaux de Foucault, de Lacan, de Derrida et de
Deleuze ne devait sur le moment laisser le champ libre à aucune pensée philoso-
phique neuve, mais au contraire jeter le discrédit sur l'ensemble des intellectuels se
réclamant des 'sciences humaines'; la montée en puissance des scientifiques dans
tous les domaines de la pensée était dès lors devenue inéluctable. (PE, 391)[89]

---

[86] '"a tiny group of men [...] are the most powerful in the world [...] they hold the
keys to rational certainty. The Western world will end up by sacrificing everything in
pursuit of rational certainty: religion, happiness, love, and eventually, life itself."'
[87] 'a handful of technicians [...] are transforming the protocols and creating the
infrastructures that over the decades to come will enable the instantaneous transmission
of all manner of data on a worldwide scale.'
[88] 'intellectual justifications for porn'.
[89] 'Far from leaving the field clear for new ways of thinking, the global ridicule which
finally greeted Foucault, Lacan, Derrida, and Deleuze after having been unjustifiably
overvalued for decades made for the blanket rejection of all intellectuals in the "human

Bruno's encounters with cultural mandarin Philippe Sollers also inter-sect with the critique of the *intellectuel médiatique* and the abdication of the responsibility of the intellectual denounced by Debray, Debord, and Bourdieu. Indeed, Houellebecq's reference to Sollers's shift from Mao-ist to conservative literary *mondain* implies a commercially driven move away from *engagement* which (in the national imagination at least) the French intellectual had been believed to incarnate. It also implies the perceived ideological bankruptcy of *fin de millénaire* thought. Further-more, Houellebecq also portrays pseudo-intellectual political stances as off-the-peg social pragmatics, as in Bruno's description of his racist tract: "'Il fallait que je garde mon positionnement 'gauche humaniste', c'était ma seule chance'" (PE, 243).[90] Indeed reality appears to imitate art, since the critical stances of the *affaire Houellebecq* are for the most part comfortable clichés, and a concern to be perceived as politically correct defends against original thought rather than encour-aging it.

Critics have also accused Houellebecq of discrediting the generation of 1968. Given that by the 1990s the inscription of the *événements* of May 1968 in the proud revolutionary narrative of the *exception française* had already been brought into critical question, that *Les Particules* evokes outrage as a critique of 'revolutionaries' turned pillars of society is hardly unprecedented. In fact the text is less an attack on *soixante huitards* than a reductive attribution of the ills of turn-of-the-millennium France to the model of American liberalism adopted by the youth of the 1960s: 'les *serial killers* des années 90 étaient les enfants naturels des *hippies* des années 60' (PE, 261).[91] What it seems Houellebecq seeks to express here are the consequences of the failure of the generation of 1968 to separate desire from consumption. However for Houellebecq, the failure of May 1968 is symptomatic of an endemic post-1945 intellectual failure to challenge the growing credo of the individual fulfilment of desire. So *Les Particules* depicts a world in which thinkers—and by implication, writers—fail to apprehend that the physical sciences, together with the mass media

sciences". Nothing could stop the physical sciences becoming dominant in all fields of thought.'

[90] "'I had to keep projecting a 'left-wing humanist' image, it was my only hope.'"

[91] 'The serial killers of the '90s were the logical offspring of the hippies of the '60s.'

and the global market, have the potential power to engineer the end of the human race. To what extent, then, do these fictions suggest any potential for critical leverage?

The accounts of Michel's hypotheses demonstrate careful research, and their outcome intersects with contemporary concerns over genetic engineering. However, in contrast with Fukuyama's latter day figuring of a post-human future and Baudrillard's proclamation that genetics is the only mode of innovation remaining, Houellebecq's eugenic solution is the result of an excess of individualistic desire. Moreover, unlike Fukuyama, the end he projects is inconclusive: a quasi-utopian turning point which undermines its own finality and credibility such that the text's ostensible *dénouement* verges on a pastiche of science fiction. The legitimizing function of the discourses of science and technology is underpinned by Michel and Bruno's discussion of Aldous Huxley's *Brave New World.* Recalling the 'struggle' of *Extension,* the discussion demonstrates the dystopian consequences of the generation of sexual desire. It highlights how writers may foreground the potential of science and technology in precipitating turning points: "'il a eu cette intuition—fondamentale—que l'évolution des sociétés humaines était depuis plusieurs siècles, et serait de plus en plus, exclusivement pilotée par l'évolution scientifique et technologique'" (PE, 196).[92] The discussion also implicitly draws parallels between the materially satisfied but sexually impoverished positions of Bruno and Michel and the outcome of Huxley's text:

"Dans une société rationnelle telle que celle décrite par *Le Meilleur des mondes,* la lutte peut être atténuée. [. . .] mais Huxley oublie de tenir compte de l'individualisme. Il n'a pas su comprendre que le sexe, une fois dissocié de la procréation, subsiste moins comme principe de plaisir que comme principe de différenciation narcissique; il en est de même du désir de richesses." (PE, 199–200)[93]

[92] "'he had the intuition—a fundamental one—that the evolution of human society had for several centuries been determined by scientific and technological advance, and would continue to be.'"
[93] "'In a rational society like the one in *Brave New World* the struggle can be relieved. [. . .] but Huxley forgot to account for individualism. He didn't understand that once you separate sex and procreation, sexual desire continues to exist less as a pleasure principle than as a form of egotism. The same goes for the desire to be rich.'"

However, by evoking a literary utopia, a genre which not only implies dissatisfaction with the present, but also a desire to challenge it, Houelle-becq suggests a questioning reading of the conclusion of *Les Particules*. Nonetheless, perhaps unwittingly, he also underpins the risk of being misread. For if by the same token that Houellebecq's protagonists claim that Huxley's contemporaries missed the significance of his insights, the pages of *Les Particules* devoted to scientific explanation often appear to be indigestible digressions, and may well be skipped as such, detracting from the threat Houellebecq represents. A threat which, if couched as an implicit warning, is also missed or misunderstood by critics.

By choosing to include a reference to quantum physics in the title of *Les Particules élémentaires*, at a first glance it may seem that Houellebecq maps his protagonists' fates onto those of two particles subjected to the same experiment, but one which may have any number of different outcomes. In such a deterministic world, Bruno and Michel's similar beginnings develop in ways which lead to opposing ends within the same restrictive universe. However *Les Particules* raises the question of the enduring agency of the individual to precipitate turning points. In the prologue the narrator suggests that whilst the lives of most sub-jects—'les individus symptomatiques'[94]—are determined, others have agency: '"les *précurseurs* [...] ne jouent cependant qu'un rôle d'accél-érateur historique—généralement, d'accélérateur d'une décomposition historique—sans jamais pouvoir imprimer une direction nouvelle aux événements—un tel rôle étant dévolu aux *révolutionnaires* ou aux *pro-phètes*"' (PE, 34, Houellebecq's emphasis).[95] Michel is reported as considering himself an agent of revolution: '"Aucune mutation méta-physique [...] ne s'accomplit sans avoir été annoncée, préparée et facilitée par un ensemble de mutations mineures, souvent passées in-aperçues au moment de leur occurrence historique. Je me considère personnellement comme l'une de ces mutations mineures"' (PE, 223).[96] Hence *Les Particules* suggests that, despite the homogenizing discourses

---

[94] 'symptomatic individuals'.
[95] '"*precursors*, [...] however, only have the function of speeding up the march of history, and for the most part, for speeding up the process of historical decomposition. They never change the train of events—that is the role of *revolutionaries* and *prophets*."'
[96] '"No metaphysical revolution [...] happens without being presaged, prepared for and facilitated by a series of minor revolutions, which often go unnoticed at the time. Personally, I see myself as one of those minor revolutions."'

of the mass media and the global market and the blindness of intellectuals, free will still exists and the trope of the turning point has enduring potential both as a sense-making narrative and as an agent of change.

Accordingly, Michel and Bruno appear to have a chance to break out of the tyranny of the sexual economy, and the failure of their love stories is caused by their own choices, so Houellebecq brings apparently deterministic trajectories into question. Meanwhile, in *Extension* the narrator suggests that although elusive, love may have counter-cultural agency: 'Phénomène rare, artificiel et tardif, l'amour ne peut s'épanouir que dans des conditions mentales spéciales, rarement réunies, en tous points opposées à la liberté de mœurs qui caractérise l'époque moderne' (EDL, 114).[97] This questioning of free will and love contradicts the ostensible thesis of both *Extension* and *Les Particules*. It therefore creates a critical opportunity, leverage for the investigation of the potential for precipitating a turning point. Leverage that counters the ostensible prognosis for *fin de millénaire* thought and which is inextricable from the question of the potential of writing.

THE EXTENSION OF THE
STRUGGLE OF THE WRITER

In both *Extension* and *Les Particules* the implied questioning of the potential of free will and love is paralleled by an investigation of the agency of the writer. In the epilogue of *Les Particules*, the clone-narrator praises the representational practice of the post-human race. Yet these apparently positive terms are jarringly self-negating: 'La science et l'art existent toujours dans notre société; mais la poursuite du Vrai et du Beau, moins stimulée par l'aiguillon de la vanité individuelle, a de fait acquis un caractère moins urgent. Aux humains de l'ancienne race, notre monde fait l'effet d'un paradis' (PE, 393–4).[98] Here, as in the

---

[97] 'A rare, artificial, and belated phenomenon, love can only blossom under certain mental conditions, which rarely occur, and are diametrically opposed to the moral freedom which characterizes the modern era.'

[98] 'Science and art still exist in our society, but without the impetus of individual vanity, the pursuit of Truth and Beauty is much less urgent. To humans of the old race, our world seems like a paradise.'

economy of the text and in its staged discussion of Huxley's *Brave New World*, utopia has a hollow ring. Thus the 'solution' to human suffering the epilogue appears to promote is brought into doubt. Certainly, the clone-narrator's description of ideal art is diametrically opposed to the conception of writing articulated by Houellebecq:

si l'art parvenait à donner une image à peu près honnête du chaos actuel, je crois que ce serait déjà énorme [. . .]. À titre personnel il me semble que la seule voie est de continuer à exprimer, sans compromis, les contradictions qui me déchirent; tout en sachant que ces contradictions s'avéreront, très vraisemblablement, représentatives de mon époque. (INV, 118)[99]

Yet in terms of an implied prognosis in *Les Particules* for the enduring sense-making capacity of literature, storytelling is one of the few ontological elements of humanity retained by the cloned race.

In Houellebecq's *fin de millénaire* prose fiction, the exploration of the crisis inherent in language is paralleled by that of (writing) subjects, exacerbated by contemporary crises and crisis discourses. The narrator of *Extension* and *Les Particules*' Bruno are both writers, and the former articulates his perception of the struggle of the writer: '[l]a forme romanesque n'est pas conçue pour peindre l'indifférence, ni le néant; il faudrait inventer une articulation plus plate, plus concise et plus morne' (EDL, 42).[100] The narrator's animal stories and digressions also provide a meta-commentary that exposes not only the unrealizable utopian promises generated by media and marketing discourses, but also the equally impossible utopian project that is fiction. As the narrator builds his thesis of the parallel material and sexual economies, his counter-arguments grow increasingly caricatured. A jibe at political correctness simultaneously undermines the credibility of his theorizing and brings into question the discourses that legitimize the production of desire:

À ce stade, il me faudra plus que jamais envelopper ma formulation des austères dépouilles de la rigueur. L'ennemi idéologique se tapit souvent près du but, et

---

[99] 'if art was able to create a more or less honest picture of the current chaos, that, I think, would already be a huge achievement [. . .]. As far as I am concerned, I think the only way forward is to carry on uncompromisingly expressing the contradictions that tear me apart, in the knowledge that they are more than likely to be representative of my times.'

[100] 'the novel is not conceived for depicting indifference or nothingness. For that a more flat, terse, and dreary discourse needs to be invented.'

avec un long cri de haine il se jette à l'entrée du dernier virage sur le penseur imprudent qui, ivre de sentir déjà les premiers rayons de la vérité se poser sur son front exsangue, avait sottement négligé d'assurer ses arrières. (EDL, 93)[101]

The narrator's description of his project emphasizes the contingency of meaning and the fallibility of representational practice, immediately undermining its own sense-making claims.

If Houellebecq establishes the theme of the struggle of the writer from the outset of *Extension*, he also begins by bringing into question the possibility of reading his fiction as reliably autobiographical: 'Les pages qui vont suivre constituent un roman; j'entends, une succession d'anecdotes dont je suis le héros. Ce choix autobiographique n'en est pas réellement un: de toute façon, je n'ai pas d'autre issue. [. . .] L'écriture ne soulage guère. [. . .] Le chaos n'est plus qu'à quelques mètres' (EDL, 14).[102] In a 1999 interview Houellebecq adopts an ostensibly pragmatic stance with regard to the question of autobiographical influence and authorial intent. He describes them as part of the fictional process, a part that in itself is self-consciously fictional: 'Tout peut, en littérature donner de bons résultats. On peut faire de la fiction, de l'autobiographie, un mélange des deux avec des dosages variables; on est en fait souverainement libre [. . .]. Circonstance aggravante [. . .] il m'arrive souvent de mentir pour améliorer l'histoire.'[103] Thus, on the one hand, Houellebecq suggests that his prose fictions should not be taken at face value. On the other, he cuts through post-Freudian debate that categorizes *autofiction* as a definable genre. Although the status of Bruno, Michel, and *Extension*'s narrator as author-doubles appears to be deliberately questionable, there is a persistent critical urge to identify them as Houellebecq's mouthpieces.

---

[101] 'At this point, I must more than ever endeavour to swathe my formulation in the stern garb of rigour. The ideological enemy often lies in wait near the finishing line, ready to throw itself with a long cry of hatred on the final bend, onto the imprudent thinker who, intoxicated from feeling the first rays of truth already alighting on his wan brow, had foolishly neglected to guard his rear.'

[102] 'The pages that follow make up a novel. By that I mean a succession of anecdotes of which I am the hero. This autobiographical choice isn't one, really: in any case I have no other way out. [. . .] Writing brings scant relief. [. . .] Chaos is but a few feet away.'

[103] Frédéric Martel, 'Michel Houellebecq: "C'est ainsi que je fabrique mes livres"', *La Nouvelle Revue française*, 548 (1999), 197–209, at pp. 197–8. 'Everything in literature can be used to good effect. You can write fiction, autobiography, or a mix of the two with different amounts of each. In fact there's absolute freedom [. . .]. The only thing is [. . .] that I often find myself lying to make the story better.'

Given the contemporary debate around the concept of the author such interpretations are at best facile, market-led attempts to categorize Houellebecq amongst writers of *autofiction*. Or at worst sinister, since they shift the attention away from the text and its challenges to questions of narcissism and to the scandal surrounding the author. Yet Houellebecq's inscription and subversion of his own personal experience in these fictions appears to be strategic, a part of the texts' problematization of at once their own status, and of the commodification of both writer and cultural product.

Writing certainly does not operate as catharsis for Houellebecq's protagonists. Bruno's career as a writer articulates a double failure: that of the attempt to fulfil his sexual desire, and that of writing as a means of assuaging the resultant frustration. Michel compares his brother's writing to the displacement activity of a caged animal, an expression of the frustration borne of unrealizable desire. During a brief flirtation with the ultra-conservative *Foi et Vie* group Bruno writes in praise of Pope John-Paul II (his motivation for joining is a misplaced hope for sexual encounters). He then turns to poetry, and his work is at once testimony to the extension of the struggle into the sexual sphere, and to its impact on self-expression and cultural production. Bruno's attempts at writing are deluded and (self-) destructive as evidenced by the racist tract penned following his humiliation by a black pupil. He sends the text to a fictional Philippe Sollers, entertaining a vain hope that literary fame will boost his sexual currency, and Bruno's risible motivations resonate with Sollers's exhortation: '"Tous les grands écrivains sont réactionnaires [. . .]. Mais il faut baiser, aussi, hein? Il faut partouzer"' (PE, 229).[104] Thus humour also dramatizes the shift from cultural to sexual equity, from *grand écrivain* to writers as *people*, and so this interlude suggests that the French literary field has become subjugated to the ideology of neoliberalism.

Intersecting with Bourdieu's critique of *intellectuels médiatiques* Houellebecq positions Sollers as media personality: 'Il était guilleret, malicieux, comme à la télé—mieux qu'à la télé, même' (PE, 242).[105] However, like his fictional Philippe Sollers, as a cultural commentator Houellebecq enacts a contradiction, at once meeting and countering

---

[104] '"All great writers are reactionaries [. . .]. But fucking is important too, isn't it? So are orgies."'

[105] 'He was perky and mischievous, just like on TV—maybe even better than on TV.'

consumer expectations. On the one hand the Sollers figure appears to be a slave to the media and to his publisher. On the other, by referring to canonical authors as reactionary; and by exposing commercially motivated censorship, his words bring the responsibility and agency of the writer into question. Indeed, whilst Houellebecq's treatment of Sollers seems playful, it may well offer a clue as to a critical intention behind the contradictory provocative discourses of the text. It certainly displays an awareness of the double bind whereby those who seek a critical voice are themselves at the mercy of the media to make their voices heard. This suggests that Houellebecq's second novel is not only intended to be critical of the power of the media in the commercially driven post-war French literary field, but also attempts to harness that power strategically. In fact Houellebecq appears to pre-empt his own critics, for Bruno flicks through Sollers's controversial novel *Femmes* in search of its notorious sexually explicit scenes. This anticipates those critics of *Les Particules* who—perhaps unwittingly revealing their own preoccupations—ascribe the success of Houellebecq's fiction to a deliberate attempt to attract such voyeuristic interest.

In *Les Particules* Bruno is cast as both a writer and teacher of literature. He muses that in a society predicated on a hierarchy of sexual allure, rap artists enjoy more cultural equity than computer magnates, and Proust seems of little relevance: "'La duchesse de Guermantes avait beaucoup moins de *thune* que Snoop Doggy Dog; Snoop Doggy Dog avait moins de *thune* que Bill Gates, mais il faisait davantage *mouiller* les filles. Deux paramètres, pas plus. [. . .] La célébrité culturelle n'était qu'un médiocre ersatz à la vraie gloire, la gloire médiatique'" (PE, 239, Houellebecq's emphasis).[106] Yet if by such criteria Proust's fiction no longer makes sense, *Les Particules* by no means infers that literature is obsolete. Just as Bruno's teenage reading of Beckett and Kafka resonates with his feeling of alienation from the world of sexual opportunity, so the crisis (both personal, and that of modernity) articulated by Baudelaire retains a power to move: "'j'ai fini par me tourner vers Baudelaire. L'angoisse, la mort, la honte, l'ivresse, la nostalgie, l'enfance

---

[106] "'The Duchess of Guermantes had a lot less *dough* than Snoop Doggy Dog. Snoop Doggy Dog had less *dough* than Bill Gates but he was better at making the girls get wet. Two judgement criteria, that's all. [. . .] Cultural renown was only a pale imitation of true fame, media fame.'"

perdue... rien que des sujets indiscutables, des thèmes solides"' (PE, 240).[107] Thus whilst writing may not provide solutions, it can, in spite of its own inherent aesthetics of crisis, at least provisionally make some limited sense of personal crises.

In Houellebecq's *fin de millénaire* prose fictions, then, statements, 'factual' injections, references, ostensibly autobiographical detail, and apparently obvious interpretations are not what they seem. However, in *Interventions* Houellebecq declares that his narrative strategies are part of a quest for truth:

En mettant le doigt sur les plaies, on se condamne à un rôle antipathique. Compte tenu du discours quasi féerique développé par les médias, il est facile de faire preuve de qualités littéraires en développant l'ironie, la négativité, le cynisme. C'est après que cela devient très difficile: quand on souhaite dépasser le cynisme. Si quelqu'un aujourd'hui parvient à développer un discours à la fois honnête et positif, il modifiera l'histoire du monde. (INV, 111)[108]

The personal risk is great: writing will not assuage the crisis of the self, the self cannot be reliably written, and to attempt to write honestly and in a way that counters the dominant discourses of the media, is to court unpopularity. Yet Houellebecq implies that if this personal risk is not taken, the consequences may be of global, apocalyptic proportions.

Such it seems are the stakes that Houellebecq plays for in *Extension* and *Les Particules*, courting criticism in the attempt to produce fictions that do not seek to toe any literary or intellectual line. Fictions that at once expose, harness, and question both their own sense-making narratives and the contradictory *fin de millénaire* crisis discourses. This is the struggle of the writer that is referenced in Houellebecq's titles: *Extension du domaine de la lutte*, *Interventions*, *Le Sens du combat*, *La Poursuite du bonheur*, *Renaissance*, and *Rester vivant*.[109] For Houellebecq then, crisis

---

[107] "'I ended up turning to Baudelaire. Anguish, death, shame, drunkenness, nostalgia, lost childhood... completely indisputable subjects, solid topics."'
[108] 'By putting your finger on open wounds you cast yourself in an unpleasant role. Given the practically magical views propounded by the media, it's easy to show literary qualities by exploiting irony, negativity, and cynicism. It's afterwards that it becomes more difficult: when you try to go beyond cynicism. If someone today was able to craft a mode of expression that was at once honest and positive, they would change the world.'
[109] The titles can be translated literally as '*The Extension of the Domain of the Struggle*'; '*Interventions*'; '*The Sense of the Combat*'; '*The Pursuit of Happiness*'; '*Renaissance*'; '*Staying Alive*'.

and contradictions—of the self, of language, and of *fin de millénaire* aesthetics—are at once inherent in the writing process, and in the reasons for writing. Indeed, it is this paradoxical faith in, but doubt surrounding writing which encapsulates the role of the writer.

However, in contradictory vein, Houellebecq claims of the parallel economies of material and sexual desire that 'quelques phrases suffisent à donner une description complète' (INV, 41–2).[110] Were this description of the parallel crisis-producing economies to suffice, there would be little point in writing a prose fiction that did the job of a few sentences in 200 pages (*Extension*), or in following it up with a more comprehensive exposé in the guise of *Les Particules* (more than 350 pages, followed by *Plateforme*'s 370, and *La Possibilité*'s 485). Thus Houellebecq's investment in these ambitious fictions implies some sense of possibilities for change beyond those evoked by the narratives themselves.

In *Rester vivant* Houellebecq warns the aspiring poet to accept the role of the writer as a necessarily difficult one. It is also not an activity that can be described in the terms of modernist experimentation or the postmodern celebration of textuality. Or indeed in terms of modest returns to history, storytelling, and the subject. Here writing is a simultaneously problematic and knowing return to the trope of crisis as a turning point, in the sense of a questioning of the fictional process, and of an attempt to expose the 'truth' of the exploitation of crisis: 'La vérité est scandaleuse. Mais, sans elle, il n'y a rien qui vaille.'[111] Thus in the context of a literary sphere where the pursuit of truth is viewed with suspicion, and the enjoyment of the materiality of the text is a fashionable focus, Houellebecq aspires to a turning point.

LITERARY COMMITMENT AND PROBLEMATIZED AND PROBLEMATIC CRISIS TROPES

If for Houellebecq struggle is inextricable from the role of the writer, to what extent do his fictions challenge the status quo, either in literary or in broader socio-political terms? This in turn invites the question of

---

[110] 'a few sentences are enough to provide a comprehensive description.'
[111] *Rester Vivant*, p. 34: 'The truth is scandalous. But, without it, there is nothing.'

whether Houellebecq's *fin de millénaire* prose fiction is conceived with any sense of literary commitment; whether he narcissistically plays out personal crises; or feeds, with the voyeuristic reader, on those of others. Moving beyond the individual struggle of the writer, in *Interventions* Houellebecq defines literature as requiring a kind of commitment to an oppositional mode of consumption, one that is seriously threatened in a society predicated on the production of the ephemeral: 'Un livre en effet ne peut être apprécié que *lentement*; il implique une réflexion [...]. Chose impossible et même absurde dans un monde où tout évolue, tout fluctue, où rien n'a de validité permanente, [...] la littérature s'oppose à la notion d'actualité permanente, de perpétuel présent' (INV, 74–5, Houellebecq's emphasis).[112] Here, he also articulates a belief in the enduring potential of the literary turning point, both as a fictional, sense-making structure, and as a challenge to the perceived domination of the mass media and neoliberal ideology:

La littérature s'arrange de tout, s'accommode de tout, fouille parmi les ordures, lèche les plaies du malheur. [...] une société ayant atteint un palier de surchauffe n'implose pas nécessairement, mais elle s'avère incapable de produire une signification, toute son énergie étant monopolisée par la description informative de ses variations aléatoires. Chaque individu est cependant en mesure de produire en lui-même une sorte de *révolution froide*, en se plaçant pour un instant en dehors du flux informatif-publicitaire, [...] [p]ar rapport au monde, dans une *position esthétique*: il suffit de faire un pas de côté. (INV, 79–80, Houellebecq's emphasis)[113]

---

[112] 'Indeed books can only be enjoyed *slowly*. They require thought [...]. Which is impossible and even seems absurd in a world where everything is changing, everything fluctuates, where nothing has any permanent value, [...] literature is the opposite of the notion of permanent novelty, of a perpetual present.'

[113] 'Literature can cope with anything, it can adapt to any circumstance, it can scrabble around in the dirt, and lick the wounds of misery. [...] a society that has reached a level of overheating does not necessarily implode, but it proves to be incapable of producing meaning, since all its energies are concentrated on attempting to provide information about all its random variations. Nonetheless, each individual is in a position to create from within themselves a kind of *cold revolution* by placing themselves, for a moment, outside the constant stream of news and advertising, [...] [b]y putting themselves in an *aesthetic position*: all it takes is to take a step aside.'

Unlike the Sartrean notion of literature as praxis, here the revolution Houellebecq envisages is self-reflexively aesthetic, a holistic question inscribed in these fictions by the appropriation of a variety of generic conventions and the juxtaposition of contradictory discourses.

Such aspirations of aesthetic resistance counter accusations of an 'absence de style' which ignores the relationship between theory and practice in these narratives.[114] The stylistic features and complexities of these fictions have been analysed by Robert Dion, Élisabeth Haghebaert, and Dominique Noguez, but for the purposes of this discussion, Houellebecq's style can be characterized by its frequent impassivity, mixed registers, intertextuality, and injections of ostensibly non-fictional texts.[115] These characteristics can be read as part of Houellebecq's quest to find an aesthetics that at once exposes, harnesses, and brings into question the discourses of the mass media and the global market. A narrative mode that seeks to respond to the problematic identified by the narrator of *Extension*: 'Cet effacement progressif des relations humaines n'est pas sans poser certains problèmes au roman' (EDL, 42).[116] This might well be one of the interpretations of the title of Houellebecq's 2001 novel *Plateforme*, interpreted by Olivier Bardolle as a quest for a 'forme plate', a flat form that by the terms of this study may also counter promotional discourses and mass media output. Indeed as underpinned by the Marxist overtones of the title and the theorizing of *Extension*, style is inextricably bound up with politics (Bardolle goes on to observe that the Arabic translation of *Plateforme*, written before the attacks of September 11 2001, is Al Qaeda).[117]

In *Interventions* Houellebecq at once warns against the seductiveness of the claims of the novel to making sense and makes some claims of his

---

[114] See Angelo Rinaldi, 'Attention brouillard!', *L'Express*, 27 August 1998: 'an absence of style'.

[115] For detailed discussion of the stylistic features and complexity of Houellebecq's *fin de millénaire* prose fiction see Robert Dion and Élisabeth Haghebaert, 'Le Cas de Michel Houellebecq et la dynamique des genres littéraires', *French Studies*, 55 (2001), 509–24; and Dominique Noguez, 'Le Style de Michel Houellebecq', *L'Atelier du roman*, 18 (1999), 17–22; 'Le Style de Michel Houellebecq: 2', *L'Atelier du roman*, 19 (1999), 121–3; and 'Le Style de Michel Houellebecq: Fin', *L'Atelier du roman*, 20 (1999), 129–37.

[116] 'This progressive erasure of human relationships creates a number of problems for the novel'.

[117] Bardolle, *La Littérature à vif*, p. 64.

own: 'Il est bon de se méfier du roman; il ne faut pas se laisser piéger par l'histoire; ni par le ton, ni par le style [. . .]. Il faudrait conquérir une certaine liberté lyrique; un roman idéal devrait pouvoir comporter des passages versifiés ou chantés' (INV, 40).[118] Here he also suggests the juxtaposition of poetry with historical and theoretical discourses as a viable mode of representing how a fragmented sense of self is compounded by the effects of atomization of life:

Voilà une chose que beaucoup de gens ressentent: par brefs instants, ils vivent; pourtant, leur vie prise dans son ensemble n'a ni direction ni sens. C'est pour cela qu'il est devenu difficile d'écrire un roman honnête, dénué de clichés, dans lequel, pourtant, il puisse y avoir une progression romanesque. Je ne suis pas très certain d'avoir trouvé une solution; j'ai l'impression qu'on peut procéder par injection brutale dans la matière romanesque de théorie et d'histoire. (INV, 116)[119]

On the one hand, such 'injections' in Houellebecq's *fin de millénaire* prose fiction—carefully researched scientific explanations and socio-historical accounts—seem to operate as totalizing narratives (sometimes page-skippingly turgid). On the other, together with marketing literature, poetry, and ancient texts they multiply interpretative possibilities and bring the unquestioning consumption of all narratives into question. Nonetheless, as *Les Particules* progresses, 'factual' injections become more evidently fictional, strategically engineered in support of the novel's conclusion but often contradicting the preceding narrative.

For example, despite the positing of the enduring agency of love and choice discussed above, Michel's fictional theory imposes a positivist rationale for the operation of free will. The emphasis on the role of individual scientists contradicts the assertion of the clone-narrator in the prologue that the 'mutations métaphysiques', critical turning points in the history of humankind, are determined. Likewise, Walcott's

---

[118] 'It is good to be wary of the novel, not to get waylaid by the story, or by the tone, or by the style [. . .]. Writers should accede to a certain lyrical freedom, so the ideal novel should be able to include passages of verse or song.'

[119] 'Here's a thing that many people feel: for a brief moment, they are alive, but in the round their lives have neither sense nor direction. That is why it has become difficult to write an honest novel, without resorting to clichés, but which nonetheless has some kind of novelistic progression. I'm not convinced that I have found the solution, but I do have the sense that the way forward is to inject elements of theory and history brutally into the fabric of the novel.'

assertion of biological determination is contradicted by the portrayal of the New Age movement as a bungled opportunity for a change: "'le New Age manifestait une réelle volonté de rupture avec le XXe siècle [...] il constituait en réalité un puissant appel à un changement de paradigme'" (PE, 388).[120] The eugenic conclusion is one such possible change of paradigm, but just as the novel's own turning points are problematized, so Houellebecq implies that it too may be challenged. Implicitly, then, this unlikely ending is brought into question throughout *Les Particules*, as are totalizing theories and discourses from advertising and autobiography to scatology and science in an implied assessment of the cultural value and resonance of both canonical and mass-market cultural products. Thus the attempt to step outside desire-generating ideology to precipitate 'une révolution froide' is made, often—and sometimes counter-productively and provocatively—from within the system Houellebecq ostensibly seeks to challenge.

A self-reflexive, implicit questioning of the enduring agency of the turning point is also inscribed via the harnessing of a range of literary tropes from Greek tragedy via science fiction to the *roman à thèse*. In a literary field perceived to be characterized on the one hand by nihilistic relativism, and on the other by a modest return to the subject, storytelling, and history, Houellebecq's *fin de millénaire* prose fictions constitute an emphatic return to potentially sense-making tropes of crisis. A return which investigates the enduring sense-making potential of the literary. In *Les Particules* different readings of Huxley's *Brave New World* are mooted, and Michel suggests that ideological and commercial expediency led to its interpretation as a denunciation of totalitarianism. The discussion goes on to posit that the utopian harnessing of the trope of crisis as a turning point by philosophers, writers, and would-be social engineers relies misguidedly on a belief in the possibility of satisfying desire: "'La solution des utopistes—de Platon à Huxley, en passant par Fourier—consiste à éteindre le désir en organisant sa satisfaction immédiate'" (PE, 200).[121] Bruno's screenplay—"'un scénario de film

---

[120] "'The New Age movement demonstrated a genuine will to break away from the twentieth century [...] in fact it was a strong appeal for a change of paradigm.'"

[121] "'The utopian solution—from Plato to Huxley via Fourier—is to dispense with desire by organizing its immediate fulfilment.'"

paradisiaque sur le thème de la Jérusalem nouvelle"' (PE, 321)[122]—also brings the viability of utopian discourses into question. On the one hand, the work, written in a psychiatric hospital, is a bathetic symbol of the mental state of the protagonist. On the other, this screenplay and the discussion of Huxley's *Brave New World* (both of which project turning points for humanity) are as lucid—or as nonsensical—as *Les Particules* itself. The question, then, compounded by the contradictions of the text and Houellebecq's manipulation of crisis rhetoric beyond it, is how to interpret *Les Particules* and its own apparently utopian narrative.

Extension is situated at perhaps the most significant turning point of the twentieth century. Not an arbitrary symbolic date, but at the juncture whereby information technology radically transforms late capitalist society. The narrator describes computerization as an 'encombrement inutile pour les neurones' (EDL, 83).[123] Moreover, it is also represented as the producer of alienation that it then seeks to conceal. In this drama of middle-class, middle-aged middle managers the narrator's colleagues either evince a naive enthusiasm for this latest technological revolution or a naive belief in their ability to resist it.

Les Particules is set on the eve of the new millennium, but features a fictional turning point marking a breakthrough in Michel's thought. On the one hand the New Year's Eve 1999 of *Les Particules* is less a symbolic marker than an embodiment of the anaesthetizing of millenarian fears: 'Partout à la surface de la planète l'humanité fatiguée, épuisée, doutant d'elle même et de sa propre histoire, s'apprêtait tant bien que mal à entrer dans un nouveau millénaire' (PE, 367).[124] On the other, the eve of the third millennium is also the eve of a breakthrough in Michel's thought: a step towards the extinction of humanity. Yet from this turning point onwards, for all its apparent determinism and scientific accuracy, the 'history' of the end of humankind in *Les Particules* is but a story. This story not only depends on Houellebecq's representation of the scientific and metaphysical conjecture of one fictional man, but also undermines its own sense-making potential by exposing how both

---

[122] "'a screenplay for a film about the paradise of a new Jerusalem'".
[123] 'useless clogging up of brain cells'.
[124] 'Tired, exhausted, loosing self-confidence and confidence in their collective history, human beings worldwide were preparing as best they could to enter a new millennium.'

history and *Les Particules* itself are but fictions, a fashioning of selected events into a linear narrative.

Houellebecq frames *Les Particules* with a prologue and epilogue, rhetorical devices of classical tragedy. Of course, various forms of framing devices have long been used by diverse French writers, subverting the convention to set up interpretative possibilities or questions for the canny reader. From a poststructuralist perspective, the use of a framing device betrays a contradictory need for the text to grasp itself: recognition of the impossibility of containing a narrative, of the inherent aesthetics of crisis of the sense-making process. Whilst Houellebecq's intention is unlikely to be overtly deconstructive, it would seem that his clone-narrator is deliberately unreliable. The prologue begins with a statement of intent: 'Ce livre est avant tout l'histoire d'un homme' (PE, 9).[125] However, the narrative consistently contradicts the claims of the prologue, and its conclusion is ambiguous. The revelation of the post-human perspective of the clone-narrator provokes questioning rather than providing closure, destabilizing the reader's own interpretation of the preceding narrative. The third part of *Les Particules* deals with the definitive stages of Michel's research and the deaths of the four protagonists. It is but twelve chapters long, and its haste underlines the artifice of the conclusion.[126] The epilogue is devoted to a credulity stretching account of the consequences of Michel's research, an unconvincing 'fast-forward' to a questionable conclusion. Yet tracing the end to Michel's story, the clone-narrator admits that 'il demeure, dans sa biographie comme dans sa personnalité, beaucoup de zones d'ombre' (PE, 383).[127] The final caution as to the unreliability of the story brings the ontological status of the narrative, and in particular, its end, into question: 'ce livre doit malgré tout être considéré comme une fiction, une reconstitution crédible à partir de souvenirs partiels, plutôt que comme le reflet d'une vérité univoque et attestable' (PE, 383).[128] This suggests that the conclusion of *Les Particules* is one such grey area.

In fact, the epilogue concludes in contradiction of the prologue. The clone-narrator now claims that, far from documenting the life of one

---

[125] 'This book is above all the story of a man.'

[126] The first part comprises fifteen chapters, and the second, twenty-two.

[127] 'there still remain many grey areas in his life story, as in his personality'.

[128] 'this book should nonetheless be thought of as fiction, a credible reconstruction made from partial memories rather than as reflecting a single, demonstrable truth'.

individual, the account is at once a historical record of the contradictions of the human race and a homage to humankind. So not only
has the declared intention changed, but the text itself has also eluded the
deterministic sense-making claims of both prologue and epilogue:
'L'histoire existe; elle s'impose, elle domine, son empire est inéluctable.
Mais au-delà du strict plan historique, l'ambition ultime de cet ouvrage
est de saluer cette espèce infortunée et courageuse qui nous a créés. [. . .]
Ce livre est dédié à l'homme' (PE, 394).[129] In the story space the clone-
narrator asserts the determinism of history, yet the 'history' represented
here is fictional. The turning point projected by *Les Particules* has not
occurred, nor have the crises depicted been resolved, for better or for
worse. And a text which claims to be paying homage to the human race
instead appears to be a critique of it within a specific socio-historical
timeframe (and indeed, a specifically francocentric one). Moreover,
with the notion of homage comes a sense that there might still be
something to be salvaged. So the 'end' of 'history' posited may be
read as another challenge to the hypotheses of Fukuyama or Baudrillard.
Thus Houellebecq brings into question both the determinism of history
and the contemporary sense of a loss of the critical turning point. Whilst
avoiding the simplistic resolution of crisis of the conventional realist
novel, Houellebecq does not exploit the putatively culturally dominant
postmodern model of perpetual crisis, instead foregrounding the potential, and, arguably, the need for problematized sense-making narratives.

Thus if their engagement with metaphysical questions, and their
ostensible theses lead Houellebecq's *fin de millénaire* prose fictions to be
judged by some critics as a return to the *roman à thèse*, what appear to be
totalizing narratives function in fact both to explain and to destabilize.
Houellebecq's representations of turn-of-the-millennium France also
afford a meta-commentary on the problematic of representational practice. Indeed, whilst drawing attention to and performing the problematic
nature of *fin de millénaire* crisis discourses, these texts, sometimes unwittingly, problematize themselves. Houellebecq, then, is interchangeably
writer-perpetrator and writer-critic, and his ostensibly totalizing discourses

---

[129] 'History exists, it commands, it dominates, it's inescapable. But beyond the
strictly historical, the ultimate aim of this work is to salute that ill-fated and courageous
race that created us. [. . .] This book is dedicated to man.'

operate as problematic and problematizing simulacra of the utopia of fiction as a sense-making narrative.

IDEOLOGICAL CHALLENGE, CENSORSHIP, AND SELF-NEGATION

To what extent, then, do Houellebecq's *fin de millénaire* prose fictions achieve his exhortation in *Interventions* to take 'un pas de côté', stepping beyond the contradictory crisis discourses of the *fin de millénaire*? Moreover, in view of the scandal surrounding Houellebecq, his fiction, and his own manipulation of crisis rhetoric within and beyond his texts, how successfully do these prose fictions negotiate the risk of appropriation and commodification by the system they seek to challenge? The fame and fortune that resulted from the *affaire Houellebecq* demonstrate that the author is indeed caught in this double bind (corroborated by the subsequent media-inflated *affaires* around *Plateforme* and *Possibilité*). Yet Houellebecq's *fin de millénaire* fictions also indicate that he has an acute awareness of the influence of the mass media and the global market on the contemporary writer, an awareness that is dramatized in his prose fictions.

Another way of reading the figure of Sollers is as a proxy for Houellebecq. Certainly in narrative terms Sollers operates as a means of articulating provocative discourses. Surprisingly, during the *affaire* the 'real' Sollers and Houellebecq appeared together in several interviews. The consummate *intellectuel médiatique*, Sollers perhaps judged it more profitable to harness the media in defence of the man of the moment than to sue for libel for his derogatory portrayal. But what of Houellebecq's alacrity in joining the media fray, priming the pump of crisis with his own inflammatory rhetoric, proffering and withdrawing contradictory statements, despite his call in *Interventions* for the adoption of a critical stance outside consumerist ideology? Houellebecq does not follow his fictional Sollers's concern for toeing the market line: "'Parce que je suis chez Gallimard, vous croyez que je peux faire ce que je veux? On me surveille, vous savez. On guette la faute'" (PE, 243).[130]

---

[130] "'Just because I'm at Gallimard doesn't mean I can just do what I like. They keep a watch on me, you know. They're waiting for me to slip up.'"

How, then, by apparently manipulating the system he seeks to challenge, might Houellebecq attempt to take what appears to be an impossible step to make?

The commercial success of *Les Particules* cannot be contested. Clearly, it paints a negative picture that seems intended to be the antithesis of political correctness. Moreover, given that sex and scandal boost sales, the text was equally clearly destined to be a prime candidate for media attention. However, whatever the commercial motivations of Houellebecq and his publisher, the reasons for the legal proceedings and trial by media of the novel are in no way commensurate with the publicity generated. The graphically sexual content of *Les Particules* has little shock value when compared, for example, with Virginie Despentes's *Baise-moi* (1993) and Catherine Cusset's *Jouir* (1997). As the novel's own *mise en abyme* of Huxley's *Brave New World* makes explicit, the 'utopian' outcome of the narrative is by no means unprecedented, and indeed, as argued above, it is pre-emptively problematized. As the *affaire Sokal* amply demonstrates, the appropriation of theories and discourses of the physical sciences is by no means a novelty in the late twentieth-century French intellectual field, whilst criticism of the ideology and outcome of May 1968 had become something of a commonplace by the thirtieth anniversary of the *événements*. It appears that the challenge lies elsewhere.

Dominick LaCapra's *Madame Bovary on Trial* provides a useful perspective for this discussion.[131] LaCapra examines the reasons generally believed to have motivated the trial of Flaubert for *Madame Bovary*: that the text represented an 'outrage à la morale publique',[132] or that the trial was a pretext for a governmental attack on the subversive *Revue de Paris* where the text originally appeared. He suggests that these hypotheses fail to account for the furore surrounding Flaubert's novel. Instead LaCapra posits that *Madame Bovary* shocked because it committed the ideological crime of putting the legitimacy of the dominant order on trial, so this radical challenge at once explains the novel's impact and the failure of the establishment to meet that challenge

---

[131] Dominick LaCapra, *Madame Bovary on Trial* (Ithaca, NY: Cornell University Press, 1982). See Cruickshank, '*L'Affaire Houellebecq*', for a detailed discussion of the ideological challenge of *Les Particules*.
[132] 'an offence to public morals'.

head on. In LaCapra's analysis *Madame Bovary* destabilized the value judgements and oppositions upon which nineteenth-century French society was founded: Church and State; and marriage versus adultery. However, since both the defence and the prosecution shared the same set of assumptions, the trial reinforced the status quo, and thus avoided the real challenge of the novel: the 'ideological crime' of a text that did not so much deviate from as radically call into question the adequacy of the norms and conventions that it portrayed and by which it was tried.

Likewise in the *affaire Houellebecq* the prosecution and the defence— both in legal terms and in terms of contradictory critical discourses and the left- and right-wing media—share the same set of market-driven assumptions. Assessing *Les Particules* by these terms protects the dominant order from the 'ideological crime' of the text, an intention to destabilize the dominant values not only of the French field of literary production, but also those of the mass media and neoliberalism. Perhaps, then, this is a literary attempt to precipitate crisis in the hope of opening up the question of alternatives. Indeed one of the factors which differentiate Houellebecq's fiction from the other *fin de millénaire* legal-cum-literary scandals discussed in Chapter 1 is what seems to be a pre-emptive attempt to manipulate the inevitable inscription of his fiction in the order of the media. In other words, by playing on its own ambivalence, *Les Particules* takes the risk of perpetuating the norms and conventions that it portrays in its attempt to radically challenge them. Yet by doing so, it is caught in a mediatized double bind made all the greater by Houellebecq's failure to problematize the discourses apparently designed to provoke both within and beyond his prose fictions. This study seeks to avoid the all-too-frequent critical pitfalls of identifying Houellebecq with his protagonists, or interpreting fictional discourses as an expression of Houellebecq's beliefs. However, because their protagonists' provocative discourses are unproblematized, the discussion seeks not only to investigate their narrative functions and the extent to which they are critically situated in relation to the discourses of the market and the media, but also to bring them into question.

The provocative strategies of *Les Particules* are prefigured in *Extension*. The narrator makes knowingly racist remarks: 'un Noir écoute son walkman en descendant une bouteille de *J and B*. [...] Un animal, probablement dangereux. J'essaie d'éviter son regard, pourtant relative-

ment amical' (EDL, 82).[133] There are also recurrent misogynist procla-
mations: 'Impitoyable école d'égoïsme, la psychanalyse s'attaque avec le
plus grand cynisme à de braves filles un peu paumées pour les trans-
former en d'ignobles pétasses, d'un égocentrisme délirant, qui ne
peuvent plus susciter qu'un légitime dégoût' (EDL, 103).[134] In *Les
Particules*, childhood memories and feelings of sexual and financial
inadequacy that solicit readers' sympathy and/or identification seem
intended to amortize Bruno's frequently odious diatribes. They can
thus be read as part of a self-conscious strategy. Meanwhile, the graphic
scenes have been dismissed as a voyeuristic sales-generating strategy,
occluding any implicit critique, and running the risk of further perpetuating the exploitation of desire and institutional misogyny. Take for
example Redonnet's comment: 'ce roman ne connaîtrait pas un tel
succès s'il ne faisait jouir le lecteur par le récit complaisant de la névrose
sexuelle de Bruno.'[135] Yet the sexually explicit content of Houellebecq's
texts is no more shocking than that routinely manipulated by the
mainstream media and the global market, strategically exemplified by
the sexual violence detailed in citations from *Newsweek*, or by Bruno's
massive bills from Minitel and telephone sex services. Perhaps, however,
by featuring a proliferation of sexual microcosms and relating in detail
Bruno's frustration, Houellebecq seeks to exceed the norms of media
voyeurism—an excess which exposes the all-consuming tyranny of
sexual competition and demonstrates how the channelling of pornogra-
phy into the mainstream decreases its potential to shock.

So, if readers are to assume that the absence of an explicit critical
stance with regard to patently provocative discourses is deliberate (and
given the above discussion of these narrative strategies, it is a fair
assumption), perhaps this is an attempt by Houellebecq to avoid the
recuperation of critical discourses by the media. Yet in doing so the
author runs other risks: not only of being identified with the words of

---

[133] 'a black guy is listening to his walkman while polishing off a bottle of J&B. [. . .]
An animal, probably dangerous. I try to avoid eye contact, although he looks quite
friendly.'
[134] 'A ruthless school of egotism, psychoanalysis cynically lays into decent, slightly
fucked-up women and transforms them into vile bitches so wildly egocentric that they
warrant nothing but contempt.'
[135] Redonnet, 'La Barbarie postmoderne', p. 60: 'there is no way the novel would
have been so successful without the cheap thrills of Bruno's sexual neuroses.'

his protagonists and narrators, but also that what may be intended as implicit criticism may become complicit with its objects.

Such is the case with the novel's disturbing emphasis on paedophilia. One way of interpreting Bruno's pursuit of teenage girls is as a critique of the changes brought about by the influence of the American model of neoliberalism and sexual liberation, whereby the fear of ageing and the cult of youth are produced alongside material and sexual desire: 'il songeait au vampirisme de la quête sexuelle [. . .]. La plupart des pédérastes [. . .] préfèrent les jeunes gens entre quinze et vingt-cinq ans; au delà il n'y a plus, pour eux, que de vieux culs flapis' (PE, 131–2).[136] Houellebecq's suggestion is that the desire for young flesh is at once produced and legitimized by the patriarchal sexual economy. The outcome of Bruno's propositioning of one of his female pupils demonstrates this collusion: 'Le dossier prenait un tour plus classique. Un enseignant dépressif, un peu suicidaire, qui a besoin de reconstituer son psychisme' (PE, 246).[137] Bruno 'gets away' with abusing an under-age girl since his act is a result of the production of unrealizable desire that must nonetheless be dissimulated because an overt sanction would entail exposing the failure of the system of which Bruno is a part.

Homophobia also undercuts what appears to be an attempt to avoid the double bind risked by critiques of the re-packaging of suffering into a spectacle, such as Farrell's analysis of 'post-traumatic culture', and Lipovetsky's critique of 'la société post-moraliste',[138] whereby buying into 'ethical' concerns becomes the only way for the subject to confer some sense of transcendence:

Une chose était certaine: plus personne ne savait comment vivre. Enfin, il exagérait: certains semblaient mobilisés, transportés par une cause, leur vie en était comme alourdie de sens. Ainsi, les militants d'*Act Up* estimaient important de faire passer à la télévision certaines publicités, jugées par d'autres pornographiques, représentant différentes pratiques homosexuelles filmées en gros plan. Plus généralement leur vie apparaissait plaisante et active, parsemée

---

[136] 'he pondered the vampiristic quality of the pursuit of sex [. . .]. Most pederasts [. . .] prefer youngsters between fifteen and twenty-five years old; older than that it's just tired old arseholes.'

[137] 'The case was taking more conventional shape. A depressed teacher, with suicidal tendencies, who needs to get his head together again.'

[138] Gilles Lipovetsky, *Le Crépuscule du devoir: L'Éthique indolore des nouveaux temps démocratiques* (Paris: Gallimard, 1992): 'post-ethical society'.

d'événements variés. Ils avaient des partenaires multiples, ils s'enculaient dans des *backrooms*. Parfois les préservatifs glissaient, ou explosaient. Ils mouraient alors du sida; mais leur mort elle-même avait un sens militant et digne. Plus généralement la télévision, en particulier TF1, offrait une leçon permanente de dignité. (PE, 149)[139]

If the suggestion here is that the media provide an artificial gloss of purpose to life and that reality television formats commodify trauma, potential critical impact is undercut by the glib evocation of AIDS as a specifically homosexual affliction, or worse still, a homophobic meting out of retribution.

So, an apparently self-conscious pre-empting of criticism significantly dilutes the strength of such arguments and their potential impact. Whilst Echenoz's perpetuation of misogynist stereotypes appears to be unintentional, Houellebecq seems to seek to forestall accusations of misogyny. Caricatures of the half-brothers' mother Janine and the female holidaymakers at the Espace du Possible/Lieu du Changement are juxtaposed with an expression of ostensible compassion for the suffering of women losing their currency in the sexual economy. Annabelle's account of her experience appears to be empathetic of women who are doubly commodified sexual objects: "'C'est pénible, à la fin, d'être considérée comme du bétail interchangeable'" (PE, 290).[140] However, neither Annabelle nor Christiane challenge the socially constructed quest for nubile female flesh, and they too embody misogynist stereotypes. Annabelle has a luminous beauty. Christiane proactively fulfils a series of male sexual fantasies. The unquestioning service of the grandmothers and their hatred of the 'bad mother' Janine at best evidences a tokenistic idealization of female sexuality, and at worst bespeaks an intractable misogyny, articulated without self-reflexivity

---

[139] 'One thing was for sure: no-one knew how to live any more. Alright, that was an exaggeration: some people seemed to be mobilized, caught up in supporting a cause, and hence their lives seemed to gain some weight of meaning. That's why *ACT UP* campaigners deemed it necessary to put certain advertisements on television, that some people considered pornographic, featuring close-ups of various homosexual practices. More generally, their lives looked pleasant and full, punctuated by a range of events. They had multiple partners, they buggered one another in backrooms. Sometimes a condom split or exploded. Then they died of AIDS, but even their deaths had a kind of militant dignity. Indeed, television generally, and TF1 in particular, delivered constant lessons of dignity.'
[140] "'It gets to you, in the end, being treated like an interchangeable piece of flesh.'"

in a comprehensive range of clichés. Meanwhile, the feminine attributes which enable love and provide the blueprint for the cloned post-human race can be read as equally clichéd, not to mention as a structural requirement of the narrative, as they are necessary to engineer the ambivalent conclusion of *Les Particules*.

Similarly the already dubious comments on paedophilia attributed to Christiane are further undermined by an analysis of a self-negating outcome for feminism: 'Le désir sexuel se porte essentiellement sur les corps jeunes [...]. Faisant partie d'une génération qui—la première à un tel degré—avait proclamé la supériorité de la jeunesse sur l'âge mur, elles ne pouvaient guère s'étonner d'être à leur tour méprisées par la génération appelée à les remplacer' (PE, 133).[141] Still more troublingly, Houelle-becq's female protagonists seem to be punished for their sexual liberation (Christiane is paralyzed in a *club échangiste*, and Annabelle develops cancer of the uterus, implicitly as a result of her abortion, multiple relationships, and childlessness). Indeed Houellebecq's treatment of abortion is particularly suspect. On the one hand, the leering male doctor who treats seventeen-year-old Annabelle is ostensibly a mouthpiece for the hypocrisy inherent in the 'therapeutic' discourses that legitimize the crises produced by the sexual economy: 'Depuis le début il soutenait la lutte des femmes [...]. C'était pour des filles comme elles qu'ils avaient lutté, indiqua-t-il; pour éviter qu'une fille d'à peine dix-sept ans ("et en plus jolie" faillit-il ajouter) ne voie sa vie gâchée par une aventure de vacances' (PE, 110–11).[142] On the other, the emotional fallout from Annabelle's abortion (luridly, the result of a one-night stand with future snuff movie director David di Méola) is not addressed. So abortion also appears to be a narrative function, harnessed as a corroboration of the novel's particular view of the *fin de millénaire*. It is not surprising then that such reactionary representations of woman as idealized sex object, mother-figure, virgin/whore, purely reproductive function, or simply inferior provokes Redon-

---

[141] 'Sexual desire is essentially directed at young bodies [...]. As part of a generation which claimed the superiority of youth over mature age—and the first to do so quite so vociferously—these women could hardly be surprised to be scorned in turn by the generation that was destined to replace them.'

[142] 'Right from the start he had been a supporter of the women's movement [...]. It was precisely for girls like her that they'd fought, he suggested; so that a girl of barely seventeen years old ("and pretty with it", he just stopped himself from adding) would never have to have her life ruined by a holiday romance.'

net, for example, to identify a 'double jeu hypocrite auquel l'auteur excelle'.[143]

These profoundly problematic discourses detract from the critical potential of Houellebecq's representation of the dual sexual and material economies featured in *Extension* and *Les Particules*. Of course, by drawing attention to how such odious discourses may deflect from the ideological challenge of Houellebecq's fiction, this study does not seek to condone prejudices, be they Houellebecq's or those of *fin de millén-aire* France. However, nor does the present analysis seek to set up an opposition of the politically correct and the politically incorrect. An opposition which, as critical responses demonstrate and Redonnet cautions, may provide a further means of avoiding the challenge of the text: 'Cette tartufferie postmoderne permet de retourner contre le lecteur trop critique le procès qu'il pourrait faire au romancier: le lecteur qui ose émettre une critique n'est qu'un adepte de la pensée unique, un censeur et un inquisiteur voulant châtrer la littérature au nom du politiquement correct et de la bien-pensance.'[144] Rather, this reading seeks to identify how Houellebecq's ideological sleights of hand constitute the dark underside of fictions which nonetheless attempt to resist their own inscription in contradictory crisis discourses. Fictions which may indeed seek to mobilize their own ambiguities in order to call into question their own manipulation of crisis tropes aside from those generated and exploited by the global market and the mass media. So the intention is also to underpin how Houellebecq's fiction challenges the status quo by bringing pressing issues to the fore, and how its reception dramatizes the inadequacy of institutional responses to them. From a perspective similar to LaCapra's on *Madame Bovary*, then, the would-be ideological crime of *Les Particules* offers an analysis of pressing contemporary anxieties to which readers may not wish to subscribe, yet in which they are inscribed. An inscription that the media

---

[143] Redonnet, 'La Barbarie postmoderne', p. 62: 'a hypocritical double-crossing the author excels at'.

[144] Ibid., p. 62: 'This postmodern hypocrisy means that the novelist can turn precisely the kind of objections made by readers considered too critical back against them: the reader who dares express a critical opinion is nothing more than a blinkered sheep, a censor, or an interrogator who wants to castrate literature in the name of political correctness and right thinking.'

and the market (and the literary and critical fields dependent on them) cannot confront without bringing their own legitimacy into question.

By these terms, whilst *Extension* and *Les Particules* evidence unproblematized misogyny, homophobia, and racism, they not only foreground the crises arising from these institutionalized prejudices, but also the critical failure to grapple with the challenges inscribed in the works. A failure in turn articulated in the critical stances adopted during the *affaire Houellebecq* wherein the discourses of the left and right are comfortable clichés, and for the most part, a concern to be perceived as politically correct defends against original thought rather than encourages it.

Thus, life imitates art, or the critical reception of *Les Particules* operates as a troubling simulacrum of the text. Not only does Houellebecq's prose fiction perpetuate misogynist, sexual, and racial prejudices, but the *affaire* it generated also encapsulates the dangerous potential of the manipulation of crisis discourses. *Les Particules* and the *affaire Houellebecq* can be read together not only as a radical challenge, but also as an at once deliberate and unintentional dramatization of the ramifications of the failure to rise to that challenge. From their misogynist, homophobic, and racist discourses to their representation of the parallel economies of material and sexual desire, and of the failure of intellectual responses to scientific and technological advance, the challenge attempted by *Les Particules* and *Extension* is more than a call to step outside of the double bind of appropriation and commodification. It implies the need for a complete change of sense-making narratives. However, since the unquestioned articulation of misogyny, homophobia, and racism in *Les Particules* and *Extension* perpetuates that of the mass media and the global market, the challenge is neutralized by the system it seeks to subvert. Paradoxically, then, at a time when the traumas of individuals and natural, economic, or ecological disasters are processed into self-contained dramas; and unsettling analyses of causes and effects of tragedies, financial crises, and the ramifications of scientific discoveries are dissimulated; the failure of Houellebecq's attempt to challenge dominant discourses that he represents as having the power to orchestrate the ultimate turning point—the end of the human race—is a cause for concern.

Yet the very problematic nature of *Extension* and *Les Particules* and the scale of the *affaire Houellebecq* suggest that these two texts should not be dismissed as examples par excellence of the *fin de millénaire* double bind of co-implication and commodification. Nor should Houellebecq's prose fiction and its critical reception be classed as symptoms of a terminal *crise du roman*. Indeed, the sense of urgency of these texts suggests a far more positive prognosis for the potential of French prose fiction. To be sure, the ideological challenge of *Les Particules* and *Extension* is at once undermined by Houellebecq's own manipulation of crisis narratives and sublimated by the order it seeks to challenge. Nonetheless, by subverting utopian narratives and projecting an apocalyptic end to *Les Particules*, Houellebecq introduces the notion of the potential and the *need* for change. Indeed, by manipulating and seeking to challenge *fin de millénaire* crisis discourses and literary tropes of crisis these strategically ambiguous texts emphatically bring the notion of the agency and the responsibility of the writer back into the intellectual arena. Thus, contrary to the perceived cultural dominant of perpetual crisis, by problematizing and problematically manipulating crisis narratives—both those of prose fiction and those of the mass media and the global market—Houellebecq demonstrates that literature still possesses the power to move, to shock, and to bring into question potentially gravely dangerous institutionalized contradictions.

4

Christine Angot: trauma, transgression, and the *write to reply*

In 1986 Christine Angot turned her back on a career in Law to write full time. Although benefiting from the advice of writers such as Le Clézio and Quignard, she spent four years seeking a publisher before her first prose fiction, *Vu du ciel,* came out in 1990 with L'Arpenteur, an offshoot of Gallimard. *Not to be* (1991) and *Léonore, toujours* (1994) followed, but poor sales led to her delisting in 1994. Fayard then took Angot on, publishing *Interview* (1995), *Les Autres* (1997), and *Sujet Angot* (1998). Critical interest in her work grew slowly until in 1999 *L'Inceste* generated intense media coverage. This, in turn, provided Angot with material for *Quitter la ville* (2000). Angot also writes for the stage, and the generic boundaries between her prose fiction and theatre are porous, thus several plays are adaptations of prose texts including *L'Usage de la vie* (1998), *Nouvelle Vague* (1998), *Même si* (1998), *Normalement* (2001), and *La Peur du lendemain* (2001). Angot remains a prolific writer of prose fiction: *Pourquoi le Brésil* (2002) provided the basis for a 2003 Laetitia Masson feature film *Pourquoi (pas) le Brésil,* and was followed by *Peau d'âne* (2003), *Les Désaxés* (2004), *Une Partie du cœur* (2004); *Rendez-vous* with Flammarion in 2006; and *Le Marché des amants* with Seuil in 2008, the last two, true to controversial form, luridly recounting unsuitable love affairs.[1]

[1] Analysed here: Christine Angot, *Vu du ciel* (Paris: L'Arpenteur, 1990); *Not to be* (Paris: L'Arpenteur, 1991); *Léonore, toujours* (Paris: L'Arpenteur, 1994); *Interview* (Paris: Fayard, 1995); *Les Autres* (Paris: Fayard, 1997); *Sujet Angot* (Paris: Fayard, 1998); *L'Inceste* (Paris: Fayard, 1999); and *Quitter la ville* (Paris: Fayard, 2000). Angot's other texts are *L'Usage de la vie* (Paris: Fayard, 1998); *Nouvelle Vague* (Paris: Fayard, 1998); *Même si* (Paris: Fayard, 1998); *Normalement* (Paris: Fayard, 2001); *La Peur du lendemain* (Paris: Fayard, 2001); *Pourquoi le Brésil* (Paris: Fayard, 2002); *Peau d'âne* (Paris: Fayard, 2003); *Les Désaxés* (Paris: Fayard, 2004); *Une Partie du cœur* (Paris: Fayard, 2004); *Rendez-vous* (Paris: Flammarion, 2006); and *Le Marché des amants* (Paris: Seuil, 2008).

With the exception of *Vu du ciel* (where the narration is shared by twenty-nine-year-old student Christine, and her guardian angel, Séverine, a six-year-old victim of a fatal sex crime), and *Not to be* (a first-person account by a male protagonist paralysed and struck dumb by a wasting illness), Angot's prose fictions feature a protagonist 'Christine Angot', who is also a writer. 'Christine Angot' is the first-person narrator of *Léonore, toujours, Interview, Les Autres, L'Inceste*, and *Quitter la ville*. She has an (ex-) husband Claude who narrates *Sujet Angot*, a daughter Léonore, a mother Rachel Schwartz, and a father Pierre Angot, names that correspond to members of the writer Angot's family. These prose fictions all feature intensely personal crises. Breakdowns of heterosexual, homosexual, family, marital, and extra-marital relationships are interwoven with the crises of a young mother and of a writer. These personal crises are set in a broader context of tangible mid- to late twentieth-century traumas including the Holocaust, the Rwandan genocide, violence in the *banlieues*, AIDS, and sexual abuse. Underpinning these different traumas and at the nexus of the six later narratives is a twelve-year period of father-daughter incest suffered by 'Christine Angot' from the age of fourteen. Accounts of crises generated and manipulated by the media and the market and those specific to the French literary field are also recurrent features. Indeed, Angot's *fin de millénaire* prose fictions increasingly interpellate the media, and 'Christine Angot' appears at once as product, pawn, manipulator, and critic. This invites an investigation of the extent to which Angot is simultaneously analyst, symptom of, and contributor to the *fin de millénaire* aesthetics of crisis.

CRITICISM, CONTRADICTION, AND ELISION

In a media circus echoing that surrounding Houellebecq's *Les Particules élémentaires* the previous autumn, *L'Inceste* became *the* literary scandal of the 1999 *rentrée littéraire*. The *affaire* took off when Angot appeared on Pivot's *Bouillon de culture* on 3 September 1999. The programme was (down) marketed as 'Les écrivains sont des êtres bizarres'.[2] It also

---

[2] 'Writers are strange beasts.'

featured Amélie Nothomb, Nicolas Genka, and Jean-Marie Laclavetine, *chef de collection* at Seuil. When Pivot canvassed his guests' opinion on the publisher's novel, he failed to ask Angot, who upbraided the presenter then slated the book. This clash was arguably stage-managed, for although Pivot claimed ignorance, 'Laclav' had turned down Angot's work. It certainly provided a boost to Angot's notoriety and to sales of *L'Inceste* whilst setting a precedent for media coverage of Angot and her prose fiction amidst which, for the most part, the question of incest is elided. Angot swiftly became a media pundit, whose frequently provocative contributions range from pieces in *Libération* and a monthly column for the FNAC's in-house magazine *Epok*, to appearing in an interview with Houellebecq in *Elle*, which literally put the two authors in bed together as the *enfants terribles* of the literary scene.[3]

Since 1999 Angot's prose fictions have been assessed by French literary critics through the lenses of the furore surrounding *L'Inceste* and of contemporary debates about *autofiction*. Writing for *Le Figaro*, Benoît Duteurtre epitomizes a tendency to deflect from the crises that recur in Angot's work, dismissing *L'Inceste* as representative of 'une littérature floue, nombriliste et intraduisible: une avant-garde de sous-préfecture entre Beckett et France Télévision'.[4] In *Le Monde* Josyane Savigneau also identifies *L'Inceste* as transgressing the norms of homogenized cultural production and political correctness: 'Voilà bien des choses qu'on ne profère pas, et surtout qu'on n' écrit pas, dans une société du soft, du light.'[5] Even before *L'Inceste*, Thierry Guichard of *Le Matricule des Anges* describes Angot as a maggot boring into the heart of consumer culture by manipulating promotional techniques and discourses: 'Ainsi, l'œuvre de Christine Angot pourrait-elle être comparée à un ver, bien installée dans le fruit de notre société du spectacle [. . .] l'écrivain fourbit toutes les armes que la télévision et une certaine

---

[3] Christine Angot and Michel Houellebecq, 'Volée de plumes', *Elle Magazine*, 20 September 1999, 146–9.
[4] Benoît Duteurtre, 'Christine Angot: Une avant-garde de sous-préfecture', *Le Figaro*, 19 November 1998: 'representative of a murky, navel-gazing untranslatable kind of literature: a second-rate avant-garde that falls somewhere between Beckett and France Télévision'.
[5] Josyane Savigneau, 'La Force Angot,' *Le Monde*, 3 September, 1999: 'Here there is a whole host of things that no-one dare mention, let alone write about in this soft-core, society *lite*.'

presse trouvent inoffensives tant qu'elles font parties de leur propre arsenal'.[6] However, critics rarely confront how, exceptionally, Angot's writing breaks through the prohibition built on silence and elision that enduringly surrounds the incest taboo.

A growing body of scholarly analyses of Angot's *fin de millénaire* prose fiction indicate that it is more than an ephemeral market-driven phenomenon. Here incest is discussed, particularly in terms of its intersection with contemporary academic concerns (notably feminism, *autofiction*, and post-Freudian notions of language and subjecthood). Alex Hughes investigates how Angot's work differs from contemporary figuring of the crises of subjectivity and of representational practice, arguing that from *Léonore, toujours* through to *L'Inceste*, incest operates intra-narratively, centring the narrating subject and constituting an attempt to tell of the experience of incestuous sexual abuse whilst simultaneously exploiting and depending upon 'the tension between fictional and referential discourse'.[7] Gill Rye figures 'Christine Angot' as a Foucauldian author figure and a Kristevan *sujet en procès*, and analyses Angot's 'rhetoric of uncertainty'.[8] She also discusses how Angot figures mothering and argues that Angot's representation of it is intended to confront readers with their own prejudices. Keith Reader situates Angot's fiction as a challenge to phallic domination, describing how 'incest' operates as 'a metonym for a textual strategy, that brings together elements normally kept apart, often by taboos of which that of biological incest is the most striking and powerful'.[9] Marion Sadoux identifies common features in Angot's *fin de millénaire* prose fictions: a meta-textual blurring and questioning of established genres; the exploitation and questioning of the status of fiction; and continuity of

[6] Thierry Guichard, 'Christine Angot: La Bâtarde libre', *Le Matricule des Anges*, November–December 1997, <http://www.lmda.net/mat/MAT02125.html> (accessed 22 May 2009): 'So Christine Angot's writing can be compared to a maggot, burrowed deep inside the fruit of our spectacular society [...] the writer brandishes all the weapons of television that cause no offence whatsoever to certain journalists when they wield them themselves.'

[7] Alex Hughes, '"Moi qui ai connu l'inceste, je m'appelle Christine" [I have had an incestuous relationship and my name is Christine]: Writing Subjectivity in Christine Angot's Incest Narratives', *Journal of Romance Studies*, 2/1 (2002), 65–77, at p. 65.

[8] Gill Rye, 'Il faut que le lecteur soit dans le doute: Christine Angot's Literature of Uncertainty', *Dalhousie French Studies*, 68 (2004), 117–26.

[9] Keith Reader, *The Abject Object: Avatars of the Phallus in Contemporary French Theory, Literature and Film* (Amsterdam and New York: Rodopi, 2006), p. 152.

172   *Fin de millénaire* French Fiction

material and of temporality in the construction of the 'Christine Angot' protagonist. Intersecting with the mainstream press coverage discussed above, Sadoux also gestures to an implicit questioning of the relationship between the mass media and the literary field: 'One of the great merits of Angot's works is the way they question, albeit indirectly, the nature of literature in an age in which intimacy, privacy and personal histories are so relentlessly mediatized and exploited, and real lives are packaged, performed and televised for an audience.'[10]

Meanwhile in France serious critical opinion is divided, in particular over the tension between Angot's transgression of taboos and her ostensible courting of the media. Contradicting Claude Arnaud's and Marc Lambron's discussion of *autofiction* as an exhibitionist '"piercing" littéraire',[11] Jean-Luc Douin, editor of *Le Monde des livres* describes Angot as a radically counter-cultural writer: 'Elle rue, dénonce, brocarde, s'extirpe de ce "bandeau social" trop souillé, [. . .] fait les procès des castes et des polices.'[12] Literary polemicist Pierre Jourde also touches on the question of the relationship between Angot's prose fiction, the media, and the market. In *La Littérature sans estomac* Jourde begins an otherwise acerbic assessment by describing *L'Inceste* as a burning aerolith searing through consumer complacency to expose a taboo that has been avoided by the manipulation of crisis by (reality) television: 'Notre société est pleine de tabous. Sexuels, surtout. Qui, dans notre monde corseté de respectabilité bourgeoise, a le courage de s'exhiber, nu, devant le public? On ne voit ça nulle part. Même pas à la télévision.'[13] *NRF* director Michel Bradeau dismisses the featuring of incest in Angot's writing as a commercial calculation: 'Un thème d'une inconvenance

[10] Marion Sadoux, 'Christine Angot's *Autofictions*: Literature and/or Reality?', in Gill Rye and Michael Worton, eds, *Women's Writing in Contemporary France: New Writers, New Literatures in the 1990s* (Manchester and New York: Manchester University Press, 2002), pp. 171–81, at p.174.
[11] Claude Arnaud and Marc Lambron, ' "Le Piercing" littéraire', *La Revue des deux mondes* (2001), p.10: 'like a literary "piercing"'.
[12] Jean-Luc Douin, 'Contre la société ou tout contre?', *La Revue des deux mondes*, March 2001, 42–7, at p. 47. 'She lashes out, denounces, taunts, and tears away society's "soiled blinkers", [. . .] putting castes and law-enforcers on trial.'
[13] Pierre Jourde, *La Littérature sans estomac* (Paris: L'Esprit des Péninsules, 2002), pp. 70–1: 'The society we live in is full of taboos. Sexual taboos in particular. Who in this world of bourgeois constraints is brave enough to reveal themselves, naked in public? You never see that. Not even on television.'

idéale pour les hebdomadaires'.[14] Claude Burgelin makes links between Duras's use of photographs of her own face and Angot's willingness to become a recognizable figure, lauding instead Angot's ability to fascinate and exasperate.[15] So the mainstream critical elision of Angot's representations of incest; the tendency to categorize her texts under the label of *autofiction* or contextualize them in relation to broader academic concerns; Sadoux's reference to an implicit critical questioning; and Jourde's and Douin's allusions to links between Angot's fiction, taboos, and the contemporary mediascape all invite the question of the relationship between Angot's *fin de millénaire* prose fictions, the market (both global and the French literary field); the mass media (print and audiovisual); and sexual trauma in general, and the incest taboo in particular.

Of her peers Angot responds most vehemently to the critical reception of her work and not only through the print and audiovisual media, but also from within her fiction. Media coverage is constantly cited: fictional, aspired for, real, self-congratulatory, and outraged. However, a craving for recognition and remuneration are juxtaposed with an expression of pain at the invasion of her privacy. Angot's extra-textual comments are equally contradictory. She argues that writers still have the responsibility and the critical potential to counter dominant discourses: 'Ce n'est pas moi qui écrit contre. C'est tout littéraire qui écrit contre la société. Toute écriture qui exprime ce qui est indivisible, ingérable par la société est littérature.'[16] Yet within the same interview Angot denies that literature has any ethical or heuristic purpose: 'En littérature, la morale n'existe pas. La notion du bien, de mal n'existe pas. La littérature n'est ni morale, ni thérapeutique.'[17]

---

[14] Michel Bradeau, 'Avec André Gide sur le pas de la porte', in Yves Mabin, ed., *Le Roman français contemporain* (Paris: Ministère des affaires étrangères, 2002), pp. 13–39, at p. 23: 'a scandalous theme perfect for getting column inches in the weeklies'.

[15] Claude Burgelin, 'Donner son corps à la littérature?: Brèves remarques sur l'écivain et son image en l'an 2000', Jean-François Louette and Roger-Yves Roches, eds, *Portraits de l'écrivain contemporain* (Paris: Champvallon, 2003), pp. 47–58.

[16] Angot in Thierry Guichard, 'En littérature, la morale n'existe pas', *Le Matricule des Anges*, November–December 1997, <http://www.lmda.net/mat/MAT02125.html> (accessed 22 May 2009): 'It's not only my writing that is a challenge. All writers of fiction challenge society. All writing which expresses the things that society cannot figure out or digest is literature.'

[17] Ibid.: 'In literature there are no ethics. The notions of good and evil do not exist. Literature is neither ethics nor therapy.'

The contradictions of Angot's comments on the potential of literature and her self-presentation within and beyond her prose fictions are
particularly clearly articulated in a March 1998 piece in *Le Monde*.
Contributing to the debate over the responsibility of the writer to
combat racism, Angot argues that media-courting intellectuals fail to
recognize elements of themselves in the behaviour of Front National
supporters. She also dismisses the unquestioning commodification of
writers as anti-racist manifesto-signers. Whilst this indicates that Angot
perceives in writing both a responsibility and a potential agency, the
article concludes by figuring a troubling relationship between writer,
text, and reader:

c'est moi qui suis dangereuse, je suis l'agresseur et la victime, la peste et le
pansement. Ne me touchez pas. J'ai vu des images impossibles, si vous me
touchiez vous en verrez aussi. Vous ne voulez pas en voir des images impossibles, où le bien et le mal sont tout confondus, où soi-même et l'étranger c'est
la même chair. Oedipe en a vu des images impossibles dans la vie, quand on
écrit on en voit aussi.[18]

Here what is ostensibly an intervention in a socio-political crisis simultaneously foregrounds conflicts between cultural producer and consumer, and, by referring to Oedipus, also establishes a clear link between
Angot's writing, the trauma of incest, and the need to bear witness to
unsayable trauma. How then do Angot's *fin de millénaire* prose fictions
figure the relationship between writer and the reader and cultural
product and consumer as they place incest at the nexus of a weave of
crises: political, historical, sexual, and personal?

FROM THE *FAIT DIVERS* TO REALITY TELEVISION

With the exception of references to presenters of cultural shows including Pivot, Durand, Poivre d'Arvor, and Ardisson, representations of

[18] Angot, 'Un Béret pour qu'on me reconnaisse', *Le Monde*, 28 March 1998: 'I'm the
dangerous one, I'm the abuser and the victim, the plague and the poultice. Don't touch
me. I've seen terrible images, if you touched me, you'd see them too. You don't want to
see such terrible images, images where good and evil are one and the same, where self and
other are one body. Oedipus, he also got to see terrible images, and when you write, you
see them too.'

television are infrequent in Angot's fictions. That is, with the notable exception of Angot's first novel *Vu du ciel*, which revolves around television news coverage of the sexual abuse and murder of six-year-old Séverine. Here Angot's *mise en scène* of sex crimes reflects the growing influence of reality television on the field of cultural production in general, and on viewers in particular. Desire and voyeurism; simultaneously compelling and repellent images; the neutralization of trauma into a trope; and the co-implication of cultural producer and consumer are all brought to the fore.

Intersecting with the televisual boom in 'true crime' stories and the spectacularization of news reporting, sexual abuse of little girls is at the core of *Vu du ciel*.[19] Angot juxtaposes the crisis of an affluent graduate student obsessed with television coverage of child victims of sexual abuse with the poverty, deprivation, and violence of the *cités*. *Vu du ciel* has two narrators: twenty-nine-year-old Christine and Séverine, six-year-old rape and murder victim from a social housing development in Amiens that goes by the grimly ironic name of *Le-Point-du-jour*. Séverine narrates from a distinctly commercial heaven, which simultaneously distances the narrative both from the televisual transformation of trauma into a trope and from the Christian ideal. The God she serves recruits guardian angels from pre-pubescent victims of sex abuse. He has assigned Séverine a 'subject', Christine, the book of whose life she must write. The text comprises Séverine's verbatim reports of Christine's monologues and her impassive commentaries on them. Christine's monologues are reported in italics and juxtapose details of the child's death and her murderer with the young woman's revelation of her own experience of sexual abuse, and the intimate details of her life. This counterpoint draws attention to the chasm between life in run-down housing developments, the dark underside of post-war modernization and consumerism, and that of the socio-economically empowered consumer. The narrative also challenges contemporary views of misogynist sex crime and paedophilia by foregrounding the tension between desire and repulsion that Angot implies is common to the sex criminal, the victim, the mass media, and the consumer. A tension and co-implication explored and exploited in Angot's subsequent prose fictions.

[19] *Not to be* likewise does not feature incest, although it makes some rather clumsy Oedipal references.

Angot is by no means the first French writer to take inspiration from *faits divers*. David Walker traces the use of trope by writers from Jarry, Gide, and Mauriac through Genet, Camus, Beauvoir, and Sartre to Duras, Robbe-Grillet, and Le Clézio.[20] Pelckmans and Tritsmans identify in the trope a link between the dark underside of consumerism and the commodification of trauma, and describe its use in contemporary French prose fiction as a tentative expression of the potential of literature to resist such mediatized commodification.[21] Taking up this challenge, Angot updates the trope to evoke a fictional television news report. The narrative draws on ghoulish media reconstructions to bring the spectacularization and consumption of trauma into question.

By contrasting Séverine's impassive narration with the media-influenced hysteria of the crowd and Christine's attraction to the murderer-media product, Angot implies that her protagonist's and the scandal-hungry spectators' behaviour is uncomfortably close to the violence of the criminal:

Daniel arrive sous bonne escorte au Palais de Justice d'Amiens [. . .]. Christine se dit: '*C'est assez mon type.*' Il a passé à la télé, on dirait que ça le gêne. Tout le monde le regarde. D'autres essaient d'attirer l'attention sur eux en réclamant sa gorge à trancher. Alors qu'ils savent très bien que ça ne se fait plus. Il arbore un air absent. Sur son T-shirt: *Life is a beautiful crime*, en lettres brillantes sur fond bleu.

'*Assassin, salaud, ordure, fumier*', la foule, dès qu'il s'agit de sexe, est dans tous ses états. Un retraité: '*Lâchez-le et vous allez voir ce que l'on va en faire*'. Le sodomiser, je suppose, en pleine place publique, en pleine gare routière d'Amiens. Amiens, mardi, capitale du monde. (VC, 20)[22]

---

[20] David Walker, *Outrage and Insight: Modern French Writers and the 'Fait divers'* (Oxford: Berg, 1995): 'news in brief'.

[21] Paul Pelckmans and Bruno Tritsmans, *Écrire l'insignifiant: Dix études sur le fait divers dans le roman contemporain* (Amsterdam and Atlanta, GA: Rodopi, 2000), p. 6.

[22] 'Daniel arrives under armed guard at Amiens court [. . .]. Christine thinks, "*I quite fancy him*". He has been on television, and it looks as though he doesn't like it. Everyone is looking at him. Some try to grab a bit of the limelight by screaming that he should be executed. Even though they know that it doesn't happen any more. He puts on a vacant look. On his teeshirt,"*Life is a beautiful crime*" in shiny letters on a blue background. "*Murderer, bastard, pervert, shitbag*", shouts the baying crowd whipped up into a frenzy because it's a sex crime. A pensioner hollers,"*Let him go, and just you see what we'll do with him*". Sodomize him, I guess, in full view of the public in Amiens bus station. Amiens, Tuesday, the centre of the universe.'

This grisly blurring of fantasy and reality bespeaks the influence of a mass media diet of violence on criminal, crowd, and narrator. The murderer's T-shirt is a *mise en abyme* of the dangerous potential of media-generated sexual desire represented in *Vu du ciel*. Séverine's account of Christine's sexualized response to the murderer further foregrounds the *jouissance* bound up in the consumption of violence that fills television screens. Moreover, her inference that media-whipped emotion might easily be converted into yet more violence also speaks volumes of the relationship between the media and the symbolic and physical violence of the world in which the little girl lived and died. Thus the double narrative operates as a trope of multiple co-implication: of protagonists, of cultural producers, and of consumers. Just as Christine is consumer and agent of the media, and Séverine is victim and servant of a sex-crime-generating God, these accounts suggest forms of co-implication with the generation and consumption of violence which readers are presumably intended to identify.

Vu du ciel also brings to the fore that which is left out by the audiovisual commodification of trauma. Rather than serving it up formulaically, Angot unflinchingly adds what is routinely elided by the news media. Instead of spectacularizing violence and neutralizing its horror, she presents the reader with a dispassionate adumbration of the unspeakable details of Séverine's death: how Daniel kissed her, penetrated her, slashed her non-existent breasts, and cut off her lips/labia. And readers are told how Vaseline, paedophile porn, and a blow-up doll are found in the murderer's cramped flat. Angot also underpins how news reporting manipulates and homogenizes unspeakable trauma, then discards it to move on to the next horrific crime, a precedent followed by Christine's obsession with Séverine's tragedy is momentarily diverted by further reports of sex crimes (the chilling frequency of which is implied by victims whose names rhyme with Séverine's: Ludovine and Céline). Although sexual abuse and murder are not specific to late twentieth-century France, Angot's representations of them underpin how in what Farrell calls 'post-traumatic culture',[23] the mass media simultaneously sensationalize and homogenize violence,

---

[23] Kirby Farrell, *Post-Traumatic Culture: Injury and Interpretation in the Nineties* (Baltimore, MD: The Johns Hopkins University Press, 1998).

converting irreparable traumas into tropes, and stoking viewers' appetites for them.

Whilst Angot foregrounds how the unspeakable experience of the female is elided by the packaging of sex crimes into televisual formulae, she also emphasizes how for all the media-reported crimes—those ending in attention-grabbing murder—there are many more hidden. Hidden because the 'good girl' Christine is acculturated to submit to violence, which despite its unspeakable horror, is of no commercial 'value':

Moi je disais oui pour éviter les complications, c'est ça qui m'a sauvée. Car c'est très dur pour un homme de s'entendre dire non, surtout par une môme [. . .]. Les journaux parlent de monstruosités. Que veulent-ils dire par là? Sucer. Non, ça, ça va encore. Caresser les fesses, l'anus, tout ça? ça va aussi. La bouche peut-être oui, le pire c'est la bouche finalement. Y a cause de la salive [. . .]. La bouche du garçon sur le sexe du petit, c'est désagréable aussi, bien sûr, mais le visage reste libre au moins. On peut couper son corps en deux, d'une part, les vraies lèvres, les plus importantes pour l'enfant, de l'autre, celles d'en bas. (VC, 65–6)[24]

Thus within the audiovisual diet of sexual suffering, Angot's protagonist reveals enduring and new misogynist taboos and mass-mediatized modes of eliding them. Christine's disturbingly ambivalent descriptions of her experiences are underpinned by Séverine's refrain: 'L'homme n'a pas bon fond.'[25] So both narrative voices point to misogynist violence, and to the manipulation and generation of it by the media. Nonetheless Christine and Séverine are both more or less co-implicated in the patriarchal systems that produce, commodify, and perpetuate misogynist symbolic violence, and, it is implied here, sex crimes. Indeed, the question of co-implication and consensuality is underpinned from the outset in Séverine's comparison of her own and Christine's experience of abuse: 'Elle, Christine était *presque consentante* [. . .]. Entre violée par un dingue et abusée par un ami, il y a une différence, non?' (VC, 21, emphasis

---

[24] '*Me, well I used to say yes to keep out of trouble, and that's what saved me. Because it's really hard for a man to be refused, especially by a kid [. . .]. The papers go on about unspeakable things. But what do they mean by that? Sucking. No, that, that's not so bad. Being touched up vaginally or anally, that kind of thing? That's not so bad either. It's the mouth, all things considered, it's the mouth that's worst. Because of the saliva [. . .]. The boy's mouth on the little girl's genitals, that's horrible too, of course, but at least your face is free. You can split your body in two, one part with the real lips, the part which really matters to a child, and the part with the lips down below.*'

[25] 'Man is not good at heart.'

added).[26] Dismissing the survivor's suffering as not commensurate with her own, Séverine's question also invites that of the dangers of relativizing acts of sexual violence. This also draws attention both to the patriarchal oppression that silences victims, and to questions television viewers would do well to ask of themselves.

Angot's protagonist namesake is cast at once as victim, manipulator, and consumer, whose comments simultaneously link and problematize the trauma of a 'presque consentante' survivor of sexual abuse with the voyeuristic commodification of trauma by the media: '*Comme Daniel, je suis une cruelle. J'adore les crimes, je suis horrible, crois-moi. Ta souffrance m'excite* [. . .]. *Je suis victime d'une malédiction. Tu m'attires. Pourquoi? Cette malédiction m'anoblit*' (VC, 35).[27] Christine's obsession with the dead child's trauma initially seems to assuage the suffering from her own experience of sexual abuse. For Séverine, meanwhile, at the beginning writing seems to offer some consolation in a heaven that, like consumer culture, privileges idealized stereotypes and dismisses goods perceived as damaged: 'Les gardiens sont tous d'anciens violés [. . .]. Les autres sont appréciés pour leur beauté, servent d'absolu. Nous, défigurés, défoncés, écorchés, émasculés, etc., en sommes réduits aux tâches subalternes: notamment, chargés d'âme. La fonction est ingrate, écrire l'anoblit' (VC, 28).[28] If the use of 'anoblir'[29] by both narrators suggests that Christine and Séverine believe that writing brings cultural equity or relief, it transpires that there is nothing ennobling or consoling about the experiences they have suffered and the suffering they go on to mete out on one another. Thus, whether deliberately or not, Angot links the audiovisual media and her own prose fiction to the commodification and arguably to the generation of sexual abuse. Both activities feed on crisis and create co-implicated victims.

---

[26] 'Christine, well she *practically consented* [. . .]. There's a difference between being raped by a nutcase and abused by a friend, isn't there?'.

[27] '*Like Daniel I'm cruel. I love crime, I'm awful, believe you me. Your suffering excites me* [. . .]. *I'm the victim of a curse. I'm attracted to you. Why? This curse ennobles me.*'

[28] 'Guardian angels are all rape victims [. . .]. The other angels, prized for their beauty, are the ideal. Meanwhile, disfigured, smashed up, bashed around, slashed open, etc., we are consigned to secondary roles, and particularly to soul caretaking. It's a thankless task, so writing ennobles it.'

[29] 'to ennoble'.

Séverine's comment 'Les anges ne sont pas tous blancs' (VC, 99)[30] operates as a metaphor for the writer, for the agent of the media, and for the consumer of audiovisual and written texts. Moreover, the desire bound up in Christine's figurative necrophilia invites the question of the consumption of the Other by the writer and by the reader. Christine's consumption of Séverine's life and death brings the trauma of both child and adult into destructive proximity. Séverine links her decision to kill off Christine to a desire to escape a return to the contemporary hell on earth: 'Ch. pour faire sa vie, reconstitue la mienne et m'en impose la vue [. . .] non, Ch. ne relèvera pas les murs de la ZUP autour de moi' (VC, 70–3).[31] When Christine's obsession prejudices Séverine's desire to be selected by God for his most important mission (choosing the next young victim of a sex crime to provide another guardian angel), Séverine begins to refer to Christine by the truncated 'Ch.'. She resolves to kill her by infecting her with a disease that is disconcertingly suggestive of AIDS.

The tension between the agency and co-implication of cultural producers is also highlighted in the representation of iconic newscaster Christine Ockrent as at once victim and manipulator of victims. Angot describes the manufacturing of Ockrent as sexually attractive, drawing attention to her expensive blouses and immaculate hair. Yet Ockrent contributes to the dissemination of media-generated symbolic and sexual violence experienced by females within and without the public eye. What is more, Christine conflates the idealized image of the newscaster with the notion that all women experience sexual initiation as rape:

Cette femme superbe qui dit 'Pauvre petite Séverine', ça frise l'indécence. Sur certains sujets, on se tait. Elle, non. Mieux, elle ouvre son journal du soir par ton horrible drame. [. . .] Je suis sûre qu'elle pensait à la première fois qu'elle a eu la main aux fesses. Ça a dû la dégoûter, la première fois. Elle a dû pleurer. (VC, 32)[32]

---

[30] 'Not all angels are pure.'

[31] 'To make something of her own life, Ch. is reconstructing mine and forcing me back into it [. . .] no, I won't let Ch. wall me up in that housing development again.'

[32] ' *This superb woman saying, "Poor little Séverine". It's practically obscene. You keep your mouth shut about certain things. But not her. What's more she leads with your appalling story on the evening news. [. . .] I'm sure she was thinking about the first time someone put their hand between her thighs. I bet it revolted her, the first time. I bet she cried.*'

Angot's representation of an iconic media figure as victim; graphic descriptions of sex crimes; the apparently strategic use of a disease recalling AIDS; and Christine's desire for Séverine's murderer are all examples of the provocative ambivalence of the sexual politics of the text. As are the recurrent instances of grim humour that drive home the co-implication of the general public: '"*Si on viole les enfants maintenant*" [...] "*Plus c'est petit, plus ça plaît.*" Les Amiénoises sont jalouses' (VC, 20).[33] This is further underpinned by the account of Christine's mother's silent complicity in the crime that figuratively consumes her daughter's life: '*elle sait que son ami a fait le mal sur moi— l'a mis en moi. Elle a toujours cru que j'aurais pu dire non*' (VC, 57).[34] In turn, the question of co-implication invites that of the relativizing of trauma, and the criteria by which sexual violence is judged to be more or less severe, and all the more provocatively, more or less consenting. Such ambivalence foregrounds the question of the co-implication of both the perpetrator and the audience.

Although also a victim of abuse, Christine is an agent of the media, making her own video of Séverine's funeral. She figures Séverine's life and death as a film, at once as a spectacle and through a self-protective lens: '*À l'enterrement, habillée de noir, je filmais. Depuis, j'ai souvent passé la vidéo*' (VC, 46).[35] Images of filming also crystallize the ghoulish voyeurism of both television news reports and Christine's obsession with '*la vidéo dans ma tête, ineffaçable*' (VC, 46).[36] The protagonist's comment encapsulates the simultaneous revulsion and compulsion evoked in the figuring of father–daughter incest in Angot's subsequent fiction. So *Vu du ciel* makes links between the mass media, the commodification of trauma, and the desiring consumer. It foregrounds the voyeurism of reality television, true-crime programming, and the audiences they attract; their complicity in the construction and consumption of victims; and the mortal danger of media-inflated fascination. Simultaneously it brings into question the co-implication of Angot as writer-victim and that of the

---

[33] '"*I can't believe they're even raping kids now*" [...]" *The younger the better.*" The women of Amiens are jealous.'

[34] '*She knows that her friend did bad things to me, put a bad thing into me. She has always thought that I could have said no.*'

[35] '*At the funeral, clad in black, I was filming. I've watched the video a lot since then.*'

[36] '*the video playing in my head, I can't erase it.*'

arguably voyeuristic reader. And yet more provocatively, that of the victim.

What is more, unintentionally, and perhaps ironically, *Vu du ciel* is a prescient performance of the reception of Angot's subsequent prose fictions. Like viewers of reality television, those critics who figuratively 'kill off' Angot as a narcissist or a shameless *provocateur* do not admit their complicity in the crisis manipulating discourses of the mass media. And just as in *Vu du ciel*, Christine's investigation threatens Séverine's advancement in a commercially driven heaven, so Angot's responses to her critics from within her subsequent prose fictions begin increasingly to consume her writing and its reception.

THE 'ANGOT SHOW'?: EXHIBITIONISM, *AUTOFICTION*, AND THE OTHER

Questions of complicity and of simultaneous compulsion and repulsion are recurrently invited throughout Angot's *fin de millénaire* prose fictions. Beyond them Angot also articulates an acute awareness of the *jouissance* involved in the representation and consumption of the crises of others: 'On inflige des douleurs à l'autre et l'on jouit soi-même de façon masochiste dans l'identification avec l'objet souffrant.'[37] Yet the arguably self-promoting writer perceives herself as a victim: 'Il y a l'idée que je me nourris d'autres mais, quand j'écris, on prend de moi.'[38] Thus Angot foregrounds not only the role of the cultural producer, but also that of the consumer. On the one hand this suggests that her texts can be read singly and severally as an implicit investigation of the relationships between the media, writers, and readers (and thus between cultural producers and consumers). On the other, it invites the question of whether Angot's *fin de millénaire* prose fictions simply reflect the development of reality television in France such that as Sadoux seems to suggest 'she has become the protagonist of a TV show of her daily life'.[39]

---

[37] Angot, 'Un Béret': 'We inflict pain on others, and get off on it masochistically by identifying with the suffering subject.'

[38] Ibid.: 'People seem to think that I am feeding off others but when I write I'm the one who is being consumed.'

[39] Sadoux, 'Christine Angot's *Autofictions*', p. 178.

Intersecting with popular television programming, contemporary academic preoccupations with the everyday, and the development of *autofiction*, Angot's fictions certainly raise urgent questions about the aesthetics and ethics of mediatized intimacy, and the neutralization of trauma by the mass media. This tension is particularly evident in *Les Autres*. Here, the influence of the media on the relationship between writer, protagonist, and others is reflected in a hybrid of the developing forms of reality television that from the late 1980s provided French viewers ever more voyeuristic access to the lives and traumas of others. *Les Autres* offers a lurid fictional line-up that outstrips France's first *reality shows*. The 'others' include an AIDS sufferer, a prematurely ejaculating masturbator, a sexoholic couple, prostitutes, sex telephone line workers, Arab women who suffer abuse (domestic and racial), and a woman addicted to plastic surgery. By representing the consequences of this latter obsession, Angot evokes a grotesque new manifestation of the violence—physical and symbolic—resulting from the imposition of idealized images.

The text also evokes the media homogenization of prostitution when 'Christine Angot' quotes the misogyny of a respected film director on a major cultural television show (a double demonstration of phallocentric dominance and of the influence of the talk show format): 'Le 26 janvier à Bouillon de culture, Bertrand Blier déclare: "Je suis sûr qu'il y a des putes qui ont la vocation, des putes heureuses"' (LA, 103–4).[40] Simultaneously *Les Autres* exposes innovations in the commodification of sex and the development of new technologies that facilitate the process: *Minitel rose, téléphone rose*, and online sex services. Angot interrogates the (lack of) distinction between private and public spaces; self-expression and exhibitionism; normality and perversion; consensual intercourse and rape; fantasy and addiction; and desire and repulsion. Intersecting with the totalizing theories of Houellebecq, she implies that compulsive behaviours are pathologies rooted in the generation of insatiable desire by the mass media and the global market. Thus, appropriating the tropes of popular television, Angot demonstrates how its subjects and viewers are both victims and co-implicated.

[40] 'On the 26 January edition of *Bouillon de culture* Bertrand Blier said,"I'm sure there are prostitutes who have a vocation, who are happy".'

However, if *Les Autres* appears to recount the lives of others, the text increasingly transpires to be 'about' 'Christine Angot'. The interwoven accounts of strangers evolve in counterpoint with that of the troubled relationship of the narrator with her parents-in-law, to whom she refers venomously as 'les autres'. And, beyond that, to the narrator's experience of incest which implicitly parallels other ambivalent relationships featured in the text. Ostensibly *Les Autres* runs the gamut of premises for *reality shows*: from sexual dysfunction and perversion, through domestic violence and family tension, to relationship breakdowns and plastic surgery. However, the personally motivated nature of this literary consumption of others is confronted on the first page of the narrative: 'Je n'avais plus d'idée. J'ai demandé aux autres de me parler. Ils ont des vies, qu'on doit pouvoir raconter. Je me disais. Les autres' (LA, 11).[41] What is more, the enduring trauma of 'Christine Angot''s experience of father–daughter incest is signalled by the use of the imperfect tense, a grammatically expressed continuum which performs how what infuses her writing is not a completed action in the past. Thus the trauma of incest is identified explicitly as the immutable lens through which the narrator's experience and writing is mediated.

This does not, however, resolve the issue of the ethics of the representation of others, either in literature or by the mass media. Indeed, it begs the question, also impossible to resolve, of whether the text seeks to dramatize the problematic of the writer whose subjects are not fictional, on whom the writer must necessarily trade to write. Or, just as daughter Léonore is used in the power games between the narrator and her parents-in-law, are the Muslim women, telephone sex workers, and prostitutes of *Les Autres* mere pawns in an autobiographical game?

Mainstream press criticism often accuses Angot of repeatedly writing the same *autofictional* thing. An accusation that is inaccurate, homogenizing, and lacking in originality, since it is one also levelled at contemporaries as diverse as Patrick Modiano and Annie Ernaux. To be sure, Angot's fictions have characteristics in common with female writers of first-person narratives labelled *autofiction* such as Ernaux, Catherine Cusset, and Marie Nimier and their intersecting concerns for the body, sexuality, and the problematic of representational practice

---

[41] 'I'd run out of ideas. I asked others to speak to me. They've got lives, and it must be possible to write about them. That's what I said to myself. Others.'

(both in terms of writing the self and of writing as a woman). Indeed, commenting on *L'Inceste*, Cusset argues that *Les Autres* can be read as at once an heuristic and an aesthetic departure: 'the bodily struggle with writing [. . .] goes hand-in-hand with an assumed rejection of the well-formed sentence and the novelistic form: a rejection of "literature"'.[42] However, this does not account for the ways in which Angot simultaneously draws attention to the questions of the possibility and the ethics of representing incest and the consensual but conflictual relationship between Angot, her 'Christine Angot' protagonist, and the media. This also invites the question of the extent to which Angot's use of an eponymous first-person narrator-writer is intended to contribute to contemporary explorations of self-writing or indeed to break out of commodified conceptions of *autofiction*.

Within and outside her fiction, Angot dismisses the categorization of her work as *autofiction*. *L'Inceste*, Angot's work most often described as *autofiction*, like *Quitter la ville*, is not labelled 'novel'. In a 1997 interview she states that writers all necessarily 'write themselves': 'Tous les écrivains ne font que ça, que "Madame Bovary, c'est moi". Même ceux qui prétendent avoir tout inventé, tout imaginé.'[43] In her earlier contribution to a Ministère de la culture event on 'le principe de la réalité'[44] Angot prefigures in extensive detail some of the material later used in *Léonore, toujours* and *L'Inceste*, and foregrounds the influence of contradictory consumer and critical expectations on the writer:

Certaines personnes protestent contre l'égocentrisme des artistes et des écrivains [. . .]. Elles voudraient des émotions sans subir l'individu derrière qui en est le principe générateur [. . .]. Les gens préfèrent les extrêmes, l'anormal qui déborde, ils aiment ça plutôt que la force égale qui persiste. Les gens n'ont ni le temps, ni la patience de constater l'immense pouvoir caché sous les apparences uniformes. Pour frapper la foule, emportée par le courant de la vie, l'artiste,

---

[42] Catherine Cusset, 'Nieces of Marguerite: Novels by Women at the Turn of the Twenty-First Century', in Roger Célestin, Eliane DalMolin, and Isabelle de Courtivron, eds, *Beyond French Feminisms: Debates on Women, Politics and Culture in France 1981 to 2001* (New York and Basingstoke: Palgrave, 2003), p. 166.
[43] Angot in Guichard, 'En littérature, la morale n'existe pas': 'That's all writers do: "Madame Bovary is me". Even those who claim they've made it all up, imagined it all.'
[44] 'the reality principle'.

l'écrivain c'est pareil, comme la passion, va toujours au-delà de son but, il exagère toujours la réalité.[45]

Albeit in an ostensible statement of authorial intention that should be mistrusted *sui generis*, here Angot foregrounds the tension between market forces and self-expression. Destined for a limited readership, the text also includes examples of father–daughter incest which later feature in *Léonore, toujours* and *L'Inceste*. Perhaps surprisingly, and contrary to critical dismissal of Angot's evocation of incest as a scandal-mongering ploy, she provides less graphic detail in fictions which are increasingly affected by and arguably court the media.

Claiming illustrious literary and (proto) *autofictional* company, in an interview Angot fleshes out the notion of the link between life and writing as organic rather than conscious: 'Les écrivains ne devraient jamais cesser d'écrire leur vie en fait. Avec le doute qui plane. Sur la vérité. Que Proust ait créé Albertine, c'est génial, car on se demande tout le temps. [...] Le corps en train de vibrer, voilà ce qu'il faudrait raconter. Jusqu'à ce que l'écriture elle-même soit cette vie'.[46] *Sujet Angot* is narrated by Claude. The literary conceit is that Claude is not only writing about 'Christine Angot' in an attempt to get over their break-up, but is also commenting on a text she is writing called *Sujet Angot*, 'excerpts' of which are reproduced in 'his' text. Claude's analyses and his references to critiques of Angot's work simultaneously plug previous novels and pre-empt critical reactions to *Sujet Angot*. Claude's voice also draws attention to a perceived difference between 'Christine Angot''s fiction and that of contemporary writers of *autofiction*, insisting on the innovative nature of the protagonist's literary output: 'Les autres, n'importe qui pourrait les l'écrire. [...] ce n'est pas le sujet Angot. [...] Tu laisses ça à Annie

---

[45] Angot, *Le Principe de la réalité* (Nice: Villa Arson, 1993), pp. 18–19: 'Some people complain about the egocentricity of artists and writers [...]. They want the emotion without having to get involved with the person who is the source of it all [...]. People prefer extremes, abnormality in excess, they like that, not chugging along equably. People neither have the time nor the patience to get to grips with the huge potential that lies beneath uniform appearances. To appeal to the masses, carried along in the wake of life, the artist or the writer, like passion, always overshoots, always exaggerates reality.'

[46] 'Angot, 'L'Usage de la vie', *La Matricule des Anges*: 'Writers should never stop writing about their lives. Cultivating doubt. Doubt about the truth. Proust's creation of Albertine is so brilliant, because you never really know. [...] A pulsating body, that's what you should write about. Such that writing itself becomes that life-force.'

Ernaux, à Catherine Cusset [. . .]. Tu es unique, ton écriture est unique' (SA, 30).[47] While speaking volumes of 'Christine Angot''s ambition, it is presumably also the desire to evade commodification as *autofiction* that Angot's text is intended to perform.

Meanwhile, *Sujet Angot*'s Claude references the impossibility of distinguishing between fact and fiction: 'Le vrai, le faux se mélangent, se fixent' (SA, 12).[48] This is reinforced by the intertextual counterpoint from autobiographical texts he is reading, including Alfred de Musset's *La Confession d'un enfant du siècle*, Gertrude Stein's *L'Autobiographie de Alice B. Toklas*, and Barthes's *Fragments d'un discours amoureux*.[49] These intertexts foreground the diversity of texts classified as autobiographical, thus implicitly bringing into question the commodification of first-person narratives. There are also excerpts from an unspecified Katherine Mansfield novel in English, and a nineteenth-century medical report on masturbation. This latter text also provides the premise for Eve Kosofksy Sedgwick's essay 'Jane Austen and the Masturbating Girl', which suggests a link between writing and sexual pleasure.[50] This question is similarly invited by Angot's citation, which either deliberately or unwittingly also raises that of whether self-writing is little more than a form of textual onanism. These intertexts are interspersed with Claude's quotes from a text within the text named *Sujet Angot*, articulating 'Christine Angot''s invective against Carole Vantroys (the journalist–protagonist of *Interview*) for representing her work as simply an autobiographical confession, and failing to question the self-identity of narrator and writer: 'Tu me connais? On se connaît? Qui t'as dit que je parlais de moi? On ne se connaît pas. Tu n'as pas entendu parler, dans tes études, de la différence auteur-narrateur, ça ne te dit rien?' (SA, 52).[51] Yet Angot's fictions adopt

---

[47] 'Other people, anybody could write like that. [. . .] but that's not for subject Angot. [. . .] You leave all that to Annie Ernaux and Catherine Cusset. [. . .] You're unique, your writing is unique.'

[48] 'True and false mix together, and cannot be separated.'

[49] Roland Barthes, *Fragments d'un discours amoureux* (Paris: Seuil, 1977); Alfred de Musset, *La Confession d'un enfant du siècle* (1836); Gertrude Stein, *The Autobiography of Alice B. Toklas* (London: Chapman & Hall, 1932).

[50] Eve Kosofksy Sedgwick, 'Jane Austen and the Masturbating Girl', *Critical Inquiry*, 17 (1991), 818–37.

[51] 'Do you know me? Do I know you? Who said I'm writing about myself? We don't know each other. Didn't they teach you about the difference between the author and the narrator? Doesn't that mean anything to you?'.

conflicting stances, mapping sometimes onto anachronistic and sometimes onto poststructuralist views of authorial intention, at once inviting
and confounding autobiographical readings.

Examples of ambivalence towards and co-implication in the recuperation of ostensibly autobiographical crises by the media abound. Contradicting 'Christine Angot''s criticism of the journalist's intrusive
questions, the final pages of *Interview* are specifically singled out as
autobiographical, providing in stark, unpalatable detail the information
voyeur Carole Vantroys sought to tease out: 'Voilà ce que je propose.
Pour les curieux, dix pages suivent, très autobiographiques' (INT,
129).[52] However, this apparently deliberately anachronistic label suggests an insolent response to market forces promoting the restrictive
category of *autofiction*, and a similar strategy is adopted for the last
section of *L'Inceste*. Thus, like the linearly narrated autobiographical
addendum to *Interview*, the 'factual' narrative recounting the incestuous
relationship with Pierre Angot contrasts starkly with the hitherto
stream-of-consciousness narration of the text. It seems unlikely that
Angot seeks simply to satisfy her customers or have them believe the
truth claims of autobiography. Indeed, rather than producing a product
conforming to expectations, she confounds them and exposes the
limitations of attempts to categorize (self-) writing.

In *L'Inceste* 'Christine Angot''s pre-emptive dismissing of the market-
driven labelling of the text as *autofiction* is juxtaposed with the consumer
brands that mark the specific memories of father–daughter incest indel-
ibly branded on her psyche: 'Ce livre va être pris comme une merde de
témoignage. Comment faire autrement? Quoi d'autre? Les bonbons
Kréma à l'orange, mais aussi: Le Codec, Le Touquet, la sodomisation,
la voiture, lui manger des clémentines sur la queue, tendue' (I, 171).[53]
This foregrounding of damaging modes of consumption links father–
daughter incest with the relationship between the consumer and the
market, and between the writer and the media. However, like *Les Autres*

---

[52] 'So here's my solution. For the curious, the next ten pages are extremely
autobiographical.'

[53] 'This book is going to be taken for some crappy memoir. But what other way is
there? There's no way around it. What else is there? Orange Kréma sweets. But also the
Codec supermarket, Le Touquet, being sodomized, the car, eating clementines off his
cock, hard.'

it seems that the writing of *Léonore, toujours* is undertaken without concern for the ramifications of the exposure resulting from representations of the intimate details of Angot's and others' lives. Moreover, in the final pages, 'Christine Angot' divulges an interest in financial gain: 'Je sais maintenant que cette sorte de journal va être publié. Gérard n'a lu que les cinquante-six premières pages, mais il pense que ça peut intéresser. Il dit "bien sûr on appellera ça roman". Et moi, quand je pense à toute la douleur, je me dis "pour en vendre combien?"' (LT, 131).[54] This suggests that Angot's *fin de millénaire* prose fictions involve knowing plays on the impossibility of distinguishing between 'Christine Angot' as a textual construct, Christine Angot as a media construct, and Christine Angot. And on the co-implication of cultural producer and consumer, victim and perpetrator. So whilst evading commodification into the product category of *autofiction*, Angot sets up ambivalent and often provocative tensions between individual (and for the most part sexual) trauma and the manipulation and commodification of it by the market-driven and mass-mediatized discourses that these texts seem intended not only to expose, but also to harness.

RECOGNITION AND THE *WRITE TO REPLY*

The ambivalence with regard to media exposure in Angot's fiction also affords a unique insight into the commercial dynamics of the literary field. *Quitter la ville* can be read at once as a vitriolic whistle-blowing targeting figures that appear to regulate the market, and as an insight into the pathology of the writer who seeks success. Here sponsors rig French literary prizes, and, chiming with Houellebecq's portrayal of Philippe Sollers as a commercially pragmatic patron of the arts in *Les Particules*, in *Quitter la ville* Sollers's support for 'Christine Angot' does not translate into a coveted (and lucrative) award. 'Christine Angot' ridicules the commodification of writers into hero and anti-hero stereotypes, seeking to set herself apart from Houellebecq, yet casting

---

[54] 'Now I know that this sort of diary will be published. Gérard has only read the first fifty-six pages, but he reckons it could do well. He said, "of course we'll call it a novel". And me, as I think about all that pain, I say to myself, "after all that how many copies will it sell?"'

herself—perhaps unwittingly—as a product of mainstream popular culture: the super-heroine: 'Une fille sur la Cinquième m'a dit: c'est comme Houellebecq, vous vous mettez minable. Je protestais naturellement. Elle a dit: c'est un compliment, dans vos livres ce sont des antihéros tout de même. Moi: je suis au contraire une super-héroïne' (QV, 150).[55] 'Christine Angot' obsessively tracks the market value of her own works, and weighs up her own cultural equity against that of contemporaries. With acrimonious competitiveness she cites François Bon's refusal to share his experience of setting up a website with a woman seeking to do likewise for her. Philippe Delerm, Jean-Claude Izzo, Amélie Nothomb, and Jean D'Ormesson are presented as outperforming sales of *L'Inceste* only because of the marketing machines behind them. Yet listing Frédéric Beigbeder, Nina Bouraoui, Olivier Cadiot, Christophe Donner, Guillaume Dustan, Anne Garréta, Houellebecq, Lesley Kaplan, and Camille Laurens, Angot (perhaps in spite of herself) provides a literary shopping list of contemporary high (market) values. Later, 'Christine Angot' rues the eventual downturn in sales of *L'Inceste*, just as in the earlier works she describes jostling for place with other writers, craving the recognition and remuneration of literary prizes. However, she also rejects the way she is being commodified as a product. To what extent, then, does Angot *knowingly* manipulate the discourses of the media and the market?

The tensions between life and writing; exhibitionism and voyeurism; and the personal and the profitable are particularly keen in *Quitter la ville*. The obsession with sales figures for *L'Inceste* articulated throughout *Quitter la ville* not only foregrounds the financial precariousness of the writer, but also brings the notion of self-construction through interaction with the media and the market into focus. The text features an example directly traceable to Angot's writing about her life outside of her fiction. In November 1999 at the height of her notoriety for *L'Inceste*, Angot agreed to write a guest column for *Libération*, ostensibly about *her* week, but by editorial convention, commenting from a personal perspective on news and cultural events. The death of her father (whose name is the same as that of the Pierre Angot figure in

---

[55] 'A woman from Channel Five said to me: you're like Houellebecq, you make yourself seem odious. Naturally, I protested. She said: I mean that as a compliment, your books are all about antiheros. My response: Quite the inverse, I'm a super-heroine.'

her fiction) coincided with her stint, whereupon she proposed to write only the briefest of sentences recording his death. When the editor refused, Angot used the space not only to provide a fuller account of her experience of her father's death, but also to bemoan the manipulation of writers by the media: '2 novembre, mon père est mort. Il me semblait que j'avais écrit ma semaine. Mais bon, vous les ferez payer jusqu'au bout d'être des écrivains, jusqu'au bout. Mon père est mort. Mais bon, je pourrais peut-être parler un peu du Stock Exchange.'[56] Angot tellingly contrasts how whilst silence was imposed on the incestuous relationship between 'Christine Angot' and her father, her own relationship with the market and the media, also represented as incestuous, is confrontational. Simultaneously, she figures the elision of the transgression of taboos and the pressure on writers to toe the market line.

A recurrent intra- and intertextual strategy of Angot's *fin de millénaire* prose fiction is the evocation of critical commentary: 'Christine Angot''s on her own writing, academic, and journalistic. In *Sujet Angot* Claude, an academic specializing in English literature, is the vehicle for 'Christine Angot''s responses to her critics (and given that 'real' criticism is cited verbatim, it would seem also the vehicle for Angot's). Although he sometimes articulates ostensibly negative judgements, Claude often operates as an ideal reader, a literary agent-cum-mouthpiece. His status as an academic perhaps belies Angot's desire to confer legitimacy on both *Sujet Angot* and other texts of hers cited. Indeed, Claude writes of a colleague who has renounced his study of Balzac since reading 'Christine Angot''s texts, thus providing fictional corroboration for the positioning of her work as superior to that of other contemporary writers. Claude also comments on the 'work in progress' *Sujet Angot*, previous novels *Les Autres* and *Interview*, and on reviews of these texts, such as Hugo Marsan's 19 September 1997 piece on *Les Autres* in *Le Monde*: 'Dans un monde où chacun se doit de penser et de jouir pareillement, ces dérisoires stratégies pour se croire le personnage unique d'un scénario original ne sauvent plus la liberté individuelle. Angot nous refuse le refuge où l'on se replie [. . .]. Elle supprime le sens de l'exclusion qui

---

[56] Angot, 'La Page noire', *Libération*, 6–7 November 1999: '2 November, my father died. So the way I saw it, I had written about my week. But they really want to make us to pay for the privilege of being a writer. My father had died. But surely I could have commented on the Stock Exchange or something.'

rend la perversion si réconfortante' (SA, 117).[57] By having her academic narrator cite an assessment which is at once positive and specifically situated in the context of *fin de millénaire* consumer culture, Angot presumably wishes to underscore that she approves of this analysis. It also implies a self-perception as a counter-cultural writer.

Moreover, although Claude criticizes aspects of 'Christine Angot''s eponymous fictional text, he singles out its challenging response to the journalist of *Interview* for fulsome praise: 'Il y a une chose, une seule chose, que j'ai bien aimée dans *Sujet Angot*. C'est tout le passage sur Carole Vantroys, la journaliste de *Lire*. Tu lui fais sa fête à celle-là. [. . .] Quand tu assènes, c'est ton style, ça. Elle s'abstiendra, à mon avis, la prochaine fois' (SA, 51).[58] Here and in other texts pre-dating *L'Inceste*, such comments are uncannily prescient of Angot's ambivalent reaction to criticism and media coverage. If a preoccupation with privacy emerges, it contradicts the desire for recognition exemplified by the ambition articulated both in *Sujet Angot* and *Interview* to appear with Pivot, Durand, and Poivre d'Arvor. This desire is fulfilled and arguably magnified by subsequent references to television pundits and appearances that jostle for space with reports of print media coverage. In *Quitter la ville* alone this ranges from weekly publications (from *Livres-hebdo* to *Le Canard enchaîné*; *Les Inrockuptibles* to *Paris-Match*; and *Le Point* to *Le Nouvel observateur*); to monthlies (from *Têtu* to *Elle*); and national and regional newspapers (from *France catholique* to *L'Humanité*; and *Le Midi libre* to *Les Informations dieppoises*).

Contrary to the negative prognoses of the *crise du roman* and to 'Christine Angot''s denigration of her contemporaries, Angot's prose fiction does not express a perception of a literary field in crisis. In *L'Inceste* 'Christine Angot' argues that writers have an enduringly exceptional status, despite their vilification and the lack of comprehension of their contemporaries: 'vous dites qu'écrire c'est toucher les ordures

---

[57] 'In a world where everyone is forced into thinking and getting pleasure in exactly the same way, all those pathetic strategies whereby we cast ourselves as the main character no longer salvage the freedom of the individual. Angot will not let us fool ourselves [. . .]. She denies us the sense of being different which is one of the attractions of perversion.'

[58] 'There's one thing, only one thing that I really liked in *Sujet Angot*. It's that whole bit about Carole Vantroys, the journalist from *Lire*. You really lay into her, don't you? [. . .] When you go in for the kill, that's what your writing is about. I bet she won't try that again.'

[. . .]. Écrivain, c'est quand même une parure' (I, 99).[59] Here, Angot
updates the myth of the *poète maudit*, recalling Baudelaire's conception
of the poet striving for transcendence, yet misunderstood, and whose
halo may tumble into the mud of the city. In Angot's version, albeit
conflated with waste, the jewel is retained: *fin de millénaire* writers keep
their knowingly tarnished halos. Moreover with literary (self-) confidence 'Christine Angot' is described and describes herself as saint and
saviour (Antigone, Mary, Elizabeth, Saint Christine, Moses, and Christ
are evoked). An unbroken stellar literary genealogy is confidently
claimed by and for her (Balzac, Zola, Proust, Beckett, and Duras are
used as favourable comparisons). Nonetheless, this confidence and quest
for affirmation clash with 'Christine Angot''s experience of intrusive
voyeurism, so Angot's *fin de millénaire* prose fictions also invite an
exploration of whether the writer may no longer be an avant-garde
precipitator of a turning point, but instead a product of and contributor
to ephemeral celebrity culture. This also begs the question of the extent
to which Angot courts the media in a way which intersects with
Bourdieu's figuring of the failure of *intellectuels médiatiques* to use
their status to challenge the mass media and neoliberalism from within.

If throughout these fictions 'Christine Angot''s contradictory attitudes towards the relationship between the writer and the conditions of
production provide insight into the negative influence of market forces
on the contemporary literary field, *Quitter la ville* offers a particularly
critical perspective. 'Christine Angot' reports being frozen out by the
Paris literati, leaving readers to surmise whether she is an outcast as a
result of literary snobbery; because of her vitriolic haranguing of established writer Jean Rouaud; because of her avidity for media coverage;
because of envy; or as a result of her transgression of the enduring silence
surrounding the incest prohibition. It is this latter that appears to
underlie *germanopratin* resistance, operating as a microcosm for broader
failures: both critics' avoidance of confronting the inscription of incest
in Angot's fiction and the institutionalized elision of the irreparable
trauma of incest victims. 'Christine Angot' also describes her quest for
literary success as a form of revenge on her father, an attempt to be more
famous, a better manipulator of language than he (a talented linguist

[59] 'you say that writing is getting down and dirty with the worst of things [. . .]. But
being a writer is the best thing.'

and interpreter). Indeed, if the narrator describes sales and notoriety both in terms of revenge and as a gauge of self worth, the techniques, vocabulary, and discourses of the media and the market are recuperated by Angot not only to respond to criticism, but also to harness the potential for critical leverage. Thus, it seems, getting media coverage is a means of having a voice.

Yet for Angot having a voice is not simply a question of being heard. On the one hand her fictions expose how the trauma of incest is still elided by the mass media. On the other, they perform—literally—a literary *write to reply*. Intertextual references to critiques of her work can also be read as an invitation to readers to judge not from mediatized criticism, but from their own reading of prose fictions which all too easily get lost amidst critical furore (*vide* Houellebecq's *Les Particules élémentaires* and *L'Inceste*). However, this strategy risks creating a perception of exhibitionist self-aggrandisement, not to mention inviting readers to judge Angot's writing harshly. It is also necessarily caught in the double bind of dependency on media coverage. Indeed, *L'Inceste* owes its success to its mediatized reception, whilst *Quitter la ville* is dependent upon the subject of its criticism for its genesis, its content, and for its chance of being published. And if the mediatized reception of *L'Inceste* is the optic Angot chooses for *Quitter la ville*, the republication of her earlier texts in *poche* versions highlights how perceptions of value can change in accordance with proven commercial potential.

Interview faces the same double bind since it is at once critical of media voyeurism and dependent upon it for its premise, going largely unread until *L'Inceste* activated precisely that voyeurism. In *Quitter la ville* readers learn that 'Christine Angot' has become such a sure media value that a puppet cited her on the *Canal plus* satirical current affairs show *Les Guignols de l'info*. That the puppet was a caricature of the French football team coach speaks volumes of changing gauges of cultural equity (as does 'Christine Angot''s appearance with David Hallyday on Thierry Ardisson's *Noir sur blanc* cultural commentary television show). The interlude may also be read as a *mise en abyme* of an author categorized by talking heads whose strings in turn are pulled by the market and the media. This suggests that Angot is a double victim: at once of incest and of the commodification of her trauma. Moreover, the trauma of incest is often occluded by 'Christine Angot''s aspirations, so Angot's *write to reply* is further caught in the double bind of co-implication. Yet 'Christine Angot''s references to her own texts and those texts which comment on them ('real' or invented) and her foregrounding of the incestuous relationships between media, text, writer, readers, and critics demonstrate—deliberately and unwittingly—how these relations cannot be separated from complicity in the conditions of textual production. For all the ostensible avidity for publicity, all the name-dropping, Angot's *fin de millénaire* prose fictions express the tension between the perceived prizes and the price of literary success, and between the desire for notoriety and the potential agency of literature to intervene in political and ethical questions.

TRAUMA, TRACE, AND TABOO

In an interview for *Libération* Angot links incest, writing, media exposure, and mental health:

Il y a deux positions pour entrer dans les choses qui ont à voir avec l'inceste, celle de l'enfant, de la douceur, et aussi celle de l'agresseur. Il y a les deux dans mon écriture. Écrire, c'est violer une intimité. Ce moment où j'ai failli basculer dans la folie; on a dit autour de moi: 'elle n'est pas folle, elle est écrivain'. C'est important d'être publié, d'avoir de la presse, c'est une reconnaissance de santé mentale.[60]

Thus Angot suggests that writing—or at least writing by an incest survivor who receives recognition—is a means of preserving some level of mental stability. However, she also suggests it involves replicating the simultaneous seduction and abuse inherent in 'Christine Angot''s account of father–daughter incest in the relationship between the writer and the reader. This invites the question of how Angot's fictions intersect with or diverge from other late twentieth-century incest narratives, and from psychoanalytical analyses of incest (both therapeutic and in terms of infant sexuality).

---

[60] Angot quoted in Mathieu Lindon, 'Trois, deux, un...Angot!', *Libération*, 26 August 1999: 'There are two ways of tackling things to do with incest. Through the child, softness, but also through the abuser. My writing does both. Writing is the violation of privacy. The time when I nearly went mad, everyone was saying, "she's not mad, she's a writer". Being published and getting coverage is important, it's a gauge of mental health.'

In 1981 Marguerite Yourcenar commented on the absence of fictions or myths featuring the desire of the victim and questions of consensuality in parent–child incest.[61] By these criteria, the figuring of incest in Angot's *fin de millénaire* prose fictions is exceptional. Moreover her representations do not fit neatly into any of the categories ascribed by Janice Doane and Devon Hodges to late twentieth-century incest narratives: the 'feminist incest story' (which they suggest runs the risk of overemphasizing the therapeutic potential of anti-patriarchal fervour); the 'recovery story'; the 'incest survivor memoir' (which they fear overstates the therapeutic potential of testimony); and the 'false-memory story'.[62] This last label carries a political charge, as according to the False Memory Syndrome Foundation: 'False Memory Syndrome describes a situation in which a person acquires a memory that is not true but which seems very vivid and real to the person who has it. The memory comes to dominate the life of the person to the detriment of the person and the people involved in the memory.'[63] Despite such troubling, revisionist discourses, Angot does not adopt an overtly politico-ethical position in relation to incest, or to the aforementioned interpretative frameworks. Nor does she overtly engage with post-Freudian thinkers such as LaCapra, Caruth, Felman, and Laub who investigate how trauma cannot be retold and discharged, yet argue that not only in terms of mental health, but also crucially, from an ethical imperative, witness must borne. And this ethical issue is all the more urgent in a field of cultural production where reality television is a dominant influence.[64]

However, the recurrence of incest in Angot's prose intersects with some aspects of the recently theorized phenomenon of Post-Traumatic

---

[61] See Marguerite Yourcenar, 'Postface', *Anna, Soror* (Paris: Gallimard, 1981), pp. 95–115, at p. 113. This 'Postface' was written for the republication of her 1925 novella, a tale of unconsummated incestuous desire between brother and sister.

[62] Janice Doane and Devon Hodges, *Telling Incest: Narratives of Dangerous Remembering from Stein to Sapphire* (Ann Arbor: University of Michigan Press, 2001).

[63] From the back page of the FMS Foundation stationery, quoted in Rosaria Champagne, *The Politics of Survivorship: Incest, Women's Literature, and Feminist Theory* (New York and London: New York University Press, 1996), p. 169.

[64] Cathy Caruth, *Unclaimed Experience: Trauma, Narrative, and History* (Baltimore, MD: The Johns Hopkins University Press, 1996); Shoshana Felman and Dori Laub, *Testimony: Crises of Witnessing in Literature, Psychoanalysis and History* (New York and London: Routledge, 1992); Dominick LaCapra, *History and Memory after Auschwitz* (Ithaca, NY: Cornell University Press, 1998).

Stress Disorder, whereby symptoms are thought to express a sense of being possessed by the traumatic event or images of it.[65] Angot's figuring of incest also intersects with Rosaria Champagne's description of the after-effects of incest as somatized and over-determined, giving rise not only to repetition, but also to multiple determinations of meaning.[66] Repetition is, of course, a recurrent inter- and intratextual feature of Angot's *fin de millénaire* prose fictions. However, whilst references to incest proliferate, they are also often strategic. Indeed, repetition, obsession, and excess are *consciously* expressed through tropes and through performative word play. Thus Angot knowingly figures at once the ways in which incest constantly invades all aspects of life; 'Christine Angot''s awareness of it; and the writer's efforts to harness and manipulate it. All this clearly situated in the context of a mass-mediatized marketplace that elides the traumatic transgression of this oldest taboo.

There are also intersections with and divergences from psychoanalytical frameworks. Psychoanalysis is figured as imbricated in both commercial concerns and in incestuous relationships. In *L'Inceste* 'Christine Angot' foregrounds the tension between recognition, sales, and sanity, revealing their co-implication in the conferring of cultural capital as she rejects psychoanalysis in favour of writing:

Je déteste avoir à écrire ça. Je vous déteste. Je vous hais. Je voudrais ne pas savoir ce que vous pensez. Je sais ce que vous pensez. [. . .] Je suis obligée. C'est la clinique ou vous parler. [. . .] L'écriture est une sorte de rempart contre la folie, j'ai déjà bien la chance d'être écrivain, d'avoir au moins cette possibilité. (I, 171)[67]

'Christine Angot''s use of the vocabulary of co-dependency also reflects the vernacularization of psychoanalytical discourses, but it does not map onto the artificially redemptive promises of a recoverable self perpetuated by reality television.

---

[65] PTSD was formally recognised by American Psychiatric Association in 1980, intersecting with the work on trauma and testimony, and in particular the Holocaust by thinkers such as Caruth, Felman, LaCapra, and Laub.

[66] Champagne, *The Politics of Survivorship*.

[67] 'I hate having to write this. I hate you. I loathe you. I don't want to know what you are thinking. But I know what you are thinking. [. . .] I have to. It's either a psychiatric ward or writing. [. . .] Writing is a sort of defence against madness, so it's a good thing I'm a writer, that at least I have that possibility.'

Neither do Angot's *fin de millénaire* prose fictions fit psychoanalytical conceptions of subjecthood and infant sexuality. Whilst the motif of incest is a key term in psychoanalytical theories, Angot's overt and implied references to psychoanalysis at once recuperate and destabilize Freudian, Lacanian, and Kleinian frameworks. In *L'Inceste* 'Christine Angot' juxtaposes definitions from Roudinesco and Plon's *Dictionnaire de la psychanalyse* and accounts of her behaviour over a three-day period which appear to fit them, but exceed the paradigmatic descriptions provided.[68] The passage begins with a definition of incest, followed by madness, paranoia, narcissism, homosexuality, the subject, suicide, perversion, sadomasochism, Nazism, hysteria, desire, Lacan's master and slave dialectic, and schizophrenia. After this excerpt of psychoanalytical doxa, the narrative resumes under the subheading 'Applications'. Phrases and sentences apparently corresponding to the dictionary definitions are underlined. However, rather than corroborating these descriptions, the text shows how the psychological trauma of incest (and by extension that of other often intersecting symptoms) cannot be contained by clinical descriptors, so Angot implies that psychoanalysis cannot account for, let alone assuage them. In the second part of *L'Inceste* a subhead 'Jeux de mots, jeux d'esprit'[69] introduces a discussion of Freud's work on the Witz. However, rather than simply playing on Freud's theorizing of the desires revealed by plays on words, verbal games in Angot's fiction exceed both Freud's theory and any ludic postmodern celebration of the crisis of language. Often consciously, they flag up the transactional co-implication of analyst and analysand, and of cultural producer and consumer: 'Lecteur, l'électeur, l'élue' (I, 84).[70]

A different kind of play—on naming—also highlights the market-driven legal constraints brought to bear on the writer. 'Christine Angot' quotes what is presented as the 'real' letter from Stock's lawyer threatening prosecution for breach of privacy, and then plays with those names she claims to have changed: 'Ça m'ennuie d'avoir changé les noms. Ça rend le livre moins bon. Mais je préfère, plutôt que de payer

---

[68] Élisabeth Roudinesco and Michel Plon, *Dictionnaire de la psychanalyse* (Paris: Fayard, 1997).

[69] 'Plays on word, mind games'.

[70] 'The lector, the elector, the elected'.

des dommages' (I, 41).[71] The inclusion and subversion of these strictures expresses the tension between the rejection of market-driven legal challenges to the freedom of speech and the writer's commercial motivations. Whether intentionally or not, another self-consciously onomastic segment bespeaks the influence of the media and the market on cultural production, for 'pivot' recalls French television's literary king-maker, Bernard Pivot: 'virgule, petite verge, ça recommence. Comme si ma tête, articulée sur un pivot, avait deux faces toujours présentes, je connecte, j'associe, tout communique, c'est ce que j'appelle ma structure mentale incestueuse. Que j'essaie de réduire un peu, comme une fracture, et une facture. Digression, à partir de fracture-facture, sur le mot d'esprit' (I, 154).[72] What is certain here is that Angot is drawing attention to her own conscious plays on words, linking them with the ever present trauma of incest.

Indeed, differentiating her prose from the figuring of language by Freud and Lacan, instead of verbal symptoms of the return of the repressed Angot's focus is on deliberate, provocative plays on linguistic traces. Conscious plays on words intersect with Derrida's deconstruction (via Lévi-Strauss's analysis of the Oedipus myth)[73] of the false binary oppositions that structure social organization.[74] Angot often foregrounds the co-implication of the reader *qua* consumer, but in a calculatedly provocative fashion she also seeks to figure the parallels between linguistic traces and the way the trauma of incest marks the victim: 'notre tête déconne Déconne, sortir, Ducon, ça veut dire, débloque. Notre tête déconne, tu comprends, elle sort du con, notre tête, mais où veux-tu qu'elle aille?' (I, 158).[75] Metaphors explicitly referencing incest offer new perspectives on post-Freudian and post-

---

[71] 'I'm annoyed that I had to change the names. It takes away from the book. But I'd rather do that than end up paying damages.'

[72] 'little comma, little cock, here we go again. It's as though my head is constantly swinging on a pivot, I make connections, I make associations, everything links up, I call it my incestuous mind. Which I try to tone down, to turn being assaulted into being insulting. But there I go, digressing into word games, assaulted into insulting'.

[73] Claude Lévi-Strauss, 'Le Problème de l'inceste', in *Les Structures élémentaires de la parenté* (Paris: Presses Universitaires de France, 1949).

[74] Jacques Derrida, 'La Structure, le signe et le jeu dans le discours des sciences humaines', *L'Écriture et la différance* (Paris: Seuil, 1967), pp. 409–28.

[75] 'Our heads talk shit Shit, comes out, Shit heads our heads talk shit, they come out from down by our shit holes, our heads, so where next?'

structuralist analyses of the crisis of language: 'J'étais arrivée à un point de non-retour, les associations de mots me menaçaient, des incestes d'idées se produisaient directement dans ma tête [. . .]. Il n'y a aucun cloison, tout se touche, rien n'est intouchable' (I, 157).[76] The notion of desiring complicity in an incestuous relationship is elsewhere expressed by positioning incest as a potentially constructive mental tool for the writer: `avec la structure mentale que j'ai, *incestueuse,* je mélange tout, tout, ça a des avantages, les connexions, que les autres ne font pas' (I, 103).[77]

So in ways that intersect with poststructuralist writing but are consciously manipulated, Angot figures incest through the performance of a slippage of language. This provides the dynamic for sentences that move, for example, from sex to writing; from the narrator's problems with the push reflex in defecation and childbirth (described as a symptom arising from the trauma of incestuous anal penetration) to Auschwitz; and from sealing a homosexual affair with a public kiss to the narrator's injury sustained during childbirth and her infant daughter's vagina:

Quand dans ces pages je confie un baiser comme place Garibaldi ou, radicalement différent, mes problèmes pour chier, surtout l'expulsion, Auschwitz, l'accouchement, mon vagin avec le nerf dans la couture et le sexe de Léonore, c'est comme dans l'amour quand on parle avec des mots vaches et les caresses de seins ou d'autres. Hors du lit, comme hors du livre. Fermée on n'en parle plus. Entre vous et moi c'est fait pour être lu. (LT, 136)[78]

All these provocative examples are linked in implicitly incestuous relations, which, by extension, are akin to those between reader and writer. Thus linguistic performance figures the inability of psychoanalytical frame-

---

[76] 'I'd got to a point of no return, word associations were assailing me, incestuous ideas popping up spontaneously inside my head [. . .]. Nothing can be kept apart, everything is connected, nothing escapes connections.'

[77] 'with the way my mind works, incestuously, I mix everything up. Though it does have its plus points, I make connections that other people don't make.'

[78] 'When I talk about the kiss on the place Garibaldi, or at the other extreme, I talk about the problems I have shitting, with expelling, Auschwitz, giving birth, the nerve in my vagina trapped in a stitch and Léonore's genitals, it's like when you talk dirty when you're making love, and stroking your lover's breasts or somewhere else. What doesn't get out of bed, doesn't go into a book. The chapter's closed, there's not a word to be said. But between you and me, it's there to be read.'

works to account for extreme physical and psychological experience, and at the same time Angot's word play knowingly figures the unknowability of trauma, foregrounding that which cannot be accounted for, or slips away from paradigms.

Critiques that dismiss Angot's narrative as devoid of imagination therefore ignore how her word play at once draws attention to the incestuous relationships of words in conscious linguistic uses; to the analogy of language as the (incestuous) structure of the unconscious; and to how the trauma of incest insistently infuses the conscious and the unconscious. In such instances Angot adds a new perspective to psycho-analytical and deconstructive interpretations, bringing to the fore how the mass media enduringly elide the incest taboo. However, in psycho-analytical terms, Angot's narrative is a secondary revision, a manipula-tion of language and of incest as a trope which links the sex crime with a range of self–Other relationships: writer and subject; cultural producer and consumer; mother and daughter; husband and wife; and lovers. This knowing manipulation necessarily invites the question of the unconscious of these texts: what Angot's fictions may disclose beyond what they consciously articulate.

CRISIS AND FEMINISM

If Angot's use and subversion of Oedipal motifs is intended to challenge psychoanalytical paradigms, they also perpetuate misogynist stereo-types. In *Quitter la ville* 'Christine Angot' casts herself literally—and rather clumsily—in the role of Oedipus. In *Not to be*, the narrator ejaculates as his estranged mother enters the room: '"l'éjaculation devant la mère [. . .]". Du crachat. Quand on a trop de souffrance. Le vomi sort du sexe' (NB, 72).[79] Perhaps unintentionally, this Oedipal *mise en scène*, like many of Angot's other Oedipal references, invites the criticism made by Jeffrey Moussaieff Masson: that Freudian and Laca-nian narratives effectively neutralize incest, describing entry into lan-guage and the constitution of the unconscious as the price of repressing

---

[79] '"in front of the mother they ejaculate [. . .]". It spits out. When the pain gets too much. Like vomit spewing out of the penis.'

incestuous desire.[80] Indeed, Angot situates the trauma of incest in a patriarchal conceptual framework, thus also inviting feminist critiques which identify the misogyny inherent in Freudian and Lacanian analyses of subjecthood. Conversely, in *Léonore, toujours* the mother–daughter relationship is represented as desiring, and the writer 'kills off' her fictional daughter. Like Angot's destabilizing of post-Freudian and poststructuralist frameworks, this begs the question of the extent to which her countering of feminist thought is a deliberate narrative strategy.

To be sure, texts that end by 'killing off' a daughter, feature collusive mothers, and represent victims of incest and sexual abuse as complicit do not correspond to the views of female sexuality expressed in the 1970s and early 1980s by 'second wave' French difference feminists and writers of *écriture féminine*. Angot's representation of childbirth has none of the lyrical celebration of Annie Leclerc's *Parole de femme* (1977).[81] Rather, by representing motherhood as ambivalent, Angot suggests that the reality of female experience does not correspond to the idealism of the female language and libidinal economy envisaged by difference feminists. Nor can these texts be neatly categorized as reflecting 'first wave' French materialist feminism. In *Le Deuxième sexe* Beauvoir described motherhood as imprisoning women, a construct of patriarchal society with which women nonetheless comply in bad faith.[82] Angot neither foregrounds women's choices nor challenges the social construct that women should become mothers. Indeed, arguably, she simultaneously perpetuates patriarchal structures, the mystification of motherhood, and the virgin/whore dichotomy.

In *Not to be* Muriel, who is obsessed with having a child, mounts the narrator in his hospital bed as he lies paralysed and unable to control his ejaculation, prompting his misogynist internalized response: 'J'aurais voulu une vraie vierge stérile' (NB, 79).[83] If this comment and the account of the narrator's lack of control might seem to intersect with the critical perspectives of difference feminists, and is intended as a critique

---

[80] Jeffrey Moussaieff Masson, *The Assault on Truth: Freud's Suppression of the Seduction Theory* (New York: Farrar Strauss, 1984).

[81] Annie Leclerc, *Parole de femme* (Paris: Grasset, 1977).

[82] Simone de Beauvoir, *Le Deuxième sexe* (Paris: Gallimard, 1949).

[83] 'I'd rather've had a real barren virgin.'

of male narcissism and fear of female sexuality (and unfortunately, there is no textual evidence to corroborate such intentions), it is at the expense of a very negative picture of the (aspiring) mother. Indeed, the text lends itself to being read as presenting a multiply misogynist view of women in its representations of the female lover desperate for a child, of men's fantasies of virgins, of the narrator's 'bad' mother, and of Muriel as would-be mother. And there is more to come. From *Léonore, toujours* onwards 'Christine Angot' unquestioningly diagnoses hysteria amongst her symptoms; evokes her dependence on her husband and subsequent partners; and parades her desire to be appreciated by male media and publishing figures. This apparently unquestioning succession of misogynist clichés arguably culminates in *L'Inceste* wherein Angot fulfils the male fantasy of lesbian sex and performs Spivak's analysis of the silencing of the developing world 'subaltern'[84] by producing arguably racist comments comparing the comfortable life of a French woman with Dalit women's voiceless poverty: 'Je suis une indienne de la classe des intouchables' (I, 98).[85] Despite the death of her father in 1999, at the end of *Quitter la ville* the voice of 'Christine Angot''s father is still correcting her use of language, suggesting that women's voices continue to be suppressed.

Angot's *fin de millénaire* prose fictions also represent—but do not challenge—the literary field as an enduring bastion of patriarchal power. Powerful figures include Mathieu Lindon of Minuit, Jean-Marc Roberts of Fayard, and Raphaël Sorin, Houellebecq's then publisher at Flammarion. The only women cited are in secondary roles. Fannette runs a bookshop, and there are brief references to female administrative staff, but publishers, editors, critics, and journalists are notably male. There is no overt criticism of these enduringly patriarchal power relations, and although some female writers are mentioned, 'Christine Angot''s comments about their fiction are for the most part critical. This may be intended as a defiant response to predictable comparisons made between female writers (male writers are rarely compared purely on the grounds of their gender), and to the notion that women in the field of cultural production are expected to show

---

[84] Gayatri Chakravorty Spivak, 'Can the Subaltern Speak', in *Colonial Discourse* (London and New York: Harvester Wheatsheaf, 1993), pp. 66–111.

[85] 'I'm an Indian woman, one of the untouchables.'

solidarity (no such expectation prevails of men). If this is the case, the implied critique also bespeaks an unsisterly competitiveness that, paradoxically, could be typified as phallocentric.

Nonetheless, Angot does update one aspect of Beauvoir's 1949 analyses. Perhaps in spite of itself, her fiction shows how female writers may be at once constructed by the media and incited to flee their responsibility in mass-mediatized forms of bad faith. 'Christine Angot' also draws attention to the difficulty of juggling writing and being a mother, and thence to other conflictual tensions that women may not admit: 'Je suis malheureuse, malheureuse. D'autant plus parce que j'écris. [. . .] Quand on a comme moi un enfant, une fille, et qu'on écrit, c'est un enfer' (LT, 123–4).[86] 'Christine Angot' performs a rejection of writing in favour of motherhood: 'Que les romans et toute cette merde, c'était fini. Que, à côté de Léonore, ça pesait zéro' (LT, 53).[87] But what the fictional writer claims and what she writes are different things: 'je n'écris pas en ce moment, je marque Léonore' (LT, 13).[88] If 'Christine Angot' claims to be recording her daughter rather than writing fiction, she is unable to sustain the decision, so instead suffers guilt.

So, on the one hand, Angot shows that although not incompatible, motherhood and writing are conflictual by the terms of socially constructed female roles. On the other, like Beauvoir, 'Christine Angot' enjoys the comforts of a bourgeois lifestyle, not to mention the practical input—both financial and in terms of childcare—of her (ex) husband Claude. The tension between freedom, guilt, and motherhood is bound up in the question of incest: 'J'ai vécu des trucs durs, le pire l'inceste par voie rectale. [. . .] Celles qui disent que l'accouchement n'est rien, on oublie, pourquoi disent-elles ça? La race? Moi, ma fille le saura. Je veux parler d'elle. Je ne parle que de moi. Mon amour pour elle. Comment marquer?' (LT, 15–16).[89] However, although she represents the blur-

---

[86] 'I'm unhappy, so unhappy. And it's worse because I write. [. . .] If like me you have a child, a girl, and you write, it's hell.'

[87] 'That novels and all that crap, it was over. All that, compared with Léonore, it wasn't worth a thing.'

[88] 'I'm not writing at the moment, I'm recording Léonore.'

[89] 'I've lived through really hard things, and rectal incest is the worst. [. . .] Women who say that giving birth is nothing, you forget about it, why do they say that? To keep us breeding? Me, I'm going to tell my daughter all about it. I want to talk about her. I only talk about myself. My love for her. How can I record it?'.

ring of pain and pleasure and self and Other to offer insights into the ambivalence of motherhood, Angot does not question the label 'incest' as have other female commentators in an attempt to foreground the specificity of father–daughter incest, and the misogyny inherent in it (Sandra Butler calls it 'incestuous assault', and to isolate incest from evasive categorization as dysfunctional, Elizabeth Ward re-names it 'Father–Daughter Rape').[90]

Nonetheless, whether deliberately or not, Angot's fictions offer new ways of considering the feminist assertion 'the personal is political'. From a Foucauldian perspective, Angot's fiction both sheds light on and contributes to the late twentieth-century construction of sexuality and of madness, and in particular the positioning of women as mad. Simultaneously intersecting with aspects of the thought of Beauvoir, Bourdieu, and difference feminists, these texts also demonstrate the ongoing symbolic violence which casts women (and may lead women to cast themselves) as hysterics, a construct that underpins phallocentric power structures but also legitimizes the culpabilizing of the female (child and mother) for male-perpetrated crimes of incest. Moreover, the media furore surrounding *L'Inceste*, the critics quoted in *Quitter la ville*, and her prose fictions pre-dating *L'Inceste* demonstrate how the media construct Angot as mad, not only because she is a woman, but also because she transgresses the incest prohibition. However, it is through courting and using the media that Angot is able to bring this trauma that cannot be resolved or elided into the open, using her prose fictions as her forum, her *write to reply*, revealing the co-implication of both the cultural producer and consumer.

Thus if Angot's gender inflects the reception of her fictions, they do not fit into extant feminist frameworks. They do, however, intersect with elements of Delphy's analyses of how institutional misogyny is enduringly generated and perpetuated by men and women.[91] Indeed, one way of interpreting the scandal surrounding *L'Inceste* and the evasion of the issue of incest within it is that this is a reaction to a transgressive female voice exposing one of the most extreme forms of

[90] Sandra Butler, *Incest* (San Francisco: Volcano Press, 1978); Elizabeth Ward, *Father–Daughter Rape* (London: The Women's Press, 1984).
[91] Christine Delphy, *L'Ennemi principal: Économie politique du patriarcat* (Paris: Syllepse, 1998).

206 *Fin de millénaire* French Fiction

misogynist oppression. A voice that seeks to wrest a *write to reply* from patriarchal institutions, transgresses the incest prohibition, and reveals the symbolic violence inherent in the mass media presentation of sexual trauma. A voice that simultaneously breaks free from and underpins— and therefore brings into question—the commodification of female sexuality and expression.

Provocatively, then but perhaps productively, Angot simultaneously brings the tensions of motherhood, feminism, the co-implication of women in institutional misogyny, and the extreme misogyny of father–daughter incest out into the open. Through her writing 'Christine Angot' exposes her father—the cultured, respected family man—as perpetrator of incest, foregrounding the crimes perpetrated by a pillar of the patriarchy. 'Christine Angot' also articulates a relationship with writing that appears to be an appropriation of patriarchal power: 'Prendre le pouvoir, avoir le dessus. Et maintenant je l'ai. Lui a perdu la tête, Alzheimer. Moi, j'ai le dessus sur l'inceste. Le pouvoir, le pénis sadique, ça y est, grâce au stylo dans ma main, sûrement, essentiellement' (I, 173).[92] However, contradictions within and between her texts beg the question of whether Angot's fictions perpetuate the patriarchal, misogynist structures which elide incest. Certainly, whether or not she intends to, Angot demonstrates how the 'turning point' of feminism has yet to be reached.

TRANSGRESSION AND CRITICAL POTENTIAL

By using incest as the nexus of a network of tropes, Angot runs the risk of reducing unspeakable trauma to figures of speech. This double bind, redoubled by the *fin de millénaire* risk of mass-mediatized commodification is most strikingly dramatized in *L'Inceste*, where 'Christine Angot' sarcastically pre-empts accusations of a cynical manipulation of incest to generate media coverage and sales:

---

[92] 'Seize power, get the upper hand. And now I've got it. He's lost his mind, Alzheimer's. I've got the upper hand over incest. Power, the sadistic penis, here it is, the pen in my hand, no doubt about it, that's it.'

Je ne sais plus avec qui parler et de quoi d'autre. Les gens pensaient 'elle prépare le prochain livre, c'est dégueulasse'. Guibert s'est injecté le sang exprès. Moi-même à quatorze ans. Je voulais devenir écrivain, je voulais démarrer fort, j'ai pensé à l'inceste, j'ai séduit mon père. [. . .] Je vais me faire exciser, peut-être infibuler, des morceaux de ma chair, de mon sexe, sécheront au soleil pour le prochain livre. (I, 26–7)[93]

Here Angot seeks to convey at once the incestuous connections of her mind, the invasive yet addictive relationship with critical responses to her fictions, and the avidity with which readers may consume and then discard them. Yet in order to do so, she appropriates the memory of Hervé Guibert whose *autofictional* accounts generated awareness-raising media exposure at a time when AIDS was surrounded by superstition and fear. Readers of *Quitter la ville* learn that 'Christine Angot''s reference to Guibert has provoked a polemic.[94] Yet the account also invites an interpretation of 'Christine Angot''s comments in *L'Inceste* as a pre-emptive—and arguably self-reflexive—swipe at the expectation that writers of first-person narratives appropriate trauma to self-promotional ends. The opening words of *L'Inceste*—'J'ai été homosexuelle pendant trois mois' (I, 11)[95]—echo those of Guibert's first-person account of his life after being diagnosed with AIDS 'J'ai eu le sida pendant trois mois'.[96] AIDS and Guibert have already featured in *Léonore, toujours*, in what appears to be a strategically motivated analogy for 'Christine Angot''s experience of motherhood such that in writing about her daughter, she is by extension writing about herself and the trauma of incest: 'Je veux faire exactement comme Hervé Guibert avec le sida. Mais moi, avec Léonore. Il savait qu'il mourrait de ça. À partir de là, il a écrit, et jusqu'à sa mort. Il n'a parlé que de ça, le sida. Ça l'a certainement

[93] 'I don't know who to talk to any more, or what else to talk about. People think "she's getting material for her next book, that's outrageous". As though Guibert injected infected blood into himself. So I did it to myself at the age of fourteen. I wanted to be a writer, to make a splash, came up with incest, seduced my father. [. . .]. I'm going to castrate myself, maybe even infibulate myself, hang out pieces of my genitals to dry in the sun for my next book.'

[94] See Hervé Guibert, *A l'ami qui ne m'a pas sauvé la vie* (Paris: Minuit, 1990), p. 9, and Daniel Martin, 'Il faut lire Angot', *Magazine Littéraire*, 380, October 1999, p. 82.

[95] 'I've been homosexual for three months.'

[96] 'I've had AIDS for three months.'

prolongé, tenu un peu plus longtemps. Je fais la même chose avec Léonore' (LT, 19).[97] The use of what appears to be a reference to AIDS to 'kill off' the writer Christine in *Vu du ciel* and the reference to the narrator's AIDS-related symptoms in *Not to be* (all the more distressing in that he stages a Lazarus-like recovery) also seem to be a form of unsavoury literary pragmatics. This invites the question of the extent to which political or ethical intervention is intended or achieved. Is Angot only concerned with the trauma of incest, appropriating other crises as analogies for it, or do her provocative modes of expression seek to exceed the contemporary neutralization and elision of trauma?

Angot articulates a deliberate strategy of provocation in a 1999 interview for *Libération*: 'Mon ambition c'est d'être ingérable; que les gens m'avalent et qu'en même temps ils ne puissent pas me digérer.'[98] She also positions her stance as one deliberately adopted to resist the homogenizing conditions she lives in: 'Toutes les choses sociales me dérangent [. . .]. Le point de vue n'existe pas au milieu d'une foule, la parole manque d'incarnation.'[99] By this logic, not being an easily consumable product goes hand in hand with challenging the 'rules' of the market: 'Je n'ai aucun sens de la contrainte sociale. Pas plus d'ailleurs que je ne l'ai dans la littérature pour tout ce qui touche à une morale.'[100] However, in addition to the multiple references to desired media coverage in *L'Inceste*, 'Christine Angot''s ostensibly homophobic account of a brief lesbian affair mirrors the product cycle of purchase followed by a lack of satisfaction and a loss of interest. Her lover also compares lesbian sex with incest: ' "Baiser avec une femme, tu as raison, c'est de l'inceste" ' (I, 36).[101] What is more, a description of the liaison homophobically and phallocentrically appears to paraphrase Klein by

---

[97] 'I want to do exactly the same as Hervé Guibert did with AIDS. But I'm going to do it with Léonore. He knew he was going to die of it. And from that moment on he wrote. Until he died. All he talked about was AIDS. It kept him going, helped him to hold on a little longer. I'm doing the same thing with Léonore.'

[98] Angot, *Libération*, 29 June 1999: 'My ambition is to be indigestible. I want people to swallow me but to find that they can't digest me.'

[99] Ibid.: 'Everything in society bothers me [. . .]. There's no room for the individual perspective amidst the crowd, there's no voice for words.'

[100] Angot in Guichard, 'Christine Angot: La Bâtarde libre': 'I've absolutely no sense of social constraint. Any more than in my writing I have anything remotely resembling an ethics.'

[101] ' "Fucking a woman, you're right, it's incest." '

describing lesbian sex as 'comme l'utilisation d'un pénis sadique. [. . .]
J'ai pas de queue mais je te sodomise quand même' (I, 158).[102] Angot
also links Freud, Nazism, incest, and her female lover in a description of
anal penetration:

> Le nazisme, je persécute M-C parce qu'elle est homosexuelle alors que c'est juste
> une variation, provoquée par un arrêt du développement sexuel. [. . .] Pour-
> quoi? Parce que mon père était homosexuel. Il ne l'était pas, je délire, j'exagère,
> je dis n'importe quoi, mais la sodomie, qu'il pratiquait sur moi [. . .] le
> rapproche d'eux. La bisexualité est humaine. Elle existe à l'état latent chez
> tous les hétérosexuels. Freud le disait, déjà en 1920. (I, 147)[103]

This incendiary description combines the trauma of incest with narcissism, anachronistic psychoanalytical interpretations, anti-Semitism,
homophobia, and misogyny.

Earlier in *Léonore, toujours* the mother–daughter relationship is figured
as incestuous: 'Je ne veux pas faire d'inceste avec elle physiquement. Mais
dans la tête, ce n'est pas possible autrement' (LT, 12).[104] The narrative
begins with a comparison of childbirth and the Holocaust: 'quand elle est
sortie, c'était de moi. [. . .] Auschwitz en mille fois pire' (LT, 12).[105] Yet
Angot seems to seek retroactively to allay accusations of anti-Semitism,
figuring a dream featuring the hallucinated rape of a German soldier called
Angst, whose name—and experience of violent anal penetration—are no
doubt deliberately close to the writer's own: 'À cet instant, Angst comprend qu'il est antisémite. Là-dessus je me suis réveillée et j'ai pensé à
éonore, ma création. Et que, l'accouchement d'une femme, c'était mille
fois pire que ça, l'antisémitisme' (LT, 105).[106] Meanwhile, in *L'Inceste*

---

[102] 'like a sadistic penis. [. . .] I haven't got a prick but I'm going to sodomise you
anyway'.
[103] 'It's like Nazism, I persecute M-C because she's homosexual when it's simply a
variation, caused by an interruption of sexual development. [. . .] Why? Because my
father was homosexual. Of course he wasn't really, I'm crazy, I'm exaggerating, talking
rubbish, but sodomy, what he used to do to me [. . .] that makes him like them. Being
bisexual is part of human life. Bisexuality is latent in all heterosexuals. Freud made that
point back in 1920.'
[104] 'I don't want to commit incest with her physically. But in my head, it's the only way.'
[105] 'When she came out, she came out of me. [. . .] Like Auschwitz, but a thousand
times worse.'
[106] 'it's at this moment that Angst realises he is anti-Semitic. At this moment [. . .] I
woke up and thought of Léonore, my creation. And that when a woman gives birth, it
much worse than that, anti-Semitism.'

there are arguably strategic references to Angot's mother, Rachel Schwartz, and to the experience of anti-Semitic comments about that name, which, mapping onto Angot's own life, 'Christine Angot' advises she carried until adopting her father's at the age of fifteen.[107] Angot's provocative juxtaposition of crises raises the question of whether the evocation of homophobia, anti-Semitism, the Holocaust, the Rwandan genocide, and AIDS is intended as a critique of the commodification of trauma by the mass media, gesturing instead towards the need to bear witness to trauma without reifying it. Or, as Adorno suggests, does Angot's *fin de millénaire* prose fiction constitute a form of barbarism, of self-satisfied contemplation and co-implication?[108]

Given the provocative content discussed above, it is not surprising that Angot's juxtaposition of individual and collective trauma attracts accusations of a dubious relativizing of crisis. Similar criticisms were levelled at Marguerite Duras for her 1959 screenplay for Alain Resnais's film *Hiroshima mon amour*, wherein footage of the bombing of Hiroshima is cut with scenes of an actress's romance with a German soldier in Nevers and her subsequent vilification during the *Épuration*. Yet Duras's work has also been interpreted as foregrounding the issue of French co-implication in the horrors of the Second World War and, as Caruth suggests, of bearing witness at once to unspeakable trauma and to the bodily experience of trauma in history.[109] This invites the question of whether Angot's juxtaposition of a personal trauma with the unspeakable crises of the Holocaust and the Rwandan genocide likewise seeks simultaneously to express the bodily trauma of incest and French co-implication in the traumas of the second half of the twentieth century.

Beyond the recurrent figuring of incest and the individual crises of 'Christine Angot', and those of female victims of sexual violence representatively portrayed in *Vu du ciel* and *Les Autres*, there are references to neo–imperial suffering, such as the plight of workers in Chinese sweat shops: 'Pour gagner le salaire de leur PDG, il faudrait aux ouvriers de chez Nike

---

[107] Angot's maternal Jewish heritage is played on overtly and insistently in the comparison of successive Jewish and non-Jewish partners in her 2006 novel *Rendez-vous*.

[108] Theodor Adorno, 'Cultural Criticism and Society', in *Prisms*, trans. Samuel and Shierry Weber (Cambridge MA: MIT Press; 1967), pp. 17–34.

[109] Caruth, *Unclaimed Experience*.

China, environ trois milliards d'années' (LA, 104–5).[110] This reference to the global market suggests that Angot is deliberately linking the crises she represents to the politics of consumption. Certainly, the references to AIDS intersect with critiques of the commodification of crisis and of cultural memory by Baudrillard, Nora, and Lipovetsky.[111] Indeed, as it has been suggested of Duras's *Hiroshima mon amour*, is it possible to read Angot's fiction as a political intervention, in her case an attempt to generate media exposure in order to exhort readers to return to the crises of the past. What is certain is that Angot's linking of incest with AIDS, anti-Semitism, Auschwitz, the Rwandan genocide, childbirth, sexual relationships (gay and straight), writer–critic, and cultural producer–consumer relationships brings into question the ethics of the representation of trauma and of the Other in cultural production at the end of the second millennium.

Thus to simply dismiss Angot's prose fictions as fame-seeking narcissism is in Adorno's terms barbaric. Paradoxically, whilst Angot courts media attention, her fiction is anti-commercial inasmuch as she does not give readers what (they think) they want. Multiple narrators, language games, disjunction of syntax, and sporadic punctuation counter conventions and stereotypes, whilst happy endings for lovers, marriages, families, writers, publishers, and readers are consistently frustrated. What appear to be turning points do not lead to the resolution of crisis. Views of motherhood, relationships, childbirth, writing, consumption, and the field of cultural production counter the idealized stereotypes produced by the mass media and the global market. Indeed, Angot's fiction shocks (even when it is not its deliberate intention) because it reveals what lies beneath homogenized media images.

One way of considering the criticism of Angot's use of incest as material and trope in her fiction is that such reactions underscore the extent to which, beyond the grisly performance of personal crises in reality television programmes (and arguably in some *autofictions*), and beyond the commodification of cultural memory, transgressions of the

---

[110] 'To earn as much as the Chief Executive it would take Nike China workers about three billion years.'

[111] Jean Baudrillard, *Simulacres et simulation* (Paris: Galilée, 1981) and *À l'Ombre du millénaire; ou, Le Suspens de l'an 2000* (Paris: Sens & Tonka, 1998); Gilles Lipovetsky, *Le Crépuscule du devoir: L'Éthique indolore des nouveaux temps démocratiques* (Paris: Gallimard, 1992); Pierre Nora, 'L'Ère de la commémoration', in Nora et al., eds, *Les Lieux de mémoire III: Les France*, Édition Quarto (Paris: Gallimard, 1992).

incest taboo are still elided. As a trauma that cannot be worked through, represented, or neutralized, incest emphatically does not fit the tropes of reality television and what has arguably become a therapeutic industry.

Angot's response is to refigure the *fin de millénaire* market-driven manipulation of crisis as analogous with incest, underpinning the elision of the inconceivable trauma of incest with references to consumer culture: from Kréma sweets and Codec supermarkets to lying sprawled on a sofa clutching a remote control or a telephone handset. These are less reality effects than links made between incest and consumerism. Inviting conflict—whether strategically or inadvertently—Angot's *fin de millénaire* prose fiction is at once (self) promotional and transgressive. It harnesses the manipulation of crisis by the mass media and the global market, and exposes modes of oppression within the literary field, and in this microcosm, aspects of the symbolic violence of turn-of-the-millennium France.

Angot's *fin de millénaire* prose fictions can therefore be read as an attempt to *write to reply*, exposing new and enduring forms of elision of transgression of the incest taboo. The simultaneously repellent and compelling tension of father–daughter incest operates as the nexus for other relationships either described or represented as analogous to it. Crisis recurs as subject, structuring principle, analogy, and outcome, intersecting with contemporary intellectual concerns as Angot foregrounds—both deliberately and unwittingly—the crises of language, of the self, and of individual and collective trauma. Angot outstrips the notion of postmodern crisis without end, instead seeking to precipitate crisis by breaching literary and other taboos.

However, if Angot seeks to expose the symbolic violence generated by the mass media and the global market, and expose their role not only in commodifying but also, arguably, generating sexual violence, and although she links these processes with the collective traumas of the late twentieth century, the reception of her work has been typified by the positioning of incest as specific to the author rather than as a product of society. This transforms 'Christine Angot''s—and arguably by extension, Angot's—experiences into singular (and therefore containable) cases, eliding elements of her texts which link father–daughter incest and questions of individual and collective co-implication in traumas such as those of the Holocaust, the Rwandan genocide, and the AIDS epidemic. Thus Angot has been accused not only of using the crisis of others as a narcissistic vehicle for the expression of her own trauma, but also of using incest as a promotional strategy, a deliberately shocking mode of generating sales. Yet the violence of this reaction draws attention by omission to the unquestioning consumption of other crisis discourses. It also shows how transgressions of the incest prohibition are ongoingly elided and naturalized.

So Angot exposes, challenges, contributes to, and indeed falls victim to the *fin de millénaire* manipulation of crisis by the media and the market. Her texts perform the double bind of recuperating trauma through the relativizing of incest by more or less implicitly comparing it with a range of other traumatic crises: from the unspeakable (the Holocaust, the Rwandan genocide, and AIDS); to the intellectualized (the crisis of the self, of the Other); the personal (crises of the couple, of family relationships, of the mother); and the commercial (the sales-driven manipulation of the literary field and the *purchase-crises* produced by marketing and media discourses). These texts are simultaneously co-implicated and destabilizing. But within Angot's fictions, between them, and beyond them, she invites the question of the relationship between literature and its conditions of production and consumption. Writing and reading are figured as a consensual, incestuous dynamic, at once voyeuristic, exhibitionist, critical, co-implicated, compelling, and repellent. Indeed Angot's *fin de millénaire* prose fictions suggest that the literary can outstrip the audiovisual media in terms of its potential for provocation, whilst drawing attention to the effects of the market-driven mass-mediatized commodification of trauma, and to the generation of a voyeuristic appetite for misogyny and sexual violence.

5

Marie Redonnet: resistance, barbarism, and self-satisfied contemplation

Marie Redonnet made her mark on the French literary field with her trilogy *Splendid Hôtel* (1986), *Forever Valley* (1987), and *Rose Mélie Rose* (1987), published by Minuit. Evoking dark fairytales without resolution, the short prose fictions feature first-person female narrators and explore questions of heritage, loss, identity, and transmission. Although not commercially successful, the trilogy evoked considerable critical interest and is variously praised or criticized for embodying a postmodern suspicion of totalizing narratives; hailed as a new departure in 'women's writing'; or cited as part of the putative 'minimalist' school. After publishing *Silsie* with Gallimard in 1990, a palpable turning point in Redonnet's fiction was confirmed in *Candy Story* (1992); *Nevermore* (1994); *Villa Rosa* (1996); and her longest work to date, *L'Accord de paix* (2000).[1] In these increasingly complex narratives explorations of grief and heritage are transposed into a recognizably contemporary context. According to Redonnet, these texts were born of a personal crisis of confidence, less in writing itself than in the *fin de millénaire* literary market. And indeed in Jérôme Lindon, who, contrary to Minuit's reputation (and in contrast with Lindon's continued support of

---

[1] Redonnet's first published works were *Le mort & Cie* (Paris: P.O.L, 1985), a collection of haïku poetry, and a collection of short tales, *Doublures* (Paris: P.O.L, 1986). The trilogy followed: *Splendid Hôtel* (Paris: Minuit, 1986), *Forever Valley* (Paris: Minuit, 1987), and *Rose Mélie Rose* (Paris: Minuit, 1987). She also published plays: *Tir et Lir* (Paris: Minuit, 1988), *Mobie-Diq* (Paris: Minuit, 1988), *Seaside* (Paris: Minuit, 1992), and *Le Cirque Pandor; suivi de Fort Gambo* (Paris: P.O.L, 1994). The prose fictions analysed here are *Silsie* (Paris: Gallimard 1990); *Candy Story* (Paris: P.O.L, 1992); *Nevermore* (Paris: P.O.L, 1994); *Villa Rosa* (Charenton: Éditions Flohic, 1996); and *L'Accord de paix* (Paris: Grasset, 2000).

Echenoz, whose early novels also did not sell well), refused to publish *Silsie*, because he deemed it would not be a commercial success. This prompted Redonnet to seek publication beyond such constraints, and also to turn to literary criticism.[2]

With little or no marketing impetus, there is limited French critical coverage of Redonnet's *fin de millénaire* prose fiction, but what there is at once draws attention to the perceptible change in Redonnet's writing and demonstrates the contradictory characteristics of the literary field. Raymond Bellour of *Magazine Littéraire* praises *Candy Story* for its representation of 'un monde dit "réel"'.[3] André Rollin writing for *Le Canard enchaîné* identifies an element of anti-consumerist denunciation in the text: 'le redoutable pouvoir de dénoncer le trafic généralisé qui gère le monde'.[4] However, Michèle Bernstein in *Libération* judges the increased complexity an unwelcome development.[5] Meanwhile, academic Colette Sarrey-Strack discusses symbolic violence in the representation of female protagonists in *Candy Story* and *Nevermore*, identifying by comparison with Redonnet's earlier prose fictions a greater ontological depth and a recognizably contemporary setting where 'le mythe fondateur perde sa force [. . .] [ce qui] dans la perspective d'un monde évoluant vers la globalisation, s'affirmerait ici comme un danger'.[6] Yet in *La Littérature sans estomac* Pierre Jourde dismisses *Candy Story* as symptomatic of what he perceives as the market-driven 'gutless' writing of his title.[7]

---

[2] See Redonnet, 'Parcours d'une œuvre: Marie Redonnet avec une introduction de Warren Motte', *Contemporary French and Francophone Studies*, 12/4 (October 2008), 487–99. Redonnet returned to Minuit (perhaps in the wake of Jérôme Lindon's death) to publish *Diego* (Paris: Minuit, 2005), which further demonstrates an engagement with contemporary culture by following the fate of an illegal immigrant in twenty-first-century France.

[3] Raymond Bellour, 'Candy Story,' *Magazine Littéraire*, 1994: 'a so-called "real" world'.

[4] André Rollin, '"Ma", "Mia", Mafia!', *Le Canard enchaîné*, 9 September 1992: 'the formidable ability to denounce the ubiquitous dealing that rules the world'.

[5] Michèle Bernstein, 'Marie Redonnet au tournant: *Candy Story*', *Libération*, 10 September 1993.

[6] Colette Sarrey-Strack, *Fictions contemporaines au féminin: Marie Darrieussecq, Marie Ndiaye, Marie Nimier, Marie Redonnet* (Paris: L'Harmattan, 2002), pp. 167–8: 'the founding myth is losing its hold [. . .] [which] from the perspective of an increasingly globalized world, is a pretty dangerous prospect'.

[7] Pierre Jourde, *La Littérature sans estomac* (Paris: L'Esprit des Péninsules, 2002), p. 156.

Jourde also cites Redonnet's own discussions of writing wherein she calls for a new form of literary commitment: resisting the violence of the mass media and the global market. However, he argues that Redonnet does the opposite, that her writing is representative of the 'roman *light* contemporain'.[8] Like Echenoz, Redonnet is also anachronistically type-cast as 'minimalist', or symptomatic of the development of that per-ceived aesthetic, described by Houellebecq as 'la débauche de techniques mises en œuvre par tel ou tel "formaliste-Minuit" pour un résultat aussi mince'.[9] The following year Redonnet attacked Houellebecq in an article on *Les Particules*, trenchantly entitled 'La Barbarie postmod-erne'.[10] This at once suggests her own perception of the agency and the responsibility of the writer, and her belief that Houellebecq is an example of detrimental agency, not only literary, but also ethical. So, whilst it does not attract the polemics surrounding Houellebecq and Angot, or the coverage enjoyed by Echenoz, Redonnet's *fin de millénaire* prose fiction attracts contradictory assessments, which, together with the relative media silence around them, occlude the critical potential of her texts.

LITERATURE, COMMITMENT, AND A NEW *(HI)STORY*

In the introduction to her first book-length critical work *Jean Genet, le poète travesti: Portrait d'une œuvre* published by Grasset in 2000, Re-donnet focuses on the crisis of literature caused, she claims, by a gap in the transmission between literary generations and a failure to confront the enduring impact of (and French co-implication in) historical traumas. For Redonnet Genet is an exception, working through the traumas of the past to inscribe a critical future for literature: 'il a mêlé son histoire [. . .] à l'Histoire (du nazisme au colonialisme en passant par les mouvements révolutionnaires). Retrouver ce lien à l'Histoire fait partie en cette fin de vingtième siècle de l'invention pour la littérature

---

[8] Jourde, *LaLittérature sans estomac*, p. 53: 'contemporary literature "*lite*"'.
[9] Michel Houellebecq, *Interventions* (Paris: Flammarion, 1998), p. 53: 'poaching techniques used by any old "Minuit formalist" to such meagre effect'.
[10] 'Postmodern barbarism'.

d'une nouvelle histoire' (JG, 8).[11] Redonnet asserts that by engaging with this new '(Hi)story', Genet demonstrates the potential of literature as an act of resistance, subverting the symbolic, sexual, religious, and political order through the use of poetic language. She describes Genet as an exemplary literary resistant, who creates new representations of reality which seek to challenge the status quo: 'Contre la société du spectacle implacablement mise à nu dans son œuvre, Genet redonne à la poésie sa chance. À partir du simulacre et du trompe-l'œil qu'il détourne et subvertit, il crée de nouvelles réalités' (JG, 318).[12] However, in a context in which identifying and bemoaning the spectacular and the hyperreal has become a cliché, to cite Baudrillard or Debord emphasizes the risk of being caught in the *fin de millénaire* double bind of appropriation and commodification (particularly given Debord's prognosis of the recuperation of dissent by the integrated spectacle).

Before her work on Genet, Redonnet coupled Sartre and Debord in a 1991 literary call to arms:

écrire redevient un acte engagé, d'un engagement qui n'a plus rien à voir avec l'engagement sartrien, puisqu'il se fonde sur la nécessité d'écrire une œuvre délivrée des héritages du passé dont il faut renaître pour recommencer. Engagement qui passe aussi par la nécessité de repenser l'histoire de la Littérature à partir des nouvelles questions qui se posent, contre la nouvelle terreur analysée par Guy Debord, celle de la dictature médiatique séductrice.[13]

If Sartre is often invoked with nostalgia as the last of the *grands écrivains*, or as an anachronism, Redonnet recognizes that the situation of the contemporary writer is very different from that of the writer in 1947

<hr/>

[11] Redonnet, *Jean Genet, le poète travesti: Portrait d'une œuvre* (Paris: Grasset, 2000): 'he blended his own story [...] with History (from Nazism to colonialism via the revolutionary movements in between). At the end of the twentieth century, rediscovering how literature relates to History is part of the process of it writing a new story.'
[12] 'Resisting the spectacular society his work exposes so implacably, Genet brings poetry back into the frame. Building on the simulacra and *trompe-l'œil* effects that he appropriates and subverts, he creates new realities.'
[13] Redonnet, 'Réponses pour une question brouillée', *Quai Voltaire*, 2 (1991), 45–8, at p. 48: 'writing is once again becoming a committed act, but a mode of commitment that no longer has anything in common with Sartre's commitment, because it is based on the need to write works which break free from the heritage of the past, from which we must be reborn to start again. A commitment which also recognizes the need to rethink literary history in relation to new questions of our times, in order to resist the new reign of terror analysed by Guy Debord: the seductive tyranny of the media.'

described in *Qu'est-ce que la littérature?*[14] The Sartrean *bête noire*—the bourgeois writer—together with the masses for whom Sartre felt the committed author should write, have been subsumed into the globalized 'class' of the consumer. The notions that writing might allow the apprehension of the freedom of the writer and the reader, and that both might, through their choices, influence their socio-political situation have little currency in an ostensibly post-ideological world. For Sartre *engagement* is a matter of action in the present, and one that rejects poetic discourse as an obstacle to communicating the implications of freedom and choice. For Redonnet, however, the writer must work through the crises of the past, and harness the poetic potential of language to reawaken the imagination of the subject to create singular, critical perspectives. Perspectives which make a travesty of the symbolic order of the mass media and the global market.

Redonnet's impassioned critique of *Les Particules* also articulates these concerns. She considers Houellebecq an example of the consequences of a two-fold failure: on the one hand to confront the question of writing a new '(Hi)story', and on the other to work through a 'très lourde histoire où se rencontrent l'Holocauste, Hiroshima, le stalinisme et la fin du colonialisme'.[15] Of course by 1999, calling for a literary return to the crises of the past did not represent a turning point. Intersecting with the work of post-Freudian theorists such as Caruth, Felman, and Laub,[16] and French writers and film-makers of the *mode rétro*, the 1990s are characterized by further developments in the literary and cinematic returns to the Occupation and the Holocaust, and by a growing number of works bearing witness to the traumas of French colonialism, decolonization, and the Algerian War, investigating such trauma and its impact on subsequent generations. However, Redonnet's dual focus—processing the crises of the past and resisting the manipulation of crisis by the market and the media in the present—appears to

[14] Jean-Paul Sartre, *Situations II* (Paris: Gallimard, 1948).

[15] Redonnet, 'La Barbarie postmoderne', *Art Press*, 244 (March 1999), 60–4, at p. 63: 'a history weighed down by convergence of the Holocaust, Hiroshima, Stalinism, and decolonization'.

[16] Cathy Caruth, *Unclaimed Experience: Trauma, Narrative, and History* (Baltimore, MD: The Johns Hopkins University Press, 1996); Shoshana Felman and Dori Laub, *Testimony: Crises of Witnessing in Literature, Psychoanalysis and History* (New York and London: Routledge, 1992).

offer a new perspective. And while her citing of Sartre, Genet, and Debord no doubt unwittingly brings to the fore the danger of the recuperation of critical discourses, Redonnet expresses a confidence in the singular, transgressive, poetic power of literature:

Quelle place unique la littérature, en tant qu'acte de résistance, pourrait-elle prendre, dans un monde envahi par l'image, où tout devient image, y compris l'écrivain et la littérature? L'écriture, parce qu'elle a le pouvoir d'engendrer dans la langue des imaginaires singuliers producteurs de nouvelles réalités vivantes, peut avoir le pouvoir de résister à l'irréalisation terrifiante du monde. (JG, 19)[17]

This *profession de foi* invites the question of the agency—represented in and, by extension, of—Redonnet's *fin de millénaire* prose fictions. To what extent does she realise her desire at once to work through the crises of the past, and to resist the travesties of the mass media and the global market? Or, given that commercial pressure led to Redonnet renouncing the media coverage that comes with the Minuit brand, and that her *fin de millénaire* fiction has consequently been less accessible to critics and readers alike, does her change in narrative style and contemporary focus mean that any intended travesty has been subsumed by market forces?

FIN DE MILLÉNAIRE PROPAGANDA AND THE LURE OF THE SMALL SCREEN

The mass media and the global market occupy an increasingly prominent place in Redonnet's *fin de millénaire* fiction. With their interchangeable promises of financial gain and freedom, billboards in *Silsie* operate in stark contrast with the misplaced commercial optimism of monsieur Codi and the eponymous narrator's first-hand experience of the moral degradation of Texe: 'Les panneaux publicitaires le long des voies font comme un guide et disent tout de Texe' (S, 26–7).[18] These

---

[17] 'What unique role could literature play, as an act of resistance, in a world deluged with images, where everything is turned into an image, including writers and literature? Writing, because it has the ability to use language to create singular imaginaries, which produce new realities that may have the power to resist the terrifying de-realization of the world.'

[18] 'The billboards along the side of the tracks are like a guide, telling all there is to know about Texe.'

advertising hoardings presage an implicit questioning of the politics of consumption that becomes increasingly insistent in Redonnet's writing. Since her next work *Candy Story* is dedicated to the memory of Giovanni Falcone, assassinated anti-Mafia judge, readers may expect a political dimension from the outset. Here, as in Redonnet's subsequent prose fictions, politics are inextricably bound up with the discourses of the media and the market, discourses which are far from anodyne. In *Nevermore* posters used in the electoral campaign chillingly echo the material used by the far Right in 1990s France, itself echoing Nazi slogans. Yet demonstrating the tension between the potential and the neutralization of crisis tropes, they also recall the slogans of May 1968. This intersects with the appropriation and neutralization of revolutionary zeal represented by the rebel army in *Villa Rosa* and the failure of the Mouvement de la Libération in *L'Accord de paix*.

Meanwhile, the two newspapers featured in *Nevermore*—the *Gazette* and *Bataille*—are propaganda machines *fin de millénaire*-fashion. The press is run by pragmatists who have no interest in politics other than the commercial gain they derive from fraudulently post-rationalizing the latest (commercially driven) machinations of the men of the moment. The people of San Rosa momentarily recognize the manipulation of crisis discourses by the *Gazette* and its sponsors. However, rather than seizing the opportunity created by the exposure of these contradictions, they turn to the equally corrupt *Bataille* and its equally self-seeking sponsors, who in turn cultivate further organs of propaganda. By implication then, these representations reveal how freedom of speech and the freedom of the press are subjugated to market forces. As in *Candy Story* and *L'Accord de paix*, the media pervert the truth to political and commercial ends, and the populace consume it unquestioningly.

This is one facet of Redonnet's dramatization of the consequences of 'l'irréalisation terrifiante du monde'.[19] Whilst representing the political and journalistic manipulation of crisis as propaganda, Redonnet's *fin de millénaire* prose fictions also show how the same tropes are repackaged by the audiovisual media. In *Silsie* cinema is linked to the lure of the new continent: 'Le nouveau continent pour nous, c'était les films en exclusivité du Cinépathé' (S, 41).[20] The girls' introduction to the silver

---

[19] 'the terrifying de-realization of the world'.
[20] 'For us the new continent meant all the new releases from Cinépathé.'

screen is also their first step towards sexual exploitation. They graduate to the Panorama, which shows pornographic films. The intrusion of cinema into their lives brings with it both the loss of their virginity to the sons of the Panorama's owner and a loss of reality replaced by the desire for the unrealizable life projected in celluloid. In *Candy Story* several protagonists attempt, unsuccessfully and painfully, to fashion themselves into film-star images. Meanwhile, Mia draws attention to the devaluation of literature in a world that privileges the audiovisual image: 'j'y suis invitée en tant que chirurgien du cerveau et pas comme l'auteur de *Sise Memories,* ce qui change tout, comme si à City Sise il fallait jouer un rôle et que la vie était du cinéma' (CS, 43–4).[21]

Redonnet also investigates the link between cinema and television, between the silver screen with its unattainable dreams and the small screen with its manipulation of tropes and trauma. In *Nevermore* the documentary maker Stive Lenz demonstrates the co-implication of individual cultural producers in the transformation crisis into a market-able product. His motivation is to commodify trauma for personal gain: 'La dernière éruption du volcan, l'embrasement du cirque Fuch, l'ex-plosion du Babylone, sur quoi se finit le film, sont des images inoubli-ables qui assurent son succès' (N, 157).[22] In *Candy Story* television is omnipresent and consistently brings bad news. Mia learns of the death of Witz and Lill from the television in her hotel room and of Kell's murder via a live broadcast. When the commander dies, and with him Ma's last hope for love, the latter sits staring at 'une chaîne qui n'existe pas' (CS, 73)[23] on her blank television screen, a potent image of the viewer's abdication of critical consciousness. Erma, a television present-er is motivated by personal gain and sexual gratification (as indeed are her guests and collaborators). The audiovisual media also treat writing as a commodity, so the value of Stev's poetry increases on his suicide as it may now be presented on television as part of a tragic story to feed viewers voyeuristically accustomed to mediatized trauma. Rotz, a

---

[21] 'I was invited there in the capacity of brain surgeon and not as the author of *Sise Memories.* That changes everything, as though in City Sise you have to play a role, and life is like a movie.'

[22] 'When the volcano last erupted, the Fuch circus going up in flames, the explosion at the Babylon (the final frame of the film), indelible images which mean the film will be a hit.'

[23] 'a channel that does not exist'.

journalist and would-be novelist has not heard of Mia's first novel *Sise Memories*, 'parce qu'il ne connaît que les auteurs invités par Erma sur Canal' (CS, 27).[24] Here, perhaps with a nod to her own experience of commercial criteria for recognition, Redonnet pre-empts Bourdieu's critique of the *intellectuel médiatique* four years later in *Sur la Télévision*.[25] Erma may also be intended as an implicitly critical representation of the sales-generating power of French television's cultural pundits epitomized by Bernard Pivot. However, by figuring this in a woman, a potentially unintentionally misogynist representation of female co-implication is introduced.

Whilst exposure of the influence of television and cinema is a discernible trend in Redonnet's *fin de millénaire* prose fiction, video and digital technology are also revealed to have a sinister power. In *Silsie* a video club is created in Dolms to keep the workers at the power station entertained and to detract from the impending crisis symbolized by the fractured dam. The video club also dissimulates the disaster that threatens Dolms; contributes to the disintegration of the community's traditions; and breeds violence. Madame Gilda migrates to the club, neglecting her hotel and her troubled son Dill, who then goes on to murder Lonie. The implication is that the films are pornographic, and that video technology further extends the ability of the celluloid image to generate misogyny, unrealizable aspirations, and unfulfilled sexual desire. Whilst in *Silsie* video technology is harnessed to deaden the critical potential of the workforce, in *Nevermore* Gobbs and Patter use it as an integral part of their electoral campaigns. Images of candidates projected on a screen hold more sway than public appearances, referencing at once the propaganda films of the 1930s and 1940s and the contemporary access to far more sophisticated and broad-reaching audiovisual rhetorical vehicles. In *Candy Story* Curtz sees video as a means of maximizing revenue by extending his product range, and as a key influence in producing marketable fiction. Curtz plans to make a video of Mia and himself performing a sex scene from the latter's first novel, *Sise Memories*. This encapsulates a question that runs through all Redonnet's *fin de millénaire* prose fictions: the extent to which life imitates art.

----

[24] 'because he has only heard of the authors Erma invites onto her show on Canal'.
[25] Pierre Bourdieu, *Sur la Télévision; suivi de L'Emprise du journalisme* (Paris: Raisons d'agir, 1996).

Curtz's video project dramatizes the dangers of reading fiction as reality, particularly where sexual exploitation is endemic, and is translated into celluloid images. Yet more sinisterly, these dangers also operate in reverse, for through the medium of video, voyeuristic sexual exploitation achieves the status of fiction. Lize secretly films the sex trade in her brothel so that the mayor can watch it with impunity, then sells the videos on to Curtz, who turns them into mass-market products in order to gain a competitive edge in a hyper-commercial literary field: 'Il veut créer chez Moréno une collection de vidéocassettes avec pour commencer la série sur *le Paradiso de City Sise*, au moment même où Rotz va publier chez Boston *le Paradiso de City Sise*, son premier roman' (CS, 120).[26] The pattern recurs in *L'Accord de paix* with even more sinister outcomes, for here the Internet provides a worldwide forum for unregulated sexual exploitation. The lighthouse-keeper plans to sell his digicam films of couples having sex both to the local 'cultural' institution and globally on the web:

il a eu l'idée d'acheter un caméscope numérique pour filmer ce qu'il observe avec un si grand intérêt. Il se fait ainsi une collection de cassettes qu'il compte aller proposer en exclusivité au futur Palais de l'Image. [...] Grâce à son branchement sur Internet, il communique avec les autres gardiens de phare. Il a le projet de créer prochainement son propre site pour diffuser des extraits de ses plus belles cassettes à des fins publicitaires. (AP, 248)[27]

With sexual exploitation locally institutionalized and globally disseminated, Redonnet implies that the twentieth century's second small screen—the computer—in tandem with digital technology and the Internet are the latest in a series of symbolically violent innovations that also constitute a tangible threat. In a representation that anticipates how Al Qaeda terrorists manipulate apocalyptic discourses and generate physical and psychological crisis at the beginning of the twenty-first century, *Villa Rosa* rebel leader José Valès uses the Internet to maintain contact with his forces, and to fan the fires of violence. In *L'Accord de*

[26] 'He wants to develop a video collection at Moréno, to launch it with *le Paradiso de City Sise*, coinciding with the publication of Rotz's first novel with Boston, *le Paradiso de City Sise*.'
[27] 'He decided to buy a camcorder to film what he is so wrapped up in watching. So he is now building up a collection of videos to offer exclusively to the forthcoming Palais de l'Image. [...] Thanks to his Internet connection, he can communicate with the other lighthouse keepers. His next plan is to launch a website featuring some of his best clips to market his videos.'

paix the Internet not only provides a means of commercializing por-
nography, but its harnessing for dubious 'educational' purposes also
highlights the effects of globalization on a community that has sacrificed
its children to the god of consumption and its critical capacity to the
images of the mass media.

With such representations of established organs and new media,
Redonnet's fictions do not simply add another nihilistic critique following in the wake of Debord's and Baudrillard's arguably already commodified accounts. Instead, they expose the ever more globalized and
sophisticated exploitation of crisis discourses, from billboards and the
print media through video to the latest digital and virtual technology.
Nonetheless, in doing so Redonnet falls short of her ideal of creating a
new '(Hi)story' through singular language. What she does, however,
expose are the particularities and the breadth of outlets for the 'la
dictature médiatique séductrice'.[28] Thus implicitly (and therefore, were
these texts to have been exposed to a wider audience, risking the *fin de
millénaire* double bind of co-implication and commodification), Redonnet raises the question of the capacity of cultural production in general,
and prose fiction in particular, to resist that pervasive seduction.

THE WORK OF ART IN THE AGE OF
VIRTUAL DISSEMINATION

Perhaps reflecting Redonnet's critical work on Genet, intersections with
twentieth-century crisis thinking emerges in these texts. Whilst Redonnet's *fin de millénaire* fiction does not overtly seek to construct a
coherent post-Marxist position, the question of the agency of cultural
production is raised by elements that recall the analyses of the Frankfurt
School. Whether deliberately or not, *Nevermore* and *Villa Rosa* in
particular intersect with the investigation of the threat identified by
Walter Benjamin in his 1935 essay 'The Work of Art in the Age of
Mechanical Reproduction'.[29] Benjamin argued that mass reproduction

[28] 'the seductive tyranny of the media'.
[29] Walter Benjamin, 'The Work of Art in an Age of Mechanical Reproduction', in
Illuminations, ed. Hannah Arendt, trans. Harry Zohn (New York: Harcourt, Brace &
World, 1968), pp. 211–35. For a detailed discussion of Redonnet's intersections with

in high commodity culture has withered the aura of the artwork: its presence and authenticity, and the time and space in which the viewer may contemplate and experience its unique affect. As increasingly ubiquitous contact forces individuals into mass subject positions, Benjamin feared the loss of critical capacity and of the potential for imagination and reflection. Whilst he identified the advent of photography and film as the latest stages in the withering of aura, he also suggested that film has potential to democratize access to the artwork. Writing on the eve of the Second World War, Benjamin considered the global ramifications of the subsuming of the artwork into the realm of politics. To avert the aestheticization of politics by fascism, he argued that the newly democratized artwork should be harnessed to revolutionary ends. Here, there are parallels with Redonnet's emphasis on the advent of video, the Internet, and digital technology, for her representation of mass production at a time of virtual dissemination simultaneously foregrounds the impact of the democratization of art and new technologies on the affect of cultural production in general and on prose fiction in particular.

In *Candy Story* Mia gives the portrait painted by her mother to a security guard, who sells it to the Rore art museum. Here although access to art is democratized, aggressive marketing neutralizes its aura. In *Nevermore* the circus—a cultural form that at once resists mass production and offers access to the broadest of audiences—is superseded firstly by sea-front brothels, and then by the politically motivated Parc des Arts et des Lettres. In *L'Accord de paix* a Chinese copy artist is routed from the city by the forces of order whose ideology is also symbolized by the hyper-commercial technocratic Palais de l'Image that rules the city's cultural life. Textually and materially, in *Villa Rosa* the reproduction of artwork is the dominant image. The text is part of the 'Musées secrets' collection at Éditions Flohic, which invites a range of French authors to write on an artist and select reproductions to accompany the text. Redonnet selected Henri Matisse, and whilst *Villa Rosa* is an exceptionally beautiful product, it is presumably not conceived as a commercial one, for 'Musées secrets' print runs are only one

Benjamin, see Ruth Cruickshank, 'Marie Redonnet, the Question of Resistance, and the Turn-of-the-Millennium Novel', *Modern & Contemporary France*, 12/4 (2004), 497–511.

thousand copies and authors have complete editorial control. Books in the collection have eighty pages, with the text printed alongside thirty-eight reproductions of the selected artist's works. So each page of Redonnet's narrative faces a reproduction of a Matisse canvas, but these do not follow the order of their representation in the narrative, or of the excerpts quoted from Matisse's notebook. This fictional dialogue has a tacit intertext: Aragon's *Henri Matisse, Roman* (1968, 1971),[30] a two-volume evolving dialogue with Matisse's plastic and verbal images that also challenges generic boundaries and by extension market classifications. Thus Redonnet subverts readers' expectations in a way that brings into question not only artificially created generic boundaries between different forms of art and linear interpretations of them, but also the critical and commercial discourses which influence the consumption of art.

In conjunction with her own verbal images, Redonnet uses both Matisse's art and his words to explore the enduring potential of creative apprenticeship and transmission. The act of copying has potentially critical leverage. Monsieur Jean's artistic journey is marked by stages in the development of a parallel intellectual and aesthetic awareness that enables him to derive inspiration from his environment and creative relationships. First, by acknowledging that art is not a magical inheritance, he must disabuse himself of the fantasy that he is the reincarnation of Matisse. This done, although unable to paint, monsieur Jean persists in his quest, poring not only over copies of Matisse's artworks but also over the painter's writings recorded by the Chinese artist. So the potential agency of the written word is consistently figured alongside that of plastic art, and just as Redonnet in her critical writing claims to have found her bearings in Genet, so her fictional would-be painter enters into a notional dialogue with the words of Matisse.

The act of transmission is one that is both visual and textual. It harnesses pain and contradictions to investigate the possibility of a turning point, releasing hope for creative and critical potential. Monsieur Jean's aesthetic turning point coincides with the inspiration provided by the love of Rosa Bell, who shares the passion for music and dance that also infuses Matisse's work. Gratefully aware of the

---

[30] Louis Aragon, *Henri Matisse, Roman*, 2 vols (Paris: Gallimard, 1968, 1971).

legacy transmitted to him by the Chinese copy artist and Matisse, monsieur Jean begins to create his own art: 'Sans les copies du vieux Chinois, jamais il n'aurait connu la joie ni l'amour, parce que jamais il n'aurait su qu'ils existaient et qu'il pouvait les peindre à son tour, avec ses propres signes. Il identifiait complètement les tableaux d'Henri Matisse aux copies du vieux Chinois, comme si la copie et l'original ne faisaient qu'un' (VR, 59).[31] Using Benjamin's terms, then, it is a question of how the artwork might yet retain, retrieve, or create aura. Monsieur Jean and Rosa Bell recognize the importance of maintaining the link between traditional means of storytelling evoked by the old painting in the cave, and new forms of representational practice. Likewise, monsieur Jean's dialogue with Matisse encompasses copying and interpretation, and visual and verbal exchange. Thus these relationships at once enact the necessity of working though the creative legacy of the past and of recognizing its traces in the present.

Given Redonnet's emphasis on the potential of love, music, and dance, and her representation of Matisse's œuvre as one spanning painting, drawing, sculpture, collage, and writing, *Villa Rosa* intersects with poststructuralist notions of representational practice as being always already inscribed in a textual weave. When little Tiss leaves the île de Gore, monsieur Jean paints a 'triptyque' (VR, 69).[32] This recalls Redonnet's description of her 1980s trilogy, suggesting that one intention of Redonnet's own writing project is to investigate the potential of art across generic boundaries. Whilst intertexuality is most often associated with postmodern aesthetics rather than with the thought of the Frankfurt School, Redonnet combines a concern for the effect of art with figures of copying and translation of words and images that are always already reproduced. This slipperiness contrasts with the often commercially driven intertextuality of cinema and television. Moreover, unlike the perpetual present of the mass media, Redonnet tentatively links past, present, and future.

---

[31] 'If it had not been for the copies made by the old Chinese man, he would never have experienced joy or love because he would have never known that the copies existed and that he in turn could copy them, using his own signs. For him there was no distinction to be made between Henri Matisse's paintings and those of the old Chinese man, as though the copy and the original were one and the same.'

[32] 'triptych'.

Through his dialogue with the old Chinese artist and Henri Matisse, monsieur Jean learns that whilst his works may not be readily accessible to present-day consumers, they represent a form of reproduction that links with the past and is a tentative expression of faith in the future: 'les artistes sont faits pour traduire les événements de leur temps, mais avec des signes qui ne sont pas lisibles pour tous. [. . .] Peu lui importait que les habitants de l'île de Gore ne comprennent pas sa peinture. Il peignait pour Henri Matisse, c'est-à-dire pour les temps qui s'annoncent' (VR, 73).[33] Such, it seems, is the faith that sustains Redonnet's fictional investigation of critical potential inherent in the necessarily intertextual production and reproduction of works of art.

In *L'Accord de paix* Redonnet also lays particular emphasis on how the value of reproduced artworks may be judged. Unlike Benjamin's discussion of the liberating potential of mechanical reproduction, *Villa Rosa* and *L'Accord de paix* imply that manual reproduction still has the potential for a regenerative dialogue with the past. Both texts feature artists who reproduce canonical artworks but who are not motivated by purely commercial reasons. Thus Redonnet's emphasis is on copying as a learning process which involves the investigation of the values of the past that might be of use in resisting the mass-mediatized cultural production of the present. Antique dealer monsieur Hito paints copies of traditional Chinese watercolours which some consumers prefer to the originals. Whilst reversing the processes of the contemporary Chinese art reproduction industry, the watercolours not only provide him with an income, but also a means of preserving and transmitting his difference and heritage in spite of the homogenizing ideology of Port l'Etoile. When administrative corruption forces him to flee, monsieur Hito leaves his copied watercolours for Marthe, and although they are pillaged, her memory of this creative transmission inspires her hope of establishing her own set of values with her family. Here it is not the physically reproduced artwork—the commodity—but the interpretation of it that has both ethical and aesthetic potential.

---

[33] 'artists exist to translate the events of their times, but they do so with signs that cannot be read by everyone. [. . .] It did not matter to him that the inhabitants of the île de Gore did not understand his paintings. He was painting for Henri Matisse, that is to say, for the years to come.'

Nonetheless, the end of *Villa Rosa* is marked with traces of loss. The protagonists all meet tragic ends due to the commercially driven civil war that is the backdrop to life on the île de Gore. Yet if the narrative deliberately avoids closure, its final verbal image of fragmentation invites discovery:

un visiteur curieux aurait pu découvrir, un peu partout, des morceaux de fresques et de tableaux, aux couleurs toujours vives. Et sur un pan de mur encore debout, caché derrière un rosier grimpant, il aurait découvert le portrait de Rosa Bell, intact, une pure merveille. Il aurait pu alors rêver à la Villa Rosa telle qu'elle avait dû être avant de tomber en ruines, et en réinventer l'histoire pour en sauver la mémoire. (VR, 81)[34]

So an auratic artwork has been created through copying, interpretation, and a notional dialogue with Matisse. However, whilst ostensibly consigned to the past, the artwork is left open for interpretation. Indeed, Redonnet's use of the conditional perfect suggests that whilst the aura of the artwork is not irretrievable, the future is necessarily precarious, and the onus is on the visitor to the now deserted island. And so, by implication, on the reader to (re)produce an original artwork by constructing their own story.

By reproducing Matisse's canvases and words as part of a fictional dialogue, Redonnet perhaps seeks to produce a new form of auratic artwork. One that incorporates traces of the past: an exception to the constant commercial quest for novelty with its inbuilt cycle of obsolescence. Yet perhaps in spite of itself, Redonnet's book dramatizes the double bind of the writer in the age of virtual and mass-mediatized reproduction. Albeit paradoxically, featuring an artist whose work receives the recognition of a global brand, *Villa Rosa* contributes to already widespread reproduction of Matisse's work and its small print run confers commercial cachet. So the text and its format also risk operating as a commodification of literary and artistic history, a *beau livre* that looks—and reads—as though the aura of art is to be commemorated as an exception. Moreover, amidst the weave of different forms

[34] 'a curious visitor would have been able to find, all over the place, remnants of frescoes and paintings, their colours still bright. And on one wall still standing, hidden behind a rambling rose, the visitor would have found the portrait of Rosa Bell, intact, an absolute marvel. The visitor would then have been able to imagine how the Villa Rosa must have been before it fell to ruin, and to reinvent its story to preserve its memory.'

of art featured it is perhaps all too easy to miss what appears to be an embedded warning. Monsieur Jean's creativity is stifled when he becomes involved in cultural production for political purposes by painting the portrait of Wadi, the new rebel leader: 'il ne savait pourquoi, quelque chose résistait. Son portrait restait raide et sans vie' (VR, 67).[35] Thus if Redonnet attempts to explore the potential of art in the age of virtual dissemination and to expose the double bind of the appropriation of cultural products that seek to resist commodification, *Villa Rosa* nonetheless falls into and arguably also perpetuates it.

THE *FIN DE MILLÉNAIRE* CULTURE INDUSTRY AND 'LA BARBARIE POSTMODERNE'

Published for a broader market two years before *Villa Rosa*, *Nevermore* also intersects with the analyses of the Frankfurt School, recasting them in the context of the global market. In the light of Redonnet's critique of Houellebecq's *Les Particules élémentaires*, 'La Barbarie postmoderne',[36] *Nevermore* can be read as a reformulation of Adorno's often misquoted assertion: 'To write poetry after Auschwitz is barbaric', taken from his 1946 essay, 'Cultural Criticism and Society'. The essay further developed Adorno and Horkheimer's 1944 analysis 'The Culture Industry',[37] and in the shadow of the Holocaust, Adorno exposed the problematic confronting the cultural producer:

The more total society becomes, the greater the reification of the mind and the more paradoxical its effort to escape reification on its own. [...] Cultural criticism finds itself faced with the final stage of the dialectic of culture and barbarism. To write poetry after Auschwitz is barbaric. [...] Absolute reification, which presupposed intellectual progress as one of its elements, is now

---

[35] 'he did not know why, but there was some kind of block. His portrait remained stiff and devoid of life.'

[36] Redonnet, 'La Barbarie postmoderne'.

[37] Theodor Adorno and Max Horkheimer, 'The Culture Industry: Enlightenment as Mass Deception', in *Dialectic of Enlightenment: Philosophical fragments*, ed. Gunzelin Schmid Noerr, trans. Edmund Jephcott (Stanford, CA: Stanford University Press, 2002), pp. 94–136. For a detailed discussion of Redonnet's intersections with Adorno and Horkheimer, see Cruickshank, 'Marie Redonnet, the Question of Resistance'.

preparing to absorb the mind entirely. Critical intelligence can no longer be equal to this challenge as long as it confines itself to self-satisfied contemplation.[38]

The paradox Adorno identifies is that the more sophisticated mass cultural production becomes, the more critical attempts to escape the homogenizing dynamic which underpins the ideologies that produced the Holocaust become complicit with that dynamic. This is because to create a cultural product which attempts to resist the culture industry is to implicitly confer a value on the culture industry. By the same token, to enter into a dialectical relationship with the culture industry by attempting to criticize it is a means of acknowledging the power of the culture industry. So to unquestioningly subscribe to the belief that culture offers the means of overcoming barbarism, of breaking free from institutionalized mass production is to be complicit in and generating of the culture industry. This is what Adorno means by self-satisfied contemplation: failing to acknowledge that even attempts to resist the commodification of culture necessarily entail the co-implication of the cultural critic, producer, and consumer in an ideology which has the potential of (re)producing inconceivable trauma.

Whilst not overtly engaging with this analysis, Redonnet's claims for working through the crises of the past seem close to Adorno's description of the dialectic of culture and barbarism and his investigation of the question of resisting the commodification of cultural production—both mainstream and dissenting. *Nevermore* in particular offers a new perspective on Adorno's analysis of capitalist cultural production, begging the question of the extent to which Redonnet herself negotiates co-implication and the risk of self-satisfied contemplation identified by Adorno. In other words, does *Nevermore* contribute a 'nouvelle H/histoire',[39] to the growing body of literature—theoretical and fictional—bearing witness to the trauma of the Second World War, the Holocaust, and subsequent conflicts and genocides? Does Redonnet avoid the double bind of co-implication by implicitly critiquing the culture of commemoration without becoming complicit with it?

---

[38] Adorno, 'Cultural Criticism and Society', in *Prisms*, trans. Samuel and Shierry Weber (Cambridge, MA: MIT Press; 1967), pp. 17–34, at p. 34.
[39] 'a new (Hi)story'.

In *Nevermore* readers discover that the population of San Rosa was involved in sending thousands to death camps just over the border in Santa Flor. Yet for the first half of the text there is no mention of this sinister legacy, and throughout there is no recognition of responsibility on the part of the inhabitants. Just as the traces of the death camps have been erased from the landscape and replaced by a golf course, so the unspeakable horror is 'grassed over' in the collective memory. The people of San Rosa and Santa Flor collaborate in this failure to face the memories and the responsibilities of the past, less from pragmatism, self-interest, or fear, than by unquestioningly consuming the rhetoric of technological progress and the promises of the mass media and the global market. If for Adorno and Horkheimer the culture industry relies on removing the idea of alternatives to repress dissent, in *Nevermore* the *impression* of choice is a key element of the *repression* of critical capacity. Whilst Adorno and Horkheimer posit that pleasure is not having to think, Redonnet implies that in late capitalism, pleasure lies in thinking that one is thinking whilst not having to think.

Nevermore can be read as Redonnet's investigation not only of the potential of writing to bear witness to the Holocaust, but also to resist the commodification of trauma that exceeds representation. The focus is particularly on writing by the generation that neither perpetrated the Holocaust, nor were its victims, but that is nonetheless co-implicated in and victim of contemporary discourses manipulating and commodifying trauma. Bost's inability to write a *travail de deuil* for his parents and songwriter Cassy Mac Key's attempts at encapsulating the suffering of the present do not assuage their personal crises or acknowledge collective trauma. Yet whilst attempts to work through the experience of the past are necessarily doomed to failure, these writing projects nonetheless constitute attempts to bear witness to unspeakable experience, and to resist the self-satisfied contemplation generated by the late twentieth-century culture industry. Redonnet also brings to the fore the question of motivation: writing for personal reasons or for the good of the community. Indeed, whether writers or involved in other forms of cultural production, protagonists fail or succeed (in a limited sense) according to the extent to which they assume responsibility for the legacy of the past, and recognize and attempt to counter their complicity in the repression of critical potential in the present.

Having turned a blind eye to the pervasive corruption of San Rosa throughout his career, Captain Roney Burke re-reads the reports left by his predecessor, and attempts to manipulate the media to denounce the regime that he has served yet by which he has been duped. If Burke's tardy challenge fails, it is implicitly because his motivation is predominantly self-absolution. Initially Bost experiences writing as identity affirming, recording events and thoughts in a notebook. Yet it is a scripted smokescreen which shields him from the responsibility of enquiring into his parents' disappearance in the death camps. Bost is forced into confronting the memory of his parents by the theft of his notebook, but his subsequent attempt to record the unspeakable trauma of the past is still personally motivated. Although seeking to bear witness, Bost also seeks catharsis: 'Ce qui rend son livre si difficile à écrire, c'est d'être un livre de mémoire qui s'écrit d'une absence de mémoire. Cette mémoire s'invente au fur et à mesure qu'il écrit. [. . .] Il ne voit pas d'autre sens à donner à sa vie que de porter témoignage sur ce dont personne ne veut rien savoir' (N, 142–3).[40] The reference here to a hole in memory, the problems of bearing witness to the unspeakable trauma of the Holocaust, without fashioning it into a totalizing—and hence barbaric—narrative intersects with what Davis and Fallaize describe as the 'crisis of testimony' figured by some French writers and film-makers from the 1970s, and discussed by thinkers such as Felman and Laub as the need to bear witness to the irretrievable nature of trauma, and to the fallibility of narratives of testimony as a means of processing it.[41] Bost's quest is no doubt intended to suggest that the trauma of genocide cannot be worked through because the inhabitants of San Rosa have not kept memory alive, and because Bost's grandfather committed suicide without ensuring the transmission of the memory. However, the irretrievable nature of trauma and the impossibility of expression are largely attributed to Bost's lack of cultural heritage. Thus joining contemporary cultural producers in bearing witness to the holes

[40] 'What makes his book so difficult to write is that it's a memory text being written because of a gap in memory. He is inventing the memory as he writes. [. . .] The only way he can see of making his life meaningful is to bear witness to that which people do not want to know about.'

[41] Colin Davis and Elizabeth Fallaize, *French Fiction in the Mitterrand Years: Memory, Narrative, Desire* (Oxford: Oxford University Press, 2000), p. 68.

in language and in memory, Redonnet figures a writer who not only tries yet fails to fill in the blanks, but whose quest to do so is also doomed to failure because it is personally motivated.

Nonetheless, the choice of the title *Nevermore* suggests that Redonnet seeks to draw attention to the double bind of recuperation risked by declarations that the Holocaust must never be repeated. Implicitly, then, without the assumption of responsibility by individuals and institutions alike, she foregrounds how such rhetoric not only cannot guard against such horrors once again becoming reality, but may also be a mass-mediatized form of self-satisfied contemplation. *Nevermore*'s title recalls Poe's poem 'The Raven', wherein the narrator cannot move on from his tortured remembrance of his lost love and is tempted to read meaning into a raven's croaking of the word 'nevermore'.[42] However, for want of explicit criticism, Redonnet's novel risks being as empty as the croaking of the raven in Poe's poem. Just as Burke, Bost, and Mac Key write for predominantly personal reasons and seek to criticize culture without an understanding of their implication in it, so in Adorno's terms, their cultural products are barbaric acts that perpetuate the barbarism they intuitively seek to progress beyond. By this understanding, Redonnet's *Nevermore* is also an act of barbarism. Whilst it may attempt to develop a critical stance beyond the homogenizing ideology of the culture industry, the text depends on the object of its criticism. Moreover, by failing to make that criticism explicit yet by creating an easily identifiable metaphor for the Holocaust, it risks joining already homogenized attempts to represent unspeakable trauma.

However, *Nevermore*'s conclusion does invite a tentatively more positive prognosis, both for Redonnet's fictional project and for the enduring critical potential of cultural production. For all its personal motivations, Bost's attempt to inscribe the missing memory of the death camps has some agency, albeit displaced, for it is he who suggests the name 'Nevermore' for the cultural space created by ex-acrobats Fabio and Lizzie in the station that served the death camps. Here testimony to the genocide of Santa Flor—and by association, that of the Second World War and those which have since followed—is given in a form of cultural production that bears witness to the location which led towards

---

[42] Edgar Allen Poe, *The Raven* (New York: N. Müller, 1874).

trauma and which neither fits Adorno's conception of modernist, autonomous art, nor his analysis of the reified products of the culture industry. Fabio and Lizzie seek to resist co-implication with the dominant order by recognizing their ethical debt, and by seeking a means of bearing witness to the crises of the past that resonates with Bakhtin's notion of the *carnivalesque*.[43] Fabio and Lizzie's performances mutate the dominant ideology, developing a cultural form that is neither complicit with nor dependent upon the order it seeks to escape. Yet Redonnet ends the novel by highlighting the fragility of this resistance through representations of the symbolic and physical violence of the *fin de millénaire* culture industry: the inflated price of the land; the prohibitive loan that threatens Nevermore with bankruptcy; the defection of erstwhile circus performers; the fickle audience; and the bomb blasts that devastate the Babylone and the Parc des Attractions.

Clearly, Redonnet cannot be charged with ignoring the weight of historical responsibility, an accusation she makes of Houellebecq and which contemporary critics variously make of the *nouveau roman*, Oulipo, *Tel Quel*, *écriture féminine*, and fictions described as postmodern. Indeed, on the one hand, *Nevermore* operates as a sobering *mise en scène* of Adorno and Horkheimer's account of the commodification of public opinion when mass cultural production becomes an integrated part of capitalist society, and of Adorno's fears for the barbaric potential of cultural criticism. From this perspective, the text shows how the crisis rhetoric that led to the Holocaust is still being produced and manipulated by the *fin de millénaire* culture industry. However, in seeking to articulate this, Redonnet in turn risks self-satisfied contemplation. Nonetheless, whilst *Nevermore* may not escape inscription in a commodified culture of commemoration, it transmits from cultural producer to consumer, and so from writer to reader, the enduring challenge of bearing witness to the unspeakable trauma of the Holocaust and of resisting not only its commodification, but also the potential for its repetition.

[43] Mikhail Bakhtin, *Problems of Dostoevsky's Poetics*, trans. Caryl Emerson (Manchester: Manchester University Press, 1984).

CORRUPTION AND LITERARY PRODUCTION

In *Candy Story* the question of the responsibility of the cultural producer comes to the fore in what appears to be intended as a critique of the *fin de millénaire* field of literary production. Here politically powerful agents of the media and their victims are all writers involved in the publishing industry. Mia the narrator is a new writer who experiences the symbolic violence of the literary arena first-hand. Following the success of her début autobiographical novel *Sise Memories*, she has suffered from a protracted period of writer's block, failing to be inspired by a trip to the Andes, and slipping into depression as she spends what is left of the advance for her second novel. Curtz, Mia's commercially and sexually rapacious editor at Moréno (and one of several 'Godfather' figures) constantly undermines her. The text features two publishing empires, Boston and Moréno, which, like rival Mafia families, vie for supremacy in the literary market and make of it a dangerously commercially driven environment. This and the dedication to Giovanni Falcone, the Italian anti-Mafia prosecutor murdered in 1992 resonate with Debord's 1988 figuring of late capitalist society into the 'le spectacle intégré', with its silent promotion of Mafia-type activities, which he describes as the epitome of commercial enterprise at its most advanced.[44] Here, drawing out the link between literary production, Mafia-style exploitation, and violence, these two publishing houses determine the output of the field of literary production and orchestrate its diversification into ever more market-driven products.

Witz has made his name by at once recycling and commodifying literary trends: 'Witz est célèbre dans le monde entier pour avoir réinventé le roman d'espionnage et fait des films de tous ses romans' (CS, 23).[45] His latest project is to write his 'Mémoires', ostensibly to record his exploits as a wartime pilot, but also with the intention of using them to denounce the mayor of Rore (and of course, with that of making money). At once weaving and caught up in the web of corruption, Witz flies his plane and his manuscript into the sea. However, his

---

[44] Guy Debord, *Commentaire sur la société du spectacle* (Paris: Gérard Lebovici, 1988).
[45] 'Witz is famous worldwide for reinventing the spy thriller and for making all his novels into films.'

sales-boosting competition with rival Curtz endures beyond his death, as Rotz replaces Witz, perpetuating the late writer's aim to maximize the commercial potential of prose fiction. Mia's analysis of the motivations of this commercially driven triumvirate (and thus implicitly Redonnet's of those who dominate the French literary field) is that each writes for financial and personal gain: 'Rotz partage tout à fait les idées de Witz et de Curtz que la seule chose qui compte, c'est les plaisirs de la vie à n'importe quel prix et par tous les moyens' (CS, 39).[46] An implicitly critical perspective is also brought to bear on a variety of recognizable contemporary French literary trends. Witz is a literary trend-spotter who has 'reinvented' the spy novel, which, like Rotz's reinvention of the *roman noir*, refers to subversions of popular fiction, a buoyant sector of late twentieth-century French publishing (and may also be a jibe at Redonnet's one-time Minuit stable mate Echenoz). Rotz's writing process—identifying a hole in the market then filling it with a daily quota of pages—at once performs both the magpie mixing of genres by a fame hungry writer, the commodification of literature, and the recuperation of novels by the audiovisual media: 'Il vient de terminer son roman dont il a faxé chaque jour les feuillets chez Boston. Tout ce qu'il veut bien me dire, c'est que c'est un roman policier à clé écrit comme un roman-film' (CS, 117).[47] Meanwhile, Mia's musing as to whether Wick's jettisoned 'Mémoires' will float down the Seine to the United States is no doubt a critical nod on Redonnet's part to the effect of American-influenced marketing strategies.

The repetition of the names Boston and Moréno and references to their domination of the market also bring to mind the power of French publishing heavyweights such as Gallimard, Grasset, and Seuil. However, the fictional publishers and the names of those of the protagonists employed by them—Witz, Curtz, and Rotz—are also redolent of foreign brands so evoke the ever-increasing globalization of the literary market, and, in turn, the threat of French publishing houses being subsumed by multinationals. Curtz can also be read as an intertext to Kurtz in Conrad's *Heart of Darkness*, wherein amidst the brutality of colonialism the prota-

[46] 'Rotz absolutely agrees with Witz and Curtz that the only thing that matters is to enjoy life's pleasures, at any cost and by any means.'
[47] 'He has just finished his novel, faxing pages every day to his publisher, Boston. All he is willing to tell me is that it's a real-life detective novel written like a film adaptation.'

gonist's quest for personal power has fatal consequences.[48] Here, a century later, Redonnet's fictional editor appears to be following in the egomaniac path of his homonym, and his neo-imperialism has implicitly disastrous ramifications for the future of non-commercial literary production: 'Curtz est en train de conquérir City Sise. [. . .] il ressent une sensation de toute-puissance' (CS, 122).[49] Meanwhile Witz shares his name with the plays on words discussed by Freud, suggesting that what might appear to be produced for entertainment is not what it seems, and that behind his literary language games is fatal desire.

Even those who are not writing for material gain do so for personal motives: exorcizing the deeds of the past (Bobby Wick and Will); blinded by passion (Stev); living by proxy (Lise); or writing for posterity (Lou and the Commander). Although for the most part they are not commercially motivated, none of these writing projects are for the good of the community. Neither do they resist the commodification of cultural production, nor work through the legacy of the past, nor seek to find a viable narrative for negotiating the present and future. What is more, the proliferation of memoirs, journals, and (semi-)autobiographical narratives parallels and implicitly problematizes the burgeoning market for *écritures de soi, récits de vie*, and works of *autofiction*. Instead of his memoirs, the Commander's notebook is filled with columns of numbers, suggesting that the decision to record life for posterity is a formulaic activity that nonetheless can never 'add up'. Bobby Wick claims to be writing the transcendental poem that would displace the market-driven novel à la Curtz, but his text appears to be no more than a record of his own sexual history:

Mais ce qui est écrit dans son carnet, ce n'est pas le poème transcendantal qu'il voulait composer [. . .], c'est le nom et l'adresse des Africaines qu'il a connues, et dans le détail ce qu'il a fait avec chacune [. . .] et tous les traitements qu'il a subis. [. . .] Ça ne sert à rien que je lise le carnet jusqu'au bout parce que c'est toujours la même histoire. (CS, 99)[50]

[48] Joseph Conrad, *Heart of Darkness* (New York: Dent, 1902).
[49] 'Curtz is winning over City Sise. [. . .] he thinks he's omnipotent.'
[50] 'But what's written in his notebook isn't the transcendental poem he wanted to write [. . .], instead there are the names and addresses of all the African women he has known, and, in graphic detail, what he did with each one of them [. . .] and all the treatments he has undergone. [. . .] There's no point me reading it all because it's always the same story.'

Hence Redonnet brings into question at once the ethics, the motivations, and the sense-making potential of the writer-protagonists' decisions to record or exhibit their own lives and to exploit those of others. And, by implication, those of their contemporary French counterparts (and beyond them the producers of and participants in *reality shows*). Wick's *Mémoires* recall Hervé Guibert, author of over twenty texts, but whose literary renown predominantly rests on the works which bear witness to the last years of his life after being diagnosed as suffering from AIDS. The inference is that Wick is dying of AIDS, so countering homophobic and racist discourses surrounding the origin and spread of the HIV virus, Redonnet figures a promiscuous heterosexual European exploiting—and indeed infecting—postcolonial Africa. First-person narratives are also linked to the cynical commodification of trauma. Witz enjoys an ever-growing posthumous fame, which in turn is paralleled by that of Stev. Meanwhile, the initial refusal to publish Stev's poetry before his death demonstrates the hypocritical pragmatism of publishers. Nonetheless, this implicitly critical perspective brings into focus the ethics of manipulating such crises to literary ends rather than confronting them, denouncing exploitation, or representing the tangible experiences of sufferers.

Candy Story also investigates the use of literary products as pawns in an extremely dangerous power game. Witz's attempt to expose the corrupt mayor of Rore is one of no less than four protagonists' book projects sharing that aim: those of the president of the Société Anonyme Petrolière (SAP), his right-hand man Lind, Witz, and finally, Mia. Witz crashes his plane, the president of the SAP suffers a suspicious stroke, and Lind abandons his project but is then killed. So the use of books in political wrangling also foregrounds how the blurring of fiction and reality has deadly potential. Here life imitates art, insomuch as the forces of violence and corruption are redoubled by these attempts at literary denunciation.

Mia's lie to Rotz that she is a brain surgeon not a writer also dramatizes the devaluation of the non-commercial writer in a field of cultural production that ascribes value according to marketability and media notoriety. Moreover, the implicit critique of the commercial obstacles to creative endeavour and critical thought extends to academe. Mia's voice is silenced by an institution that treats novels and their authors as brands: 'Je revenais d'un colloque sur le désancrage dans les romans de chez Boston où je n'avais pas osé prendre la parole, parce que dès que je suis invitée dans un colloque je ne sais plus quoi dire' (CS, 68).[51] This ironic reference to an academic 'industry' echoes Redonnet's discussion of the perceived failure of the intellectual field. She accuses academics of taking refuge in theoretical paradigms and leaving free rein to media and marketing discourses that displace focus from the text itself:

La théorie est désormais le domaine quasi exclusif de l'université, qui fait avec la littérature des thèses sur la littérature. Mais à la place de la théorie, devenue caduque, prolifère le discours 'une sorte de marketing, où l'intérêt se déplace, et ne porte plus sur des livres, mais sur des articles de journaux, des émissions, des débats, des colloques, des tables rondes à propos d'un livre incertain qui, à la limite, n'aurait même plus besoin d'exister'.[52]

The choice of topic for *Candy Story*'s fictional colloquium—*désancrage*—at once points to the commodification of crisis by intellectuals and to the experience of the (writing) subject. The domination of the mass media and the global market has led to a loss of bearings, a failure of transmission between generations. What is more, Mia's experience of the critical field recalls the self-satisfied contemplation Adorno identifies as the final stage of the dialectic of culture and barbarism.

However, although Mia differs from these examples of market-driven writers, Redonnet does not set her up as an unequivocally positive role model. Her first novel *Sise Memories* is a commercial success, but brings nothing constructive to its author or to the community. Indeed, Mia's first writing project suggests a shying away from personal responsibility (she publishes it under her mother's name, and chooses as a title the English *Sise Memories*, which may sound like an attempt to 'seize memories', but by linguistic distancing also implies a disassociation

---

[51] 'I had just come back from a conference on "rootlessness" in Boston-published novels where I hadn't dared speak, because when I'm invited to a conference, I have no idea what to say.'
[52] Redonnet, quoting Gilles Deleuze and Claire Parnet, *Dialogues* (Paris: Flammarion, 1977), p. 35, in 'Mais quel roman?', pp. 16–17: 'Theory is now practically exclusively an academic preserve, where literature is used to write dissertations about literature. But taking the place of theory, which is no longer a primary concern, there is now a burgeoning of "different kinds of marketing activities. There is not much interest any more in books themselves, but instead in articles in journals, television coverage, discussions, conferences, and round tables about books, books pushed so far into the background that it almost would not matter if they were not there at all".'

from her own material). So if *Candy Story* can be read as a fictional articulation of Redonnet's call for resistance against market-driven cultural production, the text does not offer an overtly positive model that embodies her ideal of creating a new reality. Nonetheless, the question of the potential for resistance is foregrounded in the final pages. Following Kell's murder, Mia re-writes a text called *Candy Story*, by inference the text that the reader is finishing. This second version is no longer an introspective *récit de vie*. Nor is it a ludic (or commercially motivated) subversion of the *roman noir* or the *roman d'espionnage*. For Mia, bearing witness by writing has now become an imperative, but not in the false hope of resolution: 'La seule chose qu'il me reste à faire, maintenant que Ma est morte et que Kell a été tué, c'est d'écrire la seconde version de *Candy Story*, pour qu'on sache qui est le maire de Rore. Après, je ne sais pas' (CS, 138).[53] Thus, using the example of the commodification of the literary field, *Candy Story* operates as a microcosm of the very real dangers of failing to resist institutionalized corruption and exploitation (by implication that of neoliberalism). To follow the dynamics of the market, to produce, or to consume a text as a product—be it old or new—is to collude in the institutionalized production of such symbolic violence and the mortal danger that Redonnet implies so often accompanies it.

The majority of writers motivated by either personal or commercial gain are dead by the end of the narrative. Yet if neither Redonnet's *Candy Story* nor the eponymous fiction-within-a-fiction have a happy ending, or indeed a clear conclusion, both end on a note that brings the question of the future to the fore. Embedded in this prose fiction is a grave warning: that the subjugation of writing to both commercial and personal ends has potentially fatal consequences. Using the literary field as a microcosm, *Candy Story* not only figures market-driven threats to the agency of literature as a form of resistance and transmission, but also foregrounds the consequences of symbolic violence; of the subjugation of the critical capacity of the subject; and of elimination of communities and traditions.

[53] 'The only thing I can do now Ma is dead and Kell has been killed is to write the second version of *Candy Story* so that everyone finds out who the mayor of Rore really is. After that, I've no idea.'

The relationship between the writing of the past, the present, and the future is further explored in *L'Accord de paix,* but here with a greater focus on the responsibility of the reader. Gaspard avoids confronting the crises of the present through his obsession with the old texts of Port L'Etoile. That is not to say that Redonnet suggests that the literature of the past is a sure value, since the unthinking consumption of canonical works is brought into question. Already in *Candy Story* reading the classics implies both a commodification of the art of the past and a failure to engage critically with grand narratives: 'Ma me relisait les classiques parce qu'ils sont inépuisables, et que pour réussir à l'école il fallait que je les connaisse par cœur' (CS, 64).[54] In *L'Accord de paix* the nuns avoid ethical questions by turning to their sacred texts, whilst rebel leader Jimmy Mac Law avoids responding to the concerns of his troops by prescribing the reading of writings of old revolutionaries.

Meanwhile the descriptions of Lisbeth O'Nell and Gaspard are carica-tures of the polarized rhetoric of the *crise du roman,* exposing how dichotomous evaluations of literary tradition and innovation result in stasis: 'Lisbeth O'Nell lui a dit qu'il n'était pas nécessaire d'avoir lu les vieux livres de la bibliothèque. [. . .] Gaspard n'est pas d'accord avec elle. Pour lui, la littérature contemporaine, c'est les traductions des vieux livres' (AP, 96–7).[55] Whilst Gaspard's view intersects with poststructuralist notions of textuality, he abdicates his responsibility by remaining in the literary past, and in terms echoing critiques of fiction perceived as 'post-modern' as worthless recycling, dismisses new writing as pastiche. Mean-while, despite O'Nell's declared anti-elitist stance she harnesses her relativism to collaborate with the commodification of the literary field. Her workshops involve a tightly defined 'literary product', promoting the lucrative themes of 'le sexe et la mort' (AP, 98),[56] a jibe, perhaps, at Houellebecq. And O'Nell shamelessly plagiarizes the writing of partici-pants at her workshops, which if not a reference to François Bon's use of the products of writing workshops in his fiction, certainly foregrounds the question of the ethics of appropriating the writing of others.

---

[54] 'Ma used to read the classics to me because they are inexhaustible and because to do well at school I needed to know them off by heart.'

[55] 'Lisbeth O'Nell told him that there was no point in reading the old books in the library. [. . .] Gaspard disagrees. For him, contemporary literature is just translations of old books.'

[56] 'sex and death'.

By contrast, whilst Marthe rejects O'Nell's literary projects (and with them, by implication, the artificially self-limiting category of women's writing), she neither rejects her links with the past, nor takes unquestioning refuge in its cultural products, nor remains constrained by generic boundaries. Indeed, her knowledge of the stories in the old books echoed pictorially on the votives of the cave enables her to shift Gaspard's uncritical belief in canonical notions of representation and literary value. Thus Gaspard moves to an understanding of the potential of storytelling in a broader, but more provisional sense, inscribing his child in a past tradition that has resisted commodification and is also invested with tentative hope for resistance in the future. A hope—not completely realized in *L'Accord de paix* itself—that the stories of the past will also provide future generations with bearings. The catalyst for Gaspard's insight is fatherhood: 'C'est pour lui [Noé] qu'il veut écrire de nouvelles histoires. Il n'a pas, comme Lisbeth O'Nell, d'ambition littéraire. Sa seule ambition est d'aider Noé à construire solidement son avenir. Il a trouvé un sens à sa vie' (AP, 303).[57] Here Redonnet suggests a model for cultural transmission that seeks to make a travesty of the ideology of the market: writing not for commercial or personal gain, but in order that the next generation may have the opportunity to benefit from the traditions and lessons of the past, and thus be equipped to create new ways of resisting the homogenizing forces of consumer culture in the present and in the future. Thus, contrary to the representation of the literary field in her own fiction, although Redonnet does not provide a template for literary commitment, she foregrounds responsibility and implies the enduring agency of the writer at the *fin de millénaire*.

THE POLITICS OF TRAUMA: PAST, PRESENT, AND FUTURE

Silsie, *Candy Story*, *Nevermore*, *Villa Rosa*, and *L'Accord de paix* all feature communities beleaguered by crises in the present and by traumas of the past, and contradictory images of regeneration and degradation

---

[57] 'It is for him [Noé] that he wants to write new stories. Unlike Lisbeth O'Nell, he has no literary ambitions. His only ambition is to help Noé build a solid future. He has found a meaning in life.'

proliferate. With its dichotomy of East and West and its traffic between the old and new continents, *Silsie* dramatizes the crises of the past and the present via the microcosms of the towns of Texe and Dolms. Following the *fin de millénaire* product cycle of novelty and obsolescence, Monsieur Codi's retirement plan to run a hotel by the station in Texe fails with the opening of the airport. The building of a dam for a power station in Dolms has irrevocably changed a once thriving community, submerging the old village and its castle. The electricity supply frequently fails, and the engineer lives in fear of implications of fissures in the dam. The fissures evoke fault lines in the narrative of technological progress and the violence that underlies unrealizable promises. Those in charge take no positive action against the threat of market-driven disaster, instead opening a video club. In Redonnet's subsequent *fin de millénaire* prose fictions corruption and violence (physical and symbolic) are also exposed as the by-products of market-driven 'progress'. The waste ground of Mills-le-Pont in *Candy Story* is a hot-bed for an illegal sex trade. Both literally and metaphorically, oil-rich City Sise is built on corrupt foundations: on the site of an old colonial garrison in a malaria-infested swamp. In *Nevermore* commercial coastal developments lead to the dilapidation of the town-centre of San Rosa. In Santa Flor those areas that have not been commercialized into leisure facilities are left to degenerate into scenes of 'wild-west' deprivation.

Similarly, in *L'Accord de paix* the juxtaposition of the urban jungle of Port l'Etoile with projects for regeneration provides a pressing reminder of commercially generated marginalization. Tellingly, these run-down areas are at once the victims of change, and breeding grounds for victims, not only of poverty and ill-health, but also of sexual exploitation. Yet victims are co-implicated in these processes of physical and symbolic violence. The people of Port l'Etoile fail to resist the ideology of commercial gain that underwrites the future of the town. Indeed, the norm is passive collaboration. The politically ambitious manipulate the populace's blind faith in technological progress to engineer their own success, focusing on crisis-dissimulating projects of regeneration, but failing to address the deprivation that beleaguers the town. Arguably these self-aggrandizing *Grands Projets* operate as references to the cultural policies of Mitterrand. Moreover beyond this francocentric focus, the purportedly progressive but blatantly commercial ideologies have severely detrimental ramifications for the future. In the absence of any resistance, the past is drowned in the unquestioned wave of new media that threatens to submerge the entire town and its cultural heritage: 'Dans la salle polyvalente du Palais de l'Image seront retransmis en direct les meilleurs spectacles de la planète. [...] Le Palais de l'Image sera un espace de création permanente. Il sera aussi toute la mémoire de Port l'Etoile' (AP, 262).[58] The people of Port L'Etoile perform the *fin de millénaire* quest for novelty by jettisoning the past without working through it, and without participating in the construction of a new set of values for the future. Intersecting with the critiques of the commodification of memory by Baudrillard, Lipovetsky, and Nora, this failure is an abdication of agency in favour of a market-ready 'solution' that masks a grave threat to the community.[59]

Whilst *Candy Story, Villa Rosa, Nevermore,* and *L'Accord de paix* all feature interchangeably corrupt factions who vie for political power, not one has clear policies. The motivations of those who accede to power are wealth and fame. In *Candy Story* the future of Rore lies in the hands of the Banque Centrale that bankrupts the equally corrupt SAP. The major players in these organizations and in the media are linked by their participation in the military campaigns of the colonial past. Gobbs and Fuller, the two banks in *Nevermore,* appear to vie for power in San Rosa. Yet it transpires that on the other side of the border they already operate as one, so what seems to be a case of commercial backbiting is a *mise en abyme* of crisis production to dissimulate corruption. Thus Redonnet suggests that political ideologies have become completely subjugated to commercial forces. This, together with the inhabitants' credo of self-interest appears to intersect both with Jameson's discussion of the postmodern as the cultural logic of capitalism and with the crisis discourses surrounding the subsuming of the French exception into neoliberal ideology.[60]

---

[58] 'In the hall of the Palais de l'Image the best shows from the world over will be broadcast live. [...] The Palais de l'Image will be a space of constant creativity. It will also be the repository for the memory of Port l'Etoile.'

[59] Jean Baudrillard, *Simulacres et simulation* (Paris: Galilée, 1981) and *À l'Ombre du millénaire; ou, Le Suspens de l'an 2000* (Paris: Sens & Tonka, 1998); Gilles Lipovetsky, *Le Crépuscule du devoir: L'Éthique indolore des nouveaux temps démocratiques* (Paris: Gallimard, 1992); Pierre Nora, 'L'Ère de la commémoration', in Pierre Nora et al., eds, *Les Lieux de mémoire III: Les France*, Édition Quarto (Paris: Gallimard, 1992).

[60] Fredric Jameson, *Postmodernism, or the Cultural Logic of Capitalism* (London: Verso, 1991).

However, Redonnet's emphasis is less on postmodern perpetual crisis than on the manipulation of the trope of the turning point to commercial ends, whereby new exploitative techniques overlay those which historically generated crises. The election in *Nevermore* is *fin de millénaire* 'bread and circuses' offered by all candidates. For all its nods to democracy, the election is pre-determined by the power of the market and the inertia of the populace who unquestioningly consume the rhetoric of candidates. Candidates who promise crisis resolution and progress whilst demonizing opponents for their regressive, conflict-generating use of the same rhetoric. This slick manipulation of crisis discourses recalls the Americanization of French electoral campaigns. It may also be intended to operate as a warning, for if the elections in *Candy Story, Nevermore, Villa Rosa*, and *L'Accord de Paix* set out to be democratic, they are won by men who manipulate crisis to eliminate their opponents. The forces of law and order are at best impotent, and at worst—and most frequently—co-implicated. When *Nevermore*'s Willy Bost and Roney Burke belatedly attempt to expose this, their superiors toe the market line to ensure that 'justice' (or, rather, crisis manipulation) is in the hands of the highest bidder. Meanwhile in *L'Accord de paix*, to escape from Port L'Etoile prison (with its reputation for torture that recalls the Occupation) is simply a matter of paying the right price.

Redonnet's representation of the commodification of politics in *Nevermore* also suggests that Nazism is the antecedent of late capitalist ideology. When père Anders commits suicide after being exposed as the ex-chaplain of the Santa Flor death camps, his rivals swiftly appropriate the shamed clergyman's call to eliminate the perceived sources of degeneration: crisis rhetoric resonant of Nazi Germany. The inhabitants of San Rosa are not troubled by Anders's past sins. Instead they are inconvenienced by the destruction of an off-the-peg belief system that obviated the necessity for critical thought. The distress is short-lived, for the market is flooded with similar empty promises of crisis resolution, each in slightly different packaging. Père Anders operates as a reference to the Church's complicity, or even collusion in deportations during the Second World War. His actions also suggest an ongoing political and commercial manipulation of the media by both Church and State. So not only has San Rosa failed to work through the legacy of the past to construct a better present, but this failure has also led to the re-playing of the events of the past in a present where democracy is an empty promise, and commercially driven cultural production appears to recuperate any form of resistance. So here and in Redonnet's other *fin de millénaire* prose fictions, political and commercial conflict is more than a backdrop. Warning signals are embedded in references to the failure to learn from the crises of the past. In *Candy Story* an obsolete military camp recalls the concealed atrocities of the Algerian and other colonial wars: 'c'était la faute des guerres coloniales, qui sont la plaie cachée et la honte du camp de Sise' (CS, 51).[61] Redonnet exposes an archaeology of crisis, with present-day infrastructures built on the equally corrupt foundations of the past. The army officers took early retirement to found the Société Anonyme des Pétroles, and the mosquito-infested garrison has been turned into an airport. Thus the transactions of the present articulate the danger of the return of the deadly crises of the past, exposing the very real risk of the reproduction of the conditions (and the consequences) of such conflicts.

Redonnet also represents commercially motivated fictional conflicts which have clear resonances with late twentieth-century global politics. With its sporadic civil war resumed with American backing, *Villa Rosa* recalls US involvement in the arguably neo-imperialist wars of Vietnam, Afghanistan, and Iraq (and by implication the role of the West in the generation and exploitation of these and other conflicts). In ironic contradiction of its title, conflict continues through *L'Accord de paix*. Armed militia, resistance movements, scenes of torture, and a burgeoning black market all recall the French experience of the Second World War. The artificial division between Port l'Etoile Est and Port l'Etoile Ouest evokes the Iron Curtain. Internecine violence, and the rape and murder of innocent women reflect conflicts that both precede and postdate the Second World War, but most notably, the already receding memories of massacres of Kosovo in 1996, and those, suppressed, of the 1995 Rwandan genocide.

Furthermore, the responsibility of adults is particularly brought into focus. This is pre-empted in *Silsie* where the school is left to rot, and in *Villa Rosa* where civil war curtails Rosa Bell's plan to turn the orphanage

---

[61] 'it was the wages of colonial war, the hidden wound and the shame of the Sise camp'.

into 'un centre de création et de rencontres' (VR, 75).[62] Redonnet's texts therefore strike an implicit warning note: that mass-mediatized narratives of technological progress have potentially devastating consequences for future generations. This infers that the responsibility for resistance must be ongoingly assumed by cultural producers and consumers who are 'parent figures' in the broadest sense—biological, adoptive, surrogate, religious, political, and, of course, literary—and not only for children, but for the community as a whole.

Hence recurrent elements of these fictions echo Redonnet's extra-textual discussion of the need to confront the crises of the past to create new ways of negotiating the challenges of the present. As noted in Chapter 1, fictions bearing witness to the traumas of the Occupation and the Holocaust such as Patrick Modiano's *Dora Bruder* (1997) or Lydie Salvayre's *La Compagnie des spectres* (1997) were a feature of the French literary field in the 1990s.[63] These and Redonnet's prose fictions intersect with the work of post-Freudian psychoanalytical thinkers such as Caruth, Felman, and Laub, for whom the incomprehensibility of trauma triggers language, and whilst language cannot encapsulate that trauma, cultural production should nonetheless bear witness to that which resists imagination and rationalization.[64] Yet Redonnet expresses an intention not only to bear witness to repressed horrors and figure the palpable dangers of their return, but also to resist the ideology of commercial gain, which she represents as motivating the commodification of crisis that affects all levels of social and political life.

However, the impassive tone of Redonnet's narration does not adequately convey the impossibility of expressing trauma, or the need to bear witness to that impossibility and unknowability. Instead, her fictions risk becoming inscribed in the commemoration culture described by Baudrillard, Lipovetsky, and Nora,[65] and intersect with Farrell's description of a 'post-traumatic' culture that denies the unsayability of historical

---

[62] 'a centre for creativity and a meeting place'.

[63] Patrick Modiano, *Dora Bruder* (Paris: Gallimard, 1997); Lydie Salvayre, *La Compagnie des spectres* (Paris: Seuil, 1997).

[64] Caruth, *Unclaimed Experience: Trauma, Narrative, and History*; Felman and Laub, *Testimony*.

[65] Baudrillard, *Simulacres et simulation*; idem, *À l'Ombre*; Lipovetsky, *Le Crépuscule du devoir*; Nora, *Les Lieux de mémoire III*.

crises.[66] Yet although they do not overtly problematize the recurrence of crises of the past in the present, by attempting to figure this Redonnet's *fin de millénaire* prose fictions knowingly take the risk of writing after Auschwitz, whilst both foregrounding and performing the culturally and temporally specific dangers of the return of repressed trauma.

POETIC SUBVERSION AND TEXTUAL TRAVESTY

By setting her *fin de millénaire* prose fictions in recognizably contemporary settings, Redonnet invites the question of the extent to which they make a travesty of the dominant order—sexual, symbolic, religious, and political—through poetic, singular uses of language which create realities that respond to her own call to resist the 'irréalisation terrifiante du monde'.[67] Whereas the only brand names featured in Redonnet's other *fin de millénaire* prose fictions are the fictional names of brothels and cinemas, major consumer brands are mentioned in *Candy Story*. They are sparsely deployed, perhaps to draw attention by comparison to their ubiquity in late twentieth-century France and to underscore the systematic failure of the consumer product to fulfil its unrealizable promises. Lonely Mia attempts to play the part of the successful Parisienne on her return to Sise by driving a Golf GTI. Later she buys paint to redecorate her studio at BHV. Her efforts end in tears in an enactment of the distinctly non-therapeutic phenomenon of 'retail therapy', the opiate of the late twentieth-century masses who put their faith in home improvements in the vain hope of changing their lives. Rotz, commercially motivated writer par excellence, churns out his prospective bestseller to order on a Macintosh. Erma, who is synonymous with bad news, works for 'Canal'. These brands are no doubt intended to signal the power of the market, and the nefarious potential of information technology and the mass media. However, arguably, the citing of brands operates less as a travesty or a destabilizing of the commercial order than

---

[66] Kirby Farrell, *Post-traumatic Culture: Injury and Interpretation in the Nineties* (Baltimore, MD: The Johns Hopkins University Press, 1998).
[67] 'the terrifying de-realization of the world'.

as a confirmation of it. Certainly, the narrative technique is less success-ful than the more thoroughgoing use of brands and price points in Houellebecq's *Les Particules élémentaires.*

The most frequently noted characteristics of Redonnet's narrative style are pared down language (compared to Beckett and to Barthes's notion of *écriture blanche*), a sense of detachment, and a marked lack of images.[68] However, her *fin de millénaire* prose fictions are by no means devoid of poetry. Spare and rare, its impact is intensified by the ways in which it contrasts with the apparent impassivity of the narratives. For example in *L'Accord de paix* Marthe's horror at the nuns' fate is such that she hallucinates the scene of their rape and murder. Assonance, alliteration, and repetition provide the most distressing passage of the text:

Elle s'absorbe dans sa prière [. . .]. Quand brusquement, les soldats de l'armée de Ruido font irruption dans la chapelle. Elle en distingue un [. . .] complète-ment ivre. Il titube, il rit, il crache. Puis il se précipite sur elle, déchire sa robe. Elle crie: 'mon Dieu, mon Dieu, ayez pitié de moi, ayez pitié de moi'. Le soldat hurle: 'chienne, ah, chienne, tu vas payer, payer, payer!'. [. . .] Elle entend les cris des sœurs autour d'elle. La chapelle est devenue l'un des lieux de l'enfer. Puis l'un des soldats s'approche d'elle, un poignard à la main. Elle voit la lame luisante pointée sur son ventre s'enfoncer en elle jusqu'à ce que le sang gicle. Elle hurle de douleur, d'une douleur au-delà de la douleur. Il approche main-tenant le poignard de son cou. Elle voit la lame qui va entrer dans sa chair. Elle s'évanouit. (AP, 211)[69]

---

[68] See for example Raymond Bellour, 'La Baleine blanche: *Tir et Lir; Mobie Diq*', *Magazine littéraire*, February 1989, p. 66; Warren Motte, *Small Worlds: Minimalism in Contemporary French Fiction*, p. 83; and Jeannette Gaudet in *Dalhousie French Studies*, 36 (1996), p. 150.

[69] 'She is lost in prayer [. . .]. When, suddenly, Ruido soldiers burst into the chapel. She makes one out [. . .] he is blind drunk. He staggers, he laughs, he spits. Then he throws himself on her, tears her robe. She screams: "My God, my God, have pity on me, have pity on me". The soldier hollers, "Bitch, you bitch, you're going to pay for this, I'm going to make you pay for this, pay, pay, pay!". [. . .] She can hear the sisters screaming all around her. The chapel has turned into one of the circles of hell. Then one of the soldiers comes up to her, a knife in his hand. She sees the shining blade poised over her stomach plunge in until blood spurts out. She is screaming with pain, with a pain beyond pain. Now the soldier is holding the knife up to her throat. She can see the blade about to pierce her skin. She passes out.'

Prior to this gruellingly attentive evocation of the outrage in the convent, the report of the massacre of the wife and child of the mayor of Valrosa and the rape and murder of the nuns is reported but briefly and with detachment: 'La mère supérieure et toutes le sœurs—elles étaient douze depuis la mort de Sœur Blanche et le départ de sœur Marthe—ont été violées et massacrées' (AP, 25).[70] It seems here that such contrast is deliberately designed to take the reader by surprise. Certainly both modes of description create a stark contrast with the simultaneous dramatizing, homogenizing, and neutralizing of such crises by news reports. Intersecting with Angot, Redonnet seeks to make a travesty of ubiquitous press and audiovisual images: homogenized manipulations of crisis. By harnessing the power of the written word she seeks to resist the inertia produced by a surfeit of massmediatized tropes of trauma.

In *Candy Story* a mix of irony and poetry is used to underpin the failure to perceive the threat embodied by ostensible symbols of progress: 'Au large de Rore, comme des maisons flottantes au milieu du mer, on aperçoit les plates-formes pétrolières allumées comme s'il y avait fête à bord' (CS, 127).[71] In *Nevermore* sinister beauty emanates from the scenes of destruction which self-consciously exceed cinematic tropes as bombs explode at the same time as the volcano erupts in an apocalyptic reminder of the serious ideological threat to the community of San Rosa. Redonnet adopts another implicitly critical narrative strategy in *L'Accord de paix*: the rhetorical question. The failure of the population of Port l'Etoile to challenge the rhetoric of progress is underpinned by unanswered questions. Similarly, the motivation of the choices made by Marthe and Olga and the value of their relationship are brought into question: 'Pour la première fois de sa vie, sœur Marthe a une amie. Olga pourtant ne lui ressemble pas. Qu'ont-elles en commun à part la haute vallée?' (AP, 91).[72] Unanswered questions are paralleled by exclamations which draw attention to the unharnessed critical potential of protagonists' statements. Thus, implicitly, Redonnet invites

---

[70] 'The Mother superior and all the sisters—there were twelve since Sister Blanche had died and sister Marthe had left—were all raped and murdered.'

[71] 'In the open sea beyond Rore, there are oil rigs, which look like floating houses, all lit up for a party.'

[72] 'For the first time in her life, sister Marthe has a friend. Yet Olga is nothing like her. What have they got in common apart from the high valley?'

readers to formulate questions or question assertions rather than to seek easy answers or to passively (and therefore in co-implication) to accept those imposed by the mass media and the global market.

FEMINISM IN QUESTION AND *WORK IN PROGRESS*

Predating Redonnet's monograph on Genet, Hélène Cixous cited Genet's writing as an example of the subversion of normative phallocentric identities to create a new language of sexual difference and diversity.[73] Although Redonnet is of the generation of the representation of female resistance—particularly through language—as a potent weapon against the commodification of cultural and social life, in a 1988 interview she distances herself from *écriture féminine*: 'C'est évident que je ne m'inscris pas dans la lignée de ce qui s'est dit être l'écriture féminine. [. . .] J'écris même à partir d'une très grande différence avec ces écritures-là.'[74] In this context, Marthe's exclamations and questions may evoke other concerns in the reader, for they risk being read as a travesty of feminist thought: 'Comme les femmes sont influençables!' (AP, 226);[75] 'Sœur Marthe trouve leurs textes embrouillés et mal écrits. Les femmes feraient mieux de renoncer à l'écriture!' (AP, 99).[76] When the sex-workers ill-advisedly return to their previous female employer, further underpinning a fracturing of female solidarity, Marthe asks of the egotistical docteur Clara: 'Que pense-t-elle du changement soudain des femmes?' (AP, 226).[77] Women's co-implication in symbolic violence is also foregrounded, challenging conventional conceptions of female solidarity. In *L'Accord de paix* Redonnet shows how in a culture dominated by material gain, some women exploit one another whilst priming the pump of the misogyny of consumer culture. Docteur Clara, who has

[73] Hélène Cixous, 'Sorties', in *La Jeune née* (Paris: Union générale des éditions, 1975).
[74] Pascale Hassoun and Chantal Maillet, 'Entretien avec Marie Redonnet', *Patio/Psychanalyse*, 10 (Paris: Éditions de l'Éclat, 1988), 135–43, at p. 135. 'Clearly I don't follow in the tradition of what they called *écriture féminine*. [. . .] Indeed my writing puts a great distance between me and that kind of writing.'
[75] 'The women are so easily influenced!'
[76] 'Sister Marthe found their work confused and badly written. The women ought to give up writing!'
[77] 'What did she think about the women suddenly changing their minds?'

the education and the power to galvanize the women of the Refuge, assumes no responsibility for their well-being beyond their physical symptoms. Women are also implicated in the perversion of the potential for resistance in other forms of cultural production. So both men and women sexually exploit those who sing or dance: blind Luisa by the gypsies, and the sex workers by Madame Susie.

Indeed, women and frighteningly young girls are recurrently the victims of apparently endemic sexual exploitation and violence. *Candy Story* includes a passing reference to the corpses of two little girls, victims of a paedophile ring that enjoys police protection: 'l'année dernière on a retrouvé les corps mutilés de deux petites Africaines. Il vient d'y avoir un scandale à propos d'un trafic de petits Africains, pour des soirées dans une propriété de Mells-le-Château où habite un hôte de marque protégé par la police' (CS, 79).[78] Meanwhile, Mia's childhood friend Luira is an underage recruit to a prostitution racket. Before engaging the services of an underage prostitute in a run-down part of Santa Flor, *Nevermore*'s Roney Burke encounters a little girl whose grandfather appears to be her pimp. In *L'Accord de paix* it is implied that blind orphan Luisa has been abused by Tina and Tino, the siblings who run the orphanage. Luisa seems set to find her freedom through the medium of dance but is lured via the gypsies' promise of lessons to become a 'dancing girl', a recurring motif of sexually abusive commodification in Redonnet's fiction. Yet such instances of the perversion of minors for profit are couched as inconsequential comments, and if Redonnet intends to denounce institutionalized sexual exploitation, her impassive tone risks the more or less deliberate misogyny of representations of female sexuality in Houellebecq, Echenoz, and indeed Angot. Certainly, it fails to meet her ideal of creating a new image for women by subverting the symbolic order of phallocentric exploitation.

However, Redonnet's exploration of female experience is by no means entirely negative, and it is sometimes subversive in that it resists categorization as an unequivocally feminist (or anti-feminist) stance. In *L'Accord de paix* Marthe is the vehicle for an implicitly critical representation of a non-problematized belief in 'women's writing', one that may

---

[78] 'Last year they found the mutilated corpses of two little African girls. A scandal has just broken over the trafficking of African children in Mells-le-Château for parties hosted by a dignitary with police protection.'

be appropriated to perpetuate the misogynist exploitation of women. Moreover, the text exposes how feminist stances risk becoming inscribed in the ideology of the market, appropriated as clichéd images of resistance that are consequently a form of collaboration. Marthe's questions draw attention to the motivations of Lisbeth O'Nell's commercially driven writing workshops and her paradigmatic expectations of the texts women may write there. They foreground how the workshops perpetuate at once institutionalized misogyny and the subjugation of the imagination and critical capacity. In *Candy Story* the figure of the little known female writer corresponds to the enduringly male-dominated French literary field, so it intersects with feminist critiques of the patriarchal suppression of female voices, experience, and memory. From Mia's unthinking collusion in misogynist symbolic violence to Erma's knowing manipulation of it, none of the female protagonists provides a consistently positive counter-example. So, implicitly, Redonnet parallels Delphy's critique of the recuperation and exploitation of feminist gains by the patriarchy and women's co-implication in that process, suggesting a desire to challenge commodified preconceptions of writing by women that neutralize the agency of feminism.[79]

If Redonnet thus contributes to contemporary debates about intellectuals' responsibility to resist the subjugation of critical capacity by the media, to what extent does she meet her ideal that female writers following in Genet's footsteps should make a travesty of the dominant order to create a new 'image fabuleuse de la femme' (JG, 8)?[80] *Candy Story* perpetuates misogyny in the figure of the simultaneously alluring and threatening Erma who at once corresponds to a long tradition of male sexual fantasies and colludes in the symbolic violence of the patriarchy. However, in *L'Accord de paix* the women pay for first-class tickets for Marthe and her family. Marthe is loyal to Olga, and empathizes with the women: 'Elle comprend sa sympathie instinctive pour les femmes du Refuge. Comme sa mère, elles sont des victimes' (AP, 103).[81] What differentiates Marthe from the other women is a determination to resist

---

[79] Christine Delphy, *L'Ennemi principal: Économie politique du patriarcat* (Paris: Syllepse, 1998).
[80] 'a fabulous image of woman'. Here there is a play on both 'fabulous' and 'fable'.
[81] 'She realizes why she instinctively sympathizes with the women of the Refuge. They are victims, like her mother.'

the stereotype of victim, and to construct an alternative role for herself, her family, and the generation that follows. Nonetheless, this challenge does not produce a model for resistance, nor does the language it is couched in constitute a textual challenge to phallogocentrism.

So on the one hand, the detachment of Redonnet's *fin de millénaire* prose fictions seeks to bring the dangers of the manipulation of crisis by the market and the media to the fore. Yet on the other, since these texts do not overtly adopt critical perspectives, they risk falling into both the *fin de millénaire* double bind of recuperation and commodification and the self-satisfied contemplation Adorno warns against whereby implicit denunciation risks becoming complicity. Hence whilst Redonnet's female protagonists show how both men and women perpetuate systemic misogynist exploitation, these fictions do not achieve the ideal Redonnet praises in Genet: creating a new reality for women by making a travesty of the phallocentrism of the symbolic order.

All Redonnet's *fin de millénaire* prose fictions draw to ambiguous ends, and so whether deliberately or not, they fail to give consumer satisfaction through closure. In all these texts the written word does not triumph. The *potential* of texts is nonetheless foregrounded: old or new; by men or women; written, painted or orally transmitted; intended for the benefit of the community or personally motivated; produced or consumed. The potential of narratives to resist symbolic violence and the return of the physical violence of the past is constantly brought into question. Indeed, these fictions not only highlight the threats bound up in the manipulation of crisis, but also dramatize the risk of being caught in the double bind of being commodified by the order they seek to challenge.

Perhaps, then, as eponymous protagonist Silsie articulates, Redonnet's *fin de millénaire* prose fictions show that the quest for developing singular, poetic uses of language that might subvert the symbolic order must necessarily be an ongoing project: 'Pour Silsie, la poésie, c'était sacrée. Elle cherchait ce que c'était sans trouver' (S, 54).[82] Like monsieur Jean's unfinished portrait in *Villa Rosa*—a text woven from images that transcend generic boundaries—these texts operate less as resistance, challenge, or travesty than as *work in progress*. Work which exposes the

---

[82] 'For Silsie, poetry was sacred. She sought to no avail to find out what it was.'

dangers of the subjugation of critical thought by the global market and the mass media. And work which ongoingly attempts to derive inspiration and understanding from the cultural production of the past to resist the ideology of the present and to investigate the enduring potential of art as resistance in the future.

Nonetheless, fifteen years after the death of Genet, in a world where the notion of literary commitment is considered to be long past its sell-by date; where *écriture féminine* is homogenized or packaged as a literary anachronism; and where critical discourses are commodified and recuperated by the order they seek to challenge, these fictions deliberately and unwittingly demonstrate the need for resistance and for a 'nouvelle H/histoire' for the twenty-first century. And so, as *works in progress*, and at some distance from the market-driven pressures of the literary field, Redonnet's *fin de millénaire* prose fictions transmit from writer to reader pressing but unanswered questions: how to resist the subjugation of imagination and critical capacity, to bear witness to the past, and to seek a turning point for the future.

Conclusion

The distinguishing features of the *fin de millénaire* aesthetics of crisis are the coincidence of the turn of the millennium with tangible social, economic, and political crises; a convergence of apocalyptic discourses; and the growth of the mass media and global market, which further generate and manipulate crisis. *Fin de millénaire* prose fictions are distinguishable by their different ways of representing and appropriating the exceptional conditions of their production. Indeed, Angot, Echenoz, Houellebecq, and Redonnet not only represent crises and crisis discourses, but, with varying degrees of self-reflexivity, they also draw on them. More or less knowingly, more or less critically, and more or less successfully, then, *fin de millénaire* prose fictions renew the aesthetics and the politics of literature.

In contrasting ways, Angot, Echenoz, Houellebecq, and Redonnet explore the enduring potential of the literary, and at the same time, they invite and beg the question of the ways in which writing may figure or indeed shape the future. They exploit an inherent specificity of fiction: its potential to harness the benefit of hindsight; to negotiate concerns of the here and now; and to mobilize foresight by creating new perspectives that may influence what is to come. Thus in an ostensibly post-ideological world, the engagement of these writers with the *fin de millénaire* aesthetics of crisis evidences an implicit commitment to literary agency.

While the *affaires* precipitated by Houellebecq and Angot show how the generation and manipulation of crisis by the media and the market fuels the contradictions of the *crise du roman*, they nonetheless demonstrate how at the turn of the third millennium, literature may still intervene. Certainly, the readings above give the lie to the notion that crisis without end is the cultural dominant of late twentieth-century France. So this study concludes its analyses of the returns to crisis and to crisis discourses in *fin de millénaire* prose fictions by pointing to interpretative uncertainty and to contradictions, and having also demonstrated how in a homogenized, mass-mediatized world such destabilizing returns to the trope of the turning point are not symptomatic of a postmodern sense of perpetual crisis, but instead offer some critical leverage.

Angot, Echenoz, Houellebecq, and Redonnet challenge normative discourses in their combination, blurring, subversion, and outstripping of aesthetic and intellectual paradigms. Overtly subjective, and often self-reflexively pointing to the inherent crises of language and the self, to the artificiality of their fictions, and to their own manipulation of the trope of the turning point, these very different writers' texts counter the unfulfilled promises, unrealizable stereotypes, objective pretences, and homogenizing dynamics of the mass media and global market. In addition to intertexts spanning dance, painting, and literature (canonical, popular, and contemporary), references to brand names, marketing materials, advertising jingles, films, pop music, the print media, television, video, and the Internet are appropriated to sometimes implicitly critical ends.

In Houellebecq's *Les Particules élémentaires* a slogan from a mail order catalogue and mass-market promotional techniques play a key role in engineering the end of the human race. Redonnet represents television as a vehicle for propaganda, and the Internet as a conduit for the globalized commodification of sexual violence. Echenoz reveals the dark underside of the global market, its exploitative patterns, and its imposition of alienating mass-market stereotypes. Angot's *Vu du ciel* and *Les Autres* also foreground the commodification of trauma by reality television and news reporting, but link these tropes to the generation of misogynist sexual violence. Meanwhile Houellebecq, Echenoz, and Redonnet link Hollywood output to sexual exploitation. Yet Echenoz also taps the creative potential of filmic techniques and intertexts. This is particularly evident in the playful references to Hitchcock's *Vertigo* in *Les Grandes Blondes*, which simultaneously draw attention to the fictional status of the text. Indeed, intertexts bring into question the sense-making potential and critical capacity of literature in relation to other forms of cultural production. Likewise the agency of the cultural producer: writer, television producer, screen star, newscaster, journalist, artist, and film-maker.

Intersecting with contemporary literary trends from *autofiction* and 'minimalism' to 'women's writing' and the *roman noir*, Angot, Echenoz, Houellebecq, and Redonnet destabilize the homogenizing labelling of the French literary field. Echenoz and Redonnet exceed the putative minimalist aesthetic and Redonnet's and Angot's narratives by no means correspond to the anachronistic and indeed misogynist notion that female-authored texts share consistent characteristics. Angot challenges conceptions of *autofiction*, and with variable self-reflexivity, performs the double bind of a writer at once oppressed by and dependent upon the media and the market. Also radically defying categorization, Houellebecq combines aspects of the *roman à thèse*, science fiction, and the realist novel with poetry and philosophical digressions. The figure of the writer recurs, often bespeaking a concern for the broader field of cultural production. Noting the pressures of market forces, Houellebecq's writer–narrator in *Extension du domaine de la lutte* comments that the nineteenth-century novel no longer accommodates the struggle of the writer to represent a world where competition has been extended from material achievement to a sexual economy. In *Les Particules* Bruno's attempts to become a published author are motivated by a desire to boost his sexual equity. Representations of once-committed Maoist 'real' author Philippe Sollers implicitly invite the question of the responsibility of the writer to resist the subsuming of literary *engagement* into commercial pragmatism. In Redonnet's *L'Accord de paix* commercial writer Lisbeth O'Nell and librarian Gaspard clash over dichotomous views of literature that resonate with the contradictory discourses of the *crise du roman*. Meanwhile, *Candy Story* exposes a literary field predicated on corruption and financial gain, complete with market-driven trends. The ambivalence of Angot's eponymous writer figure offers insight into the more or less complicit dependency of the writer on the media and the market. And it also invites the question of the responsibility of the reader, and hence, the consumer.

The 'consumption' of *fin de millénaire* prose fiction is necessarily individual, multiple, changing, and interpretative. It is therefore inherently a challenge to dominant discourses, and one which is maximized in some of these texts. From beginning to end, Angot's narratives underpin the impossibility of figuring and resolving trauma. Redonnet's deliberate failure to provide closure in her fictions may seek to make a travesty of the commodification of crisis by the media, and if they fail to do so, they nonetheless shine a spotlight on the responsibility for the future held by both the cultural producer and the consumer. Echenoz's inconclusive ends disrupt homogenizing cycles of crisis production and manipulation. And, by figuring an end that is self-reflexively problematic in *Les Particules*, Houellebecq, it seems, seeks to expose the perceived failure of the contemporary intellectual field to apprehend the dangers posed by the exploitation of crisis by the global market and the mass media.

Perhaps surprisingly, all four writers nonetheless figure love as having the potential to precipitate turning points. Not, however, by using the tropes of Hollywood, but by mooting a limited agency. This recurs for example in Redonnet's union of sœur Marthe and Gaspard; in the relationship of Angot's narrator and his ex-partner in *Not to be*; and in 'Christine Angot''s relationship with her daughter Léonore. To be sure, most attempts at building romantic relationships fail (following the global product cycle figured by Echenoz, or exemplifying Houellebecq's take on a putative sexual neoliberalism). Yet these failures are the result of protagonists' choices. So, along with the question of the possibility of love, those of free will and agency are raised.

Often eschewing aesthetic and intellectual paradigms, and without regard to commodifying labels and spurious distinctions between modernism and postmodernism, writers of *fin de millénaire* prose fiction extend the 'long twentieth-century' of crisis thinking precipitated by Nietzsche, Freud, Marx, and Saussure, offering new perspectives on the 'maîtres du soupçon', and on thinkers who build on or challenge their insights. Intersecting with Adorno and Benjamin, Redonnet invites an exploration of the potential of the work of art at a time of mass-mediatized and virtual reproduction. The title of Houellebecq's *Extension du domaine de la lutte* references the Hegelian dialectic yet represents a post-Marxist world and a perceived intellectual failure (he also singles out Deleuze, Lacan, and Foucault for particular ridicule). Nonetheless Houellebecq foregrounds the enduring need to precipitate a turning point. Indeed his provocative narrative strategies may be read as an ideological challenge to neoliberal thought, and to a perceived co-implication of late twentieth-century French intellectuals in it.

Both Houellebecq and Angot draw on Freudian and Lacanian theory to represent therapy in the mode of failure, recuperated as a commercial transaction, or operating as a legitimizing discourse for market- and media-generated crisis. Angot's representation of incest does not fit post-Freudian theories of trauma, feminist thought, or the conceptual frameworks developing around incest-survivor narratives. Using and exceeding deconstructive and psychoanalytical techniques, her self-conscious linguistic traces perform the impossibility of discharging trauma through language; acknowledge the ethical need to bear witness to trauma; and foreground co-implicated relationships of trauma victim, perpetrator, the media, and the market. Echenoz exposes perpetual patterns of crisis manipulation, but exceeds the already commodified tropes of the spectacular and the hyperreal, and his language games carry an implicitly critical charge. Instead of simply dismissing it as empty, all four writers cast more or less suspicious light on the thought of their near contemporaries, and in particular, Baudrillard, Debord, and Derrida. They challenge the trope of spectacularization, consciously play language games, and sometimes invite more direct comparison as, for example, does the way Redonnet's recurrent fictional wars do not correspond to Baudrillard's analysis of the first Gulf War as media-orchestrated non-event.[1] Nor are they copies unhitched from the original: Redonnet's fictional violence—physical and symbolic—is painfully immediate.

Whilst adopting very different narrative strategies, these contrasting writers of *fin de millénaire* prose fiction also bring into question the crisis discourses surrounding French exceptionalism. Their texts link the discourses of the mass media and the global market with traumas—past and present—and the danger that they may recur in the future. Avoiding the anti-Americanism that characterizes French responses to globalization, Echenoz exposes France's co-implication in economic and cultural neo-imperialism (although without harnessing the potential leverage of postcolonial thought). The neo-imperialist forces of global market economics are figured in repeated patterns of symbolic violence both experienced and perpetrated by protagonists, whether embroiled in the international drug trade, the art market, or television production; and whether in Paris, France's ex-colonies, India, or the Arctic.

In Redonnet's fictions the recurrence of internecine and ethnic violence; the legacy of war and genocide; and East–West schisms implicitly link the Second World War, the Holocaust, the Cold War, the West Bank, and Kosovo with the market-driven violence of the present. Houellebecq's narrators identify scientific advance, global market economics, and the influence of America as generators of crisis through the extension of neoliberal competition from the material to

---

[1] Jean Baudrillard, *La Guerre du Golfe n'a pas eu lieu* (Paris: Galilée, 1991).

the sexual economy (although they also point to the role played by a perceived French intellectual failure). Angot may juxtapose franco-centric representations of the personal trauma of incest with supermarket shopping, but she also draws comparisons with the Holocaust, the 1995 Rwandan genocide, and the plight of workers for Nike in China. Thus she suggests that on both an individual and a collective basis, atrocities continue to repeat themselves unchecked by late capitalism, or indeed perhaps yoked to it. So, amidst the crisis discourses surrounding French exceptionalism, *fin de millénaire* prose fiction affords some critical purchase at once on the arguably neo-imperialist ideology of the global market, and on French co-implication in it.

Of course, all critical discourses risk being caught in the redoubled *fin de millénaire* double bind of recuperation and commodification despite any intention to appropriate the discourses of the mass media and the global market to creative or critical ends. Indeed, by failing to establish critical distance from them, Angot, Echenoz, Houellebecq, and Redonnet banalize tangible crises, perpetuate symbolic violence, and underpin the significance of the objects of their implicit criticism. All these writers' representations of and attempts to appropriate crises and crisis discourses risk attracting the accusation levelled at Angot: producing a voyeuristic *jouissance* in readers and taking masochistic pleasure in crisis that parallels the generation, homogenizing, and naturalizing of trauma by the tropes of reality television and the news media. Moreover, in Echenoz and Houellebecq's fiction in particular, humour is frequently elicited without critical meta-discourses, and so risks co-implicating readers in the recuperation of any implicit challenge. Accordingly, this study does not claim that implicitly critical intent is consistently distributed or successfully carried out in the texts analysed. Instead it draws out the extent to which writers of *fin de millénaire* prose fiction aim to avoid, are co-implicated in, and perpetuate the processes they seek to expose, resist, or challenge.

Angot's *Vu du ciel* represents the crisis-generating deprivation of the *cités* and makes links between post-war housing developments, poverty, exploitation, and media-generated violence. *Les Autres* foregrounds symbolic and sexual violence and its impact on Arab women and sex workers. Yet Angot's fictions revolve around middle-class protagonists. In *Un An*, the most overtly political of Echenoz's fictions, the plight of

France's growing homeless population is exposed. However protagonist Victoire regains her socio-economic status and most of Echenoz's protagonists are agents of the global market.[2] Houellebecq represents the crises of the middle class and middle aged, and his fictional totalizing theory foregrounds the sexually impoverished but socio-economically empowered. The only marginalized subjects are the butts of racist comments or used as ancillary support for this texts' premises. Redonnet's protagonists are often victims of sexual abuse, and she evokes the institutionalized exploitation of the marginalized. Yet the implicitly critical potential of her texts is diluted by their detached tone and use of allegorical contexts that distance readers from symbolic, material, and sexual violence.[3]

If sexual abuse is frequently figured, it is misogynist symbolic violence that recurs most troublingly in all of these fictions. Indeed, contrary to the belief that on the eve of the twenty-first century, the construction of woman as negative Other identified by Beauvoir in 1949 is a prejudice of the past, *fin de millénaire* prose fictions show how it is ongoing, and, moreover, over-determined by a vast array of market-driven, unattainable idealized images.[4] The patriarchal structures of the global market and the mass media, male and female protagonists, and indeed writers of *fin de millénaire* prose fictions are co-implicated in disseminating enduring and new forms of misogyny. As well as the virgin/whore dichotomy, the stereotypes that recur in Echenoz's prose fictions include the more recent, market-driven *femme fatale*, blonde screen stars, and unnaturally endowed secretaries. If these representations are implicitly critical, without critical meta-discourses they further disseminate misogynist images, established and new. Redonnet and Angot avoid the now commodified notions of *écriture féminine*, and bring physical and symbolic misogynist violence and its links with consumer culture to the fore. Yet Angot's eponymous protagonist perpetuates the misogynist stereotype of the

[2] Following *Au Piano* (Paris: Minuit, 2003), Echenoz turned away from an engagement with the contemporary to biographical fiction with *Ravel* (Paris: Minuit, 2006), and *Courir* (Paris: Minuit, 2008), based on the life of Czech athlete Émile Zatopek.

[3] Redonnet's *Diego* (Paris: Minuit, 2005), her most overtly political prose fiction to date, tells the story of an illegal immigrant who arrives from a fictional continent in a fictional beach resort in the south of France and lives clandestinely in a fictional suburb of Paris.

[4] Simone de Beauvoir, *Le Deuxième sexe* (Paris: Gallimard, 1949).

hysteric. Meanwhile Redonnet's call to create new images that make a travesty of the patriarchal symbolic order is not carried through by female protagonists or in her representations of male attitudes towards them. The unproblematized misogynist discourses of Houellebecq's protagonists and narrators indicate at best a bungled attempt to challenge what may be politically correct clichés, or, at worst, an unreconstructed misogyny. The latter suggestion can be corroborated by noting how a sporadic lauding of female attributes appears to be intended to mitigate the way sexually active women are apparently sentenced to death once they no longer have a sexual or plot function. Intentionally or not, then, all these fictions simultaneously reveal and become new vehicles for misogyny. So at times in spite of themselves they demonstrate the ongoing need to precipitate a turning point in sexual politics.

Likewise, the representation of sexuality and of AIDS is problematic. Redonnet implicitly situates HIV as spread by a fatal mode of neo-imperialism through the account of dying Bobby Wick's promiscuous exploitation of anonymous African women in *Candy Story*. Yet if Houellebecq describes the televisual commodification of AIDS sufferers, he does so in one of a number of passages imbued with homophobia. Guardian angel Séverine injects Christine with a fatal blood-borne virus evoking AIDS in Angot's *Vu du ciel*, and the male narrator of *Not to be* suffers from a mysterious wasting illness. That narrator, who is heterosexual, recovers and in *L'Inceste* Angot equates retelling the experience of a short-lived lesbian affair with that of Hervé Guibert's diagnosis with AIDS. So whilst Redonnet and Angot may buck the homophobic trend of stereotyping of AIDS as exclusively afflicting homosexuals, they and Houellebecq also harness AIDS-related symptoms for narrative pragmatics. Meanwhile, Echenoz includes an egregious ephemeral lesbian coupling in *Les Grandes Blondes*, and his *fin de millénaire* prose fictions are resoundingly heteronormative. Heterosexual couples predominate from 'Christine Angot' and Claude to the serial failed male–female couplings in Redonnet and Echenoz; and the unfulfilled desires for or short-lived sexual relationships in Houellebecq's novels. Certainly, whether by design or default, representations of women, homosexuality, ethnic Others, and the marginalized in *fin de millénaire* prose fictions amply demonstrate that the personal must still be considered to be political.

Simply to assume that literary heterogeneity and returns to the trope of the turning point constitute evidence of resistance to the homogenizing dynamics of the mass media and the global market is a naive oversight, not to mention an elision of the *fin de millénaire* double bind of recuperation and commodification. Nonetheless, outstripping the returns to the subject, narrative, and history identified by Viart, in their different ways these *fin de millénaire* prose fictions link past, present, and future, and in particular, express or betray a concern for the return of the crises of recent history. Simultaneously intervening in aesthetic, political, and ethical debates, if they do not successfully challenge sexual stereotypes they foreground the sometimes deadly potential of the blurring of fiction and reality, and of reality imitating art. Accordingly, despite accusations of market-driven self-absorption, Angot foregrounds the commodification of trauma, linking that of victims of sexual abuse to that of victims of Auschwitz and the Rwandan genocide, suggesting a market-driven return of the repressed horrors of the past. Her fictions link the violence of the present—such as sex crimes and the plight of the *banlieues*—with the tangible threat of the replaying in the future of the most horrific man-made crises of the twentieth century.

Clearly, then, these texts do not correspond to the postmodern crisis without end described by Lipovetsky: 'Plus aucune idéologie n'est capable d'enflammer les foules, la société postmoderne n'a plus d'idole ni de tabou, plus d'image glorieuse d'elle-même, plus de projet historique mobilisateur, c'est désormais le vide qui nous régit, un vide pourtant sans tragique ni apocalypse.'[5] Far from celebrating a sense of crisis without end, the systematic generation and manipulation of crisis by the mass media and the global market is revealed, and there are also a number of apocalyptic images which feature cataclysmic turning points. In Redonnet's *Silsie* fissures appear in the man-made dam, which, like the volcano in *Nevermore*, threaten to devastate the anaesthetized population. The earthquake and tsunami in Echenoz's *Nous trois* are prescient of the extreme weather conditions of the late twentieth- and early

---

[5] Gilles Lipovetsky, *L'Ère du vide: Essais sur l'individualisme contemporain* (Paris: Gallimard, 1983), p. 16: 'There are no longer any ideologies able to carry the masses with them; postmodern society no longer has any idols or taboos, any glorious self-image, or galvanizing historical project. Henceforth it is the void that determines us, a void that is nonetheless neither tragic nor apocalyptic.'

twenty-first century; of an often unquestioning courting of ecological disaster; and of the December 2002 South-East Asian tsunami, where the suffering of those affected was arguably neutralized by the media. Such representations invite interpretation as implicit warnings of the commodification of critical capacity, the neutralization of genuine threats, and the consequences of the mismanagement of the planet. Meanwhile, in addition to developing a theory on the threats and fragilities of global market economics within his novels, Houellebecq concludes *Les Particules* with the end of the human race. Here the dangerous potential of the market and the media is underpinned by representing intellectuals and governments ceding to promotional pressure to approve eugenic policies which has irremediable consequences for humanity. So *Les Particules* represents a radical, double manipulation—at once of the media and of the human genome—that enables the human race to engineer its own extinction. Here, critical leverage and co-implication are figured as inextricable.

Although they predate at once the twenty-first-century crises of global capitalism and the emphatic return to apocalyptic narratives in the events and repercussions of September 11 2001, these *fin de millénaire* prose fictions have grimly prescient resonances with crises to come. Twenty-first-century military and paramilitary discourses and those calling for radical environmental, social, and financial change all depend upon the trope of the turning point. The environmental damage wrought by global market economics; its own crisis in the first decade of the new millennium; the fundamentalist ideology behind terrorist attacks; and the essentialist rhetoric of responses to them are examples of the dangers of a mass-mediatized, global manipulation of crisis and crisis tropes that, unlike some of those used in these *fin de millénaire* prose fictions, is neither self-reflexive nor problematized.

In *Nous trois* Echenoz harnesses the tropes of Hollywood disaster movies to describe towers falling in slow motion and dust clouds billowing as a high-rise shopping mall collapses. Redonnet's rebel forces qua terrorists in *Villa Rosa* use the Internet to plan their attacks, and *L'Accord de paix* figures a relentless series of military and paramilitary reprisals. In *Extension*, focusing on the critical inertia of the consumer, Houellebecq's narrator articulates an ironic prognosis for the third millennium: 'Sous nos yeux, le monde s'uniformise. [...] Et peu à peu le visage de la mort apparaît, dans toute sa splendeur. Le troisième millénaire s'annonce bien' (EDL, 16).[6] This is echoed by the clone-narrator in *Les Particules*: 'Partout à la surface de la planète l'humanité fatiguée, épuisée, doutant d'elle-même et de sa propre histoire, s'apprêtait tant bien que mal à entrer dans un nouveau millénaire' (PE, 367).[7] The prescience of Houellebecq's *fin de millénaire* predictions for a world anaesthetized by a consumerist ideology yet nonetheless vulnerable accumulate grim poignancy. All the more so in that his 2001 novel *Plateforme* representing the exploitation of sexual supply and demand on a global basis leading to Islamic fundamentalists bombing a sex-tourism resort in Thailand was published just days before 9/11 and a year before the 17 October 2002 bombings of a nightclub catering for Western tourists in Bali. *La Possibilité d'une île* went on to depict landscapes that, rather than evoking the late twentieth-century trope of a post-nuclear future, figure a post-capitalist, post-ecological third millennium scarred by the ravages of economically motivated war and climate change.

Tentatively, then, and beyond commodifying labels, more or less evading recuperation by the media and the market, without crisis resolution, and sometimes precipitating crisis, these prose fictions offer different uses of the trope of the turning point. They raise questions of the nature and autonomy of cultural production; of the possibilities of critical distance and agency; and of the enduring potential for challenging and resisting the ideology and aesthetics of late capitalism. Just as some of the most prominent intellectual debates of late twentieth-century France and thought which more or less overtly challenge the ideology of the mass media and the global market are predicated on the trope of the turning point, so these contrasting writers of *fin de millénaire* prose fiction demonstrate how the notion of postmodern crisis without end is neither ubiquitous nor without challenge. Continuing a 'long twentieth century' of crisis thinking, in contrasting ways, and in form and content they challenge the notion of a clear turning point between modernism and postmodernism.

---

[6] 'Right in front of our eyes the world is becoming standardized. [. . .] And gradually the face of death is revealed in all its glory. A great start to the third millennium.'

[7] 'Tired, exhausted, loosing self-confidence and confidence in their collective history, human beings worldwide were preparing as best they could to enter a new millennium.'

Like the works it analyses, this book concludes open-endedly. Angot, Echenoz, Houellebecq, and Redonnet more or less implicitly raise questions about the potential of the literary in converging debates about gender, sexuality, race, neoliberalism, the impact of the mass media, globalization, and, arguably, the future of the human race. However, their *fin de millénaire* prose fictions do not directly confront the problematic of the generation and manipulation of crises and crisis discourses. With hindsight and foresight they do, nonetheless, renew literary aesthetics and the question of the politics of literature. If Angot, Echenoz, Houellebecq, and Redonnet reflect, perpetuate, and challenge late capitalist misogyny and symbolic violence, at the same time they show how the recurrent trope of the turning point has both aesthetic and critical potential. So, whilst problematic and problematizing, and sometimes in spite of themselves, *fin de millénaire* prose fictions bespeak the need to intervene in political and ethical debates and demonstrate the enduring agency—critical and creative—of literature itself.

Chronology

May 1988	François Mitterrand re-elected president
June 1988	Legislative elections—Socialist Party returns to power; Michel Rocard prime minister
July 1988	Mitterrand announces plans for *Bibliothèque Nationale de France*
July 1989	Bicentenary of 1789 Revolution. Grand opening of *Grands Projets*: Opéra Bastille; Grand Louvre; Arche de la Défense
October 1989	First *affaire du foulard islamique*. Creation of *Haut conseil à l'intégration*
November 1989	Fall of Berlin Wall
January 1991	*Loi Evin* restricts smoking in enclosed public places
April 1991	*Affaire du sang contaminé*
May 1991	Édith Cresson France's first female prime minister
February 1992	Treaty of Maastricht signed
March 1992	Renault Billancourt closed.
April 1992	Pierre Bérégovoy replaces Cresson as prime minister. Eurodisney opens in France.
September 1992	Referendum on Treaty of Maastricht—narrow victory (51%) 'yes'
March 1993	Legislative elections—right victorious; Édouard Balladur prime minister; Mitterrand president—*cohabitation*
May 1993	Bérégovoy commits suicide
June 1993	René Bousquet assassinated ahead of his trial for crimes against humanity
May 1994	Paul Touvier convicted for crimes against humanity. Opening of Eurotunnel
August 1994	*Loi Toubon*—protecting the French language
September 1994	*Affaire Mitterrand*—Mitterrand appears on television to answer questions about his wartime record

May 1995	Jacques Chirac elected president. Release of Mathieu Kassovitz's *La Haine*
January 1996	Death of Mitterrand
May 1996	*L'appel des 234*—campaign for the legal recognition of homosexual couples published in *Nouvel observateur*
February 1997	Huge antiracism rally. Petition signed by sixty filmmakers protesting against the Debré laws on immigration. Petitions by writers, musicians, and artists followed
May/June 1997	Legislative elections—victory of the left; Lionel Jospin prime minister—*cohabitation*
April 1998	Maurice Papon convicted of complicity in crimes against humanity
May 1998	*Loi Aubry* on 35-hour working week initiated
July 1998	French national football team wins the World Cup
September 1998	*Affaire Houellebecq*
January 1999	Introduction of Euro (Franc to be phased out by May 2002)
June 1999	France officially acknowledges the 1954–62 Algerian War
August 1999	José Bové and Aveyron farmers protest against McDonald's
November 1999	PACS law passed recognizing cohabiting couples' civil union. The research section of the *Bibliothèque Nationale de France*, the last of Mitterrand's *Grands Projets*, opens
June 2000	Law on gender parity in politics
September 2001	Attacks on the World Trade Center and the Pentagon

Suggestions for further reading

The suggestions below complement references to works cited in this study.

BACKGROUND: HISTORICAL, SOCIAL, AND CULTURAL

A range of cultural studies guides to modern France are a good resource for contextual information and analysis of events and cultural products. Jill Forbes and Michael Kelly, *French Cultural Studies: An Introduction* (Oxford: Oxford University Press, 1995); Forbes and Nick Hewlett, *Contemporary France* (London and New York: Longman, 2000); Nicholas Hewitt, ed., *The Cambridge Companion to Modern French Culture* (Cambridge: Cambridge University Press, 2003); Alex Hughes and Keith Reader, *Encylopedia of Contemporary French Culture* (London: Routledge, 1998); and William Kidd and Siân Reynolds, eds, *Contemporary French Cultural Studies* (London: Arnold, 2000) are lively and accessible introductions to the cultural and social history of the period. The third volume of Georges Duby's *Histoire de la France en trois volumes* (Paris: Larousse, Bordas, and HER, 1999) provides a contrasting conventional historical perspective in French.

Robert Gildea, *France since 1945* (Oxford: Oxford University Press, 2002) provides a comprehensive analysis that includes commentary on French responses to the development of the mass media and the global market. For analyses of their social and economic impact, see Timothy B. Smith, *France in Crisis: Welfare, Inequality and Globalization since 1980* (Cambridge and New York: Cambridge University Press, 2004); John Marks and Enda McCaffrey, eds, *French Cultural Debates* (Melbourne: Monash Romance Studies, 2001); David L. Looseley, *The Politics of Fun: Cultural Policy and Debate in Contemporary France* (Oxford and New York: Berg, 1997); and Jean-Pierre Dormois, *The French Economy in the Twentieth Century* (Cambridge: Cambridge University Press, 2004).

TWENTIETH-CENTURY FRENCH LITERATURE

A growing number of studies in English and French are devoted to surveys of French literature and the twentieth-century French literary field and complement this study by providing insight into the development of French literary aesthetics. For authoritative English-language introductions to French literature see the eminently readable Sarah Kay, Terence Cave, and Malcolm Bowie, *A Short History of French Literature* (Oxford: Oxford University Press, 2003); Tim Unwin, ed., *The Cambridge Companion to the French Novel: From 1800 to the Present* (Cambridge: Cambridge University Press, 1997); and Valerie Worth-Stylianou, ed., *Cassell Guide to Literature in French* (London: Cassell, 1996).

Useful resources in French include specialist in contemporary fiction Dominique Viart's *Le Roman français au XXe siècle* (Paris: Hachette, 1999); and Dominique Rabaté, *Le Roman français depuis 1900* (Paris: Presses Universitaires de France, 1998). Other recent French resources are Patrick Brunel, *La Littérature française du XXe siècle* (Paris: Nathan, 2002); and Mireille Calle-Gruber, *Histoire de la littérature française du XXe siècle; ou Les Repentirs de la littérature* (Paris: Honoré Champion, 2001). Henri Mitterrand, *La Littérature française du XXe siècle* (Paris: Nathan 1996); and Denis Hollier, *De la Littérature française* (Paris: Bordas, 1993) are both updated classics.

Studies dovetailing with the period covered by this study include Victoria Best's *An Introduction to Twentieth-Century French Literature* (London: Duckworth, 2002); William Thompson, ed., *The Contemporary Novel in France* (Gainsville, FL: University Press of Florida, 1995); and John Taylor, *Paths to Contemporary French Literature* (New Brunswick, NJ: Transaction, 2004), a collection of essays and reviews of a wide range of writers from the second half of the twentieth century. Éliane Tonnet-Lacroix, *La Littérature française et francophone de 1945 à l'an 2000* (Paris: L'Harmattan, 2001) helpfully situates the development of prose fiction in the second half of the twentieth century alongside that of poetry and theatre.

LATE TWENTIETH-CENTURY FRENCH PROSE FICTION

There is a growing body of work on late twentieth-century French prose fiction in French, but little in English. Translated excerpts from contrasting contemporary French prose fictions can be found in Georgia de Chamberet, ed., *XCiTés: The Flamingo Book of New French Writing* (London: Flamingo, 1999). Warren Motte adopts an approach avowedly inflected by personal preference in *Fables of the Novel: Fiction Since 1990* (Normal, IL: Dalkey Archive Press, 2003). The opening chapter of Colin Davis and Elizabeth Fallaize's *French Fiction in the Mitterrand Years: Memory, Narrative, Desire* (Oxford: Oxford University Press, 2000) offers a succinct and accessible introduction to the socio-political, intellectual, and cultural context that precedes and overlaps with the period addressed in this study, followed by contrasting analyses of works by Duras, Echenoz, Ernaux, Guibert, Pennac, and Semprun which elucidate the notions of the literary 'returns' to narrative, the subject, and history, and demonstrate how they are discernible in late twentieth-century French prose fiction.

Readers of French will find this complements the analysis of a range of contemporary writers and the discussion of the phenomenon of these 'returns' in two volumes edited by Dominique Viart, *Écritures contemporaines 1: Mémoires du récit* (Paris and Caen: Lettres Modernes Minard, 1998) and *Écritures contemporaines 2: États du roman contemporaine* (Paris and Caen: Lettres Modernes Minard, 1999) with Jan Baetans; and with Bruno Vercier and Franck Évrard, covering the period from 1980 to 2005, the very good *La Littérature française au présent: Héritage, modernité* (Paris: Bordas, 2005), which covers a wide range of more or less known writers qualified as 'challenging' rather than 'middle-of-the-road' or 'commercial' (Viart also identifies a late twentieth-century 'retour au réel' in *Le Roman français au XXe siècle*).

Laurent Flieder's guide *Le Roman français contemporain* (Paris: Seuil, 1998) is an extremely helpful survey of the contemporary literary field, although by dint of its scope it does not offer detailed analysis of individual texts or writers. Another useful survey beginning in 1980 is Bruno Blanckeman, Aline Mura-Brunel, and Marc Dambre, *Le Roman français au tournant du XXe siècle: Vers une cartographie du roman français depuis 1980* (Paris: Presses de la Sorbonne Nouvelle, 2005). Other analyses of important writers (especially Echenoz) and perceived trends in contemporary prose fiction include those offered by Blanckeman in *Les Fictions singulières: Études sur le roman français contemporain* (Paris: Prétexte, 2002); Jean-Pierre Richard, *L'État des choses: Études sur huit écrivains d'aujourd'hui* (Paris: Gallimard, 1990) and *Terrains de lecture* (Paris: Gallimard, 1996); and Jean-Claude Lebrun and Claude Prévost, *Nouveaux territoires romanesques* (Paris: Messidor/Éditions Sociales, 1990). Also helpful is the collection of essays (including ones on Echenoz, Houellebecq, and Redonnet) edited by Michel Collomb, *L'Empreinte du social dans le roman depuis 1980* (Montpellier: Publications de l'Université Paul Valéry, 2005).

An interesting introduction to works by some lesser known writers is Lakis Proguidis's *De L'Autre côté du brouillard: Essai sur le roman français contemporain* (Paris: Nota Bene, 2001). Two volumes published by the Ministère des affaires étrangères offer bullish, idiosyncratic essays on the contemporary literary field: Yves Mabin, ed., *Roman français contemporain* (Paris: Ministère des affaires étrangères, 1997); and *Roman français contemporain* (Paris: Ministère des affaires étrangères, 2002).

SPECIAL ISSUES AND DOSSIERS

Some special issues and dossiers on 1990s French prose fiction offer an overview of the field, its critical debates, and key figures. Particularly useful resources are 'Writing in French in the '90s: Novelists and Poets', *Contemporary French and Francophone Studies/Sites*, (Part 1) 2/2 (1998), (Part 2) 3/1 (1999), and (Part 3) 3/2 (1999); and 'French Fiction in the 1990s', *Nottingham French Studies*, 41 (Spring 2002). Readers of French will also find the following helpful: 'Le Roman français mort et vif', *La Nouvelle Revue Française*, 557 (2001); 'La Relève des avant-gardes', *Magazine littéraire*, November 2000; 'Questions du romans, romans en question', *Europe*, 820–1 (1997); 'Que peut le roman?', *Le Débat*, 90 (1996); and 'Le Roman en question', *Prétexte*, 11 (1996).

LITERARY POLEMICS AND THE *CRISE DU ROMAN*

In addition to some of the aforementioned dossiers, readers may wish to get a taste of *fin de millénaire* literary polemics in works which articulate the contradictory crisis discourses of the *crise du roman* such as Michel Crépu, *La Confusion des lettres* (Paris: Grasset, 1999); Jean-Philippe Domecq, *Le Pari littéraire* (Paris: Éditions Esprit, 1994); Jean-Marie Domenach, *Le Crépuscule de la culture française?* (Paris: Plon, 1995); Pierre Jourde, *La Littérature sans estomac* (Paris: L'Esprit des Péninsules, 2002); and Alain Nadaud, *Malaise dans la littérature* (Paris: Champ Vallon, 1993).

GENDER, SEXUALITY, AND FEMALE-AUTHORED CONTEMPORARY FRENCH PROSE FICTION

Readers will find useful chapters on the development of feminism, feminist thought, and *écriture féminine* in Diana Holmes, *French Women's Writing 1848–1994* (London: Athlone, 1996); Elaine Marks and Isabelle de Courtivron, eds, *New French Feminisms: An Anthology* (London: Harvester, 1981); Sonya Stephens, ed., *A History of Women's Writing in France* (Cambridge: Cambridge University Press, 2000); and Abigail Gregory and Ursula Tidd eds, *Women in Contemporary France* (Oxford: Berg, 2000). For critical approaches to feminist thought, debates, and female-authored texts see Judith Still and Michael Worton, eds, *Textuality and Sexuality: Reading Theories and Practices* (Manchester: Manchester University Press, 1993); Toril Moi's updated *Sexual/Textual Politics* (London: Taylor and Francis, 2002); and Roger Célestin, Eliane Dal-Molin, and Isabelle de Courtivron, eds, *Beyond French Feminisms: Debates on Women, Politics and Culture in France 1981–2001* (New York and Basingstoke: Palgrave, 2003).

There are a number of very good monographs and edited volumes on turn-of-the-millennium French writing which include chapters on Redonnet and Angot and provide insight into the heterogeneity of female-authored texts. Particularly recommended are Shirley Ann Jordan, *Contemporary French Women's Writing: Women's Visions, Women's Voices, Women's Lives* (Bern: Lang, 2004); Catherine Rodgers and Nathalie Morello, eds, *Nouvelles écrivaines: Nouvelles voix?* (Amsterdam and Atlanta, GA: Rodopi, 2002); Gill Rye, ed., *Hybrid Voices, Hybrid Texts: Women's Writing at the Turn of the Millennium, Dalhousie French Studies*, 68 (Fall 2004); Rye, ed., *Contemporary Women's Writing in French, Journal of Romance Studies*, 2/1 (Spring 2002); Rye and Michael Worton, eds, *Women's Writing in Contemporary France: New Writers, New Literatures in the 1990s* (Manchester: Manchester University Press, 2003); and Gill Rye and Carrie Tarr, eds, 'Focalizing the Body in Contemporary Women's Writing and Film-making in France', *Nottingham French Studies*, 45/3 (Autumn 2006). A broader sweep including poets can be found in Michael Bishop, ed., *Thirty Voices in the Feminine* (Amsterdam and Atlanta, GA: Rodopi, 1996). The *Contemporary Women's Writing in French* seminar group website has helpful links and dossiers on Angot, Marie Darrieussecq, Camille Laurens, Lorette Nobécourt, and Amélie Nothomb (<http://igrs.sas.ac.uk/research/CWWF/>).

FIRST-PERSON NARRATIVES AND *AUTOFICTION*

For discussions of first-person narratives, critical approaches, and contextual information regarding *autofiction* see Michael Sheringham, *French Autobiography: Devices and Desires* (Paris: Clarendon Press, 1993); Philippe Lejeune, *L'Autobiographie en France* (Paris: Armand Colin, 1998); and in a more polemic mode, Vincent Colonna, *Autofiction et autres mythomanes littéraires* (Paris: Éditions Tristram, 2004).

'MINIMALISM'

Discussion of the putative 'minimalist' aesthetic and of works by Echenoz and Redonnet may be found in Warren Motte's *Small Worlds: Minimalism in Contemporary French Fiction* (Lincoln and London: University of Nebraska Press, 1999); Michèle Ammouche-Kremers and Henk Hillenaar, eds, *Jeunes Auteurs autour de Minuit* (Amsterdam and Atlanta, GA: Rodopi, 1994); and Fieke Schoots, *'Passer en douce à la douane': L'Écriture minimaliste de Minuit: Deville, Echenoz, Redonnet et Toussaint* (Amsterdam and Atlanta, GA: Rodopi, 1997).

Recent considerations of the development of this perceived aesthetic are Olivier Bessard-Banquy, *Le Roman ludique: Jean Echenoz, Jean-Philippe Toussaint, Eric Chevillard* (Villeneuve-d'Ascq: Presses Universitaires du Septentrion, 2003); and Bruno Blanckeman, *Les Récits indécidables: Jean Echenoz, Hervé Guibert, Pascal Quignard* (Paris: Presses Universitaires du Septentrion, 2000).

ANGOT

Since the publication of *L'Inceste* in 1999, Angot has featured in edited volumes including some of those suggested in the recommendations for reading on late twentieth-century French fiction and female-authored texts above. There is also a growing body of articles on Angot including Alex Hughes, 'Moi qui ai connu l'inceste, je m'appelle Christine' ['I have had an incestuous relationship and my name is Christine']: Writing Subjectivity in Christine Angot's Incest Narratives', *Journal of Romance Studies*, 2/1 (2002), 65–77; Shirley Ann Jordan, 'Close up and Impersonal: Sexual/Textual Bodies in Contemporary French Women's Writing', *Nottingham French Studies*, 45/3 (Autumn 2006); Gill Rye, 'A New Generation: Mothering in Christine Angot's *Léonore, toujours* and Marie Darrieussecq's *Le Mal de mer*', *L'Esprit Créateur*, 45/1 (Spring 2005), 5–15; Rye, '"Il faut que le lecteur soit dans le doute": Christine Angot's Literature of Uncertainty', *Dalhousie French Studies*, 68 (Fall 2004), 117–26; and Marion Sadoux, 'Christine Angot's *Autofictions*: Literature and/or Reality', in Rye and Michael Worton eds, *Women's Writing in Contemporary France: New Writers, New Literatures in the 1990s, Journal of Romance Studies*, 2/1 (Spring 2002), 171–81. See also Jeanette den Toonder, 'L'Autoreprésentation dans une époque massmédiatisée: le cas Angot', in Sjef Houppermans, Christine Bosman-Delzons, and Danièle de Ruyter-Tognotti, eds, *Territoires et terres d'histoire: Perspectives, horizons, jardins secrets dans la littérature française d'aujourd'hui* (Amsterdam and New York: Rodopi, 2005), 39–59. A different perspective on Angot's representation of sexuality is also to be found in Keith Reader, *The Abject Object: Avatars of the Phallus in Contemporary French Theory, Literature and Film* (Amsterdam and New York: Rodopi, 2006). Many newspaper and magazine articles in the French press are of interest only in as much as they typify the elision of incest by mass-market appraisals of Angot's *fin de millénaire* prose fictions. However, *Le Matricule des Anges* ran a special issue on Angot (November–December 1997), with useful resources and interviews available online including Thierry Guichard, 'Christine Angot: La bâtarde libre' (<http://www.lmda.net/mat/MAT02125.html>), and idem, 'En littérature la morale n'existe pas' (<http://www.lmda.net/mat/MAT02127.html>). The Contemporary Women's Writing in French website has some excellent bibliographical resources and other information on Angot, and a page dedicated to Angot contains some references and links to press articles, reviews, and other online resources (<http://igrs.sas.ac.uk/research/CWWF/Christine_Angot.htm>). One of Angot's readers has created a website devoted to her with useful bibliographical resources for most of the texts analysed in this book (<http://eva.domeneghini.free.fr>).

ECHENOZ

Press and academic articles on Echenoz are frequently good and valuable resources and are cited in this study. Echenoz also features prominently in the edited volumes and studies on late twentieth-century French prose fiction and 'minimalism' suggested above. Christine Jérusalem has published two monographs on Echenoz's prose fiction: *Jean Echenoz* (Paris: Ministère des affaires étrangères, 2006); and *Jean Echenoz: Géographies du vide* (St Etienne: Publications de l'Université de St Etienne, 2005). The volume arising from the first academic conference on Echenoz contains a wide range of articles, many by prominent literary critics: Christine Jérusalem and Jean-Bernard Vray, eds, *Jean Echenoz: Une Tentative modeste de description du monde* (St Etienne: Publications de l'Université de St Etienne, 2006). For other helpful resources see 'Minimalism' above; Sjef Houppermans, *Lectures du désir: De Madame de Lafayette à Régine Detambel et de Jean de la Fontaine à Jean Echenoz* (Amsterdam and Atlanta, GA: Rodopi, 1997); and the dossier devoted to *Les Grandes Blondes, Un An*, and *Je m'en vais* in *Roman 20–50*, 38 (2004). Online literary journal *remue.net* devotes a page to Echenoz: <http://remue.net/cont/echenoz.html>.

Sjef Houppermans, *Jean Echenoz: Étude de l'œuvre* (Paris: Bordas, 2008) is a welcome students' guide, part of a new collection on contemporary authors under Dominique Viart (other texts published to date are on Bon, Ernaux, and

278   *Fin de millénaire* French Fiction

Quignard). It situates Echenoz in relation to his influences, postmodernism, and the contemporary literary field, then addresses Echenoz's œuvre in terms of space and trajectories, and dialogues and intertexts. There are sections on *Nous trois*, *Les Grandes Blondes*, *Un An*, and *Je m'en vais*. See also Suzanne Schlinder, "'Un Réalisme en trompe l-'œil": Les Figures de perception comme principe narratif chez Jean Echenoz (*Un An, Je m'en vais*)', *Roman 20–50*, 45 (June 2008), 145–57. In English, see also Simon Kemp's sections on Echenoz in *Defective Inspectors: Crime-fiction Pastiche in Late Twentieth-century French Literature* (Oxford: Legenda, 2006).

HOUELLEBECQ

A veritable industry has developed around Houellebecq's fiction, giving rise to a proliferation of press articles and hastily published polemical volumes which exemplify the crisis discourses and commercial interest attracted by Houellebecq, but are of questionable scholarly value. Of the recent flurry of such texts, Olivier Bardolle's *La Littérature à vif: Le cas Houellebecq* (Paris: Esprit des Péninsules, 2004) and Dominique Noguez's *Houellebecq, en fait* (Paris: Fayard, 2003) are most worthwhile. Academic work on Houellebecq is also booming, and whilst quality is variable, one volume features some good material: Gavin Bowd, ed., *Le Monde de Houellebecq* (Glasgow: University of Glasgow French and German Publications, 2006); and there is some helpful content in Sabine van Wesemael, ed., *Michel Houellebecq: Études réunies par Sabine van Wesemael avec une interview inédite de l'auteur* (Amsterdam and New York: Rodopi, 2004). Martin Crowley, 'Houellebecq: The Wreckage of Liberation', *Romance Studies*, 20 (2002), 17–28; and Gavin Bowd, 'Michel Houellebecq and the Pursuit of Happiness', *Nottingham French Studies*, 42 (2002), 28–39 are also excellent. Those interested in Houellebecq's narrative technique will find the following articles particularly helpful: Robert Dion, and Élisabeth Haghebaert, 'Le Cas de Michel Houellebecq et la dynamique des genres littéraires', *French Studies*, 55 (2001), 509–24; Dominique Noguez, 'Le Style de Michel Houellebecq', *L'Atelier du roman*, 18 (1999), 17–22; 'Le Style de Michel Houellebecq: 2', *L'Atelier du roman*, 19 (1999), 121–3; 'Le Style de Michel Houellebecq: Fin', *L'Atelier du roman*, 20 (1999), 129–37. A different perspective on sexuality in Houellebecq is also to be found in Keith Reader, *The Abject Object* (see Angot above).

A dossier on *Les Particules* appeared in *L'Atelier du Roman*, 19 (June 1999). Guillaume Bridet's 'Michel Houellebecq et les montres molles', *Littérature*, 151 (March 2008), 6–20 provides a view across the scandals surrounding the two texts analysed here, and of his two subsequent novels. Its subjectivity notwith-

standing, the *Amis de Michel Houellebecq* website, <http://www.houellebecq.
info> offers some bibliographical resources and links to and details of press
articles on Houellebecq. Finally, Houllebecq and Bernard-Henri Lévy's *Ennemis publics* (Paris: Flammarion and Grasset, 2008) is worth dipping into,
with all the usual reservations concerning authorial intention (plus those
specific to Houellebecq) for the insights it offers on the commercial dynamics
of the field of cultural production.

REDONNET

Whilst there is relatively little quality coverage in the French general and
specialist press, a number of monographs feature Redonnet's prose fiction in
comparative studies of aspects of contemporary women's writing: Cathy Jelle-
nik, *Rewriting Rewriting: Marguerite Duras, Annie Ernaux, and Marie Redonnet*
(New York, Frankfurt, and Bern: Peter Lang, 2007); Michèle Chossat, *Ernaux,
Redonnet, Bâ et Ben Jelloun: Le Personnage féminin à l'aube du XXième siècle*
(New York, Frankfurt, and Bern: Peter Lang, 2002); Colette Sarrey-Strack,
*Fictions contemporaines au féminin: Marie Darrieussecq, Marie Ndiaye, Marie
Nimier, Marie Redonnet* (Paris: L'Harmattan, 2002); and Jeanette Gaudet,
Writing Otherwise: Atlan, Duras, Giraudon, Redonnet and Wittig (Amsterdam
and Atlanta, GA: Rodopi, 1999). Articles providing contrasting perspectives on
the texts analysed in this study include Sarah Fishwick, 'Encounters with
Matisse: Space, Art, and Intertextuality in A. S. Byatt's *The Matisse Stories*
and Marie Redonnet's *Villa Rosa*', *The Modern Language Review*, 99/1 (January
2004), 285–6; Gill Rye, 'Time for Change: Re(con)figuring Maternity in
Contemporary French Literature (Baroche, Cixous, Constant, Redonnet)',
Paragraph, 3 (1998), 354–75; and Aine Smith, 'Evermore or Nevermore?
Memory and Identity in Marie Redonnet's Fiction of the 1990s', in *Women's
Writing in Contemporary France: New Writers, New Literatures in the 1990s*.
Warren Motte's comments on Redonnet and her 2005 text *Diego* introduce an
illuminating piece by Redonnet on the conditions of her writing in the 1990s
and the commercial constraints of the literary, which is well worth reading
'Parcours d'une œuvre: Marie Redonnet avec une introduction de Warren
Motte', *Contemporary French and Francophone Studies/Sites*, 12/4 (October
2008), 487–99.

    For Redonnet's earlier texts see Michèle Ammouche-Kremers and Henk
Hillenaar, eds, *Jeunes Auteurs autour de Minuit*, (Amsterdam and Atlanta, GA:
Rodopi, 1994) and Fieke Schoots, '*Passer en douce à la douane: L'Écriture*

minimaliste de Minuit: Deville, Echenoz, Redonnet et Toussaint (Amsterdam and Atlanta, GA: Rodopi, 1997). Finally, Redonnet has her own website: <http://marie.redonnet.monsite.orange.fr>.

ONLINE RESOURCES

In addition to websites of the newspapers and journals cited, particularly valuable web resources include *Fabula* (<http://www.fabula.org>), an online literary community with essays and reviews; *Le Matricule des Anges* (<http://www.lmda.net>), giving online access to the archives of this literary magazine with extended reviews and interviews; *Les Inrockuptibles* (<http://www.lesinrocks.com>), a magazine covering contemporary music, cinema, and literature which was an early champion of Houellebecq and good for a greater cultural understanding of the period; and mainstream literary magazine *Lire* (<http://www.lire.fr>).

Index